DOING WHAT'S RIGHT

THE QUEST FOR REALITY AND SIGNIFICANCE

Book 1 – BEING TRULY HUMAN:
>The Limits of our Worth, Power, Freedom and Destiny

Book 2 – FINDING ULTIMATE REALITY:
>In Search of the Best Answers to the Biggest Questions

Book 3 – QUESTIONING OUR KNOWLEDGE:
>Can we Know What we Need to Know?

Book 4 – DOING WHAT'S RIGHT:
>Whose System of Ethics is Good Enough?

Book 5 – CLAIMING TO ANSWER:
>How One Person Became the Response to our Deepest Questions

Book 6 – SUFFERING LIFE'S PAIN:
>Facing the Problems of Moral and Natural Evil

BOOK 4

DOING WHAT'S RIGHT

WHOSE SYSTEM OF ETHICS IS GOOD ENOUGH?

DAVID GOODING
JOHN LENNOX

Myrtlefield House
Belfast, Northern Ireland

David Gooding and John Lennox have asserted their right under the Copyright, Designs and Patents Act, 1988, to be identified as Authors of this work.

Doing What's Right: Whose System of Ethics is Good Enough?
Book 4, The Quest for Reality and Significance
Copyright © Myrtlefield Trust, 2019

All rights reserved. No part of this publication may be reproduced, stored in a retrieval system, or transmitted, in any form or by any means, electronic, mechanical, photocopying, recording or otherwise, without the prior permission of the publisher or a license permitting restricted copying. In the UK such licenses are issued by the Copyright Licensing Agency Ltd., Barnard's Inn, 86 Fetter Lane, London, EC4A 1EN, UK.

All Scripture quotations, unless otherwise indicated, are taken from The Holy Bible, English Standard Version, copyright © 2001 by Crossway Bibles, a division of Good News Publishers. Used by permission. All rights reserved. Scripture quotations marked NIV are from the Holy Bible, New International Version® Anglicized, NIV® Copyright © 1979, 1984, 2011 by Biblica, Inc.® Used by permission. All rights reserved worldwide. Italics within Scripture quotations indicate emphasis added. Scripture quotations marked (our trans.) are as translated by David Gooding. Foreign language quotations marked (our trans.) are as translated by John Lennox.

Cover design: Frank Gutbrod.
Interior design and composition: Sharon VanLoozenoord.

Published by The Myrtlefield Trust
PO Box 2116
Belfast, N Ireland, BT1 9YR
w: www.myrtlefieldhouse.com
e: info@myrtlefieldhouse.com

ISBN: 978-1-912721-15-3 (hbk.)
ISBN: 978-1-912721-16-0 (pbk.)
ISBN: 978-1-912721-17-7 (PDF)
ISBN: 978-1-912721-18-4 (Kindle)
ISBN: 978-1-912721-19-1 (EPUB without DRM)
ISBN: 978-1-912721-30-6 (box set)

23 22 21 20 19   10 9 8 7 6 5 4 3 2

DEDICATED TO OUR YOUNGER FELLOW STUDENTS,

REMEMBERING THAT WE WERE ONCE STUDENTS — AND STILL ARE

CONTENTS

BOOK 4: DOING WHAT'S RIGHT

WHOSE SYSTEM OF ETHICS IS GOOD ENOUGH?

Series Preface xi
Analytical Outline xv

Series Introduction 1

THE STATUS, BASIS AND AUTHORITY OF ETHICS
1. Questions for Ethical Theories 43
2. What Should We Do, and Why? 53
3. The Source of Objective Moral Values 71

MAJOR CONTEMPORARY ETHICAL SYSTEMS
4. Christian Ethics 95
5. Act Utilitarianism 109
6. Intuitionism 137
7. Kantian Ethics 151
8. Virtue Ethics 165
9. Egoism 189

WHAT USE IS ETHICS?
10. Determining the Value of a Human Being 211
11. The Ethics of the Transmission of Life 221
12. Ethical Issues Raised by Science and Technology 235
13. Exercises in Ethics 255
14. Beyond Ethics 273

Appendix: The Scientific Endeavour 297
Series Bibliography 333
Study Questions for Teachers and Students 365
Scripture Index 383
General Index 385

ILLUSTRATIONS

I.1. A Rose   5
I.2. The School of Athens by Raphael   10–11
I.3. On the Origin of Species (1859) by Charles Darwin   27
I.4. A Touchstone   32
I.5. An Apple   35
Ap.1. Benzene Molecule   300
Ap.2. Model T Ford Motor Car   317
Ap.3. Milky Way Galaxy   328–9

SERIES PREFACE

The average student has a problem—many problems in fact, but one in particular. No longer a child, he or she is entering adult life and facing the torrent of change that adult independence brings. It can be exhilarating but sometimes also frightening to have to stand on one's own feet, to decide for oneself how to live, what career to follow, what goals to aim at and what values and principles to adopt.

How are such decisions to be made? Clearly much thought is needed and increasing knowledge and experience will help. But leave these basic decisions too long and there is a danger of simply drifting through life and missing out on the character-forming process of thinking through one's own worldview. For that is what is needed: a coherent framework that will give to life a true perspective and satisfying values and goals. To form such a worldview for oneself, particularly at a time when society's traditional ideas and values are being radically questioned, can be a very daunting task for anyone, not least university students. After all, worldviews are normally composed of many elements drawn from, among other sources, science, philosophy, literature, history and religion; and a student cannot be expected to be an expert in any one of them, let alone in all of them (indeed, is anyone of us?).

Nevertheless we do not have to wait for the accumulated wisdom of life's later years to see what life's major issues are; and once we grasp what they are, it is that much easier to make informed and wise decisions of every kind. It is as a contribution to that end that the authors offer this series of books to their younger fellow students. We intend that each book will stand on its own while also contributing to the fuller picture provided by the whole series.

So we begin by laying out the issues at stake in an extended introduction that overviews the fundamental questions to be asked, key voices to be listened to, and why the meaning and nature of ultimate reality matter to each one of us. For it is inevitable that each one of us will, at some time and at some level, have to wrestle with the fundamental questions of our existence. Are we meant to be here, or is it really by accident that we are? In what sense, if any, do we matter, or are we simply rather insignificant specks inhabiting an insubstantial corner of our galaxy? Is there a purpose in it all? And if indeed it does matter, where would we find reliable answers to these questions?

In Book 1, *Being Truly Human*, we consider questions surrounding the value of humans. Besides thinking about human freedom and the dangerous way it is often devalued, we consider the nature and basis of morality and how other moralities compare with one another. For any discussion of the freedom humans have to choose raises the question of the power we wield over other humans and also over nature, sometimes with disastrous consequences. What should guide our use of power? What, if anything, should limit our choices, and to what extent can our choices keep us from fulfilling our full potential and destiny?

The realities of these issues bring before us another problem. It is not the case that, having developed a worldview, life will unfold before us automatically and with no new choices. Quite the opposite. All of us from childhood onward are increasingly faced with the practical necessity of making ethical decisions about right and wrong, fairness and injustice, truth and falsity. Such decisions not only affect our individual relationships with people in our immediate circle: eventually they play their part in developing the social and moral tone of each nation and, indeed, of the world. We need, therefore, all the help we can get in learning how to make truly ethical decisions.

But ethical theory inevitably makes us ask what is the ultimate authority behind ethics. Who or what has the authority to tell us: you *ought* to do this, or you *ought not* to do that? If we cannot answer that question satisfactorily, the ethical theory we are following lacks a sufficiently solid and effective base. Ultimately, the answer to this question unavoidably leads us to the wider philosophical question: how are we related to the universe of which we form a part? What is the nature of ultimate reality? Is there a creator who made us and built into us our moral awareness, and requires us to live according to his laws? Or, are human beings the product of mindless, amoral forces that care nothing about ethics, so that as a human race we are left to make up our own ethical rules as best we can, and try to get as much general agreement to them as we can manage, either by persuasion or even, regretfully, by force?

For this reason, we have devoted Book 2, *Finding Ultimate Reality*, to a discussion of Ultimate Reality; and for comparison we have selected views and beliefs drawn from various parts of the world and from different centuries: the Indian philosophy of Shankara; the natural and moral philosophies of the ancient Greeks, with one example of Greek mysticism; modern atheism and naturalism; and finally, Christian theism.

The perusal of such widely differing views, however, naturally provokes further questions: how can we know which of them, if any, is true? And what is truth anyway? Is there such a thing as absolute truth? And how should we recognise it, even if we encountered it? That, of course, raises the fundamental question that affects not only scientific and philosophical theories, but our day-to-day experience as well: how do we know anything?

The part of philosophy that deals with these questions is known as epistemology, and to it we devote Book 3, *Questioning Our Knowledge*. Here we pay special attention to a theory that has found wide popularity in recent times, namely, postmodernism. We pay close attention to it, because if it were true (and we think it isn't) it would seriously affect not only ethics, but science and the interpretation of literature.

When it comes to deciding what are the basic ethical principles that all should universally follow we should observe that we are not the first generation on earth to have thought about this question. Book 4, *Doing What's Right*, therefore, presents a selection of notable but diverse ethical theories, so that we may profit from their insights that are of permanent value; and, at the same time, discern what, if any, are their weaknesses, or even fallacies.

But any serious consideration of humankind's ethical behaviour will eventually raise another practical problem. As Aristotle observed long ago, ethics can tell us what we ought to do; but by itself it gives us no adequate power to do it. It is the indisputable fact that, even when we know that something is ethically right and that it is our duty to do it, we fail to do it; and contrariwise, when we know something is wrong and should not be done, we nonetheless go and do it. Why is that? Unless we can find an answer to this problem, ethical theory—of whatever kind—will prove ultimately ineffective, because it is impractical.

Therefore, it seemed to us that it would be seriously deficient to deal with ethics simply as a philosophy that tells us what ethical standards we ought to attain to in life. Our human plight is that, even when we know that something is wrong, we go and do it anyway. How can we overcome this universal weakness?

Jesus Christ, whose emphasis on ethical teaching is unmistakable, and in some respects unparalleled, nevertheless insisted that ethical teaching is ineffective unless it is preceded by a spiritual rebirth (see Gospel of John 3). But this brings us into the area of religion, and many people find that difficult. What right has religion to talk about ethics, they say, when religion has been the cause of so many wars, and still leads to much violence? But the same is true of political philosophies—and it does not stop us thinking about politics.

Then there are many religions, and they all claim to offer their adherents help to fulfil their ethical duties. How can we know if they are true, and that they offer real hope? It seems to us that, in order to know whether the help a religion offers is real or not, one would have to practise that religion and discover it by experience. We, the authors of this book, are Christians, and we would regard it as impertinent of us to try to describe what other religions mean to their adherents. Therefore, in Book 5, *Claiming to Answer*, we confine ourselves to stating why we think the claims of the Christian gospel are valid, and the help it offers real.

However, talk of God raises an obvious and very poignant problem: how can there be a God who cares for justice, when, apparently, he makes no attempt to put a stop to the injustices that ravage our world? And how can it be thought that there is an all-loving, all-powerful, and all-wise creator when so many people suffer such bad things, inflicted on them not just by man's cruelty but by natural disasters and disease? These are certainly difficult questions. It is the purpose of Book 6, *Suffering Life's Pain*, to discuss these difficulties and to consider possible solutions.

It only remains to point out that every section and subsection of the book is provided with questions, both to help understanding of the subject matter and to encourage the widest possible discussion and debate.

DAVID GOODING
JOHN LENNOX

ANALYTICAL OUTLINE

SERIES INTRODUCTION 1

The shaping of a worldview for a life full of choices 3

Why we need a worldview 3

Asking the fundamental questions 9

    First fundamental worldview question: *what lies behind the observable universe?* 12

    Second fundamental worldview question: *how did our world come into existence, how has it developed, and how has it come to be populated with such an amazing variety of life?* 13

    Third fundamental worldview question: *what are human beings? where do their rationality and moral sense come from? what are their hopes for the future, and what, if anything, happens to them after death?* 14

    The fundamental difference between the two groups of answers 15

Voices to be listened to 16

    The voice of intuition 17

    The voice of science 18

    The voice of philosophy 20

    The voice of history 22

    The voice of divine self-revelation 24

The meaning of reality 29

What is the nature of ultimate reality? 34

    Ourselves as individuals 34

    Our status in the world 35

    Our origin 36

    Our purpose 36

    Our search 38

Our aim 39

PART 1. THE STATUS, BASIS AND AUTHORITY OF ETHICS 41

CHAPTER 1. QUESTIONS FOR ETHICAL THEORIES 43

Introduction 45

Modern difficulties for ethical theory 46

A fourfold analysis of ethics 48

    Question 1. What status, basis and authority does it claim? 48

    Question 2. What is its supreme goal? 48

    Question 3. What specific rules does it lay down for daily life? 49

    Question 4. What guidance does it give for application to daily life? 49

    Medical ethics as an illustration of these four questions 49

        The basis and authority of medical ethics 50

        The general principle and aim of medical ethics 50

        The specific rules of medical ethics 50

        The relevance to the practical decisions that have to be taken in actual cases 50

CHAPTER 2. WHAT SHOULD WE DO, AND WHY? 53

The status of ethics 55

    The emotivist theory 55

    Cultural relativism 56

        Cultural dependence 56

        Ethnocentrism 57

The inadequacy of subjectivism 58

    Why no one really believes that morality is subjective 59

Subjective morality would reduce all moral judgments to a matter of taste 59

Subjectivism removes the idea of moral progress 59

Subjectivism tends to be self-refuting 60

Subjectivists find it very difficult to act consistently with their own theory in daily life 60

Arguments against objectivism 62

If there are such objective moral values, how do we get to know them? 62

  Two side issues 62

    First issue: How we use the term 'justice' 63

    Second issue: The meaning of justice 63

Why are there so many different moral practices in the world? 66

  An exception? Funeral customs among the ancient Greeks and Callatiae 68

How can moral values both come from parents and be objective? 70

CHAPTER 3. THE SOURCE OF OBJECTIVE MORAL VALUES 71

On what are objective moral values grounded? 73

Universal, objective moral values are grounded in the matter of the universe 73

  Extreme, non-moral materialism 74

  Social Darwinism 74

  Sociobiology 75

  The claim that 'the struggle for survival' can account for altruistic moral behaviour 76

  Ethical naturalism 77

    The 'is' / 'ought' problem 78

    Naturalism's weakness 79

  Instinct 81

  To sum up so far 82

Universal, objective moral values are the creations of human beings 82

  Contractarianism 83

  Moral contractarianism 85

  An assessment of moral contractarianism 86

Universal, objective moral values are grounded in the character and will of God 88

  The Euthyphro Problem 89

  A residual difficulty 90

    The Ten Commandments and the old covenant (Exod 19:1–8; 20:1–24; 24:1–11) 90

    The new covenant and the writing of God's laws on the human heart (Luke 22:20; Heb 8:6–12; 10:14–18; 2 Cor 3:2–18) 91

PART 2. MAJOR CONTEMPORARY ETHICAL SYSTEMS 93

CHAPTER 4. CHRISTIAN ETHICS 95

Introduction 97

Christian ethics: its status, basis and authority 98

Its supreme goal and general principles 99

  Its supreme goal 99

    The glory of God 99

    The glorification of Christ 99

    The moral perfecting of believers in Christ 99

    The final glorification of believers in Christ 99

  Its general principles 100

Its specific rules covering various action-spheres 101

  In the Old Testament 101

    The human race in relation to God 101

    The human race in relation to daily work 101

The human race in relation to parents and the source of life 102

The human race in relation to society 102

The human race in relation to inner thoughts, desires, lusts and schemings 102

In the New Testament 103

Features of Christian ethics 103

Its guidance when we have to decide actual, complicated cases in daily life 104

Objections to Christian ethics 106

CHAPTER 5. ACT UTILITARIANISM 109

Then and now 111

A bird's-eye view of act utilitarian ethics 112

A more detailed study of act utilitarian ethics 112

Utilitarianism's basis 112

Utilitarianism's goal and general principle: pleasure maximised 113

The nature of pleasure in Bentham's theory 113

Bentham's hedonic calculus 114

The rationale of punishment according to Bentham 115

Utilitarianism's specific rule 115

Bentham's principle of utility 115

Utilitarianism's guidance for actual cases 116

An evaluation of utilitarianism: its practical difficulties 117

Disagreeing over the kind of pleasure that we should seek to maximise 118

Measuring the comparative value of incommensurable entities 118

Judging which kind of pleasure is to be aimed at 118

J. S. Mill's answer 119

Foreseeing the future 120

A Christian perspective 121

Further modifications of utilitarianism 122

An evaluation of utilitarianism: its moral problems 123

Utilitarianism's base 123

What does it mean? 124

What Bentham means by 'ought' 125

Is it true? 126

Utilitarianism's supreme good and goal 126

Drawing out some implications 127

1. Not all pleasure is good 127

2. To aim simply at pleasure is morally misleading 127

3. It can sometimes be morally wrong to seek to gratify people's pleasure 128

4. To make even good pleasure the supreme good and goal in life is a form of idolatry 128

Utilitarianism's general principle 128

Utilitarianism's one specific rule 132

First moral problem: the question of our duty to the past 132

Second moral problem: the question of distributive justice 133

Third moral problem: the question of common sense morality 134

Utilitarianism's guidance for actual cases 135

CHAPTER 6. INTUITIONISM 137

The 'end' and the 'ought' 139

Intuitionism: facts and explanations 140

The bare facts 140

Some explanations of intuitionism 140

Its champions 140
What is meant by ethical intuitionism 140
The basic prima facie duties according to intuitionism 142
Basic and derived duties 143
What is meant by calling the basic duties 'prima facie' 143

An evaluation of intuitionism: its strengths and weaknesses 145
Strengths of intuitionism 145
Its rejection of the doctrine that the end justifies the means 145
Its concern for duties arising from the past 145
Its concern for personal duty towards loved ones 145
Its concern that justice must be according to merit 145
Weaknesses of intuitionism 147
Ross's attempt to systematise the basic, and the derivative, duties 147
Ross's double claim that the basic duties are self-evident and are perceived by intuition 147
No supreme goal or overarching principle to be the final guide in practical, moral decisions 147
No base, and therefore no ultimate authority 148

CHAPTER 7. KANTIAN ETHICS 151

The basic principles of Kantian ethics 153
The indispensability of good will 153
The command which tells us to do our duty is a categorical imperative 154

The three formulations of the Categorical Imperative 155
The first formulation 155
Points to ponder 157
The second formulation 158
The distinction between means and ends 158
What Kant intends by the terms means and ends 159
Points to ponder 160
The third formulation 160

A critical assessment of Kantian ethics 161
An unanswered question 161
Kant's ambivalent stance 163

CHAPTER 8. VIRTUE ETHICS 165

A different emphasis 167

Aristotle and virtue ethics 169
Aristotle's ethics 169
The three parts of human make-up according to Aristotle 169
Aristotle's concept of virtue 169
Aristotle's doctrine of the mean 170
An analogy: food, not too much, nor too little 170
A practical example: courage 171
A sampling of Aristotle's analysis of the virtues and questions arising 171
Pleasure 172
The getting and giving of money 172
Self-assessment 172
Aim in life 173
Attitude to other people 173
Questions arising 173

Unfair criticisms of Aristotle 174
The alleged inappropriateness of his system 174
The alleged inadequacy of his system 175
A significant contrast with utilitarianism 175

The intellectual virtues according to Aristotle 176
  How can intellectual powers be virtues? 176
    How practical wisdom functions 176
    How scientific wisdom works 177
  An evaluation of Aristotle's ethics 177

Modern virtue ethics 178
  Virtue ethics' distinctive characteristic 179
    Should virtue ethics be theoretical or not? 179
    A question of deciding 180
  Hursthouse's version of virtue ethics 181
    Its general principle: what determines whether an act is right or wrong 181
    The goal of virtue ethics according to Hursthouse 183
  Slote's version of virtue ethics 184
    Slote's first suggestion 184
    Slote's second suggestion: an agent-based ethic of caring 185
    Evaluating Slote's ethic of caring 186

CHAPTER 9. EGOISM 189

Extremism in ethical theory and practice 191

The difference between self-interest and selfishness 193
  The basic difference 193
  The moral acceptability of mixed motives 194
  Christian ethics and the rightness of self-interest 195
    By definition it must be in a creature's self-interest to serve the will and purpose of his/her Creator 195
    It is positively in a person's self-interest to seek reconciliation with God, salvation and eternal life 195
    The meaning of denying oneself 196
  Self-interest is necessary in daily life 197
  Christian ethics and the wrongness of selfishness 198
    The analogy of the human body 199
    The Christian concept of reward-motivated service 200

Ethical egoism 201
  Difficulties for the theory 202
    The question of its status 202
    Universalising the basic principle 202
    Advising someone to act on the basic principle 203
    A universal breakdown of trust 203

Entrepreneurial egoism 204

Psychological egoism 205
  Evaluating psychological egoism 207
    The claim to be scientific 207
    Acting out of several, motives 207
    The grain of truth in psychological egoism 208

PART 3. WHAT USE IS ETHICS? 209

CHAPTER 10. DETERMINING THE VALUE OF A HUMAN BEING 211

Introduction 213

The value of a human being 214
  The materialist viewpoint 214
  Naturalism 215
  Contractarianism 216
  Utilitarianism 216
  Intuitionism 217
  Kantianism 217

Virtue ethics 218
The human race's transcendental value 218

The inescapable choice 219

CHAPTER 11. THE ETHICS OF THE TRANSMISSION OF LIFE 221

The ideal for sexual experience 223

The ethics of maintaining the ideal 224

Two false assumptions 225

Pressure to conform in youth 226

The values and presuppositions of Christian sexual morality 228

An exposition of 1 Corinthians 6:12–20 230

Slogans and replies 230

Basic facts about the body 233

CHAPTER 12. ETHICAL ISSUES RAISED BY SCIENCE AND TECHNOLOGY 235

New possibilities and new questions 237

Issues at the start of life 238

In vitro fertilisation 238

Third-party involvement through donation 239

Ethical problems arising 239

When does life begin? 241

Problems at the end of life 248

A good death? 249

The slippery slope 250

The stress of decision 251

The management of pain 252

CHAPTER 13. EXERCISES IN ETHICS 255

Putting ethics into practice 257

Sport 257

A professional foul 257

Honesty in playing a game 258

Deliberate match-fixing 258

Drug-taking by athletes 259

The commercialisation of sport: merchandising 259

The commercialisation of sport: big business 260

Advertising 260

Preliminary questions 260

An ethical dilemma 261

Advertising techniques 262

Professional ethics 263

Commercial ethics 265

Crime and punishment 267

Environmental ethics 269

CHAPTER 14. BEYOND ETHICS 273

Ethics reveals the problems 275

Socrates' answers 275

Aristotle's view 276

Two of Aristotle's Explanations for deliberate wrongdoing 276

Explanation 1 276

Explanation 2 277

The root-cause and the cure of wrong behaviour 278

The confession of the Apostle Paul 279

The law is spiritual 281

The demand of the law made things worse, not better 281

Inner resources inadequate to overcome weakness 282

A captive in his own castle 282

A Marxist insight 283

The place of ethics in Christian doctrine 285

Ethics is a second order exercise 285

Christian ethics are motivated by the mercies of God 286

The first two major parts of Paul's treatise 287

Part 1   287
Part 2   288
   Differences of theme   288
   The parable of the Prodigal Son revisited   289
   Part 1 of the treatise revisited   290
   Part 2 of the treatise revisited   291
   A summary of part 4 of Paul's treatise   293
Objections to Christian ethics   293

APPENDIX: THE SCIENTIFIC ENDEAVOUR   297

The clear voice of science   299

Scientific method   300
   Observation and experimentation   301
   Data, patterns, relationships and hypotheses   301
   Induction   303
   The role of deduction   306
   Competing hypotheses can cover the same data   308
   Falsifiability   311
   Repeatability and abduction   312

Explaining explanations   315
   Levels of explanation   315
   Reductionism   319

Basic operational presuppositions   323
   Observation is dependent on theory   324
   Knowledge cannot be gained without making certain assumptions to start with   325
   Gaining knowledge involves trusting our senses and other people   326
   Gaining scientific knowledge involves belief in the rational intelligibility of the universe   327
   Operating within the reigning paradigms   329

Further reading   331

DOING WHAT'S RIGHT

SERIES INTRODUCTION

Our worldview . . . includes our views, however ill or well thought out, right or wrong, about the hard yet fascinating questions of existence and life: What am I to make of the universe? Where did it come from? Who am I? Where did I come from? How do I know things? Do I have any significance? Do I have any duty?

THE SHAPING OF A WORLDVIEW
FOR A LIFE FULL OF CHOICES

In this introductory section we are going to consider the need for each one of us to construct his or her own worldview. We shall discuss what a worldview is and why it is necessary to form one; and we shall enquire as to what voices we must listen to as we construct our worldview. As we set out to examine how we understand the world, we are also trying to discover whether we can know the ultimate truth about reality. So each of the subjects in this series will bring us back to the twin questions of what is real and why it matters whether we know what is real. We will, therefore, need to ask as we conclude this introductory section what we mean by 'reality' and then to ask: what is the nature of ultimate reality?[1]

WHY WE NEED A WORLDVIEW

There is a tendency in our modern world for education to become a matter of increasing specialisation. The vast increase of knowledge during the past century means that unless we specialise in this or that topic it is very difficult to keep up with, and grasp the significance of, the ever-increasing flood of new discoveries. In one sense this is to be welcomed because it is the result of something that in itself is one of the marvels of our modern world, namely, the fantastic progress of science and technology.

But while that is so, it is good to remind ourselves that true education has a much wider objective than this. If, for instance, we are to understand the progress of our modern world, we must see it against

---

[1] Please note this Introduction is the same for each book in the series, except for the final section—Our Aim.

the background of the traditions we have inherited from the past and that will mean that we need to have a good grasp of history.

Sometimes we forget that ancient philosophers faced and thought deeply about the basic philosophical principles that underlie all science and came up with answers from which we can still profit. If we forget this, we might spend a lot of time and effort thinking through the same problems and not coming up with as good answers as they did.

Moreover, the role of education is surely to try and understand how all the various fields of knowledge and experience in life fit together. To understand a grand painting one needs to see the picture as a whole and understand the interrelationship of all its details and not simply concentrate on one of its features.

Moreover, while we rightly insist on the objectivity of science we must not forget that it is we who are doing the science. And therefore, sooner or later, we must come to ask how we ourselves fit into the universe that we are studying. We must not allow ourselves to become so engrossed in our material world and its related technologies that we neglect our fellow human beings; for they, as we shall later see, are more important than the rest of the universe put together.[2] The study of ourselves and our fellow human beings will, of course, take more than a knowledge of science. It will involve the worlds of philosophy, sociology, literature, art, music, history and much more besides.

Educationally, therefore, it is an important thing to remember—and a thrilling thing to discover—the interrelation and the unity of all knowledge. Take, for example, what it means to know what a rose is: *What is the truth about a rose?*

To answer the question adequately, we shall have to consult a whole array of people. First the scientists. We begin with the *botanists*, who are constantly compiling and revising lists of all the known plants and flowers in the world and then classifying them in terms of families and groups. They help us to appreciate our rose by telling us what family it belongs to and what are its distinctive features.

Next, the *plant breeders* and *gardeners* will inform us of the history of our particular rose, how it was bred from other kinds, and the conditions under which its sort can best be cultivated.

---

[2] Especially in Book 1 of this series, *Being Truly Human*.

FIGURE I.1. A Rose.

In William Shakespeare's play *Romeo and Juliet*, the beloved dismisses the fact that her lover is from the rival house of Montague, invoking the beauty of one of the best known and most favourite flowers in the world: 'What's in a name? that which we call a rose / By any other name would smell as sweet'.

Reproduced with permission of ©iStock/OGphoto.

Then, the *chemists*, *biochemists*, *biologists* and *geneticists* will tell us about the chemical and biochemical constituents of our rose and the bewildering complexities of its cells, those micro-miniaturised factories which embody mechanisms more complicated than any built by human beings, and yet so tiny that we need highly specialised equipment to see them. They will tell us about the vast coded database of genetic information which the cell factories use in order to produce the building blocks of the rose. They will describe, among a host of other things, the processes by which the rose lives: how it photosynthesises sunlight into sugar-borne energy and the mechanisms by which it is pollinated and propagated.

After that, the *physicists* and *cosmologists* will tell us that the chemicals of which our rose is composed are made up of atoms which themselves are built from various particles like electrons, protons and neutrons. They will give us their account of where the basic material in the universe comes from and how it was formed. If we ask how such knowledge helps us to understand roses, the cosmologists may well point out that our earth is the only planet in our solar system that is able to grow roses! In that respect, as in a multitude of other respects, our planet is very special—and that is surely something to be wondered at.

But when the botanists, plant breeders, gardeners, chemists, biochemists, physicists and cosmologists have told us all they can, and it is a great deal which would fill many volumes, even then many of us will feel that they will scarcely have begun to tell us the truth about roses. Indeed, they have not explained what perhaps most of us would think is the most important thing about roses: the beauty of their form, colour and fragrance.

Now here is a very significant thing: scientists can explain the astonishing complexity of the mechanisms which lie behind our senses of vision and smell that enable us to see roses and detect their scent. But we don't need to ask the scientists whether we ought to consider roses beautiful or not: we can see and smell that for ourselves! We perceive this by *intuition*. We just look at the rose and we can at once see that it is beautiful. We do not need anyone to tell us that it is beautiful. If anyone were so foolish as to suggest that because science cannot measure beauty, therefore beauty does not exist, we should simply say: 'Don't be silly.'

But the perception of beauty does not rest on our own intuition alone. We could also consult the *artists*. With their highly developed sense of colour, light and form, they will help us to perceive a depth and intensity of beauty in a rose that otherwise we might miss. They can educate our eyes.

Likewise, there are the *poets*. They, with their finely honed ability as word artists, will use imagery, metaphor, allusion, rhythm and rhyme to help us formulate and articulate the feelings we experience when we look at roses, feelings that otherwise might remain vague and difficult to express.

Finally, if we wanted to pursue this matter of the beauty of a rose deeper still, we could talk to the *philosophers*, especially experts in aesthetics. For each of us, perceiving that a rose is beautiful is a highly subjective experience, something that we see and feel at a deep level inside ourselves. Nevertheless, when we show a rose to other people, we expect them too to agree that it is beautiful. They usually have no difficulty in doing so.

From this it would seem that, though the appreciation of beauty is a highly subjective experience, yet we observe:

1. there are some objective criteria for deciding what is beautiful and what is not;
2. there is in each person an inbuilt aesthetic sense, a capacity for perceiving beauty; and
3. where some people cannot, or will not, see beauty, in, say, a

rose, or will even prefer ugliness, it must be that their internal capacity for seeing beauty is defective or damaged in some way, as, for instance, by colour blindness or defective shape recognition, or through some psychological disorder (like, for instance, people who revel in cruelty, rather than in kindness).

Now by this time we may think that we have exhausted the truth about roses; but of course we haven't. We have thought about the scientific explanation of roses. We have then considered the value we place on them, their beauty and what they mean to us. But precisely because they have meaning and value, they raise another group of questions about the moral, ethical and eventually spiritual significance of what we do with them. Consider, for instance, the following situations:

First, a woman has used what little spare money she had to buy some roses. She likes roses intensely and wants to keep them as long as she can. But a poor neighbour of hers is sick, and she gets a strong feeling that she ought to give at least some of these roses to her sick neighbour. So now she has two conflicting instincts within her:

1. an instinct of self-interest: a strong desire to keep the roses for herself, and
2. an instinctive sense of duty: she ought to love her neighbour as herself, and therefore give her roses to her neighbour.

Questions arise. Where do these instincts come from? And how shall she decide between them? Some might argue that her selfish desire to keep the roses is simply the expression of the blind, but powerful, basic driving force of evolution: self-propagation. But the altruistic sense of duty to help her neighbour at the expense of loss to herself—where does that come from? Why ought she to obey it? She has a further problem: she must decide one way or the other. She cannot wait for scientists or philosophers, or indeed anyone else, to help her. She has to commit herself to some course of action. How and on what grounds should she decide between the two competing urges?

Second, a man likes roses, but he has no money to buy them. He sees that he could steal roses from someone else's garden in such a way that he could be certain that he would never be found out. Would it be wrong to steal them? If neither the owner of the roses, nor the police, nor the courts would ever find out that he stole them, why shouldn't he steal them? Who has the right to say that it is wrong to steal?

Third, a man repeatedly gives bunches of roses to a woman whose husband is abroad on business. The suspicion is that he is giving her roses in order to tempt her to be disloyal to her husband. That would be adultery. Is adultery wrong? Always wrong? Who has the right to say so?

Now to answer questions like these in the first, second, and third situations thoroughly and adequately we must ask and answer the most fundamental questions that we can ask about roses (and indeed about anything else).

Where do roses come from? We human beings did not create them (and are still far from being able to create anything like them). Is there a God who designed and created them? Is he their ultimate owner, who has the right to lay down the rules as to how we should use them?

Or did roses simply evolve out of eternally existing inorganic matter, without any plan or purpose behind them, and without any ultimate owner to lay down the rules as to how they ought to be used? And if so, is the individual himself free to do what he likes, so long as no one finds out?

So far, then, we have been answering the simple question 'What is the truth about a rose?' and we have found that to answer it adequately we have had to draw on, not one source of knowledge, like science or literature, but on many. Even the consideration of roses has led to deep and fundamental questions about the world beyond the roses.

It is our answers to these questions which combine to shape the framework into which we fit all of our knowledge of other things. That framework, which consists of those ideas, conscious or unconscious, which all of us have about the basic nature of the world and of ourselves and of society, is called our worldview. It includes our views, however ill or well thought out, right or wrong, about the hard yet fascinating questions of existence and life: What am I to make of the universe? Where did it come from? Who am I? Where did I come from? How do

I know things? Do I have any significance? Do I have any duty? Our
worldview is the big picture into which
we fit everything else. It is the lens
through which we look to try to make
sense of the world.

> Our worldview is the big picture
> into which we fit everything else. It
> is the lens through which we look
> to try to make sense of the world.

ASKING THE FUNDAMENTAL QUESTIONS

'He who will succeed', said Aristotle, 'must ask the right questions'; and so, when it comes to forming a worldview, must we.

It is at least comforting to know that we are not the first people to have asked such questions. Many others have done so in the past (and continue to do so in the present). That means they have done some of the work for us! In order to profit from their thinking and experience, it will be helpful for us to collect some of those fundamental questions which have been and are on practically everybody's list. We shall then ask why these particular questions have been thought to be important. After that we shall briefly survey some of the varied answers that have been given, before we tackle the task of forming our own answers. So let's get down to compiling a list of 'worldview questions'. First of all there are questions about the universe in general and about our home planet Earth in particular.

The Greeks were the first people in Europe to ask scientific questions about what the earth and the universe are made of, and how they work. It would appear that they asked their questions for no other reason than sheer intellectual curiosity. Their research was, as we would nowadays describe it, disinterested. They were not at first concerned with any technology that might result from it. Theirs was pure, not applied, science. We pause to point out that it is still a very healthy thing for any educational system to maintain a place for pure science in its curriculum and to foster an attitude of intellectual curiosity for its own sake.

But we cannot afford to limit ourselves to pure science (and even less to technology, marvellous though it is). Centuries ago Socrates perceived that. He was initially curious about the universe, but gradually came to feel that studying how human beings ought to behave was far more important than finding out what the moon was made

DOING WHAT'S RIGHT

FIGURE I.2. *The School of Athens* by Raphael.

Italian Renaissance artist Raphael likely painted the fresco *Scuola di Atene* (The School of Athens), representing Philosophy, between 1509 and 1511 for the Vatican. Many interpreters believe the hand gestures of the central figures, Plato and Aristotle, and the books each is holding respectively, *Timaeus* and *Nicomachean Ethics*, indicate two approaches to metaphysics. A number of other great ancient Greek philosophers are featured by Raphael in this painting, including Socrates (eighth figure to the left of Plato).

Reproduced from Wikimedia Commons.

of. He therefore abandoned physics and immersed himself in moral philosophy.

On the other hand, the leaders of the major philosophical schools in ancient Greece came to see that you could not form an adequate doctrine of human moral behaviour without understanding how human beings are related both to their cosmic environment and to the powers and principles that control the universe. In this they were surely right, which brings us to what was and still is the first fundamental question.[3]

First fundamental worldview question

What lies behind the observable universe? Physics has taught us that things are not quite what they seem to be. A wooden table, which looks solid, turns out to be composed of atoms bound together by powerful forces which operate in the otherwise empty space between them. Each atom turns out also to be mostly empty space and can be modelled from one point of view as a nucleus surrounded by orbiting electrons. The nucleus only occupies about one billionth of the space of the atom. Split the nucleus and we find protons and neutrons. They turn out to be composed of even stranger quarks and gluons. Are these the basic building blocks of matter, or are there other even more mysterious elementary building blocks to be found? That is one of the exciting quests of modern physics. And even as the search goes on, another question keeps nagging: what lies behind basic matter anyway?

The answers that are given to this question fall roughly into two groups: those that suggest that there is nothing 'behind' the basic matter of the universe, and those that maintain that there certainly is something.

> Group A. There is nothing but matter. It is the prime reality, being self-existent and eternal. It is not dependent on anything or on anyone. It is blind and purposeless; nevertheless it has within it the power to develop and organise itself—still blindly and purposelessly—into all the variety of matter and

---

[3] See Book 4: *Doing What's Right*.

life that we see in the universe today. This is the philosophy of materialism.

Group B. Behind matter, which had a beginning, stands some uncreated self-existent, creative Intelligence; or, as Jews and Muslims would say, God; and Christians, the God and Father of the Lord Jesus Christ. This God upholds the universe, interacts with it, but is not part of it. He is spirit, not matter. The universe exists as an expression of his mind and for the purpose of fulfilling his will. This is the philosophy of theism.

Second fundamental worldview question

This leads us to our second fundamental worldview question, which is in three parts: *how did our world come into existence, how has it developed, and how has it come to be populated with such an amazing variety of life?*

Again, answers to these questions tend to fall into two groups:

Group A. Inanimate matter itself, without any antecedent design or purpose, formed into that conglomerate which became the earth and then in some way (not yet observed or understood) as a result of its own inherent properties and powers by spontaneous generation spawned life. The initial lowly life forms then gradually evolved into the present vast variety of life through the natural processes of mutation and natural selection, mechanisms likewise without any design or purpose. There is, therefore, no ultimate rational purpose behind either the existence of the universe, or of earth and its inhabitants.

Group B. The universe, the solar system and planet Earth have been designed and precision engineered to make it possible for life to exist on earth. The astonishing complexity of living systems, and the awesome sophistication of their mechanisms, point in the same direction.

It is not difficult to see what different implications the two radically different views have for human significance and behaviour.

Third fundamental worldview question

The third fundamental worldview question comes, again, as a set of related questions with the answers commonly given to central ideas falling into two groups: *What are human beings? Where do their rationality and moral sense come from? What are their hopes for the future, and what, if anything, happens to them after death?*

Group A. *Human nature.* Human beings are nothing but matter. They have no spirit and their powers of rational thought have arisen out of mindless matter by non-rational processes.

Morality. Man's sense of morality and duty arise solely out of social interactions between him and his fellow humans.

Human rights. Human beings have no inherent, natural rights, but only those that are granted by society or the government of the day.

Purpose in life. Man makes his own purpose.

The future. The utopia dreamed of and longed for will be brought about, either by the irresistible outworking of the forces inherent in matter and/or history; or, alternatively, as human beings learn to direct and control the biological processes of evolution itself.

Death and beyond. Death for each individual means total extinction. Nothing survives.

Group B. *Human nature.* Human beings are created by God, indeed in the image of God (according, at least, to Judaism, Christianity and Islam). Human beings' powers of rationality are derived from the divine 'Logos' through whom they were created.

Morality. Their moral sense arises from certain 'laws of God' implanted in them by their Creator.

Human rights. They have certain inalienable rights which all other human beings and governments must respect, simply because they are creatures of God, created in God's image.

Purpose in life. Their main purpose in life is to enjoy fellowship with God and to serve God, and likewise to serve their fellow creatures for their Creator's sake.

The future. The utopia they long for is not a dream, but a sure hope based on the Creator's plan for the redemption of humankind and of the world.

Death and beyond. Death does not mean extinction. Human beings, after death, will be held accountable to God. Their ultimate state will eventually be, either to be with God in total fellowship in heaven; or to be excluded from his presence.

These, very broadly speaking, are the questions that people have asked through the whole of recorded history, and a brief survey of some of the answers that have been, and still are, given to them.

The fundamental difference between the two groups of answers

Now it is obvious that the two groups of answers given above are diametrically opposed; but we ought to pause here to make sure that we have understood what exactly the nature and cause of the opposition is. If we were not thinking carefully, we might jump to the conclusion that the answers in the A-groups are those given by science, while the answers in the B-groups are those given by religion. But that would be a fundamental misunderstanding of the situation. It is true that the majority of scientists today would agree with the answers given in the A-groups; but there is a growing number of scientists who would agree with the answers given in the B-groups. It is not therefore a conflict between science and religion. It is a difference in the basic philosophies which determine the interpretation of the evidence which science provides. Atheists will interpret that evidence in one way; theists (or pantheists) will interpret it in another.

This is understandable. No scientist comes to the task of doing research with a mind completely free of presuppositions. The atheist does research on the presupposition that there is no God. That is his basic philosophy, his worldview. He claims that he can explain everything without God. He will sometimes say that he cannot imagine what kind of scientific evidence there could possibly be for the existence of God; and not surprisingly he tends not to find any.

The theist, on the other hand, starts by believing in God and finds in his scientific discoveries abundant—overwhelming, he would say—evidence of God's hand in the sophisticated design and mechanisms of the universe.

It all comes down, then, to the importance of recognising what worldview we start with. Some of us, who have never yet thought deeply about these things, may feel that we have no worldview, and that we come to life's questions in general, and science in particular, with a completely open mind. But that is unlikely to be so. We pick up ideas, beliefs and attitudes from our family and society, often without realising that we have done so, and without recognising how these largely unconscious influences and presuppositions control our reactions to the questions with which life faces us. Hence the importance of consciously thinking through our worldview and of adjusting it where necessary to take account of the evidence available.

> We pick up ideas, beliefs and attitudes from our family and society, often without realising that we have done so, and without recognising how these largely unconscious influences and presuppositions control our reactions to the questions with which life faces us.

In that process, then, we certainly must listen to science and allow it to critique where necessary and to amend our presuppositions. But to form an adequate worldview we shall need to listen to many other voices as well.

VOICES TO BE LISTENED TO

So far, then, we have been surveying some worldview questions and various answers that have been, and still are, given to them. Now we must face these questions ourselves, and begin to come to our own decisions about them.

Our worldview must be our own, in the sense that we have personally thought it through and adopted it of our own free will. No one has the right to impose his or her worldview on us by force. The days are rightly gone when the church could force Galileo to deny what science had plainly taught him. Gone, too, for the most part, are the days when the State could force an atheistic worldview on people on pain of prison and even death. Human rights demand that people should be free to hold and to propagate by reasoned argument whatever worldview they believe in—so long, of course, that their view does not injure other people. We, the authors of this book, hold a theistic worldview. But we shall not attempt to force our view down anybody's throat. We come from a tradition whose basic principle is 'Let everyone be persuaded in his own mind.'

So we must all make up our own minds and form our own worldview. In the process of doing so there are a number of voices that we must listen to.

The voice of intuition

The first voice we must listen to is intuition. There are things in life that we see and know, not as the result of lengthy philosophical reasoning, nor as a result of rigorous scientific experimentation, but by direct, instinctive intuition. We 'see' that a rose is beautiful. We instinctively 'know' that child abuse is wrong. A scientist can sometimes 'see' what the solution to a problem is going to be even before he has worked out the scientific technique that will eventually provide formal proof of it.

A few scientists and philosophers still try to persuade us that the laws of cause and effect operating in the human brain are completely deterministic so that our decisions are predetermined: real choice is not possible. But, say what they will, we ourselves intuitively know that we do have the ability to make a free choice, whether, say, to read a book, or to go for a walk, whether to tell the truth or to tell a lie. We know we are free to take either course of action, and everyone else knows it too, and acts accordingly. This freedom is such a part of our innate concept of human dignity and value that we (for the most part) insist on being treated as responsible human beings and on treating others as such. For that reason, if we commit a crime, the magistrate will first enquire (*a*) if, when we committed the crime, we knew we were doing wrong; and (*b*) whether or not we were acting under duress. The answer to these questions will determine the verdict.

We must, therefore, give due attention to intuition, and not allow ourselves to be persuaded by pseudo-intellectual arguments to deny (or affirm) what we intuitively know to be true (or false).

On the other hand, intuition has its limits. It can be mistaken. When ancient scientists first suggested that the world was a sphere, even some otherwise great thinkers rejected the idea. They intuitively felt that it was absurd to think that there were human beings on the opposite side of the earth to us, walking 'upside-down', their feet pointed towards our feet (hence the term 'antipodean') and their heads hanging perilously down into empty space! But intuition had misled them. The scientists who believed in a spherical earth were right, intuition was wrong.

The lesson is that we need both intuition and science, acting as checks and balances, the one on the other.

The voice of science

Science speaks to our modern world with a very powerful and authoritative voice. It can proudly point to a string of scintillating theoretical breakthroughs which have spawned an almost endless array of technological spin-offs: from the invention of the light bulb to virtual-reality environments; from the wheel to the moon-landing vehicle; from the discovery of aspirin and antibiotics to the cracking of the genetic code; from the vacuum cleaner to the smartphone; from the abacus to the parallel computer; from the bicycle to the self-driving car. The benefits that come from these achievements of science are self-evident, and they both excite our admiration and give to science an immense credibility.

Yet for many people the voice of science has a certain ambivalence about it. For the achievements of science are not invariably used for the good of humanity. Indeed, in the past century science has produced the most hideously efficient weapons of destruction that the world has ever seen. The laser that is used to restore vision to the eye can be used to guide missiles with deadly efficiency. This development has led in recent times to a strong anti-scientific reaction. This is understandable; but we need to guard against the obvious fallacy of blaming science for the misuse made of its discoveries. The blame for the devastation caused by the atomic bomb, for instance, does not chiefly lie with the scientists who discovered the possibility of atomic fission and fusion, but with the politicians who for reasons of global conquest insisted on the discoveries being used for the making of weapons of mass destruction.

Science, in itself, is morally neutral. Indeed, as scientists who are Christians would say, it is a form of the worship of God through the reverent study of his handiwork and is by all means to be encouraged. It is for that reason that James Clerk Maxwell, the nineteenth-century Scottish physicist who discovered the famous equations governing electromagnetic waves which are now called after him, put the following quotation from the Hebrew Psalms above the door of the Cavendish Laboratory in Cambridge where it still stands: 'The works of the LORD are great, sought out of all them that have pleasure therein' (Ps 111:2).

We must distinguish, of course, between science as a method of investigation and individual scientists who actually do the investigation. We must also distinguish between the facts which they establish beyond (reasonable) doubt and the tentative hypotheses and theories which they construct on the basis of their initial observations and experiments, and which they use to guide their subsequent research.

These distinctions are important because scientists sometimes mistake their tentative theories for proven fact, and in their teaching of students and in their public lectures promulgate as established fact what has never actually been proved. It can also happen that scientists advance a tentative theory which catches the attention of the media who then put it across to the public with so much hype that the impression is given that the theory has been established beyond question.

> Scientists sometimes mistake their tentative theories for proven fact, and in their teaching of students and in their public lectures promulgate as established fact what has never actually been proved.

Then again, we need to remember the proper limits of science. As we discovered when talking about the beauty of roses, there are things which science, strictly so called, cannot and should not be expected to explain.

Sometimes some scientists forget this, and damage the reputation of science by making wildly exaggerated claims for it. The famous mathematician and philosopher Bertrand Russell, for instance, once wrote: 'Whatever knowledge is attainable, must be attained by scientific methods; and what science cannot discover, mankind cannot know.'[4] Nobel laureate Sir Peter Medawar had a saner and more realistic view of science. He wrote:

> There is no quicker way for a scientist to bring discredit upon himself and on his profession than roundly to declare—particularly when no declaration of any kind is called for—that science knows or soon will know the answers to all questions worth asking, and that the questions that do not admit a scientific answer are in some way nonquestions or 'pseudoquestions' that only simpletons ask and only the gullible profess to be able to answer.[5]

Medawar says elsewhere: 'The existence of a limit to science is, however, made clear by its inability to answer childlike elementary questions having to do with first and last things—questions such as "How did everything begin?"; "What are we all here for?"; "What is the point of living?"' He adds that it is to imaginative literature and religion that we must turn for answers to such questions.[6]

However, when we have said all that should be said about the limits of science, the voice of science is still one of the most important voices to which we must listen in forming our worldview. We cannot, of course, all be experts in science. But when the experts report their findings to students in other disciplines or to the general public, as they increasingly do, we all must listen to them; listen as critically as we listen to experts in other fields. But we must listen.[7]

The voice of philosophy

The next voice we must listen to is the voice of philosophy. To some people the very thought of philosophy is daunting; but actually anyone

---
[4] Russell, *Religion and Science*, 243.
[5] Medawar, *Advice to a Young Scientist*, 31.
[6] Medawar, *Limits of Science*, 59–60.
[7] Those who wish to study the topic further are directed to the Appendix in this book: 'The Scientific Endeavour', and to the books by John Lennox noted there.

who seriously attempts to investigate the truth of any statement is already thinking philosophically. Eminent philosopher Anthony Kenny writes:

> Philosophy is exciting because it is the broadest of all disciplines, exploring the basic concepts which run through all our talking and thinking on any topic whatever. Moreover, it can be undertaken without any special preliminary training or instruction; anyone can do philosophy who is willing to think hard and follow a line of reasoning.[8]

Whether we realise it or not, the way we think and reason owes a great deal to philosophy—we have already listened to its voice!

Philosophy has a number of very positive benefits to confer on us. First and foremost is the shining example of men and women who have refused to go through life unthinkingly adopting whatever happened to be the majority view at the time. Socrates said that the unexamined life is not worth living. These men and women were determined to use all their intellectual powers to try to understand what the universe was made of, how it worked, what man's place in it was, what the essence of human nature was, why we human beings so frequently do wrong and so damage ourselves and society; what could help us to avoid doing wrong; and what our chief goal in life should be, our *summum bonum* (Latin for 'chief good'). Their zeal to discover the truth and then to live by it should encourage—perhaps even shame—us to follow their example.

Secondly, it was in their search for the truth that philosophers from Socrates, Plato, and Aristotle onwards discovered the need for, and the rules of, rigorous logical thinking. The benefit of this to humanity is incalculable, in that it enables us to learn to think straight, to expose the presuppositions that lie sometimes unnoticed behind even our scientific experiments and theories, to unpick the assumptions that lurk in the formulation and expressions of our opinions, to point to fallacies in our argumentation, to detect instances of circular reasoning, and so on.

However, philosophy, just like science, has its proper limits. It cannot tell us what axioms or fundamental assumptions we should

---

[8] Kenny, *Brief History of Western Philosophy*, xi.

adopt; but it can and will help us to see if the belief system which we build on those axioms is logically consistent.

There is yet a third benefit to be gained from philosophy. The history of philosophy shows that, of all the many different philosophical systems, or worldviews, that have been built up by rigorous philosophers on the basis of human reasoning alone, none has proved convincing to all other philosophers, let alone to the general public. None has achieved permanence, a fact which can seem very frustrating. But perhaps the frustration is not altogether bad in that it might lead us to ask whether there could just be another source of information without which human reason alone is by definition inadequate. And if our very frustration with philosophy for having seemed at first to promise so much satisfaction, and then in the end to have delivered so little, disposes us to look around for that other source of information, even our frustration could turn out to be a supreme benefit.

The voice of history

Yet another voice to which we must listen is the voice of history. We are fortunate indeed to be living so far on in the course of human history as we do. Already in the first century AD a simple form of jet propulsion was described by Hero of Alexandria. But technology at that time knew no means of harnessing that discovery to any worthwhile practical purpose. Eighteen hundred years were to pass before scientists discovered a way of making jet engines powerful enough to be fitted to aircraft.

When in the 1950s and 1960s scientists, working on the basis of a discovery of Albert Einstein's, argued that it would be possible to make laser beams, and then actually made them, many people mockingly said that lasers were a solution to a non-existent problem, because no one could think of a practical use to which they could be put. History has proved the critics wrong and justified the pure scientists (if pure science needs any justification!).

In other cases history has taught the opposite lesson. At one point the phlogiston theory of combustion came to be almost universally accepted. History eventually proved it wrong.

Fanatical religious sects (in spite, be it said, of the explicit prohibition of the Bible) have from time to time predicted that the end of the world would take place at such-and-such a time in such-and-such a place. History has invariably proved them wrong.

In the last century, the philosophical system known as logical positivism arose like a meteor and seemed set to dominate the philosophical landscape, superseding all other systems. But history discovered its fatal flaw, namely that it was based on a verification principle which allowed only two kinds of meaningful statement: *analytic* (a statement which is true by definition, that is a tautology like 'a vixen is a female fox'), or *synthetic* (a statement which is capable of verification by experiment, like 'water is composed of hydrogen and oxygen'). Thus all metaphysical statements were dismissed as meaningless! But, as philosopher Karl Popper famously pointed out, the Verification Principle itself is neither analytic nor synthetic and so is meaningless! Logical positivism is therefore self-refuting. Professor Nicholas Fotion, in his article on the topic in *The Oxford Companion to Philosophy*, says: 'By the late 1960s it became obvious that the movement had pretty much run its course.'[9]

Earlier still, Marx, basing himself on Hegel, applied his dialectical materialism first to matter and then to history. He claimed to have discovered a law in the workings of social and political history that would irresistibly lead to the establishment of a utopia on earth; and millions gave their lives to help forward this process. The verdict has been that history seems not to know any such irresistible law.

History has also delivered a devastating verdict on the Nazi theory of the supremacy of the Aryan races, which, it was promised, would lead to a new world order.

History, then, is a very valuable, if sometimes very disconcerting, adjudicator of our ideas and systems of thought. We should certainly pay serious heed to its lessons and be grateful for them.

But there is another reason why we should listen to history. It introduces us to the men and women who have proved to be world leaders of thought and whose influence is still a live force among us today. Among them, of course, is Jesus Christ. He was rejected, as we know, by his contemporaries and executed. But, then, so was Socrates. Socrates' influence has lived on; but Christ's influence has been and still is infinitely greater than that of Socrates, or of any other world leader. It would

---

[9] Fotion, 'Logical Positivism'.

be very strange if we listened, as we do, to Socrates, Plato, Aristotle, Hume, Kant, Marx and Einstein, and neglected or refused to listen to Christ. The numerous (and some very early) manuscripts of the New Testament make available to us an authentic record of his teaching. Only extreme prejudice would dismiss him without first listening to what he says.

> History introduces us to the men and women who have proved to be world leaders of thought and whose influence is still a live force among us today. . . . It would be very strange if we listened, as we do, to Socrates, Plato, Aristotle, Hume, Kant, Marx and Einstein, and neglected or refused to listen to Christ.

The voice of divine self-revelation

The final voice that claims the right to be heard is a voice which runs persistently through history and refuses to be silenced in claiming that there is another source of information beyond that which intuition, scientific research and philosophical reasoning can provide. That voice is the voice of divine self-revelation. The claim is that the Creator, whose existence and power can be intuitively perceived through his created works, has not otherwise remained silent and aloof. In the course of the centuries he has spoken into our world through his prophets and supremely through Jesus Christ.

Of course, atheists will say that for them this claim seems to be the stuff of fairy tales; and atheistic scientists will object that there is no scientific evidence for the existence of a creator (indeed, they may well claim that assuming the existence of a creator destroys the foundation of true scientific methodology—for more of that see this book's Appendix); and that, therefore, the idea that we could have direct information from the creator himself is conceptually absurd. This reaction is, of course, perfectly consistent with the basic assumption of atheism.

However, apparent conceptual absurdity is not proof positive that something is not possible, or even true. Remember what we noticed earlier, that many leading thinkers, when they first encountered the suggestion that the earth was not flat but spherical, rejected it out of hand because of the conceptual absurdities to which they imagined it led.

In the second century AD a certain Lucian of Samosata decided to debunk what he thought to be fanciful speculations of the early scientists and the grotesque traveller's tales of so-called explorers. He wrote a book which, with his tongue in his cheek, he called *Vera historia* (A True Story). In it he told how he had travelled through space to the moon. He discovered that the moon-dwellers had a special kind of mirror by means of which they could see what people were doing on earth. They also possessed something like a well shaft by means of which they could even hear what people on earth were saying. His prose was sober enough, as if he were writing factual history. But he expected his readers to see that the very conceptual absurdity of what he claimed to have seen meant that these things were impossible and would forever remain so.

Unknown to him, however, the forces and materials already existed in nature, which, when mankind learned to harness them, would send some astronauts into orbit round the moon, land others on the moon, and make possible radio and television communication between the moon and the earth!

We should remember, too, that atomic radiation and radio frequency emissions from distant galaxies were not invented by scientists in recent decades. They were there all the time, though invisible and undetected and not believed in nor even thought of for centuries; but they were not discovered until comparatively recent times, when brilliant scientists conceived the possibility that, against all popular expectation, such phenomena might exist. They looked for them, and found them.

Is it then, after all, so conceptually absurd to think that our human intellect and rationality come not from mindless matter through the agency of impersonal unthinking forces, but from a higher personal intellect and reason?

An old, but still valid, analogy will help us at this point. If we ask about a particular motor car: 'Where did this motor car begin?' one answer would be, 'It began on the production lines of such-and-such a factory and was put together by humans and robots.'

Another, deeper-level, answer would be: 'It had its beginning in the mineral from which its constituent parts were made.'

But in the prime sense of beginning, the motor car, of which this particular motor car is a specimen, had its beginning, not in the factory, nor in its basic materials, but in something altogether different: in the intelligent mind of a person, that is, of its inventor. We know this, of course, by history and by experience; but we also know it intuitively: it is self-evidently true.

Millions of people likewise have felt, and still do feel, that what Christ and his prophets say about the 'beginning' of our human rationality is similarly self-evidently true: 'In the beginning was the Logos, and the Logos was with God, and the Logos was God. . . . All things were made by him . . .' (John 1:1–2, our trans.). That is, at any rate, a far more likely story than that our human intelligence and rationality sprang originally out of mindless matter, by accidental permutations, selected by unthinking nature.

Now the term 'Logos' means both rationality and the expression of that rationality through intelligible communication. If that rational intelligence is God and personal, and we humans are endowed by him with personhood and intelligence, then it is far from being absurd to think that the divine Logos, whose very nature and function it is to be the expression and communicator of that intelligence, should communicate with us. On the contrary, to deny a priori the possibility of divine revelation and to shut one's ears in advance to what Jesus Christ has to say, before listening to his teaching to see if it is, or is not, self-evidently true, is not the true scientific attitude, which is to keep an open mind and explore any reasonable avenue to truth.[10]

Moreover, the fear that to assume the existence of a creator God would undermine true scientific methodology is contradicted by the sheer facts of history. Sir Francis Bacon (1561–1626), widely regarded as the father of the modern scientific method, believed that God had revealed himself in two great Books, the Book of Nature and the Book of God's Word, the Bible. In his famous *Advancement of Learning* (1605), Bacon wrote: 'Let no man . . . think or maintain, that a man can search too far, or be too well studied in the book of God's word, or in the book of God's works; divinity or philosophy; but rather let men endeavour an endless progress or proficience in both.'[11] It is this quotation which Charles Darwin chose to put at the front of *On the Origin of Species* (1859).

---

[10] For the fuller treatment of these questions and related topics, see Book 5 in this series, *Claiming to Answer*.
[11] Bacon, *Advancement of Learning*, 8.

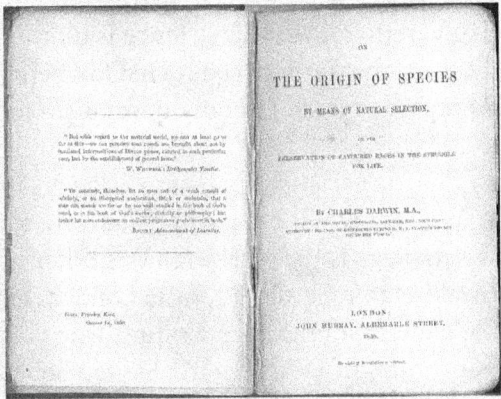

FIGURE I.3.
On the Origin of Species (1859) by Charles Darwin.

One of the book epigraphs Charles Darwin selected for his magnum opus is from Francis Bacon's *Advancement of Learning* (1605).

Reproduced from Dennis O'Neil.

Historians of science point out that it was this theistic 'Two-Book' view which was largely responsible for the meteoric rise of science beginning in the sixteenth century. C. S. Lewis refers to a statement by one of the most eminent historians of all time, Sir Alfred North Whitehead, and says: 'Professor Whitehead points out that centuries of belief in a God who combined "the personal energy of Jehovah" with "the rationality of a Greek philosopher" first produced that firm expectation of systematic order which rendered possible the birth of modern science. Men became scientific because they expected Law in Nature and they expected Law in Nature because they believed in a Legislator.'[12] In other words, theism was the cradle of science. Indeed, far from thinking that the idea of a creator was conceptually absurd, most of the great leaders of science in that period did believe in a creator.

Johannes Kepler	1571–1630	Celestial mechanics
Blaise Pascal	1623–62	Hydrostatics
Robert Boyle	1627–91	Chemistry, Gas dynamics
Isaac Newton	1642–1727	Mathematics, Optics, Dynamics
Michael Faraday	1791–1867	Magnetism
Charles Babbage	1791–1871	Computer science
Gregor Mendel	1822–84	Genetics
Louis Pasteur	1822–95	Bacteriology
Lord Kelvin	1824–1907	Thermodynamics
James Clerk Maxwell	1831–79	Electrodynamics, Thermodynamics

[12] Lewis, *Miracles*, 110.

All of these famous men would have agreed with Einstein: 'Science without religion is lame, religion without science is blind.'[13] History shows us very clearly, then, that far from belief in God being a hindrance to science, it has provided one of the main impulses for its development.

Still today there are many first-rate scientists who are believers in God. For example, Professor William D. Phillips, Nobel laureate for Physics 1997, is an active Christian, as is the world-famous botanist and former Director of the Royal Botanic Gardens, Kew in London, Sir Ghillean Prance, and so is the geneticist Francis S. Collins, who was the Director of the National Institutes of Health in the United States who gained recognition for his leadership of the international Human Genome Project which culminated in 2003 with the completion of a finished sequence of human DNA.[14]

But with many people another objection arises: if one is not sure that God even exists, would it not be unscientific to go looking for evidence for God's existence? Surely not. Take the late Professor Carl Sagan and the Search for Extra Terrestrial Intelligence (the SETI project), which he promoted. Sagan was a famous astronomer, but when he began this search he had no hard-and-fast proven facts to go on. He proceeded simply on the basis of a hypothesis. If intelligent life has evolved on earth, then it would be possible, perhaps even likely, that it would have developed on other suitable planets elsewhere in the universe. He had no guarantee that it was so, or that he would find it, even if it existed. But even so both he and NASA (the National Aeronautics and Space Administration) thought it worth spending great effort, time and considerable sums of money to employ radio telescopes to listen to remote galaxies for evidence of intelligent life elsewhere in the universe.

Why, then, should it be thought any less scientific to look for an intelligent creator, especially when there is evidence that the universe bears the imprint of his mind? The only valid excuse for not seeking for God would be the possession of convincing evidence that God does not, and could not, exist. No one has such proof.

---

[13] Einstein, 'Science and Religion'.
[14] The list could go on, as any Internet search for 'Christians in science' will show.

SERIES INTRODUCTION

But for many people divine revelation seems, nonetheless, an utter impossibility, for they have the impression that science has outgrown the cradle in which it was born and somehow proved that there is no God after all. For that reason, we examine in greater detail in the Appendix to this book what science is, what it means to be truly scientific in outlook, what science has and has not proved, and some of the fallacious ways in which science is commonly misunderstood. Here we must consider even larger questions about reality.

> The only valid excuse for not seeking for God would be the possession of convincing evidence that God does not, and could not, exist. No one has such proof.

THE MEANING OF REALITY

One of the central questions we are setting out to examine is: can we know the ultimate truth about reality? Before we consider different aspects of reality, we need to determine what we mean by 'reality'. For that purpose let's start with the way we use the term in ordinary, everyday language. After that we can move on to consider its use at higher levels.

In everyday language the noun 'reality', the adjective 'real', and the adverb 'really' have several different connotations according to the contexts in which they are used. Let's think about some examples.

First, in some situations the opposite of 'real' is 'imaginary' or 'illusory'. So, for instance, a thirsty traveller in the Sahara may see in the distance what looks to him like an oasis with water and palm trees, when in fact there is no oasis there at all. What he thinks he sees is a mirage, an optical illusion. The oasis is not real, we say; it does not actually exist.[15] Similarly a patient, having been injected with powerful drugs in the course of a serious operation, may upon waking up from the anaesthetic suffer hallucinations, and imagine she sees all kinds of weird creatures stalking round her room. But if we say, as we do, that these things which

---

[15] Mirages occur 'when sharp differences in temperature and therefore in density develop between thin layers of air at and immediately above the ground. This causes light to be bent, or refracted, as it travels through one layer to the next. . . . During the day, when a warm layer occurs next to the ground, objects near the horizon often appear to be reflected in flat surfaces, such as beaches, deserts, roads and water. This produces the shimmering, floating images which are commonly observed on very hot days.' *Oxford Reference Encyclopaedia*, 913.

she imagines she sees, are not real, we mean that they do not in actual fact exist. We could argue, of course, that something is going on in the patient's brain, and she is experiencing impressions similar to those she would have received if the weird creatures had been real. Her impressions, then, are real in the sense that they exist in her brain; but they do not correspond with the external reality that the patient supposes is creating these sense impressions. The mechanisms of her brain are presenting her with a false picture: the weird creatures do not exist. She is not seeing *them*. They are not real. On the basis of examples like this (the traveller and the patient) some philosophers have argued that none of us can ever be sure that the sense impressions which we think we receive from the external world are true representations of the external world, and not illusions. We consider their arguments in detail in Book 3 in this series, *Questioning Our Knowledge*, dealing with epistemology and related matters.

To sum up so far, then: neither the traveller nor the patient was perceiving external reality as it really was. But the reasons for their failure were different: with the traveller it was an external illusion (possibly reinforced by his thirst) that made him misread reality and imagine there was a real oasis there, when there wasn't. With the patient there was nothing unusual in the appearance of her room to cause her disordered perception. The difficulty was altogether internal to her. The drugs had distorted the perception mechanisms of her brain.

From these two examples we can learn some practical lessons:

1. It is important for us all to question from time to time whether what we unthinkingly take to be reality is in fact reality.
2. In cases like these it is external reality that has to be the standard by which we judge whether our sense perceptions are true or not.
3. Setting people free from their internal subjective misperceptions will depend on getting them, by some means or other, to face and perceive the external, objective reality.

Second, in other situations the opposite of 'real', in everyday language, is 'counterfeit', 'spurious', 'fraudulent'. So if we describe a piece of metal as being 'real gold', we mean that it is genuine gold, and not something such as brass that looks like gold, but isn't. The practical importance of being able to discern the difference between what is real in this sense and what is spurious or counterfeit, can easily be illustrated.

Take coinage, for instance. In past centuries, when coins were made (or supposed to be made) of real gold, or real silver, fraudsters would often adulterate the coinage by mixing inferior metal with gold or silver. Buyers or sellers, if they had no means of testing whether the coins they were offered were genuine, and of full value, or not, could easily be cheated.

Similarly, in our modern world counterfeiters print false bank notes and surreptitiously get them into circulation. Eventually, when the fraud is discovered, banks and traders refuse the spurious bank notes, with the result that innocent people are left with worthless pieces of paper.

Or, again, a dishonest jeweller might show a rich woman a necklace made, according to him, of valuable gems; and the rich, but unsuspecting, woman might pay a large price for it, only to discover later on that the gems were not real: they were imitations, made of a kind of glass called paste, or strass.

Conversely, an elderly woman might take her necklace, made of real gems, to a jeweller and offer to sell it to him in order to get some money to maintain herself in her old age. But the unscrupulous jeweller might make out that the gems were not as valuable as she thought: they were imitations, made of paste; and by this deceit he would persuade the reluctant woman to sell him the necklace for a much lesser price than it was worth.

Once more it will be instructive to study the underlying principles at work in these examples, because later on, when we come to study reality at a higher level, they could provide us with helpful analogies and thought models.[16]

Notice, then, that these last three examples involve significantly different principles from those that were operating in the two which we studied earlier. The oasis and the weird creatures were not real, because they did not actually exist in the external world. But the spurious coins, the fraudulent bank notes, and the genuine and the

---

[16] See especially in Book 2: *Finding Ultimate Reality*.

imitation gems, all existed in the external world. In that sense, therefore, they were all real, part of the external reality, actual pieces of matter.

What, then, was the trouble with them? It was that the fraudsters had claimed for the coins and the bank notes a value and a buying power that they did not actually possess; and in the case of the two necklaces the unscrupulous jewellers had on both occasions misrepresented the nature of the matter of which the gems were composed.

The question arises: how can people avoid being taken in by such spurious claims and misrepresentations of matter? It is not difficult to see how questions like this will become important when we come to consider the matter of the universe and its properties.

In modern, as in ancient, times, to test whether an object is made of pure gold or not, use is made of a black, fine-grained, siliceous stone, called a touchstone. When pure gold is rubbed on this touchstone, it leaves behind on the stone streaks of a certain character; whereas objects made of adulterated gold, or of some baser metal, will leave behind streaks of a different character.

FIGURE I.4. A Touchstone.

First mentioned by Theophrastus (c.372–c.287 BC) in his treatise *On Stone*, touchstones are tablets of finely grained black stones used to assay or estimate the proportion of gold or silver in a sample of metal. Traces of gold can be seen on the stone.

Reproduced from Mauro Cateb/Flickr.

In the ancient world merchants would always carry a touchstone with them; but even so it would require considerable knowledge and expertise to interpret the test correctly. When it comes to bank notes and gems, the imitations may be so cleverly made that only an expert could tell the difference between the real thing and the false. In that case non-experts, like ourselves, would have to depend on the judgments of experts.

But what are we to do when the experts disagree? How do we

decide which experts to trust? Is there any kind of touchstone that ordinary people can use on the experts themselves, or at least on their interpretations?

There is one more situation worth investigating at this point before we begin our main study.

Third, when we are confronted with what purports to be an account of something that happened in the past and of the causes that led to its happening, we rightly ask questions: 'Did this event really take place? Did it take place in the way that this account says it did? Was the alleged cause the real cause?' The difficulty with things that happened in the past is that we cannot get them to repeat themselves in the present, and watch them happening all over again in our laboratories. We have therefore to search out and study what evidence is available and then decide which interpretation of the evidence best explains what actually happened.

This, of course, is no unusual situation to be in. Detectives, seeking to solve a murder mystery and to discover the real criminal, are constantly in this situation; and this is what historians and archaeologists and palaeontologists do all the time. But mistakes can be made in handling and interpreting the evidence. For instance, in 1980 a man and his wife were camping in the Australian outback, when a dingo (an Australian wild dog) suddenly attacked and killed their little child. When, however, the police investigated the matter, they did not believe the parents' story; they alleged that the woman herself had actually killed the child. The courts found her guilty and she was duly sentenced. But new evidence was discovered that corroborated the parents' story, and proved that it really was a dingo that killed the infant. The couple was not fully and finally exonerated until 2012.

Does this kind of case mean, then, that we cannot ever be certain that any historical event really happened? Or that we can never be sure as to its real causes? Of course not! It is beyond all doubt that, for instance, Napoleon invaded Russia, and that Genghis Khan besieged Beijing (then called Zhongdu). The question is, as we considered earlier: what kind of evidence must we have in order to be sure that a historical event really happened?

But enough of these preliminary exercises. It is time now to take our first step towards answering the question: can we know the ultimate truth about reality?

WHAT IS THE NATURE OF ULTIMATE REALITY?

We have thought about the meaning of reality in various practical situations in daily life. Now we must begin to consider reality at the higher levels of our own individual existence, and that of our fellow human beings, and eventually that of the whole universe.

Ourselves as individuals

Let's start with ourselves as individuals. We know we exist. We do not have to engage in lengthy philosophical discussion before we can be certain that we exist. We know it intuitively. Indeed, we cannot logically deny it. If I were to claim 'I do not exist', I would, by stating my claim, refute it. A non-existent person cannot make any claim. If I didn't exist, I couldn't even say 'I do not exist', since I have to exist in order to make the claim. I cannot, therefore, logically affirm my own non-existence.[17]

There are other things too which we know about ourselves by intuition.

First, we are self-conscious, that is, we are aware of ourselves as separate individuals. I know I am not my brother, or my sister, or my next-door neighbour. I was born of my parents; but I am not just an extension of my father and mother. I am a separate individual, a human being in my own right. My will is not a continuation of their will, such that, if they will something, I automatically will the same thing. My will is my own.

My will may be conditioned by many past experiences, most of which have now passed into my subconscious memory. My will may well be pressurised by many internal desires or fears, and by external circumstances. But whatever philosophers of the determinist school may say, we know in our heart of hearts that we have the power of choice. Our wills, in that sense, are free. If they weren't, no one could ever be held to be guilty for doing wrong, or praised for doing right.

Second, *we are also intuitively aware of ourselves as persons, intrinsically different from, and superior to, non-personal things*. It is not a

---

[17] We call this law of logic the law of non-affirmability.

question of size, but of mind and personality. A mountain may be large, but it is mindless and impersonal. It is composed of non-rational matter. We are aware of the mountain; it is not aware of us. It is not aware of itself. It neither loves nor hates, neither anticipates nor reflects, has no hopes nor fears. Non-rational though it is, if it became a volcano, it might well destroy us, though we are rational beings. Yet we should not conclude from the fact that simply because such impersonal, non-rational matter is larger and more powerful that it is therefore a higher form of existence than personal, rational human beings. But it poignantly raises the question: what, then, is the status of our human existence in this material world and universe?

Our status in the world

We know that we did not always exist. We can remember being little children. We have watched ourselves growing up to full manhood and womanhood. We have also observed that sooner or later people die, and the unthinking earth, unknowingly, becomes their grave. What then is the significance of the individual human person, and of his or her comparatively short life on earth?

Some think that it is Mankind, the human race as a whole, that is the significant phenomenon: the individual counts for very little. On this view, the human race is like a great fruit tree. Each year it produces a large crop of apples. All of them are more or less alike. None is of any particular significance as an individual. Everyone is destined for

FIGURE I.5. An Apple.

Apple trees take four to five years to produce their first fruit, and it takes the energy from 50 leaves to produce one apple. Archaeologists have found evidence that humans have been enjoying apples since before recorded history.

Reproduced with permission of ©iStock/ChrisBoswell.

a very short life before, like the rest of the crop, it is consumed and forgotten; and so makes room for next year's crop. The tree itself lives on, producing crops year after year, in a seemingly endless cycle of birth, growth and disappearance. On this view then, the tree is the permanent, significant phenomenon; any one individual apple is of comparatively little value.

Our origin

But this view of the individual in relation to the race, does not get us to the root of our question; for the human race too did not always exist, but had a beginning, and so did the universe itself. This, therefore, only pushes the question one stage further back: to what ultimately do the human race as a whole, and the universe itself, owe their existence? What is the Great Reality behind the non-rational matter of the universe and behind us rational, personal, individual members of the human race?

Before we begin to survey the answers that have been given to this question over the centuries, we should notice that though science can point towards an answer, it cannot finally give us a complete answer. That is not because there is something wrong with science; the difficulty lies in the nature of things. The most widely accepted scientific theory nowadays (but not the only one) is that the universe came into being at the so-called Big Bang. But the theory tells us that here we encounter a singularity, that is, a point at which the laws of physics all break down. If that is true, it follows that science by itself cannot give a scientific account of what lay before, and led to, the Big Bang, and thus to the universe, and eventually to ourselves as individual human beings.

Our purpose

The fact that science cannot answer these questions does not mean, of course, that they are pseudo-questions and not worth asking. Adam Schaff, the Polish Marxist philosopher, long ago observed:

> What is the meaning of life? What is man's place in the universe? It seems difficult to express oneself scientifically on such hazy topics.

And yet if one should assert ten times over that these are typical pseudo-problems, *problems would remain*.[18]

Yes, surely problems would remain; and they are life's most important questions. Suppose by the help of science we could come to know everything about every atom, every molecule, every cell, every electrical current, every mechanism in our body and brain. How much further forward should we be? We should now know what we are made of, and how we work. But we should still not know what we are made for.

Suppose for analogy's sake we woke up one morning to find a new, empty jeep parked outside our house, with our name written on it, by some anonymous donor, specifying that it was for our use. Scientists could describe every atom and molecule it was made of. Engineers could explain how it worked, and that it was designed for transporting people. It was obviously intended, therefore, to go places. But where? Neither science as such, nor engineering as such, could tell us where we were meant to drive the jeep to. Should we not then need to discover who the anonymous donor was, and whether the jeep was ours to do what we liked with, answerable to nobody, or whether the jeep had been given to us on permanent loan by its maker and owner with the expectation that we should consult the donor's intentions, follow the rules in the driver's handbook, and in the end be answerable to the donor for how we had used it?

That surely is the situation we find ourselves in as human beings. We are equipped with a magnificent piece of physical and biological engineering, that is, our body and brain; and we are in the driver's seat, behind the steering wheel. But we did not make ourselves, nor the 'machine' we are in charge of. Must we not ask what our relationship is to whatever we owe our existence to? After all, what if it turned out to be that we owe our existence not to an impersonal what but to a personal who?

> Must we not ask what our relationship is to whatever we owe our existence to? After all, what if it turned out to be that we owe our existence not to an impersonal what but to a personal who?

To some the latter possibility is instinctively unattractive if not frightening; they would prefer

---

[18] Schaff, *Philosophy of Man*, 34 (emphasis added).

to think that they owe their existence to impersonal material, forces and processes. But then that view induces in some who hold it its own peculiar *angst*. Scientist Jacob Bronowski (1908–74) confessed to a deep instinctive longing, not simply to exist, but to be a recognisably distinct individual, and not just one among millions of otherwise undifferentiated human beings:

> When I say that I want to be myself, I mean as the existentialist does that I want to be free to be myself. This implies that I want to be rid of constraints (inner as well as outward constraints) in order to act in unexpected ways. Yet I do not mean that I want to act either at random or unpredictably. It is not in these senses that I want to be free, but in the sense that I want to be allowed to be different from others. I want to follow my own way—but I want it to be a way recognisably my own, and not zig-zag. And I want people to recognise it: I want them to say, 'How characteristic!'[19]

Yet at the same time he confessed that certain interpretations of science roused in him a fear that undermined his confidence:

> This is where the fulcrum of our fears lies: that man as a species and we as thinking men, will be shown to be no more than a machinery of atoms. We pay lip service to the vital life of the amoeba and the cheese mite; but what we are defending is the human claim to have a complex of will and thoughts and emotions—to have a mind....
>
> The crisis of confidence ... springs from each man's wish to be a mind and a person, in face of the nagging fear that he is a mechanism. The central question I ask is this: Can man be both a machine and a self?[20]

Our Search

And so we come back to our original question; but now we clearly notice that it is a double question: not merely to what or to whom

---

[19] Bronowski, *Identity of Man*, 14–5.
[20] Bronowski, *Identity of Man*, 7–9.

does humanity as a whole owe its existence, but what is the status of the individual human being in relation to the race as a whole and to the uncountable myriads of individual phenomena that go to make up the universe? Or, we might ask it another way: what is our significance within the reality in which we find ourselves? This is the ultimate question hanging over every one of our lives, whether we seek answers or we don't. The answers we have for it will affect our thinking in every significant area of life.

These, then, are not merely academic questions irrelevant to practical living. They lie at the heart of life itself; and naturally in the course of the centuries notable answers to them have been given, many of which are held still today around the world.

If we are to try to understand something of the seriously held views of our fellow human beings, we must try to understand their views and the reasons for which they hold them. But just here we must sound a warning that will be necessary to repeat again in the course of these books: those who start out seriously enquiring for truth will find that at however lowly a level they start, they will not be logically able to resist asking what the Ultimate Truth about everything is!

In the spirit of truthfulness and honesty, then, let us say directly that we, the authors of this book, are Christians. We do not pretend to be indifferent guides; we commend to you wholeheartedly the answers we have discovered and will tell you why we think the claims of the Christian gospel are valid, and the help it offers real. This does not, however, preclude the possibility of our approaching other views in a spirit of honesty and fairness. We hope that those who do not share our views will approach them in the same spirit. We can ask nothing more as we set out together on this quest—in search of reality and significance.

OUR AIM

Our small contribution to this quest is set out in the 6 volumes of this series. In this, the fourth book in the series, we remind ourselves that we are not the first generation on earth to have had to decide what are the basic ethical principles that all should universally follow. Others have wrestled with this question long before us. For that reason we present here a selection of notable but diverse ethical theories, so that we may profit from their insights that are of permanent value; and, at the same time, discern what, if any, are their weaknesses, or even fallacies.

THE STATUS, BASIS AND AUTHORITY OF ETHICS

CHAPTER 1

QUESTIONS FOR ETHICAL THEORIES

In times past, ethics was naturally faced with the age-old problems of sexual morality, war, racism, poverty and capital punishment. But nowadays, new technological advances are raising additional huge and difficult fundamental issues . . . just at the time when multitudes of people have lost (if they ever had) even the remnants of a religious belief to underpin and guide their ethical values and decisions.

INTRODUCTION

There is no doubt that for many people the world has become an ethically uncertain and bewildering place. Strong communitarian ideologies, with belief-systems and practices enforced from the centre, have faded, leaving millions of people around the world with no settled source from which to derive their ethical beliefs, their long-term values and guidance for their moral behaviour in private, social, commercial and political life.

At the other extreme, western liberalism is not without its severe critics. Since the days of its famous philosophical advocate, John Stuart Mill (1806–73), it has certainly led to great individual freedom and to prosperous economies (though it is differently interpreted in different countries). But starting with the 'negative rights' of individuals to be left free, as much as possible, from interference by others (and in particular by legal authorities) in matters of conscience, lifestyle, tastes, inclinations, commerce, property, etc., it has developed a demand for 'positive rights' to a variety of sophisticated goods, without a balancing recognition of the *duties* that are entailed by *rights*, and with a consequent reluctance to affirm any substantive moral values. Professor Brenda Almond, herself a liberal, writes:

> Contemporary criticism of liberalism, whether from the left or right, arises from a fundamental malaise occasioned by a general decline in the conditions of life in modern liberal societies—the rootlessness of the privatized individual in a mass society, crime, pornography and the decline of the family—in sum the moral and cultural vacuum to which some versions of pluralistic liberalism appear to lead . . . Many of the ills of liberal societies stem from the decline of the family and the breakdown of the contractual elements in human relationships . . . it has in effect become in a modern state, impossible to marry—if by that one means to make a long-term (or even fixed term!) commitment binding

on both parties. And states have removed ultimate responsibility for offspring, too, by well-intentioned but ill-advised measures of support for unsupported families.[1]

MODERN DIFFICULTIES FOR ETHICAL THEORY

In times past, ethics was naturally faced with the age-old problems of sexual morality, war, racism, poverty and capital punishment. But nowadays, new technological advances are raising additional huge and difficult fundamental issues related to genetic engineering, stem-cell research, embryonic implants, the cloning of human beings, customized babies, etc. just at the time when multitudes of people have lost (if they ever had) even the remnants of a religious belief to underpin and guide their ethical values and decisions.

In addition, many are succumbing to philosophical and scientific theories which teach that in each person there is no unified, continuing self that can maintain a consistent, principled stance towards life but only a kaleidoscopic succession of immediate impressions and reactions. And on this assumption the difficulty of developing stable, character-forming beliefs is aggravated by two further difficulties.

The first is one of the by-products of the astonishing development of information technology. Its benefits need not be rehearsed; but they have a downside. Through the Internet, people's minds are flooded with information from all over the world on every conceivable topic. The result is that many find it difficult to analyse the comparative worth of all the information, facts, views, theories, philosophies and religions with which they are presented. Moreover, undigested information is not true knowledge, and unanalysed knowledge is not necessarily understanding. As a result, forming a well and rationally thought out morality and worldview becomes not easier but harder.

The second difficulty in developing stable ethical belief is postmodernism's pluralism, which teaches people to think that in all this massive information there is no objective truth anywhere. One interpretation

---

[1] Brenda Almond, 'Liberty or Community? Defining the Post-Marxist Agenda', 249, 256.

is no more right or wrong than any other. All our understanding is culturally determined. We therefore cannot hope truly to interpret past cultures, or even present cultures other than our own; and since our own culture may well think differently in the future from what it thinks now, what is the point of trying to develop any permanent ethical principles?

Nevertheless, we still have to live, and that means facing unavoidable ethical decisions that are forced on us from every angle. Are we or are we not, as students, to cheat in examinations? Is it right for a husband to be unfaithful to his wife, or a wife to her husband? Is abortion murder? Is suicide sin? Is assisted euthanasia a crime? Is tax evasion wrong? Is bribery always wrong? Is the profit motive unethical? What is the purpose of punishment? Is it retribution, deterrence, reform or all three? What is forgiveness? Are we morally obliged to forgive everybody unconditionally? Has ethics anything to say to genetic engineering, eugenics and the production of designer babies? If the cloning of human beings becomes technically possible, does that automatically make it ethical? Or has society the right to control what scientists may, or may not, do? Is it morally acceptable for public television to broadcast pornography, obscene language and unnecessary violence for children to watch? Or is censorship too great a danger to the freedom of the press, and of the arts, to be acceptable? And what ought law to be? Should it simply reflect and guard current society's values, which can, and do, change from generation to generation? Or should it enshrine and enforce certain absolute, unchanging values and principles?

> What is forgiveness? Are we morally obliged to forgive everybody unconditionally? Has ethics anything to say to genetic engineering, eugenics and the production of designer babies?

These questions, then, and thousands like them, will call for answers; and unless ostrich-like we put our head in the sand and retreat from society into isolated private lives, we shall have to think through these ethical problems. On what basic principles and values shall we base our thinking? Merely responding with off-the-cuff, unthought-through solutions, based on the mood of the moment or on unrecognised prejudice, is hardly likely to come up with responsible, satisfactory answers.

A FOURFOLD ANALYSIS OF ETHICS

There are four major questions that we should ask about any ethical theory:

1. What status, basis and authority does it claim?
2. What is its supreme goal?
3. What specific rules does it lay down for daily life?
4. What guidance does it give for application to daily life?

Question 1. What status, basis and authority does it claim?

Under this heading we ask such questions as: What does this theory offer us? Is it shrewd, practical advice on how to behave, advice that we should be wise to follow? Or does it claim more than that? Does it claim authority to prescribe how we *ought* to behave and lay down commands that it is our *duty* to obey? This in turn raises the question: on what, according to this theory, is ethics based? Is it based on the individual's personal choice of moral standards? Or on the consensus of society? Or on Nature and evolution? Or on the laws of the State? Or on God's character and commands? From what source does ethics derive its authority to tell us what to do?

Question 2. What is its supreme goal?

Along with this question, we should ask what general principle or principles the ethical system lays down for the attainment of its supreme goal. Some of the ancient Greek moral philosophers laid down a supreme good as a goal at which the whole of life should be aimed. Aristotle said it was happiness. For him, as an intellectual, supreme happiness consisted in theoretical study, and to engage in such a life one needed to live the life of a gentleman, with slaves to do all the daily chores. For the Stoics the supreme goal was to live in accordance with the universal Reason that pervaded the whole universe. For the Epicureans the supreme good and goal was pleasure. For Plato it was to attain the vision of the Good. For Marxism it was the achievement of the paradise of pure communism. We are entitled, therefore, to ask of any ethical theory, what, if anything, is its supreme good or goal to which it would direct all our moral effort; and what, if any, general principles it advocates for the attainment of that goal.

Question 3. What specific rules does it lay down for daily life?

What, if any, specific rules does it lay down for all the varied action-spheres of daily life? Does it content itself with a general principle such as 'Always behave to the best of your ability in whatever circumstance you find yourself'? Or does it also lay down specific rules to be followed in love, courtship and marriage, in family life, in work, in commerce, in regard to property, in economics, welfare, health, education and politics?

Question 4. What guidance does it give for application to daily life?

What guidance does it give on how we should apply its general principles and specific rules when it comes to settling actual, complicated cases in daily life? In many actual cases decision is easy (even if carrying it out is difficult!). Shall I cheat in my examinations? There is no difficulty in knowing what answer honesty would give. Shall I steal someone's mobile phone? I could, but should I? The rule 'You shall not steal' is not ambiguous. On the other hand, we all believe in justice, but sometimes, when it comes to deciding between equally deserving but competing claims, it can be difficult to know what decision would be the most just. In such cases, how will a knowledge of the status and basis of an ethical theory, of its general principles and its specific rules, help us to make the right decisions?

Medical ethics as an illustration of these four questions

As an illustration of the helpfulness of distinguishing these four levels in ethical theory we may cite medical ethics. In many countries throughout many centuries, newly qualified doctors had to take the so-called Hippocratic oath before they were allowed to practise.[2] This oath did not, of course, prescribe the particular drug or treatment that should be employed on any particular occasion. Its purpose was to bind the new doctor's loyalty to the right and proper ethical standards of the medical profession. It can be surveyed by turning our four questions into the following four headings.

The basis and authority of medical ethics

The first thing to notice here is that, in the ancient version at least, the newly qualified doctor had to swear an oath, that is, he had to call on God, or the gods, to witness that he was solemnly promising faithfully to observe the medical ethics laid down in the oath. Simultaneously he called on God, or the gods, to punish him if he transgressed this ethical code. It was thus made obvious that the basis and authority behind medical ethics was God, or the gods.

The general principle and aim of medical ethics

This was loyalty to the life of his patients, with determination to heal and preserve that life.

The specific rules of medical ethics

These included such things as: the doctor must never use his knowledge and skills to harm, or cause the death of, anyone; he must never use any knowledge that he gained, in the course of treating a patient, to that patient's detriment; he must never betray the confidence of his patients or disclose the details of their illnesses to strangers.

The relevance to the practical decisions that have to be taken in actual cases

Here we would have to consider the relevance of the basis, of the general principle and aim, and of the specific rules to the practical decisions that have to be taken in actual cases. Under this heading we should have to ask such questions as: in the light of the Hippocratic oath would it ever

---

[2] The oath is named after Hippocrates, an ancient physician (*c*.460–377 BC). Almost nothing is known for certain about him. His name was later attached to a body of ancient Greek medical writings. It is unlikely that the oath was composed by him, but maybe it incorporates some of his principles. Parts of the oath are still used in some medical schools.

be right for a doctor deliberately to kill a terminally ill patient in order to put the patient out of his intolerable pain; or to cooperate with such a patient in doctor-assisted suicide? Or suppose a doctor discovers that a patient of his is carrying a gene that will cause him in early middle life to develop a long, incurable, and eventually terminal illness. If the patient's life insurance company got to know about this, they would terminate his life insurance policy, and no other company would take him on. If, then, the insurance company offered the doctor a large fee to disclose the patient's genetic information to them, what bearing would the Hippocratic oath have on the doctor's decision whether to disclose the information or not?

This brief study of the Hippocratic oath and its relevance for practical medical ethics, illustrates the point that in any walk of life our concept, first of the status, basis and authority of ethics, secondly of its goal(s) and general principles(s), and thirdly of its specific rules covering various action-spheres, has an exceedingly important bearing on the actual, individual cases that we have to decide in the course of daily life. In the rest of this section of this book, therefore, we shall spend a good deal of time considering the first level of ethical theory: the status, basis and authority of ethics.

CHAPTER 2

WHAT SHOULD WE DO, AND WHY?

All of us come short of the objective standard in many respects, and all (sensible) people admit it. But abandon the objective standard, and you will be left without any basis for rational debate, or guidance for reform and progress, nothing except a shouting match—or worse—between the arbitrary opinions, values and ambitions of opposing parties.

THE STATUS OF ETHICS

Moral philosophy is not simply an empirical discipline that studies *how* people behave, nor even *why* they behave as they do: it is a normative discipline that studies how people *ought* to behave. It says that some behaviour is right and some behaviour is wrong. The first thing we need to ask, therefore, is what authority moral philosophy has to tell us how we ought to behave and what exactly is meant by calling something 'right' or 'wrong'. As we might expect, opinions differ widely on this topic. Let's consider some of them.

The emotivist theory

This theory holds that moral language merely expresses, or provokes, emotion of some kind. Nothing we say in moral terms is either true or false about anything. Moral language simply vents our feelings about something. If, for example, I try to hammer a nail into a piece of wood, and accidentally hammer my thumb instead of the nail, I might well say 'Ow!' or something stronger. But no one would think of discussing whether what I meant by saying 'Ow!' was either true or false. It was but a reflex, emotional reaction to my pain.

Similarly, if a spectator at a football match cheers when his team scores a goal and boos when the other team does, he is not saying that it is wrong by some objective standard for the other side to score a goal. He is merely saying that he does not like it.

The emotivist theory claims that all our moral statements are similarly nothing more than expressions of our likes and dislikes. If, therefore, I say 'Boxing is wrong', according to this theory I am saying no more than 'Boxing? Oh no! I don't like it.' Well, it might certainly be that I am saying that; but it could be that I am saying far more. It could be that I am a neurosurgeon, and that I am claiming that it is the objective fact that constant punches to the head can cause premature brain degeneration, and that it is therefore morally wrong for people to pay large sums of money to boxers in order to enjoy watching them damaging each other's brains. Such a statement on my part would claim to be objectively true, and could then invite serious discussion as to whether it is in fact true or false.

Similarly, people who stage street protests against nuclear warfare, or globalised commerce, do certainly express their emotional feelings—sometimes, unfortunately, with unlawful violence. But the emotivist theory is exaggerating when it says that that is all they are expressing. Some such protesters, at least, would claim that nuclear warfare, with its potential to cause vastly excessive damage to civilian populations, is grotesquely disproportionate to the rights or wrongs of the cause it is defending, and morally unjustifiable. That is a truth claim that can then be debated whether it is true or false.

Cultural relativism

This theory can take two forms: cultural dependence and ethnocentrism.

Cultural dependence

This form of the theory says that a person's ethical views depend on the culture in which he or she was brought up. The person concerned has not embraced these views because she searched for some objective truth and eventually found it. Her ethical views have been produced in her by her surrounding culture. In that sense she cannot help holding these views, and she may well think they are true. But that in itself tells us nothing about whether they *are* true or not. And that, says the theory, is the status of everyone's ethical views.

But if this theory is correct, it would mean that the theory that 'everyone's ethical views are dependent on his culture and determined by that culture, and therefore not objectively true', is itself determined by the culture of whoever proposed the theory; and therefore is not objectively true either. Why, then, should we believe the theory?

But in any case it is manifestly false. Socrates' views were certainly not culturally determined: his culture executed him for his views! And so it has been with reformers and prophets all down the centuries, including Jesus Christ. They have criticised the views of their contemporaries as being false, and have proclaimed that what they themselves asserted was true. And when two parties from the same background culture disagree about what the truth is, the only way the issue can be solved is to appeal to some criterion outside the culture.

Ethnocentrism

This rather grand name denotes the view that says: 'My own nation's moral views are objectively true, and if any other nation's views differ from my nation's view, they are wrong.' Ethnocentrism is then opposed by cultural relativists as being arrogant and intolerant—as indeed it would be, if someone said that his nation's moral views were true, just because they were his nation's.

But what if someone claimed that there was such a thing as objective moral truth to which all nations should be subject; and that his nation was subject to it, and was therefore right, and any nation that was not subject to it was wrong? What would cultural relativism say about that? It would still say that this view was arrogant and intolerant. Cultural relativism maintains that there is no such thing as objective moral truth. All moral views are culturally determined, and there is no objective standard by which one culture could claim that its moral beliefs were truer than another culture's moral views. Therefore, for one culture to claim that its moral beliefs were objectively true would be grossly intolerant, and in this context intolerance is the unforgivable sin. One must always be tolerant of another culture's moral views.

> For one culture to claim that its moral beliefs were objectively true would be grossly intolerant, and in this context intolerance is the unforgivable sin.

But just here cultural relativism runs into a difficulty. We live in a culture that respects all human beings, intellectuals included. But Pol Pot's regime in Cambodia was extremely intolerant of intellectuals: thousands of them were massacred just for being intellectuals. If cultural relativism is correct, then for our culture to say that Pol Pot's moral views were wrong would be inexcusably intolerant on our part. Therefore, according to cultural relativism we must not say that Pol Pot's intolerance was wrong! What then becomes of cultural relativism's claim that intolerance *is* wrong? Cultural relativism is clearly incoherent.

There is, then, an obvious irreconcilable difference between our culture's moral view that intellectuals should be respected and Pol Pot's moral view that all intellectuals should be executed. Unless we are prepared to say that neither moral view is more true than the other, and that Pol Pot's massacre of intellectuals was equally acceptable as our respect for them, we must decide which of the two is true and which is false. On what grounds shall we decide? We cannot say that our culture's respect for intellectuals is right because it is our culture's view. We shall have to have some objective criterion that is independent of both cultures.

Thus we must face the fundamental question: is there any real right and wrong, such that an ethical belief, or an act, would be wrong, or right, independently of us, and of our culture? In other words, is there some objective standard of morality to which we all ought to submit, whatever culture we come from? Or is morality always, in the end, nothing more than a matter of each person's, or each culture's, subjective opinion?

THE INADEQUACY OF SUBJECTIVISM

It would certainly be false to claim that any of us is totally free of subjectivism when it comes to making moral judgments. All of us are influenced, more perhaps than we realise, by our cultural background, our individual personality and past experiences. On the other hand, all thoughtful people are aware of this fact, and try to make allowance for it. We try, as we say, to 'see the other person's point of view'.

An aircraft pilot is trained to trust the objective information supplied by his instruments rather than rely on his subjective feelings to determine the plane's orientation while flying through dense cloud.

Each party to a legal dispute may equally feel that he is in the right and the other in the wrong. But both would agree that it would be unfair and unwise to let one party decide the issue on the basis of his own subjective judgment. Both agree to submit the case to the objective judgment of some independent, disinterested, arbitrator.

A footballer may not like it when he is penalised for handling the ball right in front of his own goal mouth; but he, like all the other players, must submit to the objective rules of the game, regardless of whether he likes it or not. If in the course of a game the players were free to change the rules according to their personal likes and dislikes, the game would be unplayable.

Why no one really believes that morality is subjective

Subjective morality would reduce all moral judgments to a matter of taste

In matters of taste there is no question of right and wrong. If Sasha likes cheese and Jerome thinks the taste of cheese is revolting, one cannot say that Sasha is right, and Jerome is wrong, nor vice versa. If Jerome dislikes cheese, that is a simple fact. No one can say he has a moral duty to like cheese and that he is wrong not to like it. He just doesn't like it, and there's an end of the matter. Nor can we say that Jerome's taste contradicts Sasha's taste. No question of truth or falsehood is involved. Their different tastes no more contradict each other than potatoes contradict beetroot.

But if morality were simply a matter of taste, see what that would involve: we could no longer call any act or practice either right or wrong. We could not say, for instance, that forbidding women education was morally wrong. It would simply be a matter of taste whether one society forbade women education, or another allowed them it. We might not ourselves approve of the torture and sexual abuse of children, but we should have no grounds for condemning those who practise such things. It would simply be that their tastes, opinions and value judgments were different from ours.

When the leaders of Nazi Germany were brought to trial in the Nuremburg court and charged with the gassing of six million Jews, they tried to defend themselves on the ground that in their culture, such a deed was perfectly acceptable, and that other cultures had no right to say that the Nazi culture was wrong. The judges disagreed. They held that there are universal objective standards of right and wrong that are independent of what any particular culture, or group of cultures, might think. Genocide is not simply a matter of taste.

Subjectivism removes the idea of moral progress

Moreover, if it were true that all morality is subjective, we should have to abandon all idea of moral progress (or regress) not only in the history of nations, but in the lifetime of each individual. The very concept of moral progress implies an external moral standard by which not only to measure that a present moral state is different from an earlier one, but to pronounce that it is 'better' than the earlier one. Without such a standard how could one say that the moral state of a culture in which cannibalism is regarded as an abhorrent crime, is any 'better' than a society in which it is an acceptable culinary practice?

Subjectivism tends to be self-refuting

Relativists tend to argue that since, according to them, there are no moral absolutes, no objective rights and wrongs, no one ought to try to impose his or her moral views on other people. But in arguing like that, they refute their own theory. The word 'ought' implies a moral duty. They are saying in effect, that because there are no universal, objective principles, there is a universal moral principle binding on all objectivists, and everyone else, namely that no one ought to impose his moral views on other people. In so saying, relativism refutes its own basic principle.

Subjectivists find it very difficult to act consistently with their own theory in daily life

Paul Chamberlain in his book *Can We Be Good Without God?*[1] tells an amusing story that illustrates the point. A very able philosophy student wrote a capable, well-researched, well-presented essay, in which he argued strongly that there were no objective moral principles or standards such as fairness or justice. He put the finished essay in an attractive blue folder and handed it in to his instructor. The instructor gave it a fail mark, and wrote on it the comment: 'I don't like blue folders.' The student was enraged and stormed into the instructor's office, protesting, 'You can't do this to me. My essay deserves a far higher mark. You can't fail it just because you don't like the colour of the folder. It isn't fair!'

The instructor replied: 'Are you the student who wrote the essay that maintains there are no objective moral standards of fairness and justice?'

---

[1] pp. 50–1.

'I am,' said the student.

'Then I simply repeat,' said the instructor, 'that the reason I reject your essay has nothing to do with fairness or justice. You don't believe in such things anyway; and I just don't like blue folders.'

The student saw the point—and then, of course, the instructor gave the essay the good mark it deserved for being well written. But the incident illustrates the fact that however strongly people maintain the theory of moral subjectivism on intellectual grounds, they find it difficult to avoid implying objective values and judgments even in the actual process of stating their subjectivism. J. D. Mabbott comments:

> Philosophers who deny all absolute values and say values are made in individual choices, are found asserting absolute values themselves. The existentialists reject all rules and abstract propositions about duty or goodness. Each man makes his values as he makes his choices. Yet we find constant emphasis on the essential value of 'commitment' (Kierkegaard) or 'engagement' (Sartre). And the existentialists echo a very common 'subjectivist' view which one often hears among ordinary men. 'We differ on every issue but I respect his *integrity*'. (So we do *not* differ on *every* issue.) This universal and absolute value is common ground to the existentialists. 'Authenticity' (Kierkegaard and Heidegger), 'fidelity' (Marcel), 'sincerity' (Sartre) are other names for it. And the effect of many individual standards is 'tolerance', but that is itself not an individual but an absolute standard.[2]

And when it comes to the practical affairs of daily life a subjectivist philosopher will vigorously object if his theory is put into action to his disadvantage. If his bank manager entertains the idea that there is no such thing as objective fairness, and tries to cheat the philosopher out of two thousand pounds, the philosopher will certainly not tolerate the manager's subjectivist and 'culturally determined' sense of fairness.

---

[2] *Introduction to Ethics*, 101.

ARGUMENTS AGAINST OBJECTIVISM

Since there would appear to be no third position between subjectivism on the one side and objectivism on the other, the demonstration that moral subjectivism is untenable will have gone a long way towards showing that moral objectivism must be right. But, of course, it does not, strictly speaking, prove it; and people will still want to question it. Let us then ask the questions that will obviously arise.

If there are such objective moral values, how do we get to know them?

At first, this looks as if it were an academic question, and one version of it is. But at the simplest level the fact is that people are aware of these objective standards almost without thinking about them. If an older child snatches his younger brother's toy away and won't let him have it back, the younger boy soon cries out, 'It isn't fair!' Children often have a keen sense of justice and fairness. So do grown-ups: 'I went out of my way to help you when you were in need; but now I'm in difficulty, and you will not lift a finger to help me. It isn't fair!'

We therefore do not need a course in philosophical ethics before we become aware of the moral quality of fairness; and we expect other people to recognise at once what we mean by fairness. They may disagree what practical decision or action fairness would demand in a particular situation; but normal people have no difficulty with the concept of fairness itself. If when you complained to your friend that she had acted unfairly, she replied 'Fairness? What is that? I don't know what you mean,' you would find it difficult to believe she was being serious.

Two side issues

But here let us turn aside to deal with two issues that belong partly to theoretical ethics and partly to applied ethics. They both provoke an objection. What is the use of talking about abstract objective justice (or any other moral quality) since when you try to apply the concept *justice* to some practical dispute, very often the parties concerned cannot, and will not, agree on what the term *justice* means and implies in their case?

First issue: how we use the term 'justice'

It is often, and truly, said that Plato's *Republic* is not so much a practical political blueprint, as an exercise in working out what the term *justice* means. He felt that what *justice* meant would more clearly be seen if the principle were worked out in the running of the complete citizen body, rather than in the life of an individual. His basic thesis was that *justice* will not mean treating every citizen in exactly the same way, but differently according to his or her particular needs and place in society. One could illustrate his thesis with a simple analogy: in any one household, even today, you would not think that *justice* demands that the same amount of food be given to the four-year-old child as to his hard-working father.

Now our point here is not to discuss Plato's political theories. Our point is to notice how the term *justice* is being used, and to avoid making a false deduction from it. It would be easy unthinkingly to protest: 'What's the use of talking about objective moral qualities like justice, if in practice *justice* is going to mean different things to different people?'

But such thinking would be shallow. We must always keep before our mind the objective moral principle of justice. When it comes to practice, different people, political parties, governments and countries may decide very differently how justice will demand that they act. But these differences do not mean that the concept and standard of objective justice is meaningless and should be abandoned. All of us come short of the objective standard in many respects, and all (sensible) people admit it. But abandon the objective standard, and you will be left without any basis for rational debate, or guidance for reform and progress, nothing except a shouting match—or worse—between the arbitrary opinions, values and ambitions of opposing parties.

Second issue: the meaning of justice

The second issue is like the first, except that it concerns itself much more with the meaning of words like *justice*. This theory holds that justice, fairness and such like words have no intrinsic meaning. They carry the meaning given them, if not by each individual, yet by each separate society or culture, which, of course, can be less than a man's city, or even his state or his country, let alone less than all humankind. It is claimed that the meaning in any one case is not necessarily or totally subjective, because it is not the private idea of one individual. It is objective, in the sense that it is the meaning that all in the individual's community recognise and share. But it is not, and could not be, objective in the sense that it is universal, because the world at large attributes to the term *justice* as many different meanings as there are states and nations.

One might comment, in passing, that two and a half thousand years ago Greek philosophers, like Plato, had a concept of justice that existed independent of humankind, that would apply universally. The later Stoics, and the Roman jurist Cicero, in the first century BC had the inklings of a Natural Law that should apply to all humankind fairly and without discrimination. The Old Testament psalmists and prophets looked forward to a time when God would judge and administer the whole world in righteousness (e.g. Ps 96:9–13); and they warned that when God did so, he would treat Israel with equal, if not greater, severity than the other nations, because of the special favours and privileges Israel had enjoyed (Amos 3:2). It might seem odd, therefore, if modern civilisations in the twenty-first century, got so tied in to the meanings that each in his own culture gives to words like *justice*, that none of them could even conceive of a universal justice that all might one day accept. One might think that the progress of the human race—from justice in the family, in the extended family, in the tribe, in the nation, in the continent, might encourage people at least to begin to think of a universal justice throughout the world, as for instance in the Universal Declaration of Human Rights. But let's leave that aside.

The postmodernist Stanley Fish, in his book *There's No Such Thing as Free Speech, and It's a Good Thing Too*, observes that people in general falsely imagine that the meaning of terms like *justice, fairness, merit*, is perfectly clear and obvious to everyone, such that one only has to talk of applying justice to a situation, and everybody will agree what the term *justice* means. That is not so, says Fish. Such terms as these 'have different meanings in relation to different assumptions and background conditions'.[3] And that being so, Fish seems to imply, there can

> The world at large attributes to the term 'justice' as many different meanings as there are states and nations.

---

[3] *There's No Such Thing*, 4.

be no truly objective justice. Since every culture, or even individual, understands justice to mean something different, there can never be any meeting of minds. Meanwhile the powerful will use their muscle to ensure that it is their view of justice that prevails both inside and outside the courts.[4]

The picture Fish paints is all too true of many countries and, indeed, of all too many law courts. But surely it is precisely because people have a real belief in objective, absolute justice that they can see what is wrong with such countries and law courts and have grounds to work for better things and a standard by which to measure progress. If there were no such thing as absolute justice; if striving for justice had no hope of ever being more than parties in conflict, each with its own concept of justice, and unable to conceive of any higher justice than its own, and constantly fighting each other, without any meeting of minds, then all we could ever experience would be irrational shouting-matches, to which only arbitrary force could put an end.

Fish cites an example (drawn from a film) to illustrate his point: Two men are assigned to work in the mailroom of a big firm. One is the boss's nephew. An executive is appointed to choose one of them to become the head of the mailroom, and this executive announces that he is instructed to choose on the basis of merit alone. Whereupon the boss's nephew complains: 'That's not fair.'[5]

Now we might think this method of selection on merit to be eminently fair, certainly more so than nepotism. Fish's point is, however, that the nephew's idea of justice was such that he regarded selection on the basis of merit alone to be unfair. To be just, according to him, selection would have to take into account his family relationship with the boss.[6] Now it is the fact that in many countries, even within one and the same culture, in State or public factories, and in civil service and administration, nepotism is not only practised: failure to practise it would be regarded as treachery to the family.

Must we then abandon all belief in an objective justice that exists independently of any, and every, culture? Must we agree with post-modernism that it is human beings that create the idea of justice; and

---

[4] *There's No Such Thing*, viii.
[5] *There's No Such Thing*, 3.
[6] In a private, family-run business, of course, the owner would be perfectly free to appoint his own relatives if he chose to.

that, since human beings create many different and conflicting ideas of justice, there can never be such a thing as truly objective justice? If we must agree to that, we are back with moral relativism. And on what possible grounds could we then object to Hitler and his Aryans, who according to the meaning which they gave to justice, felt it was perfectly just to gas six million Jews, and regarded it as treachery to the Aryan State to protect any Jews? After all, Hitler's justice was, according to Fish's definition, objective, in the sense that it was not the justice of one individual, but the justice of his whole culture. Is there no justice independent of culture?

We now revert to our obvious questions.

Why are there so many different moral practices in the world?

If there exist objective moral values, objective right and wrong, why are there so many different moral practices in the world? Here we must take care to understand exactly what the question is. We are not asking, for instance, why, if truth-telling is supposed to be a universal, objective moral value, so many people tell lies. The plain fact is that even in cultures where truth-telling is regarded as a universal, objective moral value, many people nevertheless tell lies—and often deliberately so. But the fact is that in societies in which truth-telling is regarded as a universal, objective moral value, when people engage in deception, they try to cover it up (be they private individuals or corporate entities); and when they are caught out, they make excuses and endeavour to defend themselves. That shows, of course, that their conscience admits the existence and authority of the universal, objective moral value of truth-telling, and its demand upon everybody's obedience. Otherwise they would feel no need to make excuses.[7]

The question, then, is not why do so many people tell lies. The question must rather be: if truth-telling is supposed to be a universal, objective moral value binding on everybody, why are there so many cultures in which lying, cheating, deceiving and double-crossing one's friends, neighbours, fellow citizens and nationals is

---

[7] See also the longer discussion of this topic in Ch. 3—'The Nature and Basis of Morality', in Book 1: *Being Truly Human*.

regarded by everyone as the right, normal, and perfectly acceptable thing to do, such that no one would ever think of complaining about it when it was done to him? The answer is that in actual fact there are no such cultures anywhere in the world; or if there are, they are remarkably few.

The same holds good for many other moral values: the evidence of history right down to our present time is of a universal persistence of the awareness of the basic moral laws. In his *The Abolition of Man*,[8] C. S. Lewis collected a list of moral principles common to all the world's major civilisations. He called them 'Illustrations of the Natural Law', and grouped them under eight headings:

1. The Law of General Beneficence
2. The Law of Special Beneficence
3. Duties to Parents, Elders, Ancestors
4. Duties to Children and Posterity
5. The Law of Justice
6. The Law of Good Faith and Veracity
7. The Law of Mercy
8. The Law of Magnanimity

Under heading 1 he lists such things as not murdering, not inflicting misery; not being grasping, oppressive, cruel or calumnious; not slandering, not giving false witness, not doing to others what you would not like them to do to you; and the positive counterparts. Heading 2 is concerned with special love to one's wife, family, kin and country. Heading 5 comprises sexual justice, honesty and justice in the courts. Heading 8 covers things like courage, the willingness to suffer to protect others; counting death to be better than a life with shame; doing or thinking nothing uncomely, effeminate or lascivious. The contents of headings 3, 4, 6 and 7 are self-evident.

Or take a particular example from the ancient world. Here is a list of claimed virtues compiled from the Egyptian Book of the Dead by John A. Wilson.[9] The Book of the Dead was a kind of document that was attached to a person's body when he or she was buried. The idea was that after death a person had to face the final judgment, which

---

[8] pp. 49–59.
[9] Pritchard, *ANET*, 35.

would decide, so they thought, whether he or she would be admitted to eternal life or not. The document, therefore contained the person's 'defence statement', so to speak, claiming that he or she had not done wrong, had not broken the moral laws. Here, then, are some items from the deceased's list of claims:

> I have not committed evil
> I have not stolen
> I have not been covetous
> I have not robbed
> I have not killed men
> I have not damaged the grain measure
> I have not caused crookedness
> I have not told lies
> I have not been contentious
> I have not practised usury
> I have not committed adultery

Our point is not to conjecture how well or otherwise this ancient Egyptian lived up to the claims he is making here. Rather we should observe first in what a vastly different culture from ours he was living; and yet, secondly, how many of his moral values are exactly the same as ours are today. It is powerful, positive evidence for the objectivity and universality of moral values.

An exception? Funeral customs among the ancient Greeks and Callatiae

An instance that is often quoted by relativists in favour of the view that moral values have not been universal among all nations throughout history is the story told by Herodotus (III.38.3–4). Darius brought together Greeks, whose custom was to burn the dead bodies of their parents, and an Indian people, called Callatiae, whose custom was to eat theirs. When Darius asked the Greeks what money it would take to persuade them to eat their dead parents, and not burn them, they were outraged: nothing would induce them to do so. The Callatiae were similarly outraged when they were asked what it would take for them to burn their parents and not eat them.

But what is it right to deduce from this example? Relativists argue that it shows that moral values, ethics, and customs vary from culture to culture. It is culture and custom that give them their force, and this force is so powerful that any one generation would consider it unthinkable to change the custom. For them it is an absolute, objective moral value. But comparative anthropology shows, so relativism claims, that there is no absolute, universal moral value. Everything is relative to each tribe.

However, two mistakes beset this interpretation. Relativists are so intent on noticing the differences in the funeral customs of these two groups that they overlook the much more important thing they both had in common: both were profoundly conscious of a binding duty to honour their dead parents. Admittedly, they differed in the ways they chose to honour them; but both were equally determined not to allow anything that would desecrate them. This is a virtually universal attitude.[10]

The second mistake in this relativistic interpretation is the way it confuses a basic moral value and principle with the various ways in which that principle is expressed. If in Herodotus' story one group had honoured its dead parents, while the other group had simply flung them out on the dunghill along with all the rest of the rubbish, that would have suggested a difference in basic value and principle. As it was, their differences of practice were simply differences in application of the same basic principle.

This is of major ethical importance for us still. We saw in an earlier example that honest people who firmly believe in the basic principle of social justice can disagree on just how that principle is to be interpreted in practical situations. But to take those disagreements and on that basis to deny that there is any basic, objective, moral principle of justice would be to destroy any measuring line by which to criticise any present shortcomings and to guide future progress, and any means of settling differences other than by selfishness and force.

This, of course, is not to deny that there have been, and are still, practices among various societies that flout basic ethical principles. Cannibalism, child-sacrifice, the killing and burial of slaves along with their dead masters, abortion and infanticide—all contravene

---

[10] One thinks of Antigone in the famous play of that name by Sophocles. She held that the 'unwritten laws' of heaven demanded that her dead brother be buried, even though the State had forbidden him burial on the ground that he was a traitor.

the basic principle of the inviolability and sacredness of human life. That some of these practices have resulted from false and superstitious ideas about gods, spirits and demons reminds us that not all religions are true: some religious practices are unhealthy and evil. But at the other extreme, it is likewise beyond argument that the decline of true religion in recent decades has led to a huge decline in regard for the inviolability and sacredness of life, particularly that of the unborn. But of that more later.

How can moral values both come from parents and be objective?

Our third obvious question to arise has to do with the source of our morals. Do not most people get their moral values from their parents or school teachers? How then can they be said to have gained these values from some objective, independently existent, moral principles?

We can at once admit that we all learned many, if not all, of our moral values from our parents, or our teachers. But the things we learn from them are of different kinds. Some are merely conventions. In some countries, for instance, children are taught that traffic must drive on the right side of the road. It is the law of the land, and to drive on the left is an offence. But this is an arbitrary convention and not a universal principle. In other countries the law demands that traffic drives on the left; and teachers in those countries teach the children accordingly.

On the other hand, the laws of arithmetic are universal. A child may first discover that $2 + 2 = 4$ by learning it from its teacher. But the teacher was only pointing out to the child what was universally and objectively true, independently of the laws of any particular culture or country. So it is with the universal, objectively true, moral laws. The fact that children learn these laws from their parents or teachers does not mean that they are any less absolute for that.

But the question of the source of objective moral values deserves further discussion, and to that we turn in our next two chapters.

CHAPTER 3

THE SOURCE OF OBJECTIVE MORAL VALUES

Those who embrace extreme forms of atheistic materialism certainly face a difficult problem when they try to explain the origin of humankind's ethical and moral sense. It is difficult to see, at first glance, how mindless *matter*, without any thought, could produce *moral* consciousness.

ON WHAT ARE OBJECTIVE MORAL VALUES GROUNDED?

The theoretical possibilities are three:

1. *Universal, objective moral values are grounded in the matter of the universe.*

   According to this theory, they have simply evolved like all the other material contents and processes of the universe.

2. *Universal, objective moral values are the creations of human beings.*

   According to this theory they are principles of behaviour that have developed in the course of mankind's evolving social life and institutions.

3. *Universal, objective moral values are grounded in the character and will of God.*

   They are revealed both in Nature and through God's Word.

Let us examine each in turn, and let us remember that what we have to account for is the objectivity and universality of moral values. It will not be enough to account for the fact that various people, or nations, have various values. We have to explain how certain values seem to exist universally, independently of individual people, societies, cultures, nations and generations.

UNIVERSAL, OBJECTIVE MORAL VALUES ARE GROUNDED IN THE MATTER OF THE UNIVERSE

We now need to consider six theoretical positions related to the theory that the basis of ethics is nature and evolution.

Extreme, non-moral materialism

Those who embrace extreme forms of atheistic materialism certainly face a difficult problem when they try to explain the origin of humankind's ethical and moral sense. It is difficult to see, at first glance, how mindless *matter*, without any thought, could produce *moral* consciousness. Some materialists, therefore, solve the problem by simply denying that any moral or ethical laws exist.

William B. Provine, Historian of Science, Cornell University, declares:

> No inherent moral or ethical laws exist, nor are there absolute guiding principles for human society. The universe cares nothing for us and we have no ultimate meaning in life.[1]

At the popular level, Alasdair Palmer, scientific correspondent of the *Sunday Telegraph*, likewise assures the general public:

> But it is not just the religious explanation of the world that is contradicted by the scientific explanations of our origins. So, too, are most of our ethical values, since most of them have been shaped by our religious heritage. A scientific account of mankind has no more place for free-will or the equal capacity of each individual to be good and act justly than it has for the soul.[2]

Social Darwinism

Darwin, and some fellow evolutionists, felt that by the twin principles of 'the struggle for survival' and 'the survival of the fittest' not only could they explain the origin of species, they could safely predict the future development of the various races of humankind:

> At some future period, not very distant as measured by the centuries, the civilised races of man will almost certainly exterminate, and replace, the savage races throughout the world.[3]

---

[1] 'Scientists, Face It!', 10.
[2] 'Must Knowledge Gained Mean Paradise Lost?'
[3] *The Descent of Man*, 183.

The more civilized so-called Caucasian races have beaten the Turkish hollow in the struggle for existence. Looking to the world at no very distant date, what an endless number of lower races will have been eliminated by the higher civilized races throughout the world.[4]

Even in Darwin's day, one imagines, it would have been difficult to convince the 'Turkish', the 'lower', and the 'savage' races, as Darwin called them, that Darwin's evolutionary principles formed a sound basis for universal, objective moral values. When subsequently the theory known as *Social Darwinism*, invented by Herbert Spencer (1820–1903), was taken over by Hitler and used to justify his elimination of six million Jews, all such theories were fatally discredited.

Sociobiology

This theory is more sophisticated than Social Darwinism, but it is an equally extreme form of materialism. Associated with names like Francis Crick, Jacques Monod, Edward O. Wilson and Richard Dawkins, it holds that man is nothing but his genes. Morality, therefore, is based on the genes, though, apparently, the prime, indeed the sole, purpose of the genes is not to produce further human beings but to reproduce themselves. Generations of human beings are merely machines or vehicles for reproducing what Dawkins calls 'selfish genes'. In what sense, then, can morality be based on the genes? Michael Ruse and Edward O. Wilson explain:

> Morality, or more strictly our belief in morality, is merely an adaptation put in place to further our reproductive ends. Hence the basis of ethics does not lie in God's will . . . In an important sense, ethics as we understand it is an illusion fobbed off on us by our genes to get us to cooperate.[5]

An obvious difficulty presents itself. If a man is nothing but his genes, and his genes control his moral behaviour, how can a man ever be blamed for doing wrong, or praised for doing right? And what extraordinary promoters of morality genes must be when, on

---

[4] Letter to W. Graham, 3 July 1881, *Life and Letters*, 1:316.
[5] 'Evolution of Ethics', 51–2.

this theory, the combined genes of Europe, Asia, Australia, Africa and America caused the Second World War! Dawkins in his famous book, *The Selfish Gene*, considered that though man is nothing but his genes, he can somehow rebel against his genes when they would lead him astray:

> We are built as gene machines... but we have the power to turn against our creators. We, alone on earth, can rebel against the tyranny of the selfish replicators.[6]

But how? If we are nothing but our genes, if there is no non-material, non-genetic, element or force within us, what is there in us that could possibly rebel against our genes and behave morally? And from where would we ever get any objective moral principles to guide us in our rebellion against our genes?

This kind of genetic determinism espoused by Dawkins that claims that there is a directly causal relationship between gene and behaviour, has been severely criticised by many scientists. Here is an example. Neurobiologist Steven Rose, who has no quarrel with Dawkins over evolution itself, argues strongly against the reductionism that lies at the heart of neurogenetic determinism, concluding that such determinism is simply wrong: 'I am distressed with the arrogance with which some biologists claim for their—our—discipline explanatory and interventionist powers which it certainly does not possess, and so cavalierly dismiss the counter-evidence.'[7] Rose goes on to say: 'The phenomena of life are always and inexorably simultaneously about nature *and* nurture, and the phenomena of human existence and experience are always simultaneously biological and social. Adequate explanations must involve both.'[8]

The claim that 'the struggle for survival' can account for altruistic moral behaviour

The evolutionary model has always found it difficult to account for altruistic behaviour, since such behaviour would naturally seem to make it harder, not easier, for the race to survive. For the sake of argument we

---

[6] p. 201.
[7] *Lifelines*, 276.
[8] *Lifelines*, 279.

could suppose that since the evolutionary force was always working to promote the survival of the species, that force might somehow cause human beings to attach a moral significance to acts and practices that promoted the survival of the race. But by that same token, that same evolutionary force must have produced a moral aversion to any deed or practice that made survival more difficult or less likely.

How then can evolution explain the deep-seated moral conviction, that we have a *duty* to support the weak, the handicapped, the ill, the aged, and not only those of our kith and kin, but of people generally, even though it involves a serious drain on our resources, and makes the survival of the race more difficult and less likely? To argue that the instinctive desire to survive leads the healthy to support the weak and the ill in the hope that when the healthy themselves become weak and ill, others will support them, is not convincing. Such mutual compassion is highly commendable; but it is definitely not necessary for the survival of the race. If that survival were the *sole* aim of evolution, evolution would never produce a sense of moral duty to spend resources on the handicapped, the weak, the ill and the aged.

Ethical naturalism

In an essay entitled 'Naturalism' James Rachels revived the theory of ethical naturalism. He describes the theory thus:

> Ethical naturalism is the idea that ethics can be understood in the terms of natural science. One way of making this more specific is to say that moral properties (such as goodness and rightness) are identical with 'natural' properties, that is, properties that figure into scientific descriptions or explanations of things.[9]

There is certainly some truth in this theory. The Bible itself would, in part, agree. At Romans 1:31 and again at 2 Timothy 3:3 the Greek of the New Testament uses the adjective *astorgos*, which describes a person who lacks, not just love in general, but that love and affection that is natural between parents and children and members of the same family. Normally a mother does not have to be taught to love her children. Mother-love is built into a woman by the very physical

---

[9] In LaFollette (ed.), *The Blackwell Guide to Ethical Theory*, 75.

processes associated with the bearing of a child.[10] Similarly, members of a family have a natural affection for one another, so that it is an unnatural perversity when this affection is replaced by heartless indifference or even cruelty.

We can, therefore, to some extent, deduce ethical principles of behaviour from the way nature works; and nature's physical laws can point to principles at work at higher, ethical, levels. It is true at more than one level, that 'what we sow, we reap'.

But, that said, naturalism by itself runs into a problem.

The 'is' / 'ought' problem

David Hume was the first to describe this problem.[11] To understand what the problem is, we must first notice that the verb 'ought' is used in various senses. The sense we are interested in here is when 'you ought to do so and so' means 'you have a duty to do so and so'.

'Ought', however, has other usages, and we must be careful not to confuse them.

1. It can be used to recommend a course of action: 'You ought to go and see such and such a film. It is excellent', does not mean 'You have a duty to see it.' It means simply 'I recommend that you go and see it'.
2. It can indicate what you must do, if you wish to achieve, or avoid, a certain result: 'You ought to move your queen, otherwise it will be taken.' Good advice! But it does not imply 'you have a duty to move your queen'.
3. It can indicate what will happen if all goes according to plan: 'This train ought to arrive in St. Petersburg in thirty minutes' time'. That is, it is 4.30 p.m. now; it is timed to arrive at 5.00 p.m.; and if it keeps to the timetable, it will.

But in ethical contexts 'ought to' means 'have a duty to'. So when we say that someone ought to do, has a duty to do, something, we are voicing a valuative judgment. What Hume, then, pointed out was that you cannot base a valuative judgment on a bare factual statement.

---

[10] And when these physical processes are disturbed, e.g. by post-natal depression, natural mother-love can be suppressed.
[11] THN 3.1.1.27.

Let's take an example. Unless someone donates a kidney to Harold, Harold will die of kidney failure. That is a fact of nature. Someone reports that fact to his nephew, Thomas, and on that basis tells Thomas that he ought to donate one of his kidneys to Harold. That is a valuative judgment. The question is: how is the bare fact a valid reason for the valuative judgment? It's obvious, says someone: if Thomas does not donate the kidney, his uncle will die. Is not that valid reason enough?

Not necessarily. It assumes that it would be better for the uncle to live and not die. But Harold's liver is already ruined through a life of alcohol abuse. He is, moreover, the leader of a mafia gang who has been responsible for the murder of many victims. Thomas, by contrast, has a wife and four children who need a strong and healthy father to provide them a living. How, then, does the bare fact of nature that Harold will die, if Thomas does not donate him one of his kidneys, impose on Thomas the *duty* to donate a kidney? To establish the duty, you would have to supply an adequate reason why Thomas had a duty to stop Harold dying. To sum up, and illustrate the argument so far, we could say that the bare fact of nature that Mount Everest exists does not impose on me a duty to climb it.

Naturalism's weakness

Now as an advocate of naturalism Rachels is aware of the difficulty of deducing 'ought' from 'is'; and he offers a solution:

> The most plausible form of ethical naturalism begins by identifying goodness with satisfying our interests, while 'interests' are explained in turn as the objects of preferences. Protecting our eyesight, for example, is in our interests because we have desires that would be frustrated if we could not see; and that is why unimpaired eyesight is a good thing. Again, protecting children is a good thing because we care about children and we do not want to see them hurt. . . . Reasoning about what to do, therefore, is at bottom reasoning about how to satisfy our interests.[12]

But this immediately invites the question: what shall we say about the militias in some countries who have sought to satisfy their interests

---

[12] 'Naturalism', 75.

by equipping children with machetes and rifles, and teaching them to go around the countryside shooting, and hacking off the limbs of, other children and adults? It will doubtless be said that the rebels were mistaken about what their true interests were. But all of us can be similarly mistaken at times. Do all our ethical duties always coincide with what at the time we consider will satisfy our interests? Napoleon considered it satisfied his interests to conquer Russia. Had he an ethical duty to do so?

But Rachels argues that it is possible to deduce 'ought' from 'is'; and one of his examples runs as follows:

> Any judgment about what should be done requires reasons in its support. If I say you should get out of the room, you may ask why. If there is no reason, then it isn't true that you should leave—my suggestion is merely strange. Suppose, however, I tell you the room is on fire. That provides a reason; and if you believe me, you will no doubt leave at once. But whether this *is* a reason for you will depend on your attitudes. If you want to avoid being burned, then the fact that the room is on fire is a reason for you to leave. In the unlikely event that you don't care whether you are burned, this fact may have no importance for you. It will not provide a reason for you to leave.[13]

We have no need to deny the point that Rachels's illustration makes: that self-preservation is a powerful motive, and in many circumstances a valid and justifiable reason for action. But even so, when it comes to moral duty, physical self-preservation cannot be the final arbiter of the right course to take. Socrates held that to preserve his life at the cost of betraying truth would be traitorous to his duty. Christian martyrs by the thousand have willingly accepted their duty to lay down their lives rather than deny Christ. There are some values more important than physical life.

But the major point of Rachels's illustration is to prove that 'Hume was wrong . . . to say that we can never derive "ought" from "is",[14] and so to demonstrate that it is possible to deduce an ethic of duty from the bare facts of natural processes. How well does Rachels's example prove

---

[13] 'Naturalism', 78.
[14] 'Naturalism', 79.

his case? The answer is that it does not prove it, because the illustration he cites is not a case of duty at all. Observe how he uses the word *should* (which in this context is the equivalent of *ought*):

> If I say you should get out of the room . . . suppose I tell you the room is on fire. That provides a reason.[15]

But 'should' here does not mean 'You have a duty to get out of the room.' All it says is what you must do if you want to avoid getting burned; and it adds that if you don't mind getting burned, you have no reason to get out; in other words you have no duty to get out. It is, then, mere advice: it states no duty and does not attempt to impose a duty. Rachels, it would seem, has been misled by the ambiguities of the words 'should' and 'ought'.

But his proof fails for another reason. To deduce an 'ought' of duty from a plain statement of fact, one must supply an adequate reason why the fact entails a duty. Rachels again realises this necessity, and he suggests what he considers could be in general an adequate reason; and it turns out to be not even altruism, but our own personal interests. That is hardly the basis for an adequate ethic.

Instinct

Some people have considered that moral values are objective and universal because they are grounded in instinct that is common to all humanity. Certainly instinct is a valuable thing. A baby's cry will waken its parents out of a deep sleep. A mother hen will instinctively protect her chicks under her wings from the threat of a hawk. But by itself, instinct is no more completely adequate as a ground for objective moral values than naturalism has proved to be. We have many instincts, and the trouble is that they can sometimes conflict.

Suppose you are sitting in your home one day when you hear agonising, piercing shrieks outside calling for help. You immediately feel an instinctive urge to go to the rescue of whoever is in need. But then the contrary instinct of self-preservation urges you not to meddle with what could turn out to be a very dangerous situation. How shall

---

[15] 'Naturalism', 78.

you decide what your duty is? When instincts conflict you will need something more than instinct to settle the matter.

To sum up so far

Physical evolution, Social Darwinism, sociobiology, ethical naturalism and instinct have all proved inadequate to ground a universal, objective ethic.[16] Something more is needed. That something more, so Jews, Christians and Muslims would say, is the character and will of God, the Creator. But then, of course, many people do not believe in God. Yet at the same time they see the inadequacy of evolutionary theory and naturalism to ground a satisfactory ethic; and they have other suggestions to make. We must examine those suggestions.

UNIVERSAL, OBJECTIVE MORAL VALUES ARE THE CREATIONS OF HUMAN BEINGS

Many philosophers, though convinced atheistic evolutionists, nevertheless reject as implausible all attempts to ground ethics in the physical elements, forces and processes of Nature. They hold rather that ethical concepts, standards, principles and codes of behaviour arose naturally out of the practical exigencies of the human race's ever more complicated social development: intermarriage, trade, border-disputes, warfare, peace treaties, national constitutions, laws, etc. Ethics at that early stage was primarily a matter of practical reason, and only secondarily did reflection on many similar situations lead to theoretical ethics. Even so, the resultant ethical principles were never intended to be set in stone like God-given commandments; and therefore they could be modified, abandoned, or superseded in the light of humanity's ever increasing scientific, psychological and technological understanding.[17]

Given this understanding of the development of humanity's moral and ethical sense, there still remains, however, a practical question:

---

[16] For a fuller discussion of the topic of nature and evolution as the basis of ethics, see Ch. 4—'Comparative Moralities' in Book 1: *Being Truly Human*.

[17] A leading exponent of this view was Theodosius Dobzhansky, one of last century's foremost authorities on the modern biological theory of evolution. See his 'Chance and Creativity in Evolution'.

from where arises the human's feeling that he or she has a duty to keep the moral law? Suppose, for instance, for practical purposes and in its own interests, a nation has made a solemn treaty with another nation. Suppose circumstances change, and it would now suit the interests of the first nation to break the treaty. It might fear to do so because of possible reprisals. But suppose the second nation became so weak that it could no longer threaten reprisals. Would the first nation still have a duty to keep its treaty obligations and promises? Or with fear of reprisals removed, would it be morally free unilaterally to tear up its treaty documents? In other words, has the moral law an authority to impose a duty on a promise-maker to keep his promises? Or is ethics, in the end, simply a matter of pragmatism, such that one has no duty to keep a promise if one can break it with impunity?

Has the moral law an authority to impose a duty on a promise-maker to keep his promises? Or is ethics, in the end, simply a matter of pragmatism, such that one has no duty to keep a promise if one can break it with impunity?

The ancients, aware how easily people could be tempted to break their promises and treaties, would require both parties to a treaty to call God, or the gods, to witness, thus inviting divine sanctions if they broke it. And still today in the law courts of many countries, or at the giving of evidence before a senate hearing, people are required to take an oath that they will tell the truth, the whole truth, and nothing but the truth. Perjury is considered not only a crime, but a sin against God.

In cases, however, where people do not believe in God, and where ethical laws are regarded as merely man-made conventions, the question necessarily arises: on what is a person's duty to tell the truth, to act justly, to keep promises, and to love his or her neighbour, ultimately based?

Let us now look at one modern answer to this question.

Contractarianism

Contractarianism has had a long history. In Europe it goes back to the ancient Greeks. Their political theory held that the human race originally lived as individual families 'in the wild', completely free like wild animals. In that condition human life was crude, brutish and violent. Then humans learnt to live in cities. That meant, of course, surrendering a certain amount of freedom, and submitting to the laws, institutions and customs of the city. But most people were prepared to agree to live under these laws because of the many advantages city life gave them compared with the dangers and discomforts of living in the wild.

Socrates is a good example of contractarianism. When he was condemned to death, he could have saved his life by fleeing the city. Instead, he chose to stay. He argued that for many years he had consented to live as a citizen in Athens and to enjoy the benefits of the protection of its laws. For him, that had established a virtual contract on which he should not now renege. The city's laws were now condemning him to death. He did not agree with their sentence. But he felt he must honour his lifetime 'contract' and submit.

In the seventeenth and eighteenth centuries in Europe, contractarianism was still a heavily political theory and was used in order to convince people of their obligation to submit to the government of the day (which was generally a monarchy). Life under any government at all, with the benefits ordered society brought, was better, so it was argued, than living 'according to nature'. People, moreover, were morally obliged to give allegiance to the government because they had 'consented' to its authority, or, at least, they had good reason to assent to it, as a way to avoid the hardships of living in 'a state of nature'.

> Rousseau advocated a version of the sovereignty of the whole citizen body over itself. Its laws would then be passed by the general will of all the people, and would, so the theory went, apply to all equally.

It was, at best, a doubtful argument; for by the time of the seventeenth and eighteenth centuries, the people had not been living 'in a state of nature' for centuries. And to what extent people could have been said to have 'consented' to the particular forms of government they were under, was arguable, since the masses had no vote.

It was also a double-edged sword that could be applied in completely different directions. Jean-Jacques Rousseau (1712–78), for example, in his *The Social Contract* (1762) used the theory to condemn virtually all existing governments and to foment revolution. The claim was that people had no reason to assent to the authority of the present government, because the quality of life they could expect to face without it would be better than with it. 'Man is born free; and everywhere he is in chains', was Rousseau's slogan. He advocated a version of the sovereignty of the whole citizen body over itself. Its laws would then be passed by the general will of all the people, and would, so the theory went, apply to all equally. It would promote liberty, fraternity and equality. Man, being predominantly good by nature, would no longer be corrupted and depraved by the vices of society.

Thomas Hobbes (1588–1679), on the other hand, who is also considered by many to have been a social-contract theorist, used his version of the theory to argue the very opposite case to that which Rousseau would later adopt. In his theory, people living in a state of nature were in constant fear of some person, or groups of persons who had the power to kill them. They therefore made a free gift of their right of nature directly to some sovereign, who then had the responsibility to protect them. In return they had to submit to him and his laws, and were never morally free to go back on their gift and rebel against him.

Moral contractarianism

The original, heavily political, version of contractarianism eventually went out of fashion. It had to assume the real consent of real people in actual circumstances, when in fact it was built as a theory on the hypothetical consent of idealised people in idealised circumstances. It was, therefore, superseded by theories that fit more closely to the realities of life.

But in more recent decades contractarianism has been revived, not as a political theory, but as a serious contribution to moral theory where it aims to deal with the question of the status of ethics, the authority of the moral law and therefore also with the question we were earlier discussing: in what is our sense of duty to keep the moral law grounded? And it proposes to give an answer that will take this sense of duty seriously, and yet satisfy those who do not believe in God, and particularly those who resent the idea that behind the moral law stands a God who has the right to impose that law on us.

One of the proponents of this theory is Geoffrey Sayre-McCord. He extols its virtues in this way:

> just as political contractarianism emerged as a response to the recognition that political legitimacy and obligation could not be traced to God or nature, moral contractarianism's appeal has grown substantially with the sense that moral constraints must in some way be a reflection of human reason or social convention, not of God or (nonhuman) nature. Contractarianism holds out the seductive prospect of a theory that demystifies morality's status and shows it to be a compelling expression of humanity's nature. For if morality finds its source and authority in our capacity to embrace its demands, then understanding morality will ultimately require appealing to what we would need in any case to explain our own capacities and practices. Nothing occult or mysterious or supernatural need be implicated.[18]

Here we notice in passing that philosophical theories are recommended and accepted not simply because they are true, but because they are attractive; and many people will find a theory genuinely attractive if it eliminates God from the authority of the moral law. If, after all, the moral law emanates from ourselves and our moral capacities, then (1) we are more likely to be able to keep it; and (2) when we fail, we are answerable only to ourselves and our communities, and not to almighty God. If, on the other hand, the moral law comes from God, will not its demands be too great for us? And will not failure fill us with fear? Moreover, if the moral law is something we all agree as members of a community to consent to, then we retain our sense of freedom. If, on the other hand, moral law is imposed on us by almighty God, are we not thereby reduced to a kind of slavery?

An assessment of moral contractarianism

At the level of practical ethics there is no doubt that maximising the voluntary agreement of the maximum number of people is an ideal way of maximising social harmony and welfare. And if every party to the

---

[18] 'Contractarianism', 1st edn 254, 2nd edn 339–40.

agreement were motivated by the intention impartially to seek the good of all, the result would be ideal. One basic difficulty would of course be: how do you first persuade people to come to negotiations with those motives already formed and in that state of mind?

But when it comes to the actual working out of the theory of moral contractarianism there are even more basic difficulties. For here we are concerned not merely with day-to-day practicalities, but with the ultimate status of morality, and with the ultimate question: suppose some form of moral contractarianism is able to arrive at some general consensus about the demands of morality, what ultimate duty, or even reason, have we to give allegiance to that moral consensus? Let Sayre-McCord himself describe the problem that besets his moral theory:

> The second worry ... centres on the question: what reason is there to embrace that moral concern? Even those who are concerned to act as morality requires might, on reflection, wonder whether they have any good reason to retain or act on that concern, especially in situations where morality quite clearly requires sacrifice. Why not think of the concern as merely a reflection of socialization that one would do better to be without? If contractarianism is offered solely as a way to articulate a concern for morality that we are assumed to share, it will in effect ignore the issue. But many think this is an issue that should not be put to one side casually, not least of all because so often people's actual concerns reflect ignorance, superstition, and prejudice. Morality of course presents itself as legitimately commanding allegiance and sacrifice. But do we really have reason to offer the allegiance and make the sacrifices, when called for?[19]

Hobbes, as Sayre-McCord points out,[20] would have an answer to this problem, namely that we have prior, non-moral, reasons for yielding this allegiance and making these sacrifices. We have a need to protect ourselves from injustice, cruelty, oppression, and violence. So long, then, as everyone else in the community consents to live according to the agreed, contractarian, morality, we have a strong, practical,

---

[19] 'Contractarianism', 1st edn 259.
[20] 'Contractarianism', 1st edn 206, 2nd edn 344–5.

though non-moral, reason for giving our allegiance to the consensual morality, in spite of the sacrifices involved.

Once more as a piece of practical advice it could, within its limits, be helpful. But it has severe limits. In nation states in which democracy has allowed contractarian assent to the demands of morality its maximum influence, there are still innumerable instances of individual lying and cheating, of personal injustices, of commercial corruption, of defrauding of taxes, of mafia violence, of child abuse and such-like things. Since those who commit such offences are often able to do so with impunity, contractarian morality has no power to command their allegiance. They recognise no claim of duty.

And what shall we say when the contractarian moral consensus of the majority in a nation itself agrees to the persecution of a minority, as when the Hutu majority in Rwanda set about the genocide of the minority tribe, the Tutsis, or when Albania made belief in God a capital offence?

If there is no God behind the moral laws, and no final judgment, then morality has no ultimate authority; and contractarian morality which is built on the presupposition that there is no God, and that morality stems from, and relies on, humankind's own moral capacity, must, for all its fair ideals, prove in the end to be a rope of sand.

UNIVERSAL, OBJECTIVE MORAL VALUES ARE GROUNDED IN THE CHARACTER AND WILL OF GOD

This view holds that these values are revealed to us both in nature and in God's word. The technical name for this view is 'The Divine Command Theory of Morality'. According to this theory our duty to keep the moral law is based on the fact that God is our Creator. Its logic is simple: we should have no life to live, nor world to live in, had not he created both it and us. Reject the idea of God, and it still remains true that we did not create ourselves, let alone the universe. But in that case we are left with impersonal matter and forces as our creators, and in consequence, we cannot think of any convincing reason why we as persons, and thus superior to impersonal matter and forces, should have any ultimate duty to obey them or any social system created by our mere fellow human beings.

The unavoidable implication of the Divine Command Theory is that to live in disregard of our Creator and his laws is to live a fundamental unreality fraught with disastrous consequences. It is understandable, therefore, why this theory has often been, and still is, attacked. Very often the reason is personal and emotional. The theory conjures up the idea of an almighty tyrant, breathing down people's necks, and seriously restricting their freedom. With other people, the objection is moral: doing good out of fear of God, they say, or out of hope of reward from God, would corrupt the disinterested motivation necessary for true morality.[21] But the most basic, and the most frequently quoted, philosophical difficulty is the so-called Euthyphro problem.

The Euthyphro Problem

The problem gets this name because it was first raised in European literature, as far as we know, in Plato's dialogue, the *Euthyphro*. Euthyphro is discussing with Socrates the nature of holiness, and, at one point, he describes holiness as 'what the gods like'. Socrates asks, in effect, 'Is holiness liked by the gods because it is holiness? Or, is holiness holiness because the gods like it?'

People still ask the same question when God is said to be the authority behind morality: 'Does God command something', they ask, 'because it is morally good? Or does something become morally good, because God commands it?'

If God commands it because it is good—so the argument goes—then it must be good independently of God's command. And that would mean that 'goodness' is a standard to which God himself is subject. And that, in turn, would mean that there is something above God, so that God is not the supreme authority.

On the other hand, if something becomes morally good just because God commands it, that would mean that God could command anything at all, however bad or shocking, and it would become good simply because of God's arbitrary command. And that would mean that God was no better than the worst of dictators.

---

[21] For a discussion of this point see Ch. 4—'Comparative Moralities' (pp. 156–166) in Book 1: *Being Truly Human*.

People therefore conclude that God, even if he exists, cannot be the ultimate authority behind morality: morality must be completely autonomous.

But the argument is fallacious and springs from a failure to realise that we are here dealing with both God's will and command on the one hand, and God's essential character on the other. Let's take one of God's basic commands: 'Be holy, for I am holy' (see Lev 11:44–45; cf. 19:2; 20:7; 1 Pet 1:16). The command to us to be holy is not the arbitrary command of an unscrupulous tyrant; it is based on the essential character of God: 'I am holy'. At the same time it is not based on some standard external to God and of superior authority to him. God is in his own being the sum total and perfection of holiness. And that is why, for instance, he cannot lie, or be unfaithful, because he cannot deny himself (Titus 1:2; 2 Tim 2:13). God cannot act 'out of character' or command anything that is inconsistent with his character. This means, therefore, that the duty to keep the moral law is imposed on us not by forces of nature, nor ultimately by our fellow human beings, nor by a set of impersonal principles but by a personal God, holy, loving, compassionate and merciful.

A residual difficulty

But the answering of the Euthyphro problem still leaves in many people's minds the major difficulty that we have already mentioned. It is the difficulty from which moral contractarianism, among other theories, was intended (ineffectually as it turned out) to set us free. That is, namely, the threat to our freedom if there is some almighty God who imposes his moral law on us, and secondly the fear that his laws would be beyond our capacity, let alone our willingness, to keep, while failure would bring on us dread of the consequences.

But it would only be fair, in our present context, to notice two features of God's law-giving, as the Bible records them.

The Ten Commandments and the old covenant
(Exod 19:1–8; 20:1–24; 24:1–11)

When God gave the Ten Commandments he did not impose his laws on the people willy-nilly. He first set them free from political, economic and social slavery, and so earned their gratitude. He then offered for their free and grateful acceptance the possibility of entering into a covenant with him to be his people and to keep his laws. And ample provision was made for their forgiveness when through weakness they broke those laws.

The new covenant and the writing of God's laws on the human heart (Luke 22:20; Heb 8:6–12; 10:14–18; 2 Cor 3:2–18)

The new covenant that Christ offers for the human race's free acceptance is based on his death for the sins of the world, by which human resentment and fear of God can be overcome and humans reconciled to God. It provides not only complete forgiveness but the operation of the Holy Spirit in the human heart, imparting to those who freely accept the covenant new powers to begin to learn, to love and to keep his laws.

This more than suggests that resentment of God as a tyrannical authority behind the moral law is unjustified and misplaced.

MAJOR CONTEMPORARY ETHICAL SYSTEMS

CHAPTER 4

CHRISTIAN ETHICS

The moral law is not a set of impersonal rules and regulations: it is the declared will of the tri-personal Creator. The human race's obedience, therefore, is always, ultimately, not merely a question of conforming to a law, but of obeying a person.

INTRODUCTION

We now turn, in this section of our book, to consider six major ethical systems. Let's begin by briefly restating the four groups of questions, which in our last section we suggested, should be asked of any ethical system.

1. What status, basis and authority does it claim?
2. What is its supreme goal? And what general principle, or principles, does it lay down for the attainment of that goal?
3. What, if any, specific rules does it lay down for the varied action-spheres of daily life?
4. What guidance does it give on how we should apply its general principles and specific rules when it comes to deciding actual, complicated cases in daily life?

We shall not, of course, force every ethical theory to answer all four of these groups of questions whether they are appropriate to each particular theory or not. Some theories have no explicit supreme goal (No. 2) other than the general desire to behave ethically. Some make no hard and fast distinction between general principles (No. 2) and specific rules (No. 3); and some no distinction between specific rules (No. 3) and guidance in particular cases (No. 4). But if we bear in mind these four different levels of thought in ethical theory, it will help us to critique different ethical systems fairly. We can, at least, try to make sure that when we compare and contrast one with another, we are comparing one level of thought in one system with its corresponding level of thought in another, and not unfairly confusing the different levels.

This time, let's start with biblical ethics, which for some centuries was the major, if not the sole, system of ethics in Europe.

CHRISTIAN ETHICS: ITS STATUS, BASIS AND AUTHORITY

We saw in our last chapter that biblical ethics is ultimately grounded in the character and will of God; and therein lies its authority. Moreover, the moral law is not a set of impersonal rules and regulations: it is the declared will of the tri-personal Creator. The human race's obedience, therefore, is always, ultimately, not merely a question of conforming to a law, but of obeying a person.

Nature, for her part, can in many respects point the way to our moral duty; but the *authority* behind Nature's call to us to live in harmony with her laws is not Nature herself, but Nature's Creator. The creation (as originally made, not as distorted through man's fall and alienation) is the mind and design of God expressed and put into effect by the divine Logos, the second person of the tri-personal Godhead. And the mind and character of God have been further expressed through divinely inspired Holy Scripture, and above all through the incarnation, life, teaching, death, burial, resurrection and ascension of the incarnate Logos.

> In the last authoritative assessment of men and women's ethical behaviour the final judge will be, not God the Father, but this same perfect exemplar of God's law, Jesus Christ, the man who is God.

Moreover, the biblical declaration that men and women are made in the image of God means that we too are persons, that is, beings capable of sustaining personal relationships, not only with one another, but with our personal Creator within the parameters he himself has set us in his commandments.

Furthermore, God's law has not only been promulgated in propositional form. Through the incarnation of the God-man, Jesus the Son of God, it has been exemplified in practice in a human life. It has not remained simply a theoretical ethical system. And the authority of that exemplification has been vindicated by God's raising Christ from the dead.

Finally in the last authoritative assessment of men and women's ethical behaviour the final judge will be, not God the Father, but this same perfect exemplar of God's law, Jesus Christ, the man who is God (John 5:22–23).

ITS SUPREME GOAL AND GENERAL PRINCIPLES

Its supreme goal

The glory of God
'Do all to the glory of God' (1 Cor 10:31). 'For from him and through him and to him are all things. To him be glory for ever' (Rom 11:36). Or as one Christian catechism puts it: 'Man's chief end is to glorify God and to enjoy him for ever.'[1]

The glorification of Christ
He became 'obedient to the point of death, even death on a cross. Therefore God has highly exalted him and bestowed on him the name that is above every name, so that at the name of Jesus every knee should bow . . . and every tongue confess that Jesus Christ is Lord, to the glory of God the Father' (Phil 2:8–11).

The moral perfecting of believers in Christ
'Love your enemies and pray for those who persecute you, so that you may be sons of your Father who is in heaven. . . . You therefore must be perfect, as your heavenly Father is perfect' (Matt 5:44, 45, 48). 'He disciplines us for our good, that we may share his holiness' (Heb 12:10).

The final glorification of believers in Christ
'To be conformed to the image of his [God's] Son, in order that he might be the firstborn among many brothers. . . . those whom he called he also justified, and those whom he justified he also glorified' (Rom 8:29–30). 'We are God's children now, and what we will be has not yet appeared; but we know that when he appears we shall be like him, because we shall see him as he is. And everyone who thus hopes in him purifies himself as he is pure' (1 John 3:2–3).

From these and many similar passages in the New Testament it becomes evident that in Christianity ethics is concerned with far more than laying down rules to tell us how to behave decently one to

---

[1] *Westminster Shorter Catechism*, Q1.

another—though, of course, it is much concerned with this. Among the technical terms of the New Testament, such as salvation, redemption, justification and so on, ethics is part of what is termed sanctification. It is an integral part of the whole purpose and goal of the creation, redemption and eventual glorification of Nature and of mankind within it.

Its general principles

1. *Loving God*: "'You shall love the Lord your God with all your heart and with all your soul and with all your mind (quoting Deut 6:5). This is the great and first commandment'" (Matt 22:37).
2. *Loving your neighbour*: 'And a second is like it: "You shall love your neighbour as yourself (quoting Lev 19:18). On these two commandments depend all the Law and the Prophets"' (Matt 22:39–40). 'Love does no wrong to a neighbour; therefore love is the fulfilling of the law' (Rom 13:10).

In other words, these two commandments—love God and love your neighbour—are the two general ethical principles that underlie, and are meant to motivate and direct, behaviour in the action-spheres (Question No. 3), and in the practical decisions (Question No. 4) of life.

Or take this other summary of the general principles that biblical ethics lays down:

3. *Love and justice in the sight of God*: 'He has told you, O man, what is good; and what does the LORD require of you but to do justice, and to love kindness, and to walk humbly with your God?' (Micah 6:8).

In all situations and in all circumstances, both justice and love, plus a sense of living and acting in the sight of God, are indispensably required. Without love, justice could become heartless, impersonal and legalistic. Without justice, love could degenerate into sentimental indulgence. Without awareness of God, we lose sight of the major goal of ethics, which is to please and glorify God; and in addition, we lack a healthy restraint from doing evil. Consider, for example, Joseph's defence against temptation by Potiphar's wife: 'How then can I do this great wickedness and sin against God?' (Gen 39:9).

To all this, the New Testament adds another general principle which is peculiar to Christianity: a rationally worked out sense of obligation to live for Christ in gratitude for one's personal salvation procured by Christ's self-sacrifice:

4. *Gratitude expressed in life's choices*: 'For the love of Christ controls us, because we have concluded this: that one has died for all, therefore all have died; and he died for all, that those who live might no longer live for themselves but for him who for their sake died and was raised' (2 Cor 5:14–15).

This is what is meant by the old Christian adage: 'In Christianity salvation is grace, ethics is gratitude.'

ITS SPECIFIC RULES COVERING VARIOUS ACTION-SPHERES

In the Old Testament

The Ten Commandments that God gave to Israel at Sinai (Exod 20:1–17) cover the following action-spheres.

The human race in relation to God

1. The prohibition on worshipping other gods (and we should remember that idols need not be simply wood, stone or metal; they can be mental. Ideas and concepts can be idolatrous).
2. The prohibition on the worship or veneration of images and likenesses.
3. The prohibition on profaning the name of God with special reference to swearing oaths lightly, and breaking promises made on oath.

The human race in relation to daily work

4. The law of keeping Sabbath one day in seven, for man's physical, emotional and mental recuperation, and for him to have time to think about his Creator.

The human race in relation to parents and the source of life

5. The command to honour parents, not only with respect, but with support in their old age; and thus to maintain the sacredness of the process of handing on life from one generation to another.

The human race in relation to society

6. The sacredness of life, and the prohibition on murder.
7. The sacredness of marriage, and the prohibition on adultery.
8. The safeguarding of property, and the prohibition on stealing.
9. The sacredness of truth, and the prohibition of false witness.

The human race in relation to inner thoughts, desires, lusts and schemings

10. The prohibition not merely on actually taking other people's goods and possessions, but on coveting, that is, on allowing those inner desires that would lead to such misappropriation.

Now it is obvious that these Ten Commandments are specific rules; but it is equally evident that they are not meant to be an exhaustive set of regulations covering in detail every possible situation that could arise. They are in fact followed in the next three chapters (Exod 21–23), and in many other chapters in the Old Testament by detailed regulations and case laws showing how the broad general rules of the Ten Commandments are to be applied in various situations. For instance, the sixth commandment that forbids the unlawful taking of life is later followed by detailed instructions as to how that law is to relate to exceptional cases like capital punishment, accidental homicide, and killing in self-defence. Moreover, in the book of Proverbs we have not so much, laws, but 'rules-of-thumb' or 'practical wisdom', to be applied as is appropriate.

The Ten Commandments, then, are not intended as exhaustive detailed regulations; their importance lies in this: they describe and prescribe life's basic values and sacrednesses. And not for nothing. These are values that are at all costs to be upheld in the various action-spheres and relationships of life. It is so easy in the rough and tumble of daily life, when we have to cope with complicated situations and are under heavy pressures, to yield to pragmatism and to compromise basic values. When, for instance, a man is trying to survive in the cutthroat competition of the commercial world, it is easy for truth to become a casualty and for accounts to be falsified. In the modern climate of loose sexual behaviour it is easy for the transmission of life from one generation to another to lose its sacredness. When life is hard—and also quite often when it is successful and affluent—it is easy for daily work to squeeze out life's highest value: men and women's spiritual fellowship with their Creator. It is understandable, therefore, that biblical ethics should concentrate so heavily on what we may call 'area rules' aimed at safeguarding the broad values and sacredness of life's action-spheres.

In the New Testament

Statements of Christian ethics are to be found all over the New Testament, for it is a feature of the New Testament that it is not written as a work of systematic theology, in which one book or chapter deals exclusively with, say, God, another with Christ, another with the Church and another with ethics. In the New Testament theology, Christology, soteriology, ethics, narrative and parable are all intertwined, as indeed they ought to be both in our thinking and in our living. Theory and practice must always go hand in hand. That said, there are here and there special collections of ethical teaching such as the Sermon on the Mount (Matt 5–7) and the lists of ethical commandments relating to life in the family, at work, and in the world, that are to be found at the end of the epistles.

Features of Christian ethics

Certain features of Christian ethics are worth noticing here:

1. *The aim of Christian ethics is the fulfilment of God's law*: Though the New Testament is emphatic that salvation cannot be earned or merited by our keeping of God's law, and has to be received totally as a gift by God's grace, yet the New Testament is equally emphatic that the purpose of salvation is the empowerment of each Christian by

God's Spirit, 'in order that the righteous requirement of the law might be fulfilled in us, who walk not according to the flesh but according to the Spirit' (Rom 8:3-4. Cf. Gal 5:16-25).

2. *Christ's ethical demands are higher than mere justice*: 'You have heard that it was said, "You shall love your neighbour and hate your enemy." But I say to you, Love your enemies and pray for those who persecute you, so that you may be sons of your Father who is in heaven. For he makes his sun rise on the evil and the good, and sends rain on the just and on the unjust' (Matt 5:43-45). Christianity automatically outlaws religious persecution.

3. *Christ's ethical demands presuppose personal experience of salvation and membership of the Body of Christ, and the new motivation this produces*: 'Therefore, having put away falsehood, let each one of you speak the truth with his neighbour, for we are members one of another' (Eph 4:25). 'Put on then . . . compassionate hearts, kindness, humility, meekness, and patience, bearing with one another and, if one has a complaint against another, forgiving each other; as the Lord has forgiven you, so you also must forgive' (Col 3:12-13).

ITS GUIDANCE WHEN WE HAVE TO DECIDE ACTUAL, COMPLICATED CASES IN DAILY LIFE

We shall discuss this topic in detail in the next section of this book.[2] Here, therefore, we may seek to answer just one question: what are Christians supposed to do when they are faced with a difficult decision and the basis of their Christian ethics, its major goal and general principles, its specific rules, commands and prohibitions as contained in the Bible, give no clear and explicit indication as to what that decision should be? Where then are Christians supposed to get their ethical guidance from, and how are they supposed to act? In those cases guidance can be drawn from the following sources:

---

[2] See Section 3: 'What Use is Ethics?'

1. from Nature, as being designed by God. 'Does not nature itself teach you?' says Paul (1 Cor 11:14). The Bible is far from saying that only people who know and believe the Bible have a sincere interest in living ethically. In fact it asserts that people often do by nature what the Creator intended they should, because the Creator has put law within their hearts (Rom 2:14–15) and their conscience actively works on that basis. That is why Christians are happy to join with people of all faiths or none, in a responsible concern for Nature and Nature's environmental problems, in health, medicine, agriculture, education, relief of hunger, poverty, global warming, etc., and in opposition to all practices and processes that are unnatural and anti-natural.
2. from local culture, when that culture is healthy (1 Cor 10:32–33).
3. from the conscience of the Christian community when that conscience is healthy and truly Christian (1 Cor 10:32–33).
4. from the personal guidance of the Holy Spirit (Rom 8:14–15), dwelling in the heart.
5. through prayer (Acts 13:1–3).
6. from the collective experience of the people of God (Heb 11).

But Christian ethics teaches an additional principle that helps us understand why the Bible does not contain endless legalistic detailed regulations covering every twist and turn of daily life. God does not intend people to remain moral infants. Where the Bible does not offer specific guidance, God wants Christians to learn to take the responsibility of making the decision themselves, but to do so on this understanding: that one day each of them must stand before Christ and give account to him for their decision. And then they will need to be able to say to Christ: 'Whether my decision was right or wrong, I decided to do what I did, because I honestly thought that that was what would please you best.' Learning by practice freely to take decisions with the motive of pleasing the Lord, is the secret of developing true Christian character and lies at the heart of ethics.

Here is the Bible itself discussing questions over which Christians at one stage disagreed among themselves:

One person esteems one day as better [in a religious sense] than another, while another esteems all days alike. Each one should be fully convinced in his own mind. The one who observes the day, observes it in honour of the Lord. The one who eats, eats in honour of the Lord, since he gives thanks to God, while the one who abstains, abstains in honour of the Lord and gives thanks to God. For none of us lives to himself, and none of us dies to himself. For if we live, we live to the Lord, and if we die, we die to the Lord. So then, whether we live or whether we die, we are the Lord's. For to this end Christ died and lived again, that he might be Lord both of the dead and of the living. Why do you pass judgment on your brother? Or you, why do you despise your brother? For we will all stand before the judgment seat of God; for it is written,

'As I live, says the Lord, every knee shall bow to me,
and every tongue shall confess to God.'

So then each of us will give an account of himself to God. (Rom 14:5–12)

OBJECTIONS TO CHRISTIAN ETHICS

There are many objections to Christian ethics. Here is just a sample:

1. It presupposes, but does not first prove by reason, that God exists. For those who do not already believe in God, its basis and authority are arbitrary and unconvincing.
2. For human beings to obey a moral code imposed on them by some divine being would render them slaves, and to obey out of fear would destroy the moral quality of their behaviour.
3. On the basis of the so-called Euthyphro problem (for an exposition of the problem see the end of Ch. 3 above) it is argued that it is logically impossible to think that God is the author of the moral law. Man's moral sense must be autonomous.

Many serious moral philosophers, therefore, maintain that it is possible to build a satisfactory ethical theory without any reference to God. We shall now survey some of their major theories in detail.

CHAPTER 5

ACT UTILITARIANISM

The goal is pleasure. In other words not only are pain and pleasure our taskmasters that point out our duty and drive us to it but, in addition, pleasure is our supreme goal. That accounts for utilitarianism's underlying, general principle: always aim to effect the maximum surplus of pleasure over pain for the maximum number of people.

THEN AND NOW

Utilitarianism exists in different forms. Its original form, as invented by Jeremy Bentham (1748–1832), still persists. It is known as *act utilitarianism*, to distinguish it from a significantly modified version of it, called *rule utilitarianism*. All forms of it are types of *consequentialism*. We shall consider the meaning of these modifications later on; but in order to grasp the significance of these modifications, we need to concentrate first on the original form.

The work in which Bentham first expounded his theory was entitled *An Introduction to the Principles of Morals and Legislation* (1789). As the title indicates, his theory was originally concerned as much with the ethics of political, social, economic and legal systems as it was with personal and private ethics. We should constantly bear this in mind, since the ethics of a private individual's special care for his family and close relatives can rightly—or so many people think—be different from the impartial concern required of a government for all its citizens. Hence, when it comes to the practical application of Bentham's theory, this difference renders critique of the theory somewhat complicated.

Today, however, utilitarianism still commands widespread interest, and features of it have permeated ethical theories that are not themselves utilitarian. The little book *Utilitarianism For and Against*, in which J. J. C. Smart presents arguments for the theory, and Bernard Williams arguments against, has been reprinted twenty-seven times (the latest in 2008) since it was first published in 1973. This popularity is doubtless due, to some extent, to the fact that many economists have sought to apply Bentham's principles to the theory and practice of economics. For a more recent assessment of utilitarianism with special reference to its economics aspect, see the symposium *Utilitarianism and Beyond*, edited by Nobel Laureate Amartya Sen, and Bernard Williams. This symposium is on the whole critical of utilitarianism.

A BIRD'S-EYE VIEW OF ACT UTILITARIAN ETHICS

1. Its status, basis and authority: Nature and man's psychological make-up.
2. (*a*) Its goal: Pleasure, or happiness.
   (*b*) Its general principle: Always aim to effect the maximum surplus of pleasure over pain for the maximum number of people.
3. Its specific rule: An act is morally right if it produces a maximum of pleasure, morally wrong if it produces more pain than pleasure.
4. Guidance in actual cases: (*a*) in quantifying and distributing the pleasure effected by an act, each recipient must count as one, and none for more than one. (*b*) in calculating the amount of pleasure to be effected by an act, the agent must be neutral and altogether impartial.

A MORE DETAILED STUDY OF ACT UTILITARIAN ETHICS

Utilitarianism's basis

Michael Slote describes utilitarianism's basis as follows:

> Bentham and most subsequent utilitarians discard religious traditions and social conventions in favour of treating human well-being or happiness as the touchstone for all moral evaluation.[1]

Bentham himself tells us that his theory is founded on what he regards as the basic and inescapable psychological makeup and

---

[1] Slote, 'Utilitarianism'.

motivation of every man and woman, namely the desire to achieve pleasure or happiness and to avoid pain. He writes:

> Nature has placed mankind under the governance of two sovereign masters, *pain* and *pleasure*. It is for them alone to point out what we ought to do, as well as to determine what we shall do.[2]

In other words, pain and pleasure are not simply facts of human experience, of which, among many other things, we must take account as we attempt to fulfil our general duties to our fellow citizens such as to act justly, to tell the truth, to love, etc.; pain and pleasure are humankind's *moral guides*, our *only* moral guides in fact. They determine what we shall do, that is, they urge us, motivate us, compel us, to take the courses of action that produce pleasure and avoid pain. But not only so. They dictate what our duty is: we *ought*, we *have a moral duty*, to seek happiness and avoid pain. And we can see why that is if we consider utilitarianism's goal.

Utilitarianism's goal and general principle: pleasure maximised

The goal is pleasure. In other words not only are pain and pleasure our taskmasters that point out our duty and drive us to it but, in addition, pleasure is our supreme goal. That accounts for utilitarianism's underlying, general principle: always aim to effect the maximum surplus of pleasure over pain for the maximum number of people.

The nature of pleasure in Bentham's theory

Because Bentham posited pleasure as humankind's supreme good and goal, he is called a hedonist (from the Greek *hēdonē* = pleasure). But like the ancient Greek Epicurean philosophers, who also regarded pleasure as the supreme good, by 'pleasure' Bentham did not mean crude self-indulgence and dissipation, but something more like happiness, or wellbeing.

Now in actual life it does not always happen that an act produces nothing but pleasure for everyone concerned. Often an act will result in a mixture of pleasure and pain, or pleasure for some and pain for others. If, then, the general principle, according to utilitarianism, is so

---

[2] *An Introduction to Principles*, 1 (ch. 1.1).

to act as to produce not merely pleasure, but the maximum *amount* of pleasure and the minimum *amount* of pain, then some scheme will be needed for measuring the comparative amount of pleasure and pain produced by our various acts. Such a scheme Bentham provided by his *hedonic calculus*.[3]

Bentham's hedonic calculus

In this scheme pleasure and pain are measured each by its own:

1. Intensity.
2. Duration.
3. Certainty or uncertainty.
4. Nearness or remoteness.
5. Fecundity, that is, the chance it has of being followed by sensations of the same kind: by pleasures, if it be a pleasure; by pains, if it be a pain.
6. Purity, or the chance it has of not being followed by sensations of the opposite kind: by pains, if it be a pleasure; by pleasures, if it be a pain.
7. Extent, that is the number of persons to whom it extends (in other words, who are affected by it).

The amount of pain thus calculated, resulting from some act, is then weighed against the amount of pleasure resulting from the same act. And then it is decided whether the result is a surplus of pleasure over pain, or not.

Now obviously, if we took Bentham's calculus too literally, and imagined that he was saying that amounts of pain and pleasure can be measured precisely, like the weight of potatoes in a pair of scales, we could make his suggestion appear ridiculous. But he doubtless did not mean it in that way. He meant it in the same way that a man might weigh up in his own mind whether the pleasure which the use of a holiday home would give him and his family would be worth all the pain and effort involved in building it himself; or as a mother might consider whether the joy of having a baby outweighed the pain of childbirth. All of us weigh up things like this in our minds from time to time.

---

[3] *An Introduction to Principles*, 29 (ch. 4.2).

For Bentham, at least, this hedonic calculus had very practical applications, as appears from the way he applied it to the public policy of the State's punishment of criminals in England.

The rationale of punishment according to Bentham

A criminal, so Bentham argued, would regard crime as a way of maximising his pleasure and minimising his pain. If society responded by inflicting on him enough pain to outweigh his pleasure, the criminal might be deterred from committing crime again. On the other hand, Bentham held that society must not inflict more pain than was necessary to achieve this good result. In England in his day a man could be hanged for stealing a sheep. Bentham considered such a penalty altogether disproportionate; and on the basis of his utilitarian theory he argued strongly for prison reform.

Utilitarianism's specific rule

The rightness or wrongness, i.e. the morality, of an act is to be judged, not by any moral quality inherent in the act itself, but solely by its consequences, i.e. by whether it produces pleasure or pain.

This is the specific rule that must be applied in any and every action-sphere in order to decide whether a proposed act would be morally right or wrong. Bentham himself called it the *principle of utility*. ('Utility' comes from Latin *utilitas* = 'usefulness'; hence the name of the theory 'Utilitarianism' expresses this all-important specific rule that lies at the heart of the theory.)

Bentham's principle of utility

> By the principle of utility is meant that principle which approves or disapproves of every action whatsoever, according to the tendency which it appears to have to augment or diminish the happiness of the party whose interest is in question; or what is the same thing in other words, to promote or to oppose that happiness. I say of every action whatsoever; and therefore not only of every action of a private individual, but of every measure of government.[4]

---

[4] *An Introduction to Principles*, 2 (ch. 1.2).

It is this feature of utilitarianism that has been most attacked by utilitarianism's critics, for it implies that if an act which most people would regard as morally bad, or even repugnant, is nevertheless designed to produce happiness for the maximum number of people, that act must be regarded as morally good. In other words, if the result achieved is good, it does not matter if the means used to achieve it appear to be morally bad: the end justifies the means, and the means should not be regarded as morally bad, but good. This is the reason why this form of utilitarianism is called *act utilitarianism*.

Utilitarianism's guidance for actual cases

1. *In estimating the amount of pleasure, or happiness, that an action is intended to produce, each recipient is to count as one, and no one is to count as more than one.*

This rule would apply especially to, say, an Act of Parliament. It would not be right for such an act to be designed to provide more happiness or welfare for one group in society than for another.

2. *An agent, in any act, in making his decision what to do, must be completely neutral and impartial, not preferring his own interests to those of others, or of society in general.*

In order to see what this rule would imply let us imagine two different situations:

Situation A. Suppose two men, each on a different occasion, cause a serious accident through dangerous driving. Each in turn comes to the attention of the chief of police. How should the chief act? We surely should expect him to act with complete impartiality, and not to prosecute the one driver and to let the other off because he happened to be the chief's brother. Only strict impartiality could produce respect for the law and thus the maximum happiness for society in general. In this case most people would strongly approve of Bentham's principle.

Situation B. Suppose I am an electrician and work in a hospital in which my wife works as a nurse. An office in the hospital goes on fire, and I happen to be nearby. In the room are two people. One is a world-famous surgeon; the other is my wife. I have the chance to save one, but only one, of them before the flames become too intense. Which one shall I choose to save?

Bentham's theory says it would be immoral of me to choose to save my wife. Why? Because in making my decision I ought to be utterly neutral and impartial, and aim only to achieve the maximum happiness and welfare for the maximum number of people, regardless of my own interests. The surgeon with his skills, if he were saved, could throughout his subsequent life save far more people's lives than my wife would. My duty, therefore, is to act as a neutral disinterested party, save the surgeon and let my wife die.

In this case, most people would consider Bentham's rule utterly inhuman.

AN EVALUATION OF UTILITARIANISM: ITS PRACTICAL DIFFICULTIES

Utilitarianism has some obviously attractive features. Not the least of them is the straightforward, uncomplicated, simplicity of its general principle: always aim to maximise pleasure and minimise pain for the maximum number of people. All would surely agree that to try to anticipate the consequences of one's actions so as to maximise pleasure and minimise pain is something that all adults normally do in any case. Moreover, to aim to maximise pleasure not just for oneself but for the maximum number of one's fellow human beings is socially highly commendable. In addition, it could be heroically self-denying. For if the only way to maximise the pleasure of the maximum number of my fellow citizens, is to forego my own pleasure and to suffer loss or pain myself, then the utilitarian principle obliges me to do so. And finally, the habit of carefully anticipating the results of our actions would turn us into responsible, prudent, forward-looking people.

Nevertheless, utilitarianism runs into severe difficulties. As a result, many philosophers reject it completely, while a succession of utilitarians, dissatisfied with some of its implications, have constantly modified it, until their resultant theories are scarcely any longer utilitarian.

We may start with difficulties that arise in trying to put utilitarian theory into practice.

Disagreeing over the kind of pleasure that we should seek to maximise

First comes the criticism by J. S. Mill (1806–73). Though a fervent utilitarian himself, he maintained that it was not the *quantity* of pleasure that we should seek to maximise (as Bentham had said), but the *quality* of pleasure. Intellectual, aesthetic, spiritual pleasure, he argued, is far superior to physical pleasure and much more satisfying. 'It is better to be a human being dissatisfied than a pig satisfied,' he said; 'better to be a Socrates dissatisfied than a fool satisfied.'[5] Faced, then, with a choice between a pleasure of the body and a pleasure of the mind, the latter is to be preferred. Bentham's simplistic idea of the quantity of pleasure as our goal is thus modified.

Measuring the comparative value of incommensurable entities

Confronted with two potential acts, we are supposed to choose the one that will produce the maximum of pleasure. Suppose, then, that the one act will yield 5 nominal units of physical pleasure and 5 of intellectual pleasure, and the other act 7 nominal units of intellectual pleasure and 3 of physical pleasure. Is the total amount of pleasure the same for both acts? Or, according to Mill's theory, does a unit of intellectual pleasure count for more than a unit of physical pleasure? The answer will doubtless depend on who does the counting, since people's preferences differ widely. If each individual is free to decide his or her own personal pleasure without concern for other people, the answer is simple. But if we have a duty to maximise the pleasure of the maximum number of people, it leads to another practical problem.

Judging which kind of pleasure is to be aimed at

Who is to be the judge of which kind of pleasure is aimed at? Is it the one who performs the act, or the recipients of its results? According to Bentham's theory, an act is to be judged morally right if it produces pleasure and wrong if it produces pain. Suppose, then, an individual's act produces consequences which he judges supremely pleasurable but

---

[5] *Utilitarianism*, 8 (ch. 2).

which the recipients regard as boring or painful and therefore unacceptable. Is his act morally right or wrong? Who decides?

Moreover, when it comes to who shall decide what is to be regarded as true, acceptable, pleasure, there arises the question of the integrity of an individual's, or of a minority's, right of choice. Bentham's maxim, that all must act to produce the maximum quantity of pleasure acceptable to the maximum number of people, would seem to be satisfied if the State passed legislation that brought pleasure to an eighty-percent majority in the State and left the twenty-percent minority minimally satisfied or even distressed. We cannot forget the ruthless tactics of Hitler that gained the support of the majority in his nation at the cost of first humiliating, and then eliminating, the Jewish and gypsy minorities, among others.

Now obviously it is reasonable for parents and for the State to insist that all children must attend school and be educated, even though many children find the process painful. Parents and the State take the view that they know what is best for children, and in enforcing what seems painful to some at the time, they are aiming at maximum pleasure and happiness for them in their adult life.

But when it comes to adults, how far have individuals, or minorities, the right to choose their own concepts of pleasure and happiness, instead of having the majority's concepts and tastes forced on them by authority in the name of the maximum amount of pleasure for the maximum number of people?

Incidentally, we should notice that whatever interpretation you give of Bentham's theory, the question of which consequences are good is always answered on non-consequentialist grounds.

J. S. Mill's answer

J. S. Mill, whose preference for quality rather than quantity of pleasure gave rise to our present discussion, was a famous champion of the rights of the individual and of minorities, as we shall presently see. But in important respects he remained a Benthamite utilitarian all his days. He held, for instance, that an individual's human rights are not based on the fact that he is a creature of God, made in the image of God: his human rights are given him by the State. A person has a right to a thing, so Mill taught, if society has an obligation to protect him in his possession of that thing. But then we naturally ask, on what this obligation upon society is based. Who or what imposes it on society?

Mill's answer is truly Benthamite: the obligation must be grounded in the general 'utility'. That is to say, society grants and protects an individual's human rights solely because, and only so long as, it is 'useful', as Bentham would say, for maximising society's pleasure. One can imagine how a totalitarian State would have interpreted that.

Within these Benthamite limits Mill insisted, on the other hand, that an individual must be free to pursue his own goals in his private domain. He held that the only purpose for which power can rightfully be exercised over any member of a civilised community, against his will, is to prevent harm to others. His own good, either physical or moral, is not a sufficient warrant.

John Skorupski comments:

> Mill magnificently defends this principle of liberty on two grounds: it enables individuals to realise their individual potential in their own way, and, by liberating talents, creativity, and dynamism, it sets up the essential pre-condition for moral and intellectual progress. Yet the limitations of his Benthamite inheritance, despite the major enlargements he made to it, residually constrain him. His defence of the principle would have been still stronger if he had weakened (or liberalised) its foundation—by acknowledging the irreducible plurality of human ends and substituting for aggregate utility the generic concept of general good.[6]

Foreseeing the future

Bentham's theory maintains that the moral rightness or wrongness of an act depends on whether its results achieve pleasure or pain. But, of course, the results of an act often do not turn out as the agent intended. Along with the intended good results there can be unfortunate side effects. Sometimes the immediate good results are later on followed by disastrous consequences. Should we then judge the moral quality of an act by its intended, immediate and foreseeable consequences? Or, before deciding whether the act is morally good or not, must we wait

---

[6] 'Mill, John Stuart' in *The Oxford Companion to Philosophy*, 602.

and see what its unintended short-term and long-term consequences turn out to be?

Those who, in the 1950s, built a number of nuclear reactors sincerely felt that they were conferring on us great benefits. And to some extent they did. They could not have foreseen, however, that fifty years later these installations would become potentially lethal hazards, and the processing of their atomic waste an almost insuperable problem.

Was the initial act, therefore, morally good or bad according to utilitarian theory? It can be argued that the intention behind the act was good, whatever the eventual bad results. And that is true; but it seriously undermines act utilitarianism and turns it into what is called rule utilitarianism. For once one admits that the moral quality of the intention behind an act must be taken into account, whatever the actual results turn out to be, then one has undermined the basic rule of act utilitarianism: that the moral rightness or wrongness of an act must be decided not on any moral quality of the act itself or on the motives of the agent, but solely by the quality of its results.

Before deciding whether the act is morally good or not, must we wait and see what its unintended short-term and long-term consequences turn out to be?

Moreover, we all know that bad acts with immediate bad results can sometimes lead much later on to unintended good results. Are such acts to be regarded as good? In the famous story of Joseph and his brothers (Gen 37–50) the brothers with deliberate evil intention sold Joseph into slavery. In the end, to their great surprise, it turned out unexpectedly to be for the good of Egypt, of the surrounding nations, of Joseph's father and family and of the brothers themselves. 'You meant evil against me,' said Joseph to his brothers, 'but God meant it for good, to bring it about that many people should be kept alive' (Gen 50:20). Certainly the long-term result of their act was the eventual maximisation of pleasure. Are we then to say that the brothers' act was itself morally good?

A Christian perspective

A Christian might well comment at this point that in making the morality of an act depend solely on its results, atheistic utilitarianism puts upon people a burden they were never intended to bear. We must all be responsible for our actions, and are duty-bound to act with due foresight, care and precaution. But we cannot fully foresee the future with utter certainty. Only God can do that.

A man may, with the very best intentions, decide to take his wife and family out in his car for their pleasure. He drives with great care. But suddenly a child runs out in front of the car. The driver swerves to avoid the child. The car skids, runs into a telegraph pole, and his wife, sitting in the passenger's seat, is killed. If the morality of taking his family out in the car is to be judged by its results, then the man has committed a morally wrong act, and he will torture himself with blame for years. Reasonable people will protest: the man's intentions were good, he could not foresee the accident, and it was not his fault. Even in swerving to avoid the child his intention was good. To say that his initial act in taking the car out was morally wrong simply because it resulted in enormous pain would be grossly unfair. Similarly, a surgeon operating with the utmost care, and intending nothing but good for his patient, may make an accidental slip that proves fatal for the patient. Shall we say on that ground that his surgery was morally bad?

The fact is that we live in an uncertain world. None of us can foresee the bad results that our well-intentioned acts might produce. If the morality of our acts had to be judged simply by whether they produced pleasure or pain, action would be severely inhibited and responsibility intolerable. Christians find the courage to live boldly from the assurance that, come what may, 'for those who love God all things work together for good' (Rom 8:28), that is, for their ultimate and eternal good.

Many modern utilitarians, it should be noticed, modify Bentham's original theory at this point. They hold that in judging the morality of any act, the agent's motivation and intention, and much else beside, must be taken into consideration, and not merely the results of the act. That is much fairer; but, as we have already noticed, it undermines the basic principle upon which Bentham's act utilitarianism rests.

Further modifications of utilitarianism

It is in view of these practical difficulties that we have been discussing that modern utilitarians have sought to modify the basic theory still further.

Some abandon Bentham's idea that an act, to be morally right, must aim at the *maximum* amount of pleasure for the *maximum* number of people. Instead they adopt what has been called *outcome utilitarianism*. This form of the theory claims that the goodness of any state of affairs is solely a matter of how much overall, or average, wellbeing is enjoyed by people and also by sentient animals. This is the view which many economists take.

Others relax Mill's high standard of the quality of pleasure that should be aimed at. They are content to regard human or personal good as whatever satisfies people's desires or preferences, or makes them happy.

Still others relax the amount of good/pleasure that an agent is duty bound to aim to produce. If in order to qualify for being morally good, a man must aim at maximising the good of the maximum number of people, then he would be duty bound to give away his last crumb of food and piece of money in order to save the maximum number of people who are currently dying of starvation throughout the world. But this is thought by many utilitarians (and others as well!) to be unreasonable and impossibly demanding.

They substitute for it, therefore, what is called *satisficing utilitarianism*. This allows an act to count as morally good if it produces 'enough on-balance' of pleasure/good, even if the agent could have produced more on-balance of pleasure/good, if he had chosen to. The satisfactory nature of this minimal, but obligatory, good then leaves open the possibility, for the enthusiast, of works that go beyond the call of duty, works of supererogation and special merit.

AN EVALUATION OF UTILITARIANISM: ITS MORAL PROBLEMS

Utilitarianism's base

Here, once more, is Bentham's own formulation:

> Nature has placed mankind under the governance of two sovereign masters, *pain* and *pleasure*. It is for them alone to point out what we ought to do, as well as to determine what we shall do.[7]

---

[7] Bentham, *Introduction to Principles*, 1 (ch. 1.1).

We must first make sure that we rightly interpret what this means, and then we must ask: 'Is it true?'

What does it mean?

As we learned earlier, 'Bentham and most subsequent utilitarians discard religious traditions and sacral conventions'.[8] But we notice that their theory, in discarding God as its base for ethics, does not leave them as free agents to choose their duty and impose it upon themselves. Now they are subject to two 'sovereign masters', and mindless masters at that, set over them by Nature to dictate what their duty shall be and to enforce it by rewarding obedience with pleasure and chastening disobedience with pain. One might well wonder, then, how this impersonal, *amoral* state of affairs—Nature, pleasure and pain—without a personal creator behind them, can impose a *moral* duty on us.

But perhaps this would be unfair to Bentham. Perhaps his rhetoric means no more than that, pain and pleasure being the circumstances in which we are obliged to live, it soon becomes clear to us what our duty to our fellow men and women is in these circumstances. Let's use an analogy. Suppose I am driving a carload of passengers when I come upon a stretch of road covered with black ice and very slippery. The state of the road now makes me aware that I have a duty to my passengers to drive with special care. If I do not, I run the risk of accident, injury and death for them. The icy condition of the road, then, is the basis of my ethics, in that, in Bentham's terms, it alone points out what I ought to do, what my duty is, by making me aware that if I don't drive carefully, it will impose pain and injury on me and on my passengers, whereas if I drive cautiously, all will be pleasurable. This then, according to Bentham, is the way Nature controls us, by indicating what our duty is and by imposing severe sanctions on us if we fail or refuse to do our duty. But, of course, the duty that in these circumstances we owe, is not to Nature but to our fellow human beings and to ourselves. At the same time it is mindless, amoral

> When Bentham says that it is for pain and pleasure alone to point out what we ought to do, what does he mean by 'ought'?

---

[8] Slote, 'Utilitarianism'.

Nature, not God, that makes us aware of what life's supreme good is, the ultimate goal at which we have a moral duty to aim, namely pleasure.

What Bentham means by 'ought'

But to be fair to Bentham we must make sure that even so we have still not misunderstood him. When he says that it is for pain and pleasure alone to point out what we ought to do, what does he mean by 'ought'? In Chapter 2, when we were discussing ethical naturalism and the is/ought problem, we saw that the word 'ought' can be used in several different senses. Does Bentham mean that pain and pleasure show us what we ought to do, in the weaker sense that, if we want to avoid pain and enjoy pleasure, *we should be wise to act in such and such a way*? Or does he mean 'ought' in the stronger sense: pain and pleasure point out that *we have a moral and ethical duty to act in such and such a way*?

The answer seems beyond doubt. First, in July 1822 Bentham added a note to page 1 of his *Introduction to the Principles of Morals and Legislation*, confirming the view,

> which states the greatest happiness of all those whose interest is in question, as being the right and proper, and only right and proper and universally desirable, end of human action.[9]

Then on page 4 he writes:

> When thus interpreted, the words *ought*, and *right* and *wrong*, and others of that stamp, have a meaning: when otherwise, they have none.[10]

But on page 6, contemplating the possibility that a person might reject the utilitarian principle in favour of his or her own feelings, Bentham puts the meaning of 'ought' beyond doubt:

> 5. In the first case, let him ask himself whether his principle is not despotical, and hostile to all the rest of the human race.

---

[9] Bentham, *Introduction to Principles*, 1 n. 1 (ch. 1.1).
[10] Bentham, *Introduction to Principles*, 4 (ch. 1.10).

6. In the second case, whether it is not anarchical, and whether at this rate there are not as many different standards of right and wrong as there are men.[11]

It seems clear then, that Bentham means 'ought' in the strongest possible sense of a moral and ethical duty; and that is how his followers have generally understood him. The 'ought' which Nature indicates to men and women by means of pain and pleasure is not the ought of good advice: 'you would be well advised to behave towards society in this way', but the 'ought' of moral duty: 'it would be immoral, anarchic and despotic, if you did not act in this way toward society.'

Is it true?

Is it true that man's moral duty to effect the maximum of pleasure for society is not only indicated but imposed by Nature, pain and pleasure?

Christians will certainly not dispute that they have a duty to 'do good to everyone' (Gal 6:10), to 'be subject to the governing authorities', to 'pay to all what is owed to them: taxes to whom taxes are owed, revenue to whom revenue is owed, respect to whom respect is owed' (Rom 13:1, 7); to make 'supplications, prayers, intercessions and thanksgivings . . . for all people, for kings and all who are in high positions' (1 Tim 2:1–2), in other words to love their neighbours as themselves (Rom 13:9). But Christians will say that their duty to seek the good of society is based, not in Nature, nor even in pain and pleasure, but in God. In making Nature the basis of man's ethical and moral duty to society, utilitarianism suffers the same fatal weakness as the contractarian system suffers from: Nature simply exists. It is an 'is'; and you cannot derive an 'ought' from an 'is'.[12]

Utilitarianism's supreme good and goal

As the supreme good and goal for both the individual and society, Bentham designates 'pleasure'. He himself later suggested 'happiness', and still later utilitarians have described it as 'welfare' or 'desire-satisfaction'.

---

[11] Bentham, *Introduction to Principles*, 6 (ch. 1.14.5–6).
[12] See the long discussion of the matter in Ch. 3.

Now normal people like pleasure and dislike pain, and Christians are no exception. They delight both in the pleasures of this life and in the prospect that in God's presence there are 'pleasures for evermore' (Ps 16:11). But pleasure is a notoriously slippery thing, not simply because it can take different forms, physical, emotional, aesthetic, intellectual or spiritual; nor merely because what gives pleasure to one person might be painfully boring to another; but because pleasure itself, as an experience, can be very elusive.

You can't set out to grasp pleasure by itself, *in vacuo*, so to speak. Wise heads have long discovered and pointed out that pleasure is something that you find when you are looking for something else. It is like that kindred experience, enjoyment. You can't have enjoyment without something to enjoy. You can enjoy football, or swimming, or mountaineering, or painting, or chess, or studying or a hundred other things. But you can't just have enjoyment by itself without some thing, person, activity or other to get the enjoyment from. So it is with pleasure.

Drawing out some implications

1. Not all pleasure is good

It all depends on what we get pleasure from. Some people find pleasure in inflicting pain on other people—we call it sadism; some in sexually abusing children—we call it paedophilia, and it is an ever growing crime. Criminals often take pride and pleasure in their crimes, as Bentham himself observed. When it comes to our personal aims, not all pleasure is good. It depends on what the source and moral quality of our pleasure is. It is not enough to posit pleasure as our supreme good, value and goal. It needs to be morally qualified. By what principle, then, shall we decide what pleasure is good?

2. To aim simply at pleasure is morally misleading

It is right, for instance, for a man and woman to look for pleasure from their marriage. But suppose one partner becomes ill and more of a burden than a pleasure to the other partner. If then that other partner's main aim is simply pleasure, that partner may well feel he or she has a right to abandon the other spouse and seek some other partner. But true love will condemn and despise such mere pleasure-seeking as not being true love at all.

*3. It can sometimes be morally wrong
to seek to gratify people's pleasure*

Let's take some historical examples. Socrates would have given the Athenian populace great pleasure if he had consented to cease his quest for the truth. He refused. It was his duty, he felt, to urge them to join him in seeking the truth. They executed him for it.

Christ could have given the crowd much pleasure if he had led them in armed revolt against the Romans. He refused; and they shouted for his crucifixion.

*4. To make even good pleasure the supreme
good and goal in life is a form of idolatry*

The Bible does not condemn aiming at pleasure; but it would dispute Utilitarianism's designating pleasure as the human race's supreme good and goal. It condemns in fact those who are 'lovers of pleasure rather than lovers of God' (2 Tim 3:4). Adam and Eve, so the story goes, were in a garden full of all the delights and pleasures that the love and ingenuity of God could provide. They fell for the oldest temptation in history: that physical, aesthetic and intellectual pleasure are the chief goal in life, and can be enjoyed to the full, and more, by ignoring the Creator, his will and word.

To sum up so far then: when it comes to our personal quest, the Christian, as distinct from the utilitarian, view is that it is certainly not wrong to seek for pleasure; but it is wrong to make pleasure the supreme goal. In all our seeking, love for God and for our neighbour, and the duty and morality that spring from that love, must take precedence over seeking pleasure for its own sake. And when it comes to our duty to society then again many philosophers argue that certain things must take precedence over Bentham's utility principle, as we shall see in a moment.

Utilitarianism's general principle

It is easy to lay down the general principle that when we have a choice what to do, we must always choose to act in a way that will maximise pleasure for the maximum number of people. But in practice the actual choice can be anything but simple.

To start with, it would be an impossibly heavy task if, for each and every act we do every day, we had individually to stop and calculate *de novo* whether or not the act in question would produce the maximum of pleasure for everybody concerned. And when it comes to the major decisions that society has to take, involving as they do many fields of expert knowledge, it is obvious that most private citizens would in any case have to leave decision to the experts. But it is not easy for the experts always to know for certain what actions will definitely produce the maximum of happiness for the maximum number of people. Let's take some examples.

1. Cutting down the rainforests in various parts of the world, and extracting the hardwood timber without replacement, certainly maximises the profits of the timber companies, of their employees and of the government officials who wink at the illegality of it; and certainly also it provides beautiful hardwood furniture for the homes of those who can afford it. On the other hand its long-term effect on world ecology, and on the welfare of the local populace, is potentially disastrous. If our only motive is to maximise pleasure for the maximum number of people, what course of action should we take?

2. Suppose accountants working for a big industrial conglomerate discover that the directors have falsified the accounts and have reported to the public that their profits are far in excess of what they actually are; and they have done so to boost the price of their shares and keep their shareholders happy. What ought the accountants to do? Should they cooperate with this fraud and publicly sanction it, and thus keep their jobs? Or should they publish the truth and bring the company's shares crashing down, with great losses to pension funds and widespread loss of jobs? What action should be taken if our motive is not justice, but only to maximise the happiness of the maximum number of people?

3. Widespread pre-marital sex, refusal to be tied to a marriage contract, easy divorce, adultery, and abortion of unwanted children are all advocated and practised in the name of minimising pain and maximising pleasure. Do they maximise the pleasure of all those whose interests are concerned? And will they maximise the long-term welfare, health and happiness of a nation or society as a whole?

Faced with decisions like these, and hundreds more, it would seem obvious that we need more than a general rule: 'act so as to maximise pleasure for the maximum number of people.' We need some specific rules relating to the various action-spheres of life to guide us as to what decisions and behaviour are likely to lead to the maximum happiness. And it is likewise obvious, from the nature of the problems that face us, that the guidance we need will inevitably include moral guidance.

That is why in biblical ethics, for example, we are given not only a general goal to aim at—'You shall love the Lord your God with all your heart and with all your soul and with all your mind and with all your strength.... You shall love your neighbour as yourself' (Mark 12:30–31), but also specific rules for various action-spheres, for example, 'You shall not murder. You shall not commit adultery. You shall not steal' (Exod 20:13–15), 'Take no part in the unfruitful works of darkness, but instead expose them' (Eph 5:11).

> It would seem obvious that we need more than a general rule: 'act so as to maximise pleasure for the maximum number of people'. We need some specific rules relating to the various action-spheres of life to guide us as to what decisions and behaviour are likely to lead to the maximum happiness.

The utilitarian J. S. Mill himself saw this point and agreed that we cannot always calculate the consequences of our actions, and therefore we need rules and norms. Of course, he did not regard these rules and norms as coming from God but as being the result of human experience through the centuries. In his work *Utilitarianism*, originally published in 1863, he wrote:[13] 'During all that time, mankind have been learning by experience the tendencies of actions' (p. 20), and therefore 'mankind must by this time have acquired positive beliefs as to the effects of some actions on their happiness' (p. 21), and 'the beliefs which have thus come down are the rules of morality for the multitude, and for the philosopher until he has succeeded in finding better' (p. 21). But he adds, 'the received code of ethics is by no means of divine right' (p. 21).

---

[13] Mill, *Utilitarianism*, 20–22. The first separate publication was in 1863 but the work had previously been published in *Fraser's Magazine* in 1861.

He held, in fact, that these rules and norms were capable of indefinite improvement, though they should not in practice be lightly set aside in their entirety on the pretext of deciding every single action by Bentham's principle of utility.

> But to consider the rules of morality as improvable, is one thing; to pass over the intermediate generalizations [he means 'the rules and norms' that have come into being by generalising the results of the human race's long experience] entirely and endeavour to test each individual action directly by the first principle [he means Bentham's principle of 'utility'], is another.[14]

There was then to be no irresponsible disregard of the norms and rules—especially, it seems, by ordinary people: it was for the philosophers, apparently, to improve the common morality. Nevertheless, Mill, as a convinced utilitarian, held that none of the norms and rules was absolute. There was only one fundamental principle of morality, and that was the utilitarian principle: 'does the proposed action produce maximum happiness?' When, therefore, any of the norms and rules seemed (to the philosophers particularly) to call for improvement, and particularly when any one of them seemed to conflict with some other one, the sole decisive criterion had to be happiness.

Once more there is in this version of utilitarianism a certain apparent, and appealing, simplicity. It is, in fact, a form of *rule consequentialism* as distinct from *direct consequentialism*. The latter maintains that the rightness or wrongness of an act must be judged *not* by any moral quality of the act itself, but solely by the quality of its consequences—and that is the pure and original form of Benthamite theory. Rule consequentialism on the other hand says that, in deciding the rightness or wrongness of an act, you must, on most occasions, judge the act by the rules and norms of traditional morality and not simply by the act's intended and expected results.

Most modern utilitarians, however, adhere to Bentham's direct consequentialism and reject rule consequentialism. What theoretical justification can be given, they argue, for claiming that *rules* should be evaluated simply by their consequences (i.e. does following these rules lead to happiness?) and yet *acts* themselves not be evaluated simply by

---

[14] Mill, *Utilitarianism*, 21.

their consequences (i.e. do these acts lead to happiness?)?[15]

But there is a far more serious, practical objection to Mill's theory. Its force can be measured from recent history since Mill's time. Neither Marxist Communism nor Hitler's National Socialism lacked powerful and influential philosophers who assured the world that there was no divine authority behind the traditional rule, 'Thou shalt not murder innocent people.' They claimed, therefore, that it was morally right to break it. Their justification for their action in breaking the rule was that it would help to produce the maximum happiness for the maximum number of people in the utopia they guaranteed was coming. So they broke the rule millions of times. What kind of happiness it consequentially produced we all know too well.

Utilitarianism's one specific rule

Here once more, in accordance with Bentham's principle of utility, we state a summary of that one specific rule again: The rightness or wrongness, i.e. the morality, of an act is to be judged, not by any moral quality inherent in the act itself, but solely by its consequences, i.e. by whether it produces pleasure or pain. If it produces a surplus of pleasure it is morally right; if a surplus of pain, it is morally wrong.

First moral problem: the question of our duty to the past

In bidding us judge the morality of an act solely by its future consequences, act utilitarianism overlooks our duty to the past. Suppose I am a businessman. An older friend of mine, who is also a businessman, often helped me in times past to get established in my own business when I was a young man. I owed him a great debt of gratitude. When he was dying he appealed to my sense of gratitude and made me promise to help his inexperienced son who then had to take over the running of his father's business. But after the father's death, instead of helping the young man, I think up a way—quite legally—of taking over the business from him and then of dismissing him. I decide to do it. I will thereby break my past promise to his father and woefully fail to repay my duty of gratitude to him. But I

---

[15] See Slote, 'Utilitarianism'.

shall make a vast sum of money and, with that money in the future, I can become a public benefactor and bring a great deal of pleasure to a large number of people. I will have effected a surplus of happiness over pain. According to Bentham, then, my action must be regarded as morally right. But is it?

Second moral problem: the question of distributive justice

The aim of Bentham's utility principle is to act in such a way as to achieve a surplus of pleasure over pain. If then, we take a nation as a whole, calculate the total amount of pain and the total amount of pleasure suffered by all its citizens, and find that the total of pleasure surpasses the total of pain, that would seem to satisfy Bentham's utility principle. Is that enough, however, to satisfy distributive justice? Might there not still remain gross inequalities in the amount of good enjoyed by the very rich and the very poor? Would that be just?

Benthamite though he was, even J. S. Mill argued that the rights of justice *must take priority* over the direct pursuit of general utility. J. M. Skorupski sums up Mill's attitude in this respect in this way:

> The rights of justice reflect a class of exceptionally stringent obligations on society. They are obligations to provide each person 'the essentials of human well-being'. The claim of justice is the 'claim we have on our fellow-creatures to join in making safe for us the very groundwork of our existence'. Because justice-rights protect those utilities which touch that groundwork *they take priority over the direct pursuit of general utility* as well as over the private pursuit of personal ends.[16]

John Rawls (1921–2002), in his very influential book *A Theory of Justice*, argues even more strongly against Bentham's utility principle at this point. Philosopher Thomas Nagel comments:

> Rawls opposes utilitarianism, holding that the maximum total good may not be pursued by means which impose unfair disadvantages on minorities, including the unskilled.[17]

---

[16] Skorupski, 'Mill, John Stuart', emphasis added.
[17] Nagel, 'Rawls, John'.

Third moral problem: the question of common sense morality

There exists a difficulty in justifying the divergence between act utilitarianism's moral views and common sense morality. Act utilitarianism holds that the end justifies the means. The wrongness or rightness of an act depends not on the moral quality of the act itself but on its results, on whether it produces the maximum good for the maximum number of people. Opponents of utilitarianism have not been slow in thinking up extreme examples to show that utilitarianism's basic principle here is morally unacceptable.

> There exists a difficulty in justifying the divergence between act utilitarianism's moral views and common sense morality.

Imagine four men who are terminally ill: one with heart-lung failure, two with kidney failure, and one with liver failure. Suppose then a team of surgeons seizes a healthy young man without his permission and, against his will, kills him, and transplants his heart-lung into the first man, his kidneys, one each, into the second and third men, and his liver into the fourth man. Would this be a morally right thing to do? According to utilitarianism it would be perfectly right, because the end result would be one man dead, but four men alive, instead of one young man alive and four men dead. The resultant surplus of good would justify the act of murdering the young man.

To common sense morality, utilitarianism at this point is morally repulsive. To start with, assume the surgeons' motives are as benevolent as possible, but who gave them the right to take the life of the young man? And what kind of a society would it be if some lives could be arbitrarily sacrificed for the greater pleasure of others? And who has the authority to decide that a human life at best is only of finite worth, so that four lives are by definition more valuable than one? Suppose a human life is of infinite worth!

It is easily understandable, then, when Michael Slote states that most present-day utilitarians are engaged 'in one way or another attempting to reduce or play down the importance of the divergence between utilitarian moral views and common sense moral thinking.'[18] Not all are, of course. In *Utilitarianism For and Against* by J. J. C. Smart and Bernard Williams, Smart writes: 'Admittedly utilitarianism does

---
[18] 'Utilitarianism'.

have consequences which are incompatible with the common moral consciousness, but I tended to take the view, "so much the worse for the common moral consciousness."'[19] And later, 'It is not difficult to show that utilitarianism could, in certain exceptional circumstances, have some very horrible consequences.'[20] Citing the hypothetical case in which the sheriff of a small town can prevent serious riots (in which hundreds of people will be killed) only by 'framing' and executing (as a scapegoat) an innocent man,[21] Smart confesses he would be most unhappy to adopt this utilitarian solution to the problem, though he adds that he would be unhappy with an anti-utilitarian solution that allowed hundreds of people to suffer misery and death rather than execute an innocent man.[22]

Bernard Williams, however, ends that same volume with the remark:

> But the demands of political reality and the complexities of political thought are obstinately what they are, and in face of them the simple-mindedness of utilitarianism disqualifies it totally.
>
> The important issues that utilitarianism raises should be discussed in contexts more rewarding than that of utilitarianism itself. The day cannot be too far off in which we hear no more of it.[23]

Utilitarianism's guidance for actual cases

Here the moral problem lies with utilitarianism's insistence that in all circumstances everyone must deny his or her special duty to the family in favour of seeking the maximum good of everybody else. Strictly applied, this would destroy the family as the basic unit in society. From time to time various philosophers, like Plato, and totalitarian politicians have recommended the breaking of the natural family bond as though it were hostile to the prosperity of the State. Mercifully, Nature has proved stronger than these idealists. The Bible teaches that concern for one's family is a prior, though not exclusive, duty (see 1 Tim 5:4, 8).

---

[19] p. 68.
[20] p. 69.
[21] It was on this principle that Caiaphas had Christ executed (John 11:50).
[22] pp. 69–73.
[23] p. 150.

With that, we will now stop our specific consideration of act utilitarianism. In the following chapters, we will have reason to observe how it compares and contrasts with other ethical theories.

CHAPTER 6

INTUITIONISM

Intuitionism . . . insists on duties of *fidelity* arising from promises I have made, or debts I have taken on, in the past; duties of *reparation*, that is, making amends for wrongs I have done in the past; duties of *gratitude* owed to people that have helped me in the past; and duties of *justice* to overturn injustices that have been done in the past.

THE 'END' AND THE 'OUGHT'

In our previous chapter, we spent a long time studying various versions of utilitarianism because their central ideas still pervade the thinking of many people who would not necessarily hold the full-blown utilitarian theory, or regard themselves formally as being utilitarians of any sort. Moreover, utilitarianism also serves well as a basis of comparison by means of which to grasp more clearly the special features of other theories which we must now go on to consider. With that in mind, it will be helpful to acquaint ourselves at this point with two technical terms.

1. Teleological theories. The Greek word *telos* means 'an end' in the sense, not merely of the point at which something stops or ceases, but of the goal or consequences at which one directs one's actions. Ethical theories are classified as 'teleological' when they hold that the rightness or wrongness of our actions should be assessed solely by their results or consequences, and not according to any moral quality in the actions themselves. Pragmatism and all forms of consequentialism are obviously teleological theories; and so is act utilitarianism that we have just been studying.

2. Deontological theories. *Deonto* is part of a Greek word that means 'the things which ought to be done', in other words 'one's duty'. Ethical theories are classified as deontological when they maintain that we all have a duty to behave in certain ways; and that, therefore, our acts are to be judged morally right, not according to their results, but according to whether we have acted in the way in which it was our duty to act. It is the moral quality of the act that is all-important. Morally right acts, of course, may normally be expected to lead to good results. But it is not the good results that make the acts morally right. What makes an act morally right is whether the act itself complies with certain moral duties and standards.

Now in this and the next chapter we are to study two ethical theories that, in contrast to utilitarianism, are both classified as deontological.

We will consider intuitionism in this chapter, and Kantian ethics in the next.[1]

INTUITIONISM: FACTS AND EXPLANATIONS

The bare facts

1. It is a deontological theory.
2. It holds that there are a number of principles or duties that bear on the rightness or wrongness of any act.
3. These principles or duties are fundamental and underivative.
4. These principles or duties are known by intuition.
5. From these underived, fundamental principles or duties, we derive further principles or duties that we must apply in various action-spheres and particular situations.

Some explanations of intuitionism

Its champions

In modern times it is associated with the names of G. E. Moore (1873–1958), H. A. Prichard (1871–1947), W. D. Ross (1877–1971), and A. C. Ewing (1899–1973), of whom Ross has proved to be the most influential. After much hostile criticism and neglect, it has more recently been revived, in particular by David McNaughton.

What is meant by ethical intuitionism

In logic and science 'intuition' is used in specialist senses. In philosophy, and particularly in epistemology, it was employed by the so-called 'intuitivists', N. O. Lossky (1870–1965) and S. L. Frank (1877–1950), to denote a system of integral intuitivism, which is explained by Lossky as

---

[1] These classifications are not hard and fast. In laying down that an agent must always aim at producing maximum pleasure, utilitarianism may be said to impose a duty on the agent, and is, therefore, to that extent deontological. Similarly, Kantian ethics, which stresses our moral duty to treat all other human beings as ends in themselves, and not simply as a means to an end, can be said to have in mind the results of actions. To that extent, it may be said to be teleological.

'the doctrine that all species of knowledge are an immediate contemplation of reality by the knowing subject.'[2]

When it comes to modern ethical intuitionism, it is easier to say first what it does not mean. It does not denote a sudden flash of inspiration, nor a premonition, nor a sudden idea that such and such might be the case. The word 'intuition' comes from a Latin word which originally meant 'to look at' in the physical sense. Then it came to mean to 'see' something intellectually, e.g. to 'see' that the whole is greater than a part, or that 3 + 5 = 8, and to see it without having to work it out by discursive reasoning; and to see it as self-evidently true without any need for it to be proved by any argument or further evidence. We see it, it is said, by direct intuition; and what is seen by direct intuition is self-evident.

David McNaughton explains what intuiting the basic moral principles means:

> The very name 'intuitionism' was a handicap, since it encouraged the popular misconception, that the theory was committed to the existence of a mysterious faculty of moral intuition, unknown to science, by which we detect moral properties....
>
> The fundamental prima facie principles can, as noted, be known with certainty. Ross does not suppose that moral agents are aware of them from the moment they first make a moral judgment. We can come to know them by a process of *intuitive induction.* Particular moral truths come first in the order of judging. We take some act to be right in virtue of being, say, an act of promise-keeping. After reflecting on a number of acts involving promise-keeping, we come to the conclusion that promise-keeping is a right-making characteristic. If this were simply an inductive inference, then its strength would depend on the number and variety of cases I had considered. But, Ross holds, having formed the principle, we can then come to have direct insight into its truth... It is a necessary truth, knowable a priori because self-evident and thus requiring no proof. A truth is self-evident if understanding it is sufficient for being justified in believing it. One knows the proposition provided one believes it on the *basis* of understanding it.[3]

---

[2] Lossky, *History of Russian Philosophy*, 296.
[3] 'Intuitionism', 270, 281; 289, 300 (in 2nd edn).

McNaughton goes on to explain that such self-evident principles are not necessarily immediately obvious to everyone. One may have to think through a lot of particular cases before seeing that there is a universally valid principle involved. But he adds:

> this is the important point in defending intuitionism against its detractors—Ross is not claiming that moral principles are known by some special and mysterious faculty ... Ross is here placing himself squarely in the mainstream philosophical tradition that holds there are substantial claims, including ethical ones, whose truth we can know by direct rational insight.[4]

The basic prima facie duties according to intuitionism

In his book *The Right and the Good*,[5] Ross lists the fundamental, underived, prima facie duties, which McNaughton summarizes as follows:

1. Duties resting on a previous act of my own. These in turn divide into two main categories:
   (a) duties of *fidelity*; these result from my having made a promise or something like a promise.
   (b) duties of *reparation*; these stem from my having done something wrong so that I am now required to make amends.
2. Duties resting on previous acts of others; these are duties of *gratitude*, which I owe to those who have helped me.
3. Duties to prevent (or overturn) a distribution of benefits and burdens which is not in accordance with the merit of the persons concerned; these are duties of *justice*.
4. Duties which rest on the fact that there are other people in the world whose condition we could make better; these are duties of *beneficence*.
5. Duties which rest on the fact that I could better myself; these are duties of *self-improvement*.

---

[4] 'Intuitionism', 282; 301 (in 2nd edn).
[5] p. 21.

6. Duties of not injuring others; these are duties of non-maleficence.[6]

Basic and derived duties

By calling these duties basic, Ross meant, for instance, that by intuition you can see that justice is a basic duty. This insight requires no further justification, and no reasons can be, or need be given for it. If, by contrast, I ask why it is my duty to obey the laws of my country, I can be given several reasons for doing so. But if I ask why justice is always the right thing to do, no answer can be given, other than: justice is right, because it's right, because it's right. It is self-evidently right.

In addition to these basic duties, Ross held that there are certain other duties that are derived from them. The derived duties are not general enough in their scope to be regarded as fundamental principles; they are merely specific instances of one, or more, of the basic principles.

> The derived duties are not general enough in their scope to be regarded as fundamental principles; they are merely specific instances of one, or more, of the basic principles.

For instance, Ross held that the duty to obey the laws of one's country arises from three distinct basic duties: gratitude, fidelity and beneficence (Nos. 2, 1a, and 4). Normally, we owe a debt of gratitude to our country for the benefits and protection we have received from it (No. 2). By living in the country we have, as Socrates considered, made an implicit promise to obey its laws (No. 1a); and we have a duty to keep its laws, because law keeping makes things go better for one's fellow citizens as a whole (No. 4). Similarly, the duty not to lie is derivable from two basic principles: non-maleficence (No. 6) and fidelity (No. 1a).

What is meant by calling the basic duties 'prima facie'

The reason Ross called the basic duties 'prima facie' was not because he regarded them as being tentative in any way, such that fidelity, for

---

[6] 'Intuitionism', 275.

instance, which seems to be a basic duty, might turn out in the end not to be a duty at all. It was because he could not think of a better word to describe them.

He regarded all the basic 'duties' rather as sound and, in themselves, invariable principles that must always be taken into consideration when arriving at a moral decision. On the other hand, in a given situation two of the basic principles might point in different directions, so that it would be impossible for a person to obey both. In that case, then, the person concerned could not be said to have a duty to obey both (simultaneously, at least) and would then have to choose under which of the two basic principles he or she must act.

Take the duty not to lie as an example. As we have just seen, Ross regarded this as a derivative duty drawn from the two basic principles of fidelity and non-maleficence. Suppose a doctor is treating a patient with serious, and possibly terminal, cancer, and the patient says: 'Tell me, doctor, have I got cancer?' What shall the doctor say? By undertaking to treat the patient the doctor has given an implicit promise not to deceive the patient in any way. Basic principle No. 1a, fidelity, would demand that he not betray her trust by deceiving her. But if he respects this duty and tells her the truth, he will destroy the very hope and courage she needs to continue to fight the disease, and therefore any hope of her recovery. But that would be seriously to injure her, and basic principle No. 6, the duty of non-maleficence, forbids it. He cannot, then, be said to have a duty to do the impossible and obey both. He may well decide to obey No. 6, and tell the patient less than the truth.

> When two basic 'duties' conflict, a person must decide which of them on this occasion must be given the greater weight.

Ross would have approved; but that does not mean that he thought that the basic principle of fidelity only appeared to be a basic duty and was now shown not to be. It remained a genuinely basic duty that must be taken into account in all moral decisions. Only, when two basic 'duties' conflict, a person must decide which of them on this occasion must be given the greater weight.

AN EVALUATION OF INTUITIONISM: ITS STRENGTHS AND WEAKNESSES

Among the loudest critics of intuitionism are utilitarianism and consequentialism, but compared with them intuitionism has some noticeably superior features.

Strengths of intuitionism

Its rejection of the doctrine that the end justifies the means

Along with this feature we should include its insistence that to be regarded as morally right an act must itself conform to certain moral principles, quite apart from any good results it achieves.

Its concern for duties arising from the past

Act utilitarianism and act consequentialism are concerned solely with achieving the maximum happiness in the present and future. An act is morally right if it achieves the maximum pleasure for the maximum number, never mind if it involves disowning obligations arising from the past. Intuitionism, by contrast, insists on duties of *fidelity* arising from promises I have made, or debts I have taken on, in the past; duties of *reparation*, that is, making amends for wrongs I have done in the past; duties of *gratitude* owed to people that have helped me in the past; and duties of *justice* to overturn injustices that have been done in the past.

Its concern for personal duty towards loved ones

Under the basic duty of gratitude to those who have helped us in the past, intuitionism would hold that our sense of special duty to parents and loved ones is not only permissible but morally required. In this again it differs from utilitarianism (recall here the case of the hospital fire).

Its concern that justice must be according to merit

In the context of the law, justice according to merit would absolutely forbid the execution of an innocent man, or indeed any injury at all being done to a person who did not deserve it, for the sake of some greater good of society at large. Utilitarianism and consequentialism, we remember, have a great weakness here. Since the only absolute they recognise is the maximum pleasure or good of the maximum number, they have no absolute prohibition against injuring, torturing, or even executing an innocent person, if it is regarded as necessary for the good of society at large. Protesting against this feature of consequentialism Anthony Kenny writes:

> Consequentialists, like Bentham, judge actions by their consequences, and there is no class of actions which is ruled out in advance. A believer in natural law, told that some Herod or Nero has killed five thousand citizens guilty of no crime, can say straightway 'that was a wicked act'. The consequentialist, before making such a judgment, must say 'tell me more'. What were the consequences of the massacre? What would have happened if the ruler had allowed the five thousand to live?
>
> The consequentialism which can trace its origin to Bentham is nowadays widespread among professional philosophers. Thoroughgoing consequentialism is probably more popular in theory than in practice: outside philosophy seminars most people probably believe that some actions are so outrageous that they should be morally ruled out in advance, and reject the idea that one should literally stop at nothing in the pursuit of desirable consequences. But in present-day discussions of, for instance, topics in medical ethics, it is consequentialists who have the greater say in the formation of policy, at least in English-speaking countries. This is because they talk in cost-benefit terms which technologists and policy-makers instinctively understand. And among the general non-professional public, many people share Bentham's suspicion of the idea that some classes of action are absolutely prohibited.[7]

Compared, then, with utilitarianism and consequentialism, intuitionism, with its insistence that justice be according to merit, is markedly superior. But, as Anthony Kenny goes on to point out, to claim

---

[7] *An Illustrated Brief History of Western Philosophy*, 312.

that something is absolutely forbidden, raises the question: since you cannot have an absolute prohibition without a prohibiter, who, then, is the prohibiter that lays down these absolute prohibitions? Kenny has his own answer, and we shall later see what that is. But for the moment we must turn to see how and whether intuitionism can answer this question satisfactorily.

Weaknesses of intuitionism

Ross's attempt to systematise the basic, and the derivative, duties

Ross himself was not satisfied with his list of basic duties. He regarded it as a first attempt, which could later be improved on. Not even all intuitionists agree with all the items in the list. Some, for instance, suggest that truth-telling is not a *derivative* duty arising from the basic duty to keep an implicit promise. It is the other way round. Truth-telling is a *basic* duty, and from it arises the derivative duty of keeping promises.

Others hold that some of the items that Ross lists as separate basic duties, such as justice, beneficence and non-maleficence (Nos. 3, 4 and 6) could easily be combined into one duty of seeking the pleasure and happiness of people, in the same way as utilitarians do.

Ross's double claim that the basic duties are self-evident and are perceived by intuition

When even intuitionists disagree among themselves about what the basic duties are, it is understandable that their critics should argue that these duties cannot be self-evident. Christians would suggest that the intuitionists would do better to say along with the New Testament that we know certain basic moral principles because they have been written into our very nature by our creator (Rom 2:14–15).

No supreme goal or overarching principle to be the final guide in practical, moral decisions

Christianity's supreme goal is the glory of God, and its overarching principle is to love God with heart, mind, soul and strength, and one's neighbour as oneself. Utilitarianism's supreme goal is pleasure, and its overarching principle is to maximise the pleasure of the maximum number.

Intuitionism, by contrast, seems to have no supreme goal—other than, perhaps, good behaviour and the general good of mankind; and it has no overarching principle to guide in a moral dilemma.

No base, and therefore no ultimate authority

Christian ethics are based in the character and will of God; utilitarian ethics in Nature and man's psychological make-up. But intuitionist ethics seem not to be based in anything. True, it claims that the basic duties are perceived by intuition. But to the question, what put them there for intuition to perceive, it appears to have no answer. It, therefore, has no adequate answer to the even deeper question: granted that these basic duties can be perceived by intuition, why should anyone take them seriously? What authority do they have? Is there no super basic principle or duty that commands us to fulfil all the lesser basic principles? Why, then, should anyone care?

This is the same problem that arose with contractarianism. McNaughton considers that he has an adequate answer. He writes:

> I turn now to the fourth objection raised against intuitionism . . . It claims that we can know certain moral facts, but . . . Why might not someone simply notice these moral facts and carry on regardless?
>
> This hoary old objection to intuitionism is a complete non-starter. Facts can, in appropriate contexts, supply us with reasons, either to believe something or reasons to do something. That a large lorry is hurtling towards you is a reason to move out of its path. That she is honest and reliable is a reason to believe what she says. We can, of course, recognise that some fact obtains without recognising that it gives us a reason to act. . . . But we often realise not only that a fact obtains, but that its obtaining gives us a reason to do something. . . . The intuitionist claims that we are able to recognise that certain kinds of fact, such as that I have made a promise, or that this person needs help, provide us with reason to act.[8]

---

[8] 'Intuitionism', 283.

But this argument fails to distinguish between a *reason* to do something and a *duty* to do that thing.[9] If I want to buy a packet of sweets, the fact that the sweet shop will close in ten minutes gives me a reason for hurrying to get there. But the fact does not impose on me a moral duty to hurry. And after all, Ross claims that what we perceive by intuition is not a number of *facts*, but a number of basic prima facie *duties*. He claims that they are not logically deduced from other considerations. In that sense they are underived. But they must be based in something if they are going to have the authority to impose duties on us. Thin air never imposed a duty on anyone.

Kenny's comments on the idea that some classes of action are absolutely prohibited, are to the point:

> Where, people ask, do these absolute prohibitions come from? No doubt religious believers see them as coming from God; but how can they convince unbelievers of this? Can there be a prohibition without a prohibiter?[10]

Quite so. Many sincere ethical thinkers do not believe in God; but they still have to find an answer to the question: who or what has the authority to lay down these prohibitions that we have an absolute duty to observe? Kenny's answer is:

> The answer is to be found in the nature of morality itself. There are three elements which are essential to morality: a moral community, a set of moral values, and a moral code. . . . the moral life of the community consists in the shared pursuit of non-material values such as fairness, truth, comradeship, freedom.[11]

Quite so, again. But where does the community get this set of moral values from, which its members then share? Does the community invent them out of its own collective head? Kenny again:

> The answer to the question, 'Who does the prohibiting?' is that it is the members of the moral community: membership of a common moral society involves subscription to a common code.[12]

---

[9] See the same weakness in Rachels's argument for ethical naturalism in Ch. 2.
[10] *An Illustrated Brief History of Western Philosophy*, 312.
[11] *An Illustrated Brief History of Western Philosophy*, 312.
[12] *An Illustrated Brief History of Western Philosophy*, 312.

But this is exactly what we found Geoffrey Sayre-McCord arguing on behalf of modern contractarianism (Ch. 2), and we heard him there confess the inadequacy of the answer. And we may add that if it is the community that first originates the moral code to which all its members then subscribe, and if it is the community that does the commanding and the prohibiting, what happens if the community in question is Hitler's Germany?

It is the fact that many serious thinkers find it difficult to accept God as the authority behind morality; but it is also the fact that they find it difficult to find an adequate substitute Commander and Prohibiter.

CHAPTER 7

KANTIAN ETHICS

So act that you treat humanity, both in your own person and in the person of every other human being, never merely as a means, but always at the same time as an end.

—Kant, *Groundwork*

THE BASIC PRINCIPLES OF KANTIAN ETHICS

In a previous book in this series we have studied in some detail Immanuel Kant's epistemology;[1] here we must consider his ethical theory. Along with utilitarianism, it has proved over the last two centuries to be one of the most influential of ethical theories. Some of its principles have become part and parcel of the thinking of many people who would not necessarily regard themselves as thoroughgoing Kantians, or even be aware that they were following Kant's principles. The major source of Kant's ethics is his *Groundwork of the Metaphysics of Morals*, which was first published in 1785.[2]

Kant was the greatest of the philosophers of the Enlightenment. His approach to ethics was that of rationalism rather than empiricism. It was by reason that one worked out what was morally right and wrong. He felt, moreover, that reason was universal; and therefore everyone, if guided solely by reason, would come to the same view of morality as he himself.

The indispensability of good will

In contrast to utilitarianism, Kant's ethical system is severely deontological. Kant holds that the highest form of good is *good will*. He writes: 'It is impossible to conceive anything at all in the world, or even out of it, which can be taken as good without qualification, except a good will.'[3] And having a good will means to do one's duty, that is to do those morally good things that duty requires one to do, and to do them for no other reason or purpose than to fulfil one's duty.

To give a gift to a poor person out of compassion, for example, is not a morally good act; because giving out of compassion implies that

---

[1] See Ch. 2—'The Epistemology of Immanuel Kant' in Book 3: *Questioning Our Knowledge*.
[2] The German edition was originally published in 1785; here cited mostly from the English translation by H. J. Paton.
[3] *Groundwork*, 393; Eng. tr., 59.

if you did not feel compassion, you would not give the gift, whereas it was your duty to give the gift whether you felt compassion or not. You should have given it simply because it was your duty to do so.

To do some act simply because you desire its good consequences, is likewise not a morally good act. It is simply to act out of self-interest. You should do an act simply because it is your duty to do it, whether it has good consequences or not. (This, we note, is the very opposite of utilitarianism and consequentialism.) Kant himself uses the following example:

> it certainly accords with duty that a grocer should not overcharge his inexperienced customer; and where there is much competition a sensible shopkeeper refrains from so doing and keeps to a fixed and general price for everybody so that a child can buy from him just as well as anyone else. Thus people are served honestly; but this is not nearly enough to justify us in believing that the shopkeeper has acted in this way from duty or from principles of fair dealing, his interests required him to do so. We cannot assume him to have in addition an immediate inclination towards his customers, leading him, as it were out of love, to give no man preference over another in the matter of price. Thus the action was done neither from duty nor from immediate inclination, but solely from purposes of self-interest.[4]

Moreover, an evilly intentioned act that unexpectedly caused good results would not thereby be regarded as a morally good act. Whatever the good results, the perpetrator's will was not good but evil; and it is not the good results of an act that make it morally good. The act must be morally good in itself and done with the sole motive of doing one's duty.

The command which tells us to do our duty is a categorical imperative

To see what this means we must notice the difference between categorical imperatives and hypothetical imperatives. These latter take the form: 'if you want X, do Y'. 'If you want to be an Olympic gold medallist, train six

---

[4] *Groundwork*, 397, Eng. tr., 63.

hours every day without exception.' 'To lose weight, eat less.' This kind of imperative is called hypothetical, because it tells you what to do if you want to be or do something, e.g. to be an Olympic gold medallist, or to lose weight. But, of course, you may not want to be an Olympic gold medallist, or to lose weight, in which case you don't have to follow the advice. After all, it was only advice, and it was conditional upon your wanting. It was not telling you that it was your *duty* to train six hours a day, and to lose weight, whether you wanted to or not.

Similarly: 'If you want to be respected, always tell the truth' is a hypothetical imperative. It is very sound advice; but once more, it depends on a hypothesis, namely, that you want to be respected. A categorical imperative, by contrast, issues its command independently of any hypothesis. It tells you that it is your absolute duty to do something, whether you want to do it or not, whether you hope to achieve good results or not, whether you like it, or dislike it intensely. 'Always tell the truth.' 'Never murder anyone.' 'Pay your debts.' 'Keep your promises.'

According to Kant, then, the basic principle that underlies and motivates all right action is the Categorical Imperative. 'Always do your duty, and do it with good will, that is, with the intention of doing it solely because it is your duty.'

This, however, raises the question: in the thousand and one situations in life, how shall I know what my duty is? By what general criterion, or criteria, shall I decide it? In other words, what we need here is not a list of specific commandments for various action-spheres, but a general principle to guide our basic thinking. In answer to this question Kant's Categorical Imperative resolves itself into three formulations.

THE THREE FORMULATIONS OF THE CATEGORICAL IMPERATIVE

The first formulation

The Categorical Imperative says:

> There is . . . only one categorical imperative. It is: Act only according to that maxim by which you can at the same time will that it should become a universal law.[5]

---

[5] *Groundwork*, 421, Eng. tr., 80–7.

In other words, you are to act as if you were legislating for everybody else. Kant gives several examples to illustrate what he means. Here is one:

> Suppose I run out of money, I may decide to borrow money, promising to repay it, even though I know that I will be unable ever to repay it. Then I shall be acting on the maxim 'Whenever I believe myself short of money, I will borrow money and promise to pay it back, though I know that this will never be done. I cannot will that everyone should act on this maxim, because if everyone did so, the whole institution of promising would collapse.'[6]

Here the Categorical Imperative rules out (1) *partiality*: I must not act as if there were one law for me, and another law for everybody else. (2) *logical inconsistency*: if everybody acted like me and broke promises, no one would lend money again, not to me nor to anyone else, for no one would ever believe any promises any more. In other words my action could not be universalised, because universalising it would involve logical and practical contradictions, which Kant calls *contradictions in the law of nature*.

But Kant gives another example, and this time it involves a slightly different principle:

> [A man] is himself flourishing, but he sees others who have to struggle with great hardships (and whom he could easily help); and he thinks 'What does it matter to me? Let everyone be as happy as Heaven wills or as he can make himself; I won't deprive him of anything; I won't envy him; only I have no wish to contribute anything to his well-being or to his support in distress!' Now admittedly if such an attitude were a universal law of nature, mankind could get on perfectly well—better no doubt than if everybody prates about sympathy and good will, and even takes pains, on occasion, to practise them, but on the other hand cheats where he can, traffics in human rights, or violates them in other ways. But although it is possible that a universal law of nature could subsist in harmony with this

---

[6] cf. *Groundwork*, 421, Eng. tr., 80-6.

maxim, yet it is impossible to will that such a principle should hold everywhere as a law of nature. For a will that decided in this way would be in conflict with itself, since many a situation might arise in which the man needed love and sympathy from others, and in which, by such a law of nature sprung from his own will, he would rob himself of all hope of the help he wants for himself.[7]

In this case, unlike the first, the maxim 'Don't help others in their need' could be universalised without any logical or practical contradiction in nature. Society would still survive. But, Kant's point here is: the man himself, who acted on this maxim, could not will it to be universalised. If he did, the maxim, once universalised, would cut off from him the very help that he himself might one day need. Kant calls this, not a contradiction in nature, but *a contradiction in the will*.

Points to ponder

Kant's Categorical Imperative, as applied in the first example, is without doubt an excellent maxim, since it rules out the ugly partiality that says 'One law for the rich, another for the poor', or which lays down the law for other people, but behind the scenes itself breaks the law.

Similarly, the Categorical Imperative, as exemplified in the second example, sets an excellent moral standard. At first sight, it might seem to be saying almost the same thing as the so-called Golden Rule: 'Whatever you wish that others would do to you, do also to them, for this is the Law and the Prophets' (Matt 7:12). It warns us against self-centredness that expects other people to help us, though we ourselves are not prepared to help others.

Some critics, however, have alleged that here Kant has unintentionally abandoned his principle of 'doing one's duty for duty's sake regardless of the consequences, and without seeking from it any benefit for oneself,' and has inadvertently fallen into utilitarianism: 'always help others in need, for if you don't, the consequences of your inaction will be painful for you; nobody will help you, when you are in need.'

---

[7] *Groundwork*, 423, Eng. tr., 86.

But, strictly speaking, this criticism is not fair. Kant is not saying 'You should act out of self-interest and always help others, so that in turn others will help you.' Nor is he issuing a hypothetical imperative: 'If you want others to help you, first help them.' He is illustrating the first formulation of his Categorical Imperative: 'If you will to do, or not to do, something, you should, by implication, simultaneously will that everyone else in the world should will to do, or not to do, that same something. If you, then, refuse to help those in need, you are willing, by implication, that no one in the whole wide world should ever help anyone in need, not even yourself.' Kant, then, is not telling us to help others *so that* they will in turn help us. He is saying that if, on principle, you refuse to help others, your own principle universalised would positively forbid everyone else in the world ever to help you or anyone else—and that is absurd.

The second formulation

The Categorical Imperative says:

> So act that you treat humanity, both in your own person and in the person of every other human being, never merely as a means, but always at the same time as an end.[8]

The distinction between means and ends

The distinction between *means* and *ends* goes back, in philosophical thought, to Aristotle. He considered that every living thing in Nature had its 'end', in the sense that the end of an acorn, for instance, is to develop into an oak tree. Then he transferred the idea to human beings, in the sense of the end, or the supreme good, towards which they aim, or should aim, in life. And he further defined an 'end' in this sense, as something that is sought for its own sake and not as a means towards some greater end.

Now in practical life a person may have many minor ends, which then in turn become means to some greater ends. So a man goes to work as a means to earn money. But the money is not an end in itself. He needs it as a means to buy food for himself and his family, so that they can live. But he may also play the violin, not as a means to make

---

[8] Cf. Kant, *Groundwork*, 428, Eng. tr., 45.

money, not as a means to develop a career, but simply as an end in itself, for the sheer joy of making music.

What Kant intends by the terms means and ends

We must never, says the Categorical Imperative, use other human beings simply as means, as instruments, for the achieving of our own ends. Notice the phrase 'simply as means'. There is nothing wrong with using a human being as a means. We all do it, when, for instance, we use a hairdresser to cut our hair, or a taxi driver to drive us somewhere, or a baker to bake our bread. Similarly, the State uses teachers as a means to educate students, and doctors to cure people's illnesses.

But the point is, we must never use human beings *simply* as means. Aristotle, like many of his contemporaries, used some human beings as slaves. He called them 'living tools', and treated them simply as means to achieve his own ends. When we, by contrast, employ a builder as a means for building us a house, we recognise that he is more than just an instrument for achieving our purpose. He is a human being, with his own desires and purposes in life; and he must be free to choose and serve his own ends. So if we employ him to build a house for us, we come to an agreement with him; and he freely undertakes to serve us, because it serves his own immediate end of making money and earning a living, and perhaps also of achieving satisfaction in the use of his skills.

> So act that you treat humanity, both in your own person and in the person of every other human being, never merely as a means, but always at the same time as an end.
> —Kant, *Groundwork*

The second formulation of the Categorical Imperative, then, bids us always respect the independence, value, significance, integrity and dignity of every human being. No human being was put on this earth simply as a means for achieving other people's ends. Each human being is an end in himself or herself and requires no other reason for his or her existence other than that he or she exists.

To treat people as ends, therefore, means recognising that they exist as ends in themselves, and not only allowing them, as far as possible, to exercise their own choices and desires, and to achieve self-fulfilment, but also, as far as we can, helping them to achieve their own ends.

Points to ponder

Once again, the principle that Kant is enunciating here is immensely important. It carries implications in private life. We normally despise people who simply use other people for their own ends, and then drop them when they have got what they want. It has implications too for industry. All too often in the industrial revolution factory owners used their workers as though they were nothing more than cogs in a machine. And when the cogs wore out, or were no longer needed, they just dumped them. Even little children were forced to work, with total disregard for the true ends of a child, which is to develop in body and mind into a healthy and educated adult.

What we said above—'No human being was put on this earth simply as a means for achieving other people's purposes' is perfectly true. But the further statement: 'Each human being is an end in himself or herself, and requires no justification for his or her existence other than that he or she exists' is true in the sense that this is how society should regard each individual. But to be the whole truth according to the biblical view of human beings, that statement would have to be expanded. The chief end of man is, as we have noticed before, 'to glorify God and to enjoy him forever'. And, according to the New Testament, the end which God has in view for each human being, if he or she will accept it, is union with Christ, and final glorification, that is, conformity to the image of God's Son in body, soul and spirit, and that by God's grace and the working of God's Spirit. Our treatment of our fellow human beings should always have regard to this end; anything that impedes or opposes it is by definition evil.

The third formulation

The Categorical Imperative says:

> So act as if you were *through your maxim a law-making member of a kingdom of ends.*[9]

This third formulation puts the balance to the first and second. The first and second emphasise the effect my principles of action will have

---

[9] cf. *Groundwork*, 438, Eng. tr., 74.

on other people: I must act according to maxims that I could logically wish to become a universal law for all other people; and I must treat other people as ends in themselves. This third formulation reminds me that I am not the only member of the country to which I belong. I am not the only one who has the right and duty to follow behavioural maxims that should, I believe, be the universal law for everybody. Everyone else in the State has the right and duty to behave in this way; and I must respect their right. Obviously, if everyone behaved in this way, no one would take unfair advantage of others. But what happens when equally rational people disagree about the maxims that should be universalised? Perhaps the best political answer that has been found to date is genuine democracy, in which people are left free as far as possible to make their own decisions as to their own ends and yet, out of respect for other people's ends, are prepared to make the necessary compromises.

A CRITICAL ASSESSMENT OF KANTIAN ETHICS

We have so far examined the strong and valuable elements in Kantian ethics. Now we must consider criticisms that have been levelled against it. The chief criticism concerns its status, basis and ultimate authority.

An unanswered question

Kant was a rationalist, and for him morality was based in reason. It was the self-evident principles that human reason discovered that were the basis of his ethics. Naturally, empiricists disagree with him. D. D. Raphael comments on Kant's rule that we should treat other people as ends in themselves:

> How do we reach the principle of ends? Is it supposed to be self-evident? Kant himself was a rationalist. He maintained that the categorical imperative is known to be true by the exercise of reason. We do not have to follow him in that view. If, on general philosophical grounds, we think it is best to follow the path of empiricism, i.e. to explain ideas and beliefs in terms of the

experience of sense and feeling, then we can explain our fundamental ethical principle in this sort of way, just as an empiricist utilitarian does with his principle. The capacity for imaginative sympathy is what enables us to judge and act as moral beings. We can imagine ourselves in other people's shoes; we can imagine what we should want and how we should decide if we were in their situation. Sympathy is what leads us to act so as to serve other people's ends, to feel towards their ends as we naturally feel towards our own.[10]

Doubtless, what Raphael says about imaginative sympathy, its value and effect, is true; and many people will prefer his warm-hearted explanation to Kant's coldly rational one. Certainly, we should all learn to practise it. But there remains a question which imaginative sympathy cannot explain, as Raphael now admits:

> The empiricist approach to the principle of ends does not give a complete answer to the question, how do we know the truth of our fundamental principle. As with the empiricist form of utilitarianism, it does not show how we are to proceed from positive psychological explanation to normative judgment. The account tells us that sympathy produces a judgment and a motive of altruistic obligation to be set alongside the innate motive of self-interest. But it has not explained why the claims of sympathy should be regarded as superior to those of self-interest. . . . The empiricist version gives a positive psychological explanation of the feeling of obligation to others but fails to give us good reason for making a normative judgment about altruistic obligation in relation to natural self-interest.[11]

Just as we earlier found with atheism, naturalism, contractarianism, utilitarianism and intuitionism, so now we find with Kantian ethics, whether interpreted by rationalist or empiricist thinkers—none of them is able adequately to explain the rock-bottom basis of morality. In other words, given our psychological make-up, our empirical feelings of sympathy, our rational insights, what is it that imposes on us not just an inclination but an absolute duty to behave morally? As Hume

---

[10] *Moral Philosophy*, 59.
[11] *Moral Philosophy*, 59–60.

would put it, how do we turn the 'is' of the facts and feelings into the 'ought' of absolute duty?

Christians, of course, would maintain that our moral duty finds its basis and grounding in God our Creator, in his character and will; and that that will has been expressed not only in Nature, but in God's written self-revelation in Scripture and in the person of Christ. Here lies, Christians would admit, the gulf between an ethics based on faith in God and an ethics that rules out God in advance and tries to found itself and its ultimate authority on some secular basis. But it is at this point that Kantian ethics becomes seriously ambivalent.

Kant's ambivalent stance

Kant was a believer in God, and was so on moral grounds.[12] He observed that a life lived strictly according to the moral duties of the Categorical Imperative was often not vindicated in this present life; nor was an immoral life necessarily punished in this life as it deserved. He therefore argued that there must be another world and a final judgment at which God would suitably acknowledge and vindicate the righteous and punish the wicked.

In spite of that, however, Kant virtually denied all God's self-revelation in Scripture and indeed in Christ himself. Kant argued that the law-like processes that we observe in the workings of nature must have been put there by a divine ruler. But he explicitly denied that we have any direct commands from God beyond the moral rules that our reason deduces from the nature of things.

> We may not, therefore, . . . regard them [*scil.* the laws in nature] . . . as derived from the mere will of the Ruler, especially as we have no conception of such a will . . . we shall not look upon actions as obligatory because they are the commands of God . . . We shall study freedom according to the purposive unity that is determined in accordance with the principles of reason, and shall believe ourselves to be acting in conformity with the divine will in so far only as we hold sacred the moral law which reason teaches

---

[12] We have considered this at the beginning, and then again towards the end, of our study of Kant's epistemology in Ch. 2—'The Epistemology of Immanuel Kant' in Book 3: *Questioning Our Knowledge*.

us from the nature of the actions themselves; and we shall believe that we can serve that will only by furthering what is best in the world, alike in ourselves and in others. Moral theology is thus of immanent use only.[13]

Here speaks a typical Enlightenment thinker. He professes to believe in God, but demands that man's will shall be completely autonomous.[14] He does not merely mean that God has given man free will so that he can choose whether he will obey God or not. He means that man's reason must be the final arbiter as to what the commands shall be that he is willing to obey. He does not regard actions as obligatory because they are the commands of God; he studies the nature of things, and if his reason decides that something is morally obligatory, he concludes that it possesses a kind of divine obligatoriness; and so he obeys simply and only what his own reason decides. Man is the central arbitrator in the ethical world.

It was but a short logical road from this to the existentialism of Sartre, who rejected God completely and any external moral authority, and aimed to make himself an authentic self-made man by arbitrarily making his own moral decisions.

·

---

[13] *Critique of Pure Reason*, A818, B846—A819, B847, tr. Smith.
[14] See *Groundwork of the Metaphysics of Morals* (1795), section 3.

CHAPTER 8

VIRTUE ETHICS

Some virtue-ethicists appeal to Aristotle's view that it is the person who has developed the virtues who perceives what the 'mean' is at which he, or she, should aim, and what would be the right or wrong thing to do in any given situation. The right decision cannot be prescribed by rules: it depends on perception; and that can be acquired only by experience and by developing a virtuous character.

A DIFFERENT EMPHASIS

As soon as we begin to study virtue ethics, we immediately become aware that it carries a strikingly different emphasis from most of the ethical systems that we have studied so far. They were mainly concerned with the rightness or wrongness of our actions. Virtue ethics is concerned, not so much with the kind of actions we do, as with the kind of people we are, with our inner disposition and our character.

It should be at once obvious that the kind of person we are inwardly greatly affects the kind of actions we do outwardly, the way we behave towards others, our attitude to work, and our general demeanour. One student, for instance, may be intellectually brilliant but is lazy and weak-willed. He cannot discipline himself to persevere with the hard work of mastering his subject but too often gives way to the temptation of 'having a good time'. He relies on spur-of-the-moment extemporising to get him through his examinations; but thereafter can never hold down a responsible post because he cannot be relied on to fulfil his commitments. Another student may be technically less brilliant, but is determined, persevering, thorough and reliable. She succeeds where the other student fails.

Moreover, inner motives and intentions can change the moral significance of an act. Suppose at some public function people are asked to make contributions to a well-deserving charity. One person gives but inwardly begrudges it. He gives simply because he would look miserly if he refused. Another person gives lavishly because he wants to make everyone else look small by comparison. Another gives more than she can afford, strictly speaking, because she is moved by genuine compassion. All who receive the money genuinely benefit from it, whatever the motives were behind the giving. But how would you assess the moral worth of the three acts of giving?

The Bible comments:

> If I give away all I have, and if I deliver up my body to be burned,[1] but have not love, I gain nothing. Love is patient and kind; love does not envy or boast; it is not arrogant or rude. It does not insist on its own way; it is not irritable or resentful; it does not rejoice at wrongdoing, but rejoices with the truth. Love bears all things, believes all things, hopes all things, endures all things. (1 Cor 13:3–7)

Love is an inner virtue; so is patience and kindness. Envy, boasting, pride and self-seeking are vices. Now the New Testament does not approve of quietism that contents itself merely with the development of inner attitudes. It insists on the necessity of practical action and good works. 'Let us not love', it says, 'in word or talk but in deed and in truth' (1 John 3:18). But at the same time, it likewise insists on the development of the inner virtues of character: 'The fruit of the Spirit is love, joy, peace, patience, kindness, goodness, faithfulness, gentleness, self-control' (Gal 5:22). And these are all virtues. Right living, then, is not simply a matter of outwardly conforming to a set of rules, but of developing inner character.

In thinking about our inner states, however, we need to distinguish between motives and intentions that might drive particular actions on the one hand, and settled disposition and character on the other. Arthur E. Holmes expresses it this way:

> Motives, intentions and underlying dispositions. What these have in common, first, is that they are all inner states rather than overt behaviours and, second, that they are affective rather than purely cognitive states. A virtue is a right inner disposition, and a disposition is a tendency to act in certain ways. Disposition is more basic, lasting and pervasive than the particular motive or intention behind a certain action. It differs from a sudden impulse in being a settled habit of mind, an internalised and often reflective trait. Virtues are general character traits that provide inner sanctions on our particular motives, intentions and outward conduct.[2]

---

[1] The reference is probably to martyrdom.
[2] *Ethics*, 116.

After some centuries of almost exclusive concentration on the theoretical side of ethics, interest in Virtue Ethics as a valid academic discipline has been revived in the West by philosophers such as Elizabeth Anscombe, Philippa Foot, Rosalind Hursthouse, John McDowell, Alasdair MacIntyre, Martha Nussbaum, Amélie Rorty, Michael Stocker and Michael Slote. But in Europe this emphasis goes back to the ancient Greek philosophers, especially to Aristotle.

ARISTOTLE AND VIRTUE ETHICS

Aristotle's Ethics

The three parts of human make-up according to Aristotle

1. *The nutritive part* has to do with physical nourishment, food, drink, growth, etc. This part we share with the animals; it concerns physical, rather than moral, processes, and they are non-rational, and fall largely outside the range of moral responsibility.
2. *The passionate part* covers feelings of fear, hate, pride, love, compassion, envy, jealousy, desire, ambition, etc. This is the context in which the moral virtues have to be exercised and developed in order to control our behaviour.
3. *The intellectual part* is concerned with philosophical wisdom and understanding, and then with practical wisdom.

Accordingly, Aristotle distinguished two kinds of virtue: moral virtues whose province is the proper control of the passions, and intellectual virtues whose task is the proper use of philosophic wisdom and understanding and of practical wisdom.[3]

Aristotle's concept of virtue

To Aristotle virtues were neither passions like, say, anger or fear that suddenly rise up within us and, if we are not careful, overwhelm us. Nor were they faculties like, say, speech, smell or hearing that are inbuilt into the mechanisms of the body. Virtues are what he called 'states of character'.

---

[3] *Nicomachean Ethics*, I.13.19; 1103a ll. 3–10.

Again, the Greek word for virtue, *aretē*, originally meant the quality that makes something good at doing something. So the *aretē* of a knife would be its sharpness that makes it a good knife and good at actually cutting things. When applied to human beings, the *aretē* of a soldier was that trait of character that made him good at fighting; the *aretē* of a politician was what made him good at governing the nation. When used at a moral level, then, the *aretē* of a man was that state of character that made him a good man in himself, and good at living properly and well, so as to achieve as far as possible life's chief, supreme good.

Now for Aristotle the supreme good was what the Greeks called *eudaimonia*, a word that is difficult to translate. If it is rendered 'happiness', it must be carefully distinguished from mere pleasure, or amusement, and certainly from self-indulgence. One might perhaps describe it as 'getting and enjoying the best out of life'. This happiness, moreover, was not a passive experience of pleasurable feelings. It was, or at least involved, activity. Happiness was, so Aristotle said, an activity of the soul according to virtue. That, in turn, carried the implication that when it comes to moral virtues virtue consists in actively choosing the middle state, or course, between two extremes, as we shall now see.

Aristotle's doctrine of the mean

Aristotle's doctrine of the mean is famous. It has also often been misunderstood and misrepresented. We must take care, therefore, to try to understand it and not to press it beyond what Aristotle intended. So let's begin with actual, practical examples; and first, an analogy from food.

An analogy: food, not too much, nor too little

Food and feeding belong in Aristotle's scheme, we remember, to the nutritive or vegetative level of the human make-up. But feeding ourselves serves as a simple illustration of the need always to aim at the mean between excess on the one hand and deficiency on the other. Eat too much, and you injure your health. Eat too little and you do the same, like those who suffer from anorexia nervosa. Both extremes are bad. The thing to aim at is the happy mean: not too little, not too much.

Aristotle is at pains to point out that telling people to aim at the mean in eating does not prescribe the exact amount of food that should be taken. That amount will vary with each person: a weight-lifter will need a greater quantity than a petite young lady, a full-grown adult more than a child of five. But in every case the right amount will always be the mean between the two extremes of too much and too little.

Now come to the moral virtues that have to do with the control of our passions and desires; and let us begin with a practical example.

A practical example: courage
Courage is the moral virtue that has to do with the control of our reaction to fear. Now fear is inbuilt into every human being as it is into animals and birds. It is a very healthy mechanism, designed to protect us in face of danger and to start pumping the adrenalin into the body's system to empower us either to face the danger, whatever it is, or to flee.

Fear, however, is not an enjoyable emotion: it is more like a pain than a pleasure. It is, therefore, a test of character. In interpersonal relationships it can make us more aggressive, or more defensive, than we need be, and unready to admit our faults when we are in the wrong. Or it can make us run away from doing our duty, or fail to stand up for a just cause or for what we know to be the truth.

> The true reaction to fear, according to Aristotle, is courage. But what is courage?

The true reaction to fear, according to Aristotle, is courage. But what is courage? It is not an attempt to eliminate all fear or to ignore danger. A parachutist must never completely lose all fear of jumping: if he does, he will be in danger of carelessness, and hence of losing his life. A man who acts as if there were no dangers to be feared when there are real dangers all around is not truly courageous but foolishly rash. On the other hand, a person who fears danger excessively and deserts his duty is a coward.

A sampling of Aristotle's analysis of the virtues and questions arising
To do justice to Aristotle's analysis of the virtues, we should need to quote his long discussions of the many examples and their opposites that he cites; and we have not the space to do that here. Interested students should get a translation of his *Nicomachean Ethics* and read the appropriate passages for themselves. We cite a few examples here, however, to illustrate the width of his coverage of human behaviour.

Pleasure

We have just seen that in the context of our fears the relevant virtue is courage. Now we consider the relevant virtue in the context of our pleasures.

1. *The deficiency.* This is the rejection of pleasure of any kind, as though it were a bad thing. Some religious people have adopted this attitude, imagining that to enjoy pleasure is something intrinsically evil. And some misers, like Scrooge in Dickens's *A Christmas Carol*, regard enjoying pleasure as irresponsibility. This is false. God himself has given us many pleasures to enjoy. Take eating. God could have made the feeding of our body no more enjoyable than a car finds the process of being filled with petrol. But a good appetite, the anticipation of food, the actual satisfying of desire, is a God-given pleasure that is meant to be enjoyed. Some pleasures—like the sudden and unexpected smelling of the fragrance of a flower—are not aimed at filling up a consciously felt need. We do not normally feel the need to smell a fragrance before we actually smell one. God has gone out of his way to surprise us with unexpected pleasures. To deny it, or disregard it, or to regard it as bad, is false, and shows both insensibility and ingratitude.

2. *The excess.* This is intemperance: the immoderate indulgence of one's appetites and pleasures, pursuing pleasure for pleasure's sake, until in extreme cases like gluttony and drunkenness it destroys the very pleasures being sought, and leads to satiety and disgust, ill-health and premature death.

3. *The mean.* This is temperance, moderation and self-control.

The getting and giving of money
  1. *The deficiency*: miserliness, illiberality.
  2. *The excess*: prodigality, reckless, irresponsible wastefulness.
  3. *The mean*: responsible generosity, liberality.

Self-assessment
  1. *The deficiency*: ironical, insincere, self-deprecation.
  2. *The excess*: boastfulness.
  3. *The mean*: sincerity, realism, truthfulness.

Aim in life
1. *The deficiency*: no ambition, aimlessly drifting through life.
2. *The excess*: over-ambitious, ruthless, and totally regardless of fairness to other people, their interests and feelings.
3. *The mean*: right-ambition: setting realistic objectives that challenge one to develop one's potentials, but with due consideration of others.

Attitude to other people
1. *The deficiency*: surliness.
2. *The excess*: obsequiousness.
3. *The mean*: friendliness, civility.

Questions arising

1. If we ought always to aim at the mean between two extremes, *how do we decide what exactly the mean is?* Aristotle's answer is 'by perception'. That is, one cannot lay down exact rules. People and situations differ. One learns by experience. A person learning to drive a car will tend at first to pull the steering wheel too far in one direction, and then attempt to correct it by pulling it too far in the other. Experience will teach the driver to perceive how much turning of the steering wheel is necessary at any particular speed to keep the car on its desired course. One cannot lay down rules for it.

2. *How does one become virtuous?* It is not just by being taught, or by learning, the theory, but by actual practice. Some people have felt a difficulty here. If courage is a virtue, they argue, how can you act courageously unless you first possess the virtue of courage? If, then, to acquire the virtue you have first to practise behaving courageously, you appear to be in an impossible situation. But the impossibility is more apparent than real. It's like learning to ride a bicycle. You cannot ride a bicycle unless you learn to balance. But you cannot learn to balance unless you get on the bicycle and begin to ride it. Yet most people who try soon learn to ride, though at first they may fall off now and again.

So with courage. A child learns to face what to an adult is no danger at all, but to the child is very frightening. The child gradually overcomes his or her fears and so, becoming courageous, is able to face other, real dangers, grapple with fear and overcome it, and thus increase its courage so that courage becomes a settled trait of adulthood character.

The New Testament says similarly. We do not become virtuous by simply reading in the Bible that we ought to live virtuously. Virtue has to be practised, just as an athlete trains in order to run well. 'Train yourself to be godly,' says Paul; '. . . pursue righteousness, godliness, faith, love, endurance and gentleness' (1 Tim 4:7; 6:11 NIV). 'For this very reason,' adds Peter, 'make every effort to supplement your faith with virtue, and virtue with knowledge, and knowledge with self-control, and self-control with steadfastness, and steadfastness with godliness, and godliness with brotherly affection, and brotherly affection with love'; though Peter, as a Christian, and not just a philosopher, reminds his readers that God has first granted them all things that pertain to life and godliness, that is, all the resources with which to develop their virtues (2 Pet 1:5–7).

Unfair criticisms of Aristotle

The alleged inappropriateness of his system

Critics allege that to reduce the concept of the great and noble virtues like, say, courage and love to a nicely calculated mean between too much and too little is altogether inappropriate and petty-minded. Courage and love, they protest, should be practised with large-hearted abandon, not with the penny-pinching calculations of a grocer weighing out packets of tea.

This criticism is fair enough in itself, but it is based on a misunderstanding of Aristotle. He himself points out that in calling courage, for example, a mean, he is simply defining *what courage is*: it is a virtue which stands in contrast with, and in opposition to, two vices. These two vices lie each at an opposite extreme from courage, and each at an opposite extreme from the other vice. That, then, is what courage *is*. But when it comes to its *value* and *extent*, it is an extreme, and should so be practised. One cannot have too much genuine courage. Aristotle says of each virtue:

in respect of its substance and the definition which states its essence virtue is a mean, with regard to what is best and right an extreme.[4]

The alleged inadequacy of his system

Many have complained also that to force all vices and virtues into Aristotle's scheme of a mean with two extremes, one of excess and one of deficiency, is both unhelpful and impossible. Murder, for instance, is not an excess or a deficiency of some quality that if practised as a mean would be a virtue. But then Aristotle himself says the same thing:

> But not every action nor every passion admits of a mean; for some have names that already imply badness, e.g. spite, shamelessness, envy, and in the case of actions adultery, theft, murder; for all of these and suchlike things imply by their names that they are themselves bad, and not the excesses or deficiencies of them. It is not possible, then, ever to be right with regard to them; one must always be wrong. Nor does goodness or badness with regard to such things depend on committing adultery with the right woman, at the right time, and in the right way, but simply to do any of them is to go wrong ... however they are done, they are wrong.[5]

A significant contrast with utilitarianism

Here we notice a highly significant difference between utilitarianism and Aristotle's ethics. Utilitarianism, as we earlier saw, is not prepared to rule out in advance any action whatsoever. Given a special circumstance, it is prepared to say that the killing of an innocent man, for instance, would be justified, if it prevented the killing of a large number of other people, and so maximised the pleasure of the maximum number. Aristotle, by contrast, rules out in advance certain acts and attitudes as absolutely evil, and unjustifiable in any circumstance.

---

[4] *Nicomachean Ethics*, II.6.17; 1107a, ll. 6–8.
[5] *Nicomachean Ethics*, II.6.18; 1107a, ll. 8–24.

The intellectual virtues according to Aristotle

According to Aristotle there are two parts to man's intellectual powers. One is what the Greeks call *phronēsis*, that is, practical wisdom. This is brought into play when we deliberate about what choice to make, what course of action to take, what means to adopt to achieve a desired end. In other words, it is involved in making the right choice among variables. Aristotle called it the 'calculative power'.

The other intellectual power is what the Greeks called *sophia*, that is, philosophic wisdom. It is by *sophia* that we contemplate (the Greek word for 'contemplate' is the source of our modern word 'theorising'), and come to understand the originating, invariable, principles and causes that underlie all things. Aristotle called it the 'scientific part'.

How can intellectual powers be virtues?

In the first place we should recall that *aretē* (virtue) was, for the Greeks, the quality of being 'good for doing something'. Then we should observe that the proper function of both intellectual powers is, says Aristotle, to come at the truth:

> The work of both the intellectual parts, then, is truth. Therefore the states that are most strictly those in respect of which each of these parts will reach truth are the virtues of these two parts.[6]

How practical wisdom functions

When it comes to the moral virtues that ought to control our actions, it is practical wisdom that has to decide where the 'mean' lies, and therefore what we should aim at, in order to avoid the vices that lie on each side of the mean. Moreover, in any action we propose to take, we ought to consider why we are doing it, what end we have in view, and whether that end is good or bad; for according to Aristotle, the end we have in view becomes the reason, or the 'originating cause', for doing it.

It is the function, then, of practical wisdom to deliberate and decide about these aims, reasons, and ends; and that is why practical reason

---

[6] *Nicomachean Ethics*, VI.2.6, 1139b, ll. 13–15.

must itself be virtuous. If it isn't, practical reason itself will be corrupted, and connive at, permit, and excuse, evil behaviour.

> For the originating causes of the things that are done consist in the end at which they are aimed; but the man who has been ruined by pleasure or pain forthwith fails to see any such originating cause—to see that for the sake of this or because of this he ought to choose and do whatever he chooses and does; for vice is destructive of the originating causes of action.[7]

How scientific wisdom works

Scientific wisdom, Aristotle holds, is concerned with the study of basic unchanging principles and universal necessary truths—but with this reservation: scientific investigation and demonstration cannot establish first principles. Certain truths have first to be taken as given before science can begin its researches and demonstrations. According to Aristotle, we grasp these basic first principles, not by scientific proof, but by intuition.[8]

The Bible agrees with this. It claims that we can 'see' by direct 'contemplation', that what lies behind the visible processes of nature is the eternal power and Godhood of the Creator (Rom 1:20). Others, of course, state that they intuit no such things. It raises the question to what extent the functioning of our intuition is influenced by our prior dispositions.

An evaluation of Aristotle's ethics

We have no need to argue the value of Aristotle's ethical insights: they are self-evident. That said, some parts of his theory are obviously limited by the culture of his time and by his own temperament and inclinations. Particularly that is so with regard to what he considered to be the chief good in life, namely, *eudaimonia*, that is, happiness. *Eudaimonia* was, he maintained, an activity according to virtue; but it is not clear whether he thought that this happiness consisted in behaving virtuously, or was the goal and reward to which virtuous

---

[7] *Nicomachean Ethics*, VI.5.6; 1140b, ll. 16–19.
[8] *Nicomachean Ethics*, VI.6.1–2; 1140b, ll. 31–1141a, l. 8

behaviour led. He felt however that rational contemplation must be God's chief activity, and likewise the most god-like activity that man is capable of; and that, therefore, supreme human happiness must be intellectual activity. Man, though, mortal, must emulate the activity of God.

But then Aristotle was an academic, and a comparatively wealthy man, who had the leisure to engage in philosophical contemplation because he had slaves to look after all his daily needs. He certainly betrays the influence of his social background when he writes:

> And any chance person—even a slave—can enjoy the bodily pleasures no less than the best man; but no one assigns to a slave a share in happiness—unless he assigns to him also a share in human life. For happiness does not lie in such occupations, but, as we have said before, in virtuous activities.[9]

But this is a mistake to which the academic and philosophical disposition is particularly inclined, namely to suppose that reason is the highest thing in the universe, and—if there is a God—reason must be his chief occupation. The Bible asserts otherwise. God is love, it says; and the enjoyment of that love is open to all, and is, along with holiness, the chief motivator of all true ethical behaviour.

MODERN VIRTUE ETHICS

The modern revival of interest in virtue ethics was sparked off by an article by G. E. M. Anscombe entitled 'Modern Moral Philosophy'. In it she argued that since the utilitarianism that was so prevalent in the first half of the twentieth century had no way of relating the 'ought' to the 'good' (i.e. it could not explain why we have a *duty* to do what is good), it might as well have abandoned the concepts of moral obligation and moral duty. They were but relics of the ethical concepts of years gone by. She also felt that the excessive rationalisation of ethical theory since the Enlightenment had become unfruitful. It was time, therefore, to go back to the ancient tradition of Aristotle and concentrate once again on concern for the development of the inner virtues of the person.

---

[9] *Nicomachean Ethics*, x.6.8; 1177a, ll. 6–11.

Since Anscombe's article, interest in virtue ethics has mushroomed and has developed to the point where there are now several different versions of it. A very helpful survey of the main branches of modern virtue ethics, plus a carefully reasoned statement of his own interpretation, is given by the virtue-ethicist Michael Slote in his article 'Virtue Ethics'. We shall here use that article as our main source.

Virtue ethics' distinctive characteristic

We can grasp the distinctive characteristic of virtue ethics by contrasting it first with utilitarianism and then with Kantianism:

(1) Utilitarianism judges right or wrong according to the results produced by a given action.

(2) Kantianism judges right or wrong by whether the agent has conformed to certain moral rules or principles.

Virtue ethics, by contrast, talks about what is right or wrong in terms of personal inner factors such as character and motive. Fundamental to its discussion of ethics are not deontological concepts like 'ought', 'right', 'obligatory', 'duty-bound', but rather ideas of what is 'virtuous', (called, in technical language, *aretaic* ideas, from *aretē*, the Greek word for 'virtue') or 'admirable', or 'excellent'. Slote offers the following as a rough preliminary characterisation of virtue ethics:

> a view counts as a form of virtue ethics if and only if it treats aretaic terms as fundamental (and deontic notions as either derivative or dispensable) and it focuses mainly on inner character and/or motive rather than on rules for or consequences of actions.[10]

Within this general definition, however, virtue-ethicists disagree over a number of basic issues.

Should virtue ethics be theoretical or not?

Some virtue-ethicists appeal to Aristotle's view that it is the person who has developed the virtues who perceives what the 'mean' is at which he, or she, should aim, and what would be the right or

---
[10] 'Virtue Ethics', 325.

wrong thing to do in any given situation. The right decision cannot be prescribed by rules: it depends on perception; and that can be acquired only by experience and by developing a virtuous character. Virtue-ethicists of this persuasion, therefore, maintain that no attempt should be made to reduce virtue ethics to a formal theory, with fixed general principles and specific rules for various action-spheres. All decisions in any given situation should be left to the sensitivities—some have called it 'moral connoisseurship'—of the virtuous individual.

A question of deciding

This view raises an obvious question, which can be put like this: to perceive the right decision, one first has to be virtuous. To become virtuous, one has to acquire or develop the necessary virtues. How, then, does one know what those necessary virtues are, if one has no moral theory? Are they self-evident, like intuitionist theory claims? How would one decide between the virtues that Hitler approved of, and those that Marx recommended? Even Aristotle theorised a great deal about what the virtues are.

> To become virtuous, one has to acquire or develop the necessary virtues. How, then, does one know what those necessary virtues are, if one has no moral theory?

Michael Slote and many other virtue-ethicists hold that some attempt must be made to develop an overall general structure and theory for virtue ethics. As an example of attempts that are currently being made, he cites that of Rosalind Hursthouse ('Virtue theory and abortion') and then his own ongoing attempts.

To help ourselves grasp what they are saying, let us recall the four questions that we have suggested can be asked of any ethical theory:

1. What is its status, basis and authority?
2. What is its major goal, and what general principle(s) does it lay down for achieving that goal?
3. What specific rules does it prescribe to guide behaviour in various action-spheres?
4. What guidance does it give for deciding particular moral problems in day-to-day situations?

Hursthouse's version of virtue ethics

Its general principle: what determines whether an act is right or wrong

According to Slote, Hursthouse holds that whether acts are right or wrong depends on whether the virtuous individual would choose them; and in this she follows what she thinks Aristotle taught, namely that acts count as right *because a virtuous person would choose them*.

Even at first sight this is obviously different from utilitarianism, which teaches that whether an act is morally right or wrong depends solely on its consequences. It is also different from Kantianism, which holds that whether an act is morally right or wrong depends on whether or not it was done solely with the motive of obeying the moral law. Even so, what exactly does it mean to say that acts count as right *because* a virtuous person would choose them? To clarify the question in our minds let's use an analogy.

Suppose I know virtually nothing about art, but I am standing in an art gallery surrounded by twenty oil paintings of widely different worth. I am told I am to be given one of these paintings, whichever I choose. I naturally want to choose the most valuable. But which is that? Knowing nothing about art, I cannot tell. But presently there comes in a world famous art critic, and I ask him to choose which one is best, and I base my choice on his. If, when I get home with my painting, I am asked how I know it is valuable, I naturally reply: 'I know it is the most valuable of all the paintings in the gallery, because the art critic chose it out of all the rest.'

But what does my answer imply? Did the painting *become* a very good painting *because* the art critic chose it? Surely not. It was a very good painting *before* he even saw it and quite independently of his choice. It was simply that, being a very knowledgeable art critic, he at once recognised the excellence of the painting and chose it because it was intrinsically valuable.

Now let's apply the analogy. Supposing we are faced with an act that we and everyone else recognise to be an evil deed. We can rightly say: 'Whoever perpetrated that deed must have been an evil man.' Why? 'Because no virtuous person would have chosen to do an act like that.' We don't mean, of course, that the act *became* an evil act *because* virtuous people would never do it. It is the other way round: because the act was objectively—and always will be—an evil act, no virtuous person would ever choose to do it.

What, then, does it mean to claim that 'acts count as right *because a virtuous person would choose them*'? It surely cannot be true to say that an act *becomes* right simply because a virtuous person chooses to do it. Admittedly, a young and inexperienced person, uncertain whether a proposed course of action would be morally right or wrong, might understandably look to the example of a senior friend and say 'She does so-and-so, and obviously thinks it right, else she would never choose to do it. I will therefore follow her example.' But when it comes to defining right and wrong, it would be dangerous indeed to *define* right as 'what virtuous people choose to do'. Their choosing to do it doesn't make it right; and virtuous people can sometimes do very bad things.

And besides, if whether an act is right or wrong *depends on* whether or not a virtuous person would do it, then before one could evaluate an act, one would first have to evaluate the person who did it, and decide whether he, or she, was virtuous *at the time* when the act was done. And that, as Robert Louden argues,[11] could be difficult to ascertain. Outwardly virtuous acts can sometimes be done by people who inwardly are far from virtuous. Judas Iscariot preached and behaved like a true disciple of Christ for three years, and everyone, except Christ, regarded him so, before his act of betrayal exposed him to be what in reality he always had been.

The upshot of all this is that, far from replacing the objectivity of moral standards and absolute values, virtue-theory ultimately assumes and depends on them. Things and acts have to be objectively good and right before a virtuous person could rightly choose to do them; though, of course, a virtuous person will more readily perceive the goodness and rightness of something than an habitual criminal will, just like the expert art critic recognised the value of the painting when the non-expert didn't.

> When it comes to defining right and wrong, it would be dangerous indeed to *define* right as 'what virtuous people choose to do'. Their choosing to do it doesn't make it right; and virtuous people can sometimes do very bad things.

---

[11] 'On some vices of virtue ethics'.

The goal of virtue ethics according to Hursthouse

According to Slote, Hursthouse holds that: 'virtues are qualities of character that an agent needs in order to attain *eudaimonia*, overall wellbeing or a good life.'[12]

Now as we saw earlier, it is not beyond doubt whether Aristotle thought that *eudaimonia* consisted in living and acting according to virtue, or whether he thought of *eudaimonia* as the goal and reward of living and acting virtuously.

Let's illustrate the difference. One young man trains hard, practises and constantly plays football: his aim and goal is the sheer enjoyment of eventually being able to play football at the highest level. In this case the happiness he seeks is not something different from playing football: it is playing football at the highest level. Another young man similarly enjoys playing football, and aims to play at the highest level. But his ultimate aim is not just playing football. It is something in itself different from actually playing. It is the happiness of being awarded, as captain of the world champions, the trophy of the world cup and taking it in his own hands.

How then is *eudaimonia* related to the practice of virtue ethics? Is it the sheer joy of living virtuously? Or is it something beyond that, some further goal to be attained by living virtuously, but in addition to virtuous living? Slote understands Hursthouse to regard it as something beyond living virtuously and different from it. Living according to virtue ethics is thus ultimately only a means to attaining this supreme goal of *eudaimonia*.

If that is so, what exactly is this *eudaimonia*, and how is it to be defined? Whatever it is, it would mean—and this is what vexes Slote—that virtue ethics would no longer be self-standing and self-sufficient. Its supreme goal and purpose would be something else. In that sense, then, it would depend on that something else for its final purpose, significance and value.

Christian ethicists would have no difficulty with this concept. They hold that behaving virtuously, good and desirable though it is, is not self-sufficient. It has a supreme goal beyond itself and not definable simply in terms of ethics, that is to glorify God and to enjoy him forever. But ethicists who do not believe in God, still have to try to answer the

---

[12] 'Virtue Ethics', 327–8.

question: why be good? And for an answer they have either to invent some other supreme goal, like, say happiness (however defined), or to regard behaving virtuously as worthwhile, and enjoyable enough in itself, to be an end in itself, indeed to be the supreme goal of life.

Slote's version of virtue ethics

Slote's search is for one basic principle that would constitute virtue ethics a genuine unified theory that could stand comparison with unified ethical theories like utilitarianism and Kantianism, and show it to be superior.

Like all virtue-ethicists, Slote argues for an agent-based evaluation of right and wrong. That is to say, that whether an act is morally right or wrong depends not on an assessment of its consequences as in utilitarianism, but on an evaluation of the virtuousness of the agent. How then is the virtuousness of the agent to be assessed?

Slote's first suggestion

One could, by intuition, decide that morality boils down to one single basic motive: *universal benevolence*. In that case, you would not judge whether an action done by someone was morally right or wrong by assessing its results. Nor would you judge it by asking whether in doing it she obeyed the 'ought to' of some moral rule. You would judge it by how close her personal virtue came at the time to the *moral quality* of universal benevolence. No other justification of her act would be needed. Universal benevolence is not grounded in any more basic thing, principle, moral law (or person, presumably): it is itself basic. Even if her act, through some unforeseen happening, had disastrous results, she would not be blameworthy, so long as she was motivated by the virtue of universal benevolence.

Slote, however, eventually confesses his dissatisfaction with universal benevolence as the one basic principle. His reason is that it would have the same weakness as utilitarianism. According to Bentham, as we have seen, one must not only so act as to maximise the amount of pleasure for the maximum number of people, but in computing these maxima one must be impartial and neutral. One must neglect one's close relatives, mother, wife, children, etc. and let them perish in fact, if that were necessary for maximising the quantity of pleasure for the maximum number of people.

To most people that would seem inhuman. Yet if universal benevolence were the basic principle behind virtue ethics, it could run into a similarly inhuman difficulty. It would insist that one's benevolence should always be universal. It would not allow special concern for one's close relatives, as distinct from the rest of the people in one's city; or for one's own country, as distinct from all the other countries in the world. And since nowadays an ethical theory is considered unsatisfactory unless it can be applied not only to one's personal life and the immediate circle of one's friends and colleagues, but also to national and international needs, Slote searches for one, basic principle that will unify virtue-ethics theory, and yet combine love and concern for one's close relatives, with a genuine humanitarian concern for the rest of the world.

Slote's second suggestion: an agent-based ethic of caring

Slote himself points out that in recent decades Carol Gilligan (*In a Different Voice: Psychological Theory and Women's Development*) and Nel Noddings (*Caring: A Feminine Approach to Ethics and Moral Education*) have both advocated a morality, or ethic, of caring as being essentially feminine and thus as opposed to traditional (masculine) approaches to morality that stress rights, justice or quantified utility. Slote has, however, taken over this idea of caring as the basic principle of morality and applied it to his version of agent-based virtue ethics.

He starts with the instinctive love of a loving father for his children. He then supposes a father who has two grown-up sons in their twenties. One of them is healthy, vigorous and ambitious; the other has a learning disability. Slote further supposes that there is little that the father can, or needs to, do to help the healthy son, but a lot that he can and must do to help the son with a learning disability. Slote then asks us to consider how the father will apportion his love, help and time between his two sons.

Slote suggests that a loving parent will not decide according to the demands of some abstract principle of justice. He will be moved by his instinctive parental care for both sons. And though he may need to spend much more on the son with a learning disability, he will naturally want to spend as much love, time and help as possible on the other son as well.

Slote then applies this well recognised way that caring parents behave, to the broader level of the behaviour of the general populace. He points out that there is a big difference between our care for our close relatives, for people we know, and for our own country which we love, and our care for other countries and their millions of people whom we do not know. In the first case our care is for known individuals, for an individual person, an individual family, an individual nation with which we are personally involved. In the second case we care not for individuals we know, but for people en masse, none, or very few, of whom we know personally. Our caring in this instance is in the nature of general, humanitarian benevolence.

Slote's point in all this is that a genuine, basic ethic of caring explains, allows and validates our special, personal care for our nearest and dearest (in a way that utilitarianism does not), and at the same time it motivates us to give some proportion of our time, energy, and money to general humanitarian concern for people in need the whole world over.

Evaluating Slote's ethic of caring

One can have nothing but praise for the aim of an ethic that not only fosters the development of the virtue of practical caring but seeks to justify it intellectually by building it into a philosophical theory. Certainly its humanity is to be welcomed in contrast to the cold, heartless logic-chopping of much philosophical theorising.

Nevertheless, when we begin to ask about the basis of virtue ethics and about what grounds it has, and hence what authority it has, difficult questions arise both with its theory and with its practice.

First comes Slote's statement that (his version of) virtue ethics is agent-based. That is, to evaluate an action it considers not the results of the action, nor, apparently, the intrinsic moral quality of the action, but rather the motives of the agent. Take Slote's advocacy of universal benevolence (it will also apply equally to his preferred ethic of caring). He writes:

> agent-based *morality as universal benevolence* will regard universal or impartial benevolence as in itself the highest and best of motives and will evaluate actions solely in terms of *how close their motives are to universal benevolence.*[13]

---
[13] 'Virtue Ethics', 330.

We need not dispute the excellence of the motive of universal benevolence, still less the motive of caring. But we must ask about the *status* of these motives. Take caring, for instance. What exactly is it? Is it a thing which most people do naturally, but which a lot of other people ought to do, but don't?

Let's illustrate the point of the question by once more using our analogy with painting. Some people are born with a gift for painting; and then by constant practice and training they develop their gift, with the result that when people observe their attitude and technique they judge them to be admirable and excellent. They have what the Greeks called the *aretē* of a painter, in other words they are good at painting; and people assess their work in *aretaic* terms.

I, by contrast, have no gift for painting, and I very rarely try to paint. If I did try to paint, people would assess my *aretē* for painting as being very poor indeed. But—and here is the point of the analogy—no one would dream of telling me that I had *a duty* to paint, and that my habit of not painting, or of painting badly, was a dereliction of duty on my part.

Then what about caring? The vast majority of women, particularly mothers, naturally care for their family, and particularly for the children; and so do a lot of fathers. But if our ethical theorising is going to be realistic, we must face the fact that nowadays thousands of fathers refuse to get married. They are not prepared to obligate themselves to care for a wife and children. And even if they marry, thousands of them divorce their wives, abandon their children, refuse to maintain them, and go off and father other children by another woman, some of them by a succession of other women. Unfortunately, it is no longer possible to argue that these cases are exceptions to the normal rule. In some countries the number of divorces in any one year almost equals that of marriages.

Such fathers, then, can scarcely be said to care for their children or their wives. The point is: ought they? Have they any *duty* to care for them? Or should we say of them, what people would say of my painting: 'You are obviously no good at caring; but, then, of course, you have no *duty* to care.'

The question could be asked in many other situations. Has a bank any duty of caring for its bank managers, for instance? Or is it all right, if after years of loyal service they ruthlessly dismiss the man in middle life, and replace him with a younger man at half his salary?

But there is no point in multiplying examples; the main point is clear enough; have we a duty to care? Virtue ethics' answer seems clear: concepts of duty—deontic concepts, as they are called—do not really have a place in virtue ethics; certainly they are not fundamental. We may recall Slote's 'rough' characterisation that we encountered earlier:

> virtue ethics specifies what is moral in relation to such inner factors as character and motive, and unlike most modern views, it treats *aretaic* notions like 'admirable' and 'excellent'—rather than deontic concepts like 'ought', 'right', and 'obligatory'—as fundamental to the enterprise of ethics.
>
> A view counts as a form of virtue ethics if and only if it treats aretaic terms as fundamental (and deontic notions as either derivative or dispensable).[14]

To the Christian way of thinking this is a fatal weakness in this form of modern virtue ethics. At any rate it certainly renders it radically different from biblical ethics. Cain, we are told, said to God, 'Am I my brother's keeper?' If God in reply had propounded virtue ethics, he would have said: 'Well, Cain, if you were motivated by universal benevolence, or by an ethic of caring, your attitude would be aretaically admirable and excellent. If, therefore, you wish it to be so regarded, you should care for your brother. But I cannot say that you have a fundamental duty to be your brother's keeper, for that would be a deontic concept.'

What God actually said to Cain was something very different. And so is God's law. 'You shall love your neighbour as yourself' is unapologetically deontic.

---

[14] 'Virtue Ethics', 325.

CHAPTER 9

EGOISM

Ethical egoism is not merely a description of what most people ordinarily do. Being an ethical theory it is *normative*. Its basic principle states what people always *ought* to do: namely everyone ought to act *solely to serve his or her own interests, and not to consider the interests of other people.*

EXTREMISM IN ETHICAL THEORY AND PRACTICE

Two admirable qualities characterise Aristotle's ethical theory: one is his impressive power of observation and analysis, and the other is his practical realism. Nowhere is that realism more obvious than when he remarks how difficult it is in ethical practice to hit the mean; it is all too easy to veer off in the direction of one extreme or the other.

What is true of ethical practice is true also of ethical theory, as we have observed in our survey of the more famous systems. After the Enlightenment, for example, ethical theorising tended to concentrate heavily on defining the rightness or wrongness of people's acts and on people's responsibility to do their duty. Now in recent decades virtue ethics has swung to the opposite extreme. It lays its emphasis on the quality, not of people's acts, but of their inner virtues, almost to the exclusion of any deontic element. Better ethical thinking would surely favour neither one extreme nor the other but a balanced combination of both.

Act utilitarianism and Kantian ethics, we found, likewise stand at two extremes. In the formal statements of their positions, at least, utilitarianism is altogether teleological and uncompromisingly not deontic, while Kantianism is altogether deontic and uncompromisingly not teleological. Life and logic being what they are, however, rigid extremes are hard to maintain. In their detailed exposition of their doctrines, we found that a deontic element had crept surreptitiously into Bentham's theory, and a teleological element into Kant's.

From another point of view, act utilitarianism and Kantianism stand together at one and the same extreme. Both eventually deny the legitimacy of any self-interest. Utilitarianism says that in estimating the maximum amount of pleasure for the maximum number of people, the individual agent must be absolutely impartial and neutral. He must show no special interest for his nearest and dearest loved ones. Mother, father, siblings, wife and children must be sacrificed, if need be, for the sake of maximising the pleasure of the greatest number.

Kantianism, for its part, likewise outlaws self-interest. The only morally right act, says Kant, is one that is done solely out of the motive of doing one's duty. A good and kind act, motivated by compassion rather than duty, is morally invalid. A grocer, he argued, might treat his customers justly and fairly; but because he did so out of self-interest (if he treated them unjustly, he would lose all his customers and his business) his just and fair behaviour was morally valueless. The proverb 'honesty is the best policy' must have seemed to Kant morally corrupt. Kant could not conceive of the possibility that the grocer could rightly act both out of justice and out of self-interest at one and the same time.

From this extreme, we must now go on to consider an ethical theory that lies at the very opposite extreme. It is called ethical egoism, and it holds that the only ethically valid act is one that is done solely out of self-interest.

It is understandable, therefore, if in the minds of many people, 'ethical egoism' suggests that 'egoism' and 'acting out of self-interest' are one and the same thing. The result is that both are regarded with the same disapproval. Kurt Baier describes egoists as

> self-centred, inconsiderate, unfeeling, unprincipled, ruthless, self-aggrandizers, pursuers of the good things in life whatever the cost to others, people who think only about themselves or, if about others, then merely as means to their own ends.[1]

This is strong language; and if 'acting in self-interest' were always and necessarily the same thing as 'egoism', then 'acting in self-interest' would deserve the same condemnation.

But strictly speaking 'acting in self-interest', as we shall presently see, is not always and necessarily the same thing as 'egoism'. 'Selfishness' might correctly be identified with 'egoism'; but 'self-interest' is not the same as 'selfishness'. Imprecise language that treats 'self-interest' and 'selfishness' as if they both meant the same, can only lead to confusion of thought, and to unfair and extreme interpretations of ethical systems.

An instructive example of this are two extreme, but opposite, interpretations that from time to time are given of Christian ethics.

---

[1] 'Egoism', 197.

At one extreme some Christian theologians, influenced perhaps more than they should be by Kant's concept of 'acting solely out of a sense of duty', tend to give the impression that to serve God out of self-interest is morally wrong. According to them, the Bible teaches that the only acceptable attitude and motivation is to deny oneself, take up one's cross and serve God with utter and complete disinterest.

At the other extreme are philosophers who are critical of Christian ethics. They too regard self-interest (in this context at least) as something morally bad. They, however, point to certain passages in the Bible that explicitly exhort Christians to serve God in hope of the reward they will receive for their service. In light of this, these philosophers conclude that this Christian doctrine is morally deficient.

> Imprecise language that treats 'self-interest' and 'selfishness' as if they both meant the same, can only lead to confusion of thought, and to unfair and extreme interpretations of ethical systems.

If, then, we are to evaluate fairly ethical systems that appeal to the motive of self-interest, we must make the effort to think through the part that self-interest plays in these systems, and especially what they mean by self-interest.

THE DIFFERENCE BETWEEN SELF-INTEREST AND SELFISHNESS

The basic difference

James Rachels alerts us to the fact that acts that are plainly done out of self-interest are not necessarily selfish.[2] We may illustrate it in this way. It is certainly in a man's self-interest to consult a doctor when he is sick; but it is not selfish. It harms no one else, nor deprives any other person of benefit. On the other hand, if the amount of food available to a family on a certain day were limited, it would be selfish of any one member to devour it all, or to demand more than his fair share regardless of the others.

---

[2] *Elements of Moral Philosophy*, 72–4.

The moral acceptability of mixed motives

Kant's theory was, we remember, that the only act that is morally acceptable is one that is done strictly out of a sense of duty. Done from any other motive an act is morally invalid. Giving to the poor, because one is moved by compassion, rather than by a sense of duty, is morally unsatisfactory. But consider the following example.

At the time of year when people bottle fruit, Sarah bottles far more fruit than she needs for her family. Her motives are:

1. *Duty*. She has a husband and four children and it is, she feels, her duty to feed her family throughout the following year.
2. *Self-interest*. Most of the bottles not needed for the family she intends to sell at the local market, and with the profit she gets, she will buy herself a new dress which she has seen in a shop and greatly admires.
3. *Compassion*. The remaining bottles she intends to give to a recently widowed young woman who has almost no income and three ill children.

Her motives, then, in bottling such a very large quantity of fruit are mixed. Had she been content to bottle only enough fruit for her family, but had done so out of no other motive than 'doing it because it was her duty', Kant would have regarded her act as morally good.

But she bottled some out of compassion! Truth to tell, she was not driven to it out of a sense of duty. It was simply that she felt sorry for the widow and acted out of sympathy. What is more she enjoyed doing it and gained much satisfaction from seeing the gratitude on the faces of the widow and her children. Must we agree with Kant that this part of her bottling enterprise was morally substandard because she did not do it strictly and solely out of a sense of duty?

Undeniably, however, she bottled some of the fruit in order to get herself a nice, though not extravagantly priced, dress; and to that extent she acted out of self-interest. We can say at once that this was not selfishness: she deprived no one of anything that they had a right to. Moreover, the fact that she paid for it herself helped her family, because the money did not come out of the general family budget. Admittedly, she did not act out of a sense of duty, that is, she did not feel that she had a duty to buy this particular dress. She acted out of self-interest and bought the dress because she liked it. On the other hand, even Kant might allow that people have a duty to dress themselves and not go about the streets naked. In this case, then, self-interest served the purpose of an underlying duty.

Examples such as these show that Kant's principle, that only those acts deliberately and consciously done solely out of a sense of duty are morally acceptable, is extreme and simplistic. It fails to take account of the complexities of human behaviour.

To grasp more clearly what ethical egoism means by self-interest, it will be helpful first to examine what Christian ethics means by it. The two systems do not mean exactly the same thing; the difference will be revealing.

Christian ethics and the rightness of self-interest

By definition it must be in a creature's self-interest to serve the will and purpose of his/her Creator

If all that we are—body, soul, spirit, abilities and powers—and the very air we breathe were created by God by his loving act and will, how could it possibly be not in our self-interest to serve his will and pleasure?

Granted, a believer does not serve God primarily, or even chiefly, for the joy and reward that he/she gets out of it. In our disordered world, often hostile to any idea of God, and hostile to Christ, it can cost a believer heavily to be faithful to God. But even so, it would be a slander on the character of God to suggest that living to serve God must necessarily be for the believer a joyless, unrewarding, experience. Christ said the very opposite: 'My food is to do the will of him who sent me and to accomplish his work' (John 4:34). He obviously gained personal satisfaction and sustenance from serving God. It would be presumptuous of us to make out that we were morally superior to him and did not need such satisfaction. Christ, moreover, as the Bread of Life, invites all to come to him on purpose to satisfy their pangs of spiritual hunger.

It is positively in a person's self-interest to seek reconciliation with God, salvation and eternal life

Christ himself said so. Appealing to the crowds, he urged them:

> Strive to enter through the narrow door. For many, I tell you, will seek to enter in and will not be able. When once the master of the house has risen and shut the door . . . there will be weeping and gnashing of teeth, when you see Abraham and Isaac and Jacob and all the prophets in the kingdom of God but you yourselves cast out. (Luke 13:24, 25, 28)

Many ethicists, however, maintain that this teaching is morally objectionable. If it were a question of working hard in order to get a degree, they would approve of it. Or if it were necessary to work overtime to earn extra money to pay for entrance to a famous concert—they would approve of that too. But they feel it is morally unacceptable to *be good* for what you get out of it, namely, as they think, heaven. They claim that it subverts the very basis of morality, which should be a completely disinterested intention of being good for good's sake, and not for what you get out of it.

The criticism, however, rests in the first place on a misconception. One cannot, in fact, earn entrance to God's heaven by 'being good'. Reconciliation with God, redemption, salvation and heaven: these all are free gifts:

> By grace you have been saved through faith. And this is not your own doing; it is the gift of God, not a result of works, so that no one may boast. (Eph 2:8–9)

Secondly, when God our Creator offers the human race a free gift, it would be absurd to pretend that it was not in men and women's self-interest eagerly to accept it, and likewise foolishly arrogant to ignore or reject it for lack of interest in it. Said Christ to a woman who was deeply dissatisfied with life and also with religion as she knew it: 'If you knew the [free] gift of God . . . you would have asked him, and he would have given you living water' (John 4:10). True self-interest at this level, therefore, is not only morally permissible: it is positively good and necessary.

The meaning of denying oneself
But if this is so, the question arises: why, then, does the Bible teach the necessity of self-denial? The answer is to be found in the context in which Christ taught this lesson to his disciples:

> From that time Jesus began to show his disciples that he must ... suffer many things from the elders and chief priests and scribes, and be killed, and on the third day be raised. ... Then Jesus told his disciples, 'If anyone would come after me, let him deny himself and take up his cross and follow me. For whoever would save his life will lose it, but whoever loses his life for my sake will find it. For what will it profit a man if he gains the whole world and forfeits his soul? Or what shall a man give in return for his soul? For the Son of Man is going to come with his angels in the glory of his Father, and then he will repay each person according to what he has done. (Matt 16:21, 24–27)

The context, then, was Christ's announcement of his imminent official rejection by his nation's authorities, his crucifixion and resurrection, and then of his eventual second coming. He was forewarning his disciples that they could not necessarily expect any better treatment from the world than the world had given him. 'If they persecuted me, they will also persecute you' (John 15:20). This was no exaggeration: millions of Christians have been persecuted and executed because of their faith in Christ, and not just in the early centuries when the Romans threw them to the lions. Any would-be disciple of Christ must, therefore, face this possibility. He must be prepared to deny his natural desire to live, and be ready to lose his life in this world for the sake of loyalty to Christ; but in so doing, he will keep his life, in the sense that he will enjoy eternal life plus a reward in the kingdom of God when Christ comes again. But if anyone, under a false sense of self-interest, denies Christ in order to keep his life in this world, he will in fact lose it, for he will never enjoy eternal life with Christ in his coming kingdom.

But it is to be noticed that even in this solemn context, it is to self-interest that Christ appeals: 'What will it profit a man', he asks, 'if he gains the whole world [i.e. by denying Christ] and yet loses life in the world to come?'

Self-interest is necessary in daily life

It is no use disguising the fact that it is basically self-interest that drives us to our daily work. People are fortunate if their daily work is enjoyable and becomes a virtual hobby that they would engage in even if it were not necessary for making a living. But at the basic level it is an empty stomach and the need for clothes and shelter that drive us to work. The Bible's general rule for all able-bodied people is, that if someone will not work, neither shall he eat (2 Thess 3:10).

At the same time, of course, the Bible is not content that people should work *simply* out of self-interest. It exhorts converted thieves, for instance, 'Let the thief no longer steal, but rather let him labour, doing honest work with his own hands, *so that he may have something to share with anyone in need*' (Eph 4:28, emph. added). In our daily work, therefore, it is not a question of *either* being motivated by self-interest *or else* of being completely altruistic. It can rightly be, and often is, a mixture of both. What is altogether wrong is a life lived solely for oneself without regard, or in total disregard, of other people, of their needs and interests and of the pain and loss one's selfishness might cause them. There is, after all, an obvious difference between a miser who, after making a vast fortune, retires as a recluse within his castle and uses his money simply to surround himself with treasures of all kinds, and a man like Andrew Carnegie (1835–1919) who having built up a considerable fortune devoted his wealth to charitable purposes, supported many educational institutions, libraries, and the arts, and created the Carnegie Peace Fund to promote international peace.

Christian ethics and the wrongness of selfishness

Human beings are different from other animals in this, among other things, that compared with the young of other animals, human infants remain for a long while absolutely dependent on their parents and other human beings. Indeed, for the vast majority of us who live in complex civilisations it is doubtful that we are ever free from dependence, to a greater or lesser degree, on the services of a multitude of other people. A man, therefore, who lives solely for his own self-interest, in disregard of the interests and needs of others, is guilty of gross abuse of the basic conditions of human life and society. Moreover, he is grievously distorting his own function and purpose in life, and seriously crippling his potential.

The analogy of the human body

To bring this point home, both pagan and Christian thinkers in the ancient world used the analogy of the human body to illustrate the relation of the individual person in the one case to the body politic of the State, and in the other to the universal spiritual body of Christ.[3] We may summarise the lessons here:

Individuals need not be ashamed of their own self-interest and concern for their own wellbeing. If a foot, for instance, has suffered some injury, or is being mistreated in any way, it will immediately send a pain signal to the brain, demanding care and attention. It is in fact in the interest of the good health and proper functioning of the State, or of the church, or of a factory, or of a family as a whole, that the well-being of its individual members is looked after. After all, that is what a state, or a church, or a factory, or a family, *is*: a communion, or a team, an organic whole even, composed of individuals.

Individuals need not be ashamed of their own importance. They should certainly not undervalue their abilities (nor overvalue them either). A human body can exist without any hands or with no eyes; but in that case it is not a complete body and cannot function as efficiently as a complete body can. It is to the enrichment of the community, if each individual is helped to develop to the full his or her potential.

> Individuals need not be ashamed of their own importance. . . . On the other hand it would be arrogant for individuals to think that they are so important that they do not need the rest of the community.

On the other hand it would be arrogant for individuals to think that they are so important that they do not need the rest of the community; and it would be outrageous for them to act as if they existed simply for their own sake and had a right to pursue their own selfish interests no matter how it damaged others in society. If a man gives way to his body's craving for excessive alcohol or drugs no matter how it damages his liver, pancreas and brain, he will end up by destroying the whole of himself. If it were possible for our feet to revolt and to refuse to serve the rest of the body unselfishly by transporting it, they would deprive

---

[3] See Menenius Agrippa's political parable in Livy, *Ab urbe condita* II.32.8–12; and Paul's extended metaphor in 1 Cor 12:12–31.

themselves of their true and only significance. If they persisted in that refusal they would atrophy. Total selfishness is unnatural, impractical, unliveable and self-destroying.

The Christian concept of reward-motivated service

It is undeniable, nonetheless, that the New Testament does in places exhort people to live, serve and work motivated by a hope of personal reward hereafter in the coming kingdom of Christ.

> Whatever you do, work heartily, as for the Lord... knowing that from the Lord you will receive the inheritance as your reward. You are serving the Lord Christ. (Col 3:23–24)

Once more, secular ethicists are inclined to wince at this: serving Christ self-interestedly for personal reward later on seems to them morally a very poor motivation. If Christians loved Christ, as they profess to do, they would serve him unselfishly out of love with no thought of reward. And, of course, to a Marxist, the idea of a reward in heaven seems to be a deception perpetrated on the workers by the capitalists. Marxists, however, felt no difficulty themselves in motivating the proletariat to work and sacrifice for the reward later on of bringing in an eventual utopia! We need, therefore, to understand what is involved in the New Testament's concept of reward.

First, comes the relationship between Christ as master and his disciples as servants. On earth many employers do not justly and amply reward their workers. It is a serious moral fault in the employers. Christ being who he is, and his character what it is, it is morally impossible for him not to reward and recompense his servants for what they have done and sacrificed for his sake.

Second, there is the nature of the reward. At one stage, two of Christ's disciples requested that in return for their service and self-denying work, he would grant them as their reward to occupy the two greatest positions next to his in his coming kingdom. But they had false ideas of what such a reward would involve. Christ explained:

> You know that those who are considered rulers of the Gentiles lord it over them, and their great ones exercise authority over them. But it shall not be so among you. But whoever would be great among

you must be your servant, and whoever would be first among you must be the slave of all. (Mark 10:42–44)

The reward for serving Christ, and others for his sake, now, is that one is thus trained and qualified to serve vastly more people more perfectly later on. There is nothing strange in this principle. The reward for training hard and playing football well in the second division is the ability eventually to enjoy playing football at the international level. But in the coming kingdom of Christ the opportunity to serve others will be the greatest reward that even the most self-interested persons would desire, if only they knew the truth. Here lies the paradox of Christianity.

Thirdly, there is the Christian role model. The Christian idea of a coming kingdom of God, in which each shall count it his/her greatest joy to serve the other, is no fantasy. The role model for such behaviour has been demonstrated here on earth. 'The Son of Man', said Christ to his disciples, 'came not to be served but to serve, and to give his life a ransom for many' (Mark 10:45).

Accordingly his disciples are exhorted:

> Let each of you look not only to his own interests, but also to the interests of others. Have this mind among yourselves, which is yours in Christ Jesus, who, though he was in the form of God, did not count equality with God a thing to be grasped, but poured himself out, taking the form of a servant, being born in the likeness of men. And being found in human form, he humbled himself by becoming obedient to the point of death, even death on a cross. (Phil 2:4–8 own trans.)

ETHICAL EGOISM

The first thing to notice here is that ethical egoism is not merely a description of what most people ordinarily do. Being an ethical theory it is *normative*. Its basic principle states what people always *ought* to do: namely everyone ought to act *solely to serve his or her own interests, and not to consider the interests of other people.*

Of course, this principle allows an ethical egoist to help other people, for example, not to steal from them, not to break promises made to them, etc. *if* it serves the egoist's interests. He might, for example, consider it good tactics to help someone on some occasion because that would induce that someone to help him when he needed help. But the principle of ethical egoism says that he should not help anyone if it is not in his interest to do so; and it does not forbid him to do anything at all that it is in his interest to do.

Difficulties for the theory

There is no disputing that many people do in fact seem to follow this principle in their behaviour, even if they do not openly admit it. But as a theory ethical egoism runs into some obvious difficulties.

The question of its status

'Acting in one's own interests' is not, in this theory, one among many specific rules that could be applied in certain situations to solve a moral dilemma. It is the single fundamental principle in which the whole theory is grounded. There is no moral principle superior to it that could, and should, on times overrule it. It means, therefore, that if I judged it was in my interest to kill someone, then I ought to do it.

Suppose, for instance, I am in competition with another businessman to take over a very lucrative business. So much potential profit is at stake, that I might think that it was very much in my interest to eliminate my competitor by surreptitiously hiring a contract killer, like the Mafia do, to kill him. There is nothing in the theory of ethical egoism that would necessarily forbid me to do this, or to do a thousand and one lesser, but still malevolent, acts either.

Universalising the basic principle

There is also a difficulty when it comes to the logical and practical contradictions involved in universalising the basic principle of ethical egoism. Take, as an example, the situation between me and my competitor in the story above. I, being an ethical egoist, hold not only that I should always act in my own interests, but that everybody else should act in his or her interest too. That universal rule, therefore, would apply to my competitor as well. It would be in his interest to stop me eliminating him, and therefore morally right for him to do so. But if it is morally right for me to eliminate him, how could it be morally right for him to stop me doing what is morally right for me? Such an action must surely be morally wrong. Yet how could one and the same action—stopping me from eliminating my competitor—be both morally right and morally wrong at one and the same time?[4]

Advising someone to act on the basic principle

It is potentially immoral to advise someone to act on the basic principle of ethical egoism. It involves advising him or her to do an act because it is in his or her interest, regardless of whether the act is intrinsically good or evil.

A universal breakdown of trust

Universal practice of ethical egoism would lead to a universal breakdown of trust. Suppose I wish to get a mortgage for a house so that I can one day sell it and make a profit on the sale. Knowing little about mortgages, I could consult an independent mortgage adviser. Now the size of the commission he receives from a mortgage company for advising a client to use that company varies greatly from company to company. A company that gave him a large commission might in fact not be providing me the best terms for a mortgage; and a company that gave him a small commission might be the best company for me. As an ethical egoist myself I want to act solely in my own interest. Then I must hope that he is not an ethical egoist; for if he is, he will act, not in my interest, but in his, and therefore I could not trust his advice. He will simply advise me to use in the company that gives him the biggest commission, even though it is a bad company from which to get my mortgage. Therefore, though an ethical egoist myself, I must hope that he acts, not according to ethical egoism but according to ethical altruism, for that is the only condition on which I could trust him. Ethical egoism, then, as an ethical theory is inconsistent and contradictious; and its inconsistency springs from the principle on which it is based. If I want to be able to act solely in my own interests regardless of the interests of other people, I cannot logically wish that everyone else should act toward me on that same principle.

---

[4] For a fuller development of this argument, see Kurt Baier, *The Moral Point of View*, 189–90.

ENTREPRENEURIAL EGOISM

Entrepreneurial egoism is a form of economics theory that goes back to the famous work by Adam Smith, *An Enquiry into the Nature and Causes of the Wealth of Nations* (1776). Smith advocated egoism as applied to business. He maintained that entrepreneurs should be granted freedom, untrammelled by government control or restriction, to develop their businesses in their own interests and to maximise their profits for themselves and for their shareholders (if they had any). He argued that though their motive was to act in their own interests, the benefits of their activities would 'trickle down' to the community at large, through the wages they gave to their employees, through the prices they paid to their suppliers, and through the sums they paid to the builders that constructed their premises. Smith wrote:

> It is not from the benevolence of the butcher, the brewer, or the baker, that we expect our dinner, but from their regard to their own interest. We address ourselves, not to their humanity but to their self-love, and never talk to them of our own necessities but of their advantages.[5]

Advocates of this form of laissez-faire economics point to the increase in wealth it produces for the general public; and it has become central to the workings of the so-called free market. It is, of course, undeniable that in the last century countries that have given free rein to the principle of entrepreneurial egoism have noticeably prospered more than strict command economies.

On the other hand, serious questions can be asked about completely unregulated commercial egoism. It is true that even extreme egoism must have some regard for the interests of the public it serves. But it is not everywhere evident, particularly in developing countries, that the wealth produced by entrepreneurial egoism always 'trickles down' in significant quantities to the public at large.

One thinks of how in some developing countries the wealth produced by the multinational oil companies has not in fact trickled down to the population at large but has come to rest in the bank

---

[5] *Wealth of Nations*, 1.2.2 (Glasgow edn, 27).

accounts of various officials. Nor can one forget that in Bhopal in central India, in December 1984, leakage of poisonous gas from an American-owned pesticide factory, apparently through insufficient safety precautions, caused the death of several thousand people and tens of thousands of injuries. Even more were left chronically ill.

Or again, certain powdered milk for babies was found in the West to be harmful to babies because it was not giving the babies the nutrition that mothers supposed it was. It was therefore rejected in the West; nevertheless its manufacturers continued to sell it in some countries to mothers who knew no better than to feed it to their babies.

We could compile a list of dozens of not dissimilar cases from a variety of industries in countries around the world in the decades since. It is not everywhere apparent, then, that unbridled commercial egoism invariably benefits the people at large.

PSYCHOLOGICAL EGOISM

Strictly speaking, psychological egoism is not a moral theory; but it impinges on ethics because it claims to give an account of human nature, based on a scientific insight into the true motivation behind all human behaviour. Its basic contention is that a human being is so constructed that it is psychologically impossible for him or her to do anything that is not in his or her own self-interest. It is not concerned with whether what people do is right or wrong. It says merely that people always do solely what is in their own interest, because they are so made that they are incapable of acting otherwise. Therefore, any ethical theory that says that people ought to do something that does not promote their own self-interest must be false: it is telling people to do something that they cannot in fact do.

It is, of course, a universally acknowledged principle that to tell someone that he has a moral duty to do something must imply that he has the ability to do it. If he cannot do it, he cannot have a duty to do it, and cannot be blamed for not doing it. A person whose legs are paralysed cannot be said to have a duty to climb down the face of a cliff and rescue a child that has fallen over and come to rest on a ledge. No one would blame him for not even attempting to do it; nor could any rightly say that he could have done it, if only he had been willing to try.

Psychological egoism, then, maintains that people can do only what they desire to do; and further, that their psychological mechanisms are so inescapably determined that they can desire to do only what serves their own interests.

Psychological egoism admits, of course, that people often appear to behave unselfishly. Many work without pay for charities, or, like Mother Teresa or Albert Schweitzer, they devote their lives to caring for the sick and poor; and most parents spend endless energy and time unselfishly looking after their children. Psychological egoism does not deny all this. What it does deny is that their basic desires that lie behind this apparently unselfish behaviour are themselves actually and truly unselfish. It maintains that they are always and invariably selfish. And people cannot help it. They may even think that they are acting altruistically with the very best of unselfish intentions. But that is impossible. Psychological egoism knows the real facts, and knows them scientifically: people are so constructed psychologically that they literally cannot do anything other than act in their own interests.

> Psychological egoism impinges on ethics because it claims to give an account of human nature, based on a scientific insight into the true motivation behind all human behaviour.

Suppose, then, a house is on fire and inside there are two children upstairs shouting, 'Help me!' Two men are standing outside. One makes no attempt to save them. Psychological egoism tells us why. It is not in his interest to save them, for he might lose his own life in the attempt; and he cannot do anything that is against his own interest. The other man rushes in and manages to save them, but himself dies as a result of his burns. Once more psychological egoism professes to be able to tell what made the man do it. It was not pity for the children, and it was not unselfish readiness to sacrifice his life for others. That would be psychologically impossible. It was his basic psychological desire to act in his own self-interest: he could not have lived with himself, if he had made no attempt to save them. He did not do it for their sake: he did it simply to get peace of mind for himself.

Evaluating psychological egoism

The claim to be scientific

Psychological egoism claims to be scientific, but is not truly so. The claim that 'All people always act out of self-interest' is at best an empirical generalisation based on experience and observation—and on very limited experience and observation at that. It suffers from the notorious weakness of induction. One single instance to the contrary would demolish its claim. How does it know from experience that there has never been anyone in history who at any time has acted, not out of self-interest, but out of genuine self-sacrificial love? And how does it manage to peer into the depths of the hearts of all contemporary people so that it can assert beyond reasonable doubt that none of them ever acts out of any other motive than self-interest?

Consider also the illustration given above. Psychological egoism claims to explain why one man made no attempt to save the children. But the same explanation, without any adjustment, equally explains why the other man did the very opposite. Indeed it can explain exactly why every person that has ever lived or ever will live, has done or ever will do any act whatever. But a theory which in this kind of way gives the same explanation for a thing and for its opposite, is worthless. Far from being scientific, it is more likely to have arisen in hearts that have never themselves known what it is to act other than selfishly; and, in consequence, it tries to debunk all evidence of unselfish behaviour in others.

Acting out of several motives

Empirical evidence suggests that human beings act not out of one, but out of several, motives. When psychological egoism claims that human beings act out of one solitary motive, namely, the desire to serve their own self-interest, we must ask what is meant by self-interest.

Reason. A man who drinks too much alcohol, smokes excessively or takes drugs, will insist that he is serving his own self-interest. Maybe it gives him short-term pleasure. But how can it be said to be genuinely self-interest when in the long-term it will ruin his liver, pancreas, lungs and brain? Presently, we hope, he will see his mistake and stop yielding to his false short-term interest, and aim at his long-term interest. But that shows at least that a man is not helplessly and indiscriminatingly driven by his desire. He has another driving power, namely reason, that can control and redirect his self-interested desire.

Sympathy. And then a human being has a faculty of sympathy, which enables him to 'put himself in the other man's shoes', and to understand how he feels, and what he needs and longs for. Not infrequently that sympathy will lead the first man, at his own cost, to act benevolently to help the second man, with no thought whatever that he is doing it out of self-interest, and with no expectation of getting something back in return.

Love. And beyond sympathy there is the greatest motive in the world, love: not passionate love, nor the love of friendship, but disinterested love that loves deliberately because it is its very nature to love, and, as the Bible puts it, 'seeks not its own' (1 Cor 13:5 own trans.). Christ demonstrated it to the full, but by his grace many have been able to act to some extent out of that same love. Humans are not driven by one unvarying motive.

The grain of truth in psychological egoism

In spite of what has been said so far, there are many people who genuinely feel that psychological egoism is true of them, at least to some extent. As far as they are concerned, the claims of non-egoistic ethical theories are unrealistically too demanding, and the moral demands of the Bible hopelessly out of reach. There is honesty, and a good deal of truth, in this admission. In one sense it is true of everyone. It was, in fact, one of the greatest saints who ever lived who bewailed his own inability to keep the moral law:

> For I know that nothing good dwells in me, that is, in my flesh. For I have the desire to do what is right, but not the ability to carry it out. For I do not do the good I want, but the evil I do not want is what I keep on doing. (Rom 7:18–19)

This is a predicament that faces everyone sooner or later. What the answer to it is, we must consider in our final chapter.

WHAT USE IS ETHICS?

CHAPTER 10

DETERMINING THE VALUE OF A HUMAN BEING

Different people value things differently. . . . If ethics is based, consciously or unconsciously, on values, the fundamental question that arises in our everyday attitude towards other people is: what is the value of a human being? And how shall we decide it?

INTRODUCTION

We have now spent a long time considering some of the leading theories in moral philosophy. The question arises: what use is ethics when it comes to deciding the practical questions that face us in everyday living? And what difference will it make whether we follow one theory or another?

There are some thinkers who say that, when it comes to decisions about practical everyday life, ethical theory is no use whatsoever. Such a view is stated by John D. Caputo:

> Waiting for firm theoretical premises to bolster and back up our ethical beliefs is a little like waiting for a proof of the veracity of perception before dodging out of the way of a projectile barrelling at our head.... The singular situations of daily life fly too close to the ground to be detected by the radar of ethical theory. Ethical life is a series of... accidents and casualties, against which ethical theory can supply little insurance.[1]

If Caputo's view is true, a further question arises: how shall we proceed when faced with an ethical decision? Some people seem to think that they will automatically know what to do. Past experience and common sense will be sufficient to guide them. Each person must be free to take the decision for himself and for herself, without drawing upon any particular ethical theory to guide that decision.

The fact is, however, that such an attitude does not avoid ethical judgments. There may be no well thought out ethical theory in the person's mind, but past experience and common sense, upon which the person relies in any situation, is itself made up of all kinds of decisions that have now formed the person's attitude to life and the general principles on which he or she treats other people. Now the way one treats oneself and other people depends on how one values oneself and

---

[1] 'The End of Ethics', 111, 112.

other people. To put it briefly: ethics depends on value judgments. And value judgments already give us an ethical framework whether we are consciously aware of it or not.

Different people value things differently. For instance, faced with what looks like a diamond, the immediate reactions of various individuals will differ. One man will look at it and say that it is not a diamond, but probably merely paste. Another man will say, 'No, it's not paste. It is a common gemstone of no special value.' An expert may look at it and recognise it to be a real diamond, which is therefore valuable. But what is its value? A machine-tool engineer will say that its value lies in this—that it is useful as an instrument for cutting hard materials. Another person will protest, 'That is a very low view of a diamond. Its value is aesthetic. Look how beautifully it sparkles and refracts the light!' Someone else looks at it and says, 'I see no beauty in it at all, I wouldn't let it take up space in my house.' A businessman looks at it and says, 'Yes, but, if some people value this thing, I could make a lot of money out of it.' A thief looks at it and says, 'How can I steal it and turn it into cash?'

If, then, ethics is based, consciously or unconsciously, on values, the fundamental question that arises in our everyday attitude towards other people is: what is the value of a human being? And how shall we decide it? So let us examine this question in the light of the various ethical systems that we have studied.

THE VALUE OF A HUMAN BEING

The materialist viewpoint

A human being is nothing but primeval 'paste' and virtually valueless—an animated piece of matter that has arrived at its present state as a result of the mindless forces of evolution. For some people, this abolishes all ethical considerations.[2] Some races have succeeded more than others in the evolutionary struggle. Those that survive have a right to survive. There is no morality involved. Human beings after all are nothing but machines by which genes reproduce themselves.

---

[2] See Ch. 3.

Naturalism

No, says naturalism, nature is to be respected. Nature has genuine value and we are part of its great system.

Yes, that is good. Nature is valuable and is to be respected. But who is to interpret nature's values? According to the thinking of one ethicist, Peter Singer, the human is valuable; but it is only one animal along with all the other animals and in some circumstances less valuable than they are. For instance, Singer writes: 'the life of a newborn baby is of less value to it than the life of a pig, a dog or a chimpanzee is to the nonhuman animal.'[3] What this could mean in practice is exemplified by the suggestion that he and his colleague Helga Kuhse make that a period of 28 days *after* birth should be allowed before an infant is accepted as having the same right to live as others, so that, for example, infants born with debilitating defects could be killed.[4]

Well, certainly, a month-old baby is arguably not so magnificent or strong as a lion. But why stop there? For a full-grown lion may well be more majestic and beautiful than a young woman who is a semi-permanent invalid. Why, then, would it not be right to eliminate the invalid as a drain upon society? John Hardwig writes:

> Since lives are deeply intertwined, the lives of the rest of the family can be dragged down, impoverished, compromised, perhaps even ruined because of what they must go through if she lives on. When death comes too late because of the effect of someone's life on her loved ones, we are, I think, forced to ask, 'Can someone have a duty to die?' . . . Assisted suicide would then be helping someone to do the right thing.[5]

But that raises the question: on what basis do you value the lion and the human being? Are we assuming that a human being has no intrinsic value but is to be evaluated on the basis of some quality or other: beauty, strength, prowess, intelligence or something else? Who shall do the deciding, and on what basis?

---

[3] *Practical Ethics*, 169.
[4] See Singer and Kuhse, *Should the Baby Live?*, 191. See also *Practical Ethics*, 190, where Singer discusses the timeframe for such cases as being 'a week or a month after birth'.
[5] 'Dying at the Right Time', 101.

J. S. Mill, as we saw, held that the State had a duty to protect the basic rights of the individual, but that ultimately the rights of the individual were given by the State. In his view, therefore, the value of the individual ultimately depends on the State's evaluation.

Well yes, certainly that is better than the value of the individual being dependent simply on his next door neighbour or on the whim of the Mafia, as to whether he ought to be allowed to live and work. Better the State control it.

Yes, but history has shown that different States have put different values upon the individual. In some States certain classes of people are treated as second-rate citizens. Hitler decided that the Aryan race was supremely valuable and the rest, like Jews and gypsies, ought to be eliminated for the good of the State.

Contractarianism

Contractarianism can see the danger of allowing the value of an individual to be dependent on a totalitarian state. It says the way to preserve the value of the individual is for all the citizens of a state to form a contract one with the other and with the State, and agree a common value to be put on all its citizens.

Yes, but, as we found, contractarianism itself admits the weakness of such a system.[6] Vigorous entrepreneurial people will eventually observe that others in the State are not pulling their weight, are scrounging upon the efforts of others, and they will ask themselves: 'why should we bother to sign up to this contract?' They will prefer to go their own way and maximise their own interests no matter what happens to others. And what is there to stop them?

Utilitarianism

No, no, say the utilitarians. The best way to behave is for everybody to seek the maximum welfare and happiness for the maximum number of people.

Yes, if everybody did so, certainly it would lead to a very happy state of affairs. But utilitarianism, as we saw, says that if a situation arose

---

[6] See Ch. 3 for the assessment.

where the good of the maximum number of people could be achieved only by the execution of an innocent man, then he must be executed. In that case the individual has no intrinsic value. His value depends on what is good for the majority.

Intuitionism

Intuitionism is certainly an improvement on utilitarianism. Utilitarianism says that the morality of an act depends solely on its outcome. If the outcome results in the maximum amount of pleasure for the maximum number of people, then the act is morally right even if the act itself was, in common sense morality, an evil act, as in the example just given. Intuitionism says that this cannot be right. We have, for instance, duties from the past to keep our promises, and even if much happiness could be caused to oneself and many other people by breaking one's promises, it would nevertheless be an immoral thing to do. For that would break people's trust in each other and thus undercut the value of truth upon which society is built.

Kantianism

Kant joins the intuitionists in protest against utilitarianism. He demands on the basis of his universalising principle that all people have equal rights. If you claim the right to steal from other people, you must be prepared to grant them the right to steal from you, and that would be foolish.

Secondly, and even more importantly, he holds that the proper way to evaluate people is to regard human beings as ends in themselves. Their value and right to life does not depend on their being a useful means to some other person's ends. He allows us, of course, to use people with their consent as a means to an end as, for instance, we use a mechanic to mend our cars. But we must never treat human beings merely as means to an end, like an engineer who uses a diamond simply as an instrument for his own purposes.

This, then, according to Kant, is the only rational way to behave: for him reason is the force behind ethics.

Yes, but not all people are prepared to listen to reason. If they have the power to devalue their fellow citizens and to treat them as mere cogs in a machine and are able to get away with it, they don't see why they shouldn't.

Virtue ethics

But then come the virtue ethicists, who say that all this concentration on the morality of actions is comparatively unimportant. We should concentrate, not so much on the quality of the *deeds* that are done, as on the moral quality of the *person* who does them, since a virtuous person will naturally value and care for people, and therefore will treat them virtuously.

Yes, but, who says that I ought to value other people and treat them virtuously? Who defines virtue, anyway? Why shouldn't I pretend to care for someone and use the opportunity to steal her diamond? What is the ultimate authority behind virtue? Who enforces it?

The human race's transcendental value

With this we come to the Bible's evaluation of the human race. The human race derives its intrinsic value from God, and, in the end, God will vindicate that value. The Bible insists that ethics is based upon this transcendental value, namely, that humans are created by God. But not merely that we are created by God, for so are the animals. The human creature is a special creation and has been given a special relationship with God. He is made in the image of God, and what that entails can be seen from the context in which it is said: 'Then God said, "Let us make man in *our* image, after *our* likeness"' (Gen 1:26, emph. added). Man therefore bears a certain likeness to God. He is in some way an expression and representative of God, as the passage goes on to state: 'and let them have dominion over the fish of the sea and over the birds of the heavens and over the livestock and over all the earth and over every creeping thing that creeps on the earth' (Gen 1:26).

A later passage declares that because man is God's responsible steward over the earth and God's representative on earth, to kill

> The Bible insists that ethics is based upon this transcendental value, namely, that humans are created by God. But not merely that we are created by God, for so are the animals.

a man is an affront to God: 'Whoever sheds the blood of man, by man shall his blood be shed; for God made man in his own image' (Gen 9:6).

THE INESCAPABLE CHOICE

How, then, shall we value human life? How shall we value ourselves? How shall we value others? We cannot escape the choice. We cannot say that we are not interested in ethics, for the simple reason that to say so is itself already a value judgment, which determines our ethics.

Now there is, as we have seen, some truth in most of the views we have discussed. But there is no doubt that the last one puts the highest value on human beings. So the crucial question to be asked is: is it true? As Christians, the authors of this book believe that it is. In what follows we shall see how it works out, and compares and contrasts with other value systems in dealing with the practical problems of everyday life. People of other faiths, too, hold, though on a very different basis, that you cannot have satisfactory values on which to base an ethic without some concept of the transcendental.

Yet others will hold, on the contrary, that you can have a system of ethics without any transcendental values. On the extreme of this wing stand people like Singer who writes:

> The new vision leaves no room for the traditional answer to these questions, that we human beings are a special creation, infinitely more precious, in virtue of our humanity alone, than all other living things. In the light of our new understanding of our place in the universe, we shall have to abandon that traditional answer, and revise the boundaries of our ethics. One casualty of that revision will be any ethic based on the idea that what really matters about beings is whether they are human.[7]

Singer, apparently, makes the doubtful assumption that the evolutionary view has been proved and hence that there is an unbroken continuity between animals and humans that removes any special

---
[7] *Rethinking Life and Death*, 183.

God-given status for human beings.[8] In the end, of course, it is up to each one of us to make up his or her own mind about the truth of any of these competing views.

In the next two chapters we shall think of some of the major ethical questions that cluster around the beginning and the end of human life. The first major issue is the transmission of life.

---

[8] We will not discuss this issue further here, but we have touched on this matter in the Appendix 'The Scientific Endeavour' and it is addressed at length in the books by John Lennox referenced there.

CHAPTER 11

THE ETHICS OF THE TRANSMISSION OF LIFE

Many people in our modern world . . . find the Christian prohibition of sex outside marriage strange, unnatural, unhealthy maybe, or even unthinkable. Non-Christians, however, might nevertheless find it interesting and instructive to discover from Paul's response what experiences, values, and motivations actually lie behind the Christian abjuration of casual sex.

THE IDEAL FOR SEXUAL EXPERIENCE

The obvious fact is that, without life, there would be no human values. Life, therefore, is regarded by all people as the most valuable thing. It is no wonder, then, that the transmission of life is surrounded on all sides by ethical constraints.

The second obvious fact of nature is that the transmission of human life is by sexual reproduction. But, from the very start, the Bible makes it clear that this is far more than a mere physical process, let alone a merely mechanical one. It involves a special, intimate, relationship between two persons.

> Therefore a man shall leave his father and his mother and hold fast to his wife, and they shall become one flesh. (Gen 2:24)

We must be careful to notice what this is saying. First of all, a man leaves his father and mother. This phrase does not simply mean that he shall remove himself physically from the presence of his parents. It is speaking about the special relational grouping that has set the parameters of his life so far. This he now leaves, in order that he may enter a new relational unit that shall be the dominant relationship in his life. He shall be joined to his wife. And when it says 'and they shall become one flesh' it is not merely saying that they shall be one when they are actually engaged in sexual intercourse. It is denoting a new relationship that is much more than the union of two bodies, although that is important in itself. It is nothing less than the union of two persons—a new relational unit.

Furthermore, when it says 'the man shall *hold fast to* his wife', the verb means to 'stick with' or 'keep close to'; that is to say, the relationship is designed to be permanent—in modern terminology, marriage. One thing is absolutely clear from this: the relationship is not a casual one. It is not a question of a man remaining, so to speak, in his parents' group, and simply emerging from time to time to satisfy his desires with casual liaisons.

This, then, is the biblical blueprint for the transmission of new life. It begins with the establishment of a new relational unit that involves a new permanent relationship between two persons. It is only within that unit that the sexual relationship can properly fulfil its intended purpose.

It is to be emphasised that there are two elements in sex. There is first the mutual pleasure and enjoyment, one of the other. Witness the beautiful love poetry of the Bible's Song of Songs. This needs to be underlined, since there have been times in history when some people, sometimes in the name of religion, have regarded the pleasure and joy of sex as unworthy, if not positively sinful. The second element, of course, is to be the means in the Creator's hand of creating new persons.

The ethics of maintaining the ideal

Now this biblical pattern for marriage is an ideal that cannot be maintained and enjoyed without a great deal of self-discipline, since there is another implication of 'being one flesh'. This ethical demand is stated in the New Testament as follows:

> Husbands, love your wives, as Christ loved the church and gave himself up for her . . . In the same way husbands should love their wives as their own bodies. He who loves his wife loves himself. For no one ever hated his own flesh, but nourishes and cherishes it . . . 'Therefore a man shall leave his father and mother and hold fast to his wife, and the two shall become one flesh.' (Eph 5:25–31)

It is because sometimes men seek in marriage only self-gratification, and neglect this ethical responsibility, that many marriages end in misery.

Here again, the ethical dimension becomes exceedingly important. For malpractice at this point has two serious effects. Disloyalty of one partner to the other does profound damage to the persons concerned at the deepest and most intimate level of their personalities. It also seriously detracts from the ideal conditions that the stable union of husband and wife was meant to provide for the transmission and nurture of new life.

However, to many people, especially in the West since the so-called sexual revolution of the 1960s, this attitude to marriage is regarded as completely out of date; and that for two reasons. Many men want pleasure without the responsibility of a life-long contract. They want to be free, when a more attractive partner comes along, to abandon the first partner in favour of the second. They father children by one woman and then abandon them and father children by another, and have no sense of responsibility for caring for these children. Here virtue ethics, with its emphasis on caring, would object very strongly.

Some women also resent these ethical restrictions. They see them as a code developed by society to force women to submit to the tyranny of unreasonable men. Yet nature drives them to seek the pleasure; and so they try to derive it from casual relationships.

They feel that the 'old-fashioned' morality of marriage may have made some sense when there was a real threat of sexually transmitted diseases and unwanted pregnancies, and when there were no adequate methods of protection against them. But now that modern science has provided us with antibiotics, contraception and abortion, there is nothing to stop us giving full expression to our sexuality how and when and with whomsoever we want. There is no Creator behind marriage to set its ethical limits. There is simply the powerful and beautiful sexual drive with which nature has marvellously endowed us by some freak accident of remote biological history.

Sex, they say, is a natural activity like eating, and just as we satisfy our appetite for food whenever we feel hungry, so we should satisfy our appetite for sex whenever we feel like it. To repress it would be psychologically damaging. But there are false assumptions here.

Two false assumptions

First of all, in the biblical view, *marriage was never designed simply to avoid sexually transmitted diseases*. Marriage is the union and self-giving of two persons, as we have seen. Indeed, the word that the Bible uses to describe physical union is the verb 'to know'. This is not simply a euphemism. It denotes one of the main ways in which the ever-increasing knowledge one of the other grows as their two personalities are blended. Sex is not simply a physical mechanism for inducing pleasurable physical and emotional sensations, although those sensations are part of its joy. Sex is the natural expression of a deep bonding of two persons, a deep knowing one of another. You cannot have that in a casual relationship. It can only be enjoyed in the loyal steadfast commitment of one person to the other person in marriage. It is therefore an unnatural degradation of sex to remove it from the context of the 'knowing each other' of two persons.

The second false assumption is that *casual sex does no damage to those involved*. There is, in fact, a high emotional cost. For there is actually no such thing as casual sex even if those involved have only casual intentions.

There are always deep emotional scars and traumas that may never completely heal, and that can make it difficult to form future stable relationships. Far from enhancing the joy of sex, the ultimate effect of casual sex is to ruin it: the mere physical act will in the end prove unsatisfying. Writing of the damage that casual sex does to the true enjoyment of intimate love in marriage, Mike Starkey remarks:

> The generation searching for intimacy more pitifully than any other in history has taken the central sacrament of interpersonal intimacy and killed it dead. We have the dubious privilege of living in the culture that is presiding over the death of eroticism.[1]

Pressure to conform in youth

Teenagers are tempted to engage in premarital sex. It has always been so, and nowadays is even more so in many parts of the world. The biblical ethic on this matter is clear and unambiguous: 'Flee youthful passions' (2 Tim 2:22). This is not a tyrannous prohibition. It comes, as the Apostle Paul who wrote it claims, from the inventor and Creator of sex himself, who by definition is concerned that sex should be properly enjoyed, and that nothing should be done prematurely that could eventually damage that proper enjoyment.

One cannot overlook, however, the enormous unethical pressure that is brought to bear on teenagers to anticipate the joys that properly belong to marriage.

---

[1] *God, Sex, and Search for Lost Wonder*, cited from Kilner et al., *Cutting-Edge Bioethics*, 130.

The sexual revolution of the 1960s had as part of its intention to remove all restraints upon sexual behaviour. That revolution has been so successful that many of school age think that sexual experience among their peers is normal; and that anybody who has not experienced sex by the age of sixteen is somehow abnormal. In addition to this peer pressure, the vulgarisation and commercialisation of sex in the media has deliberately excited sexual activity for the purpose of making fortunes for the media moguls, who have no concern for the damage that they might cause young people. On top of that, some psychologists have falsely taught that repression of sexual desire, even among young people, can lead to psychological disturbance.

> The vulgarisation and commercialisation of sex in the media has deliberately excited sexual activity for the purpose of making fortunes for the media moguls, who have no concern for the damage that they might cause.

As to the sinister reality of all this peer pressure on teenagers, a survey in the UK has shown that peer pressure alone was the reason why over 40% of teenagers had their first experience of sexual intercourse.[2]

This sexual pressure and exploitation have been immorally cruel because there is mounting evidence that points in the other direction: premature sexual experience can produce long-term injurious effects upon teenagers. The founder of the US Sex Information and Education Council, Dr Mary Calderone, highlights the central issue:

> Sex experience before confidentiality, empathy and trust have been established can hinder and may destroy the possibility of a solid permanent relationship.[3]

In light of all of this information, some governments (including some in the West) have, in spite of the scepticism of the press, encouraged sex education programmes in schools, with the key objective of encouraging pupils to delay sexual intercourse. Part of their message is that there is nothing wrong, and everything right, about being a virgin. They also point out that sexually active teenagers are exposed to additional health risks.

---

[2] Social Exclusion Unit, *Teenage Pregnancy*, 46 Figure 23.
[3] Cited by R. Collins in 'A Physician's View of College Sex', 392.

THE VALUES AND PRESUPPOSITIONS OF CHRISTIAN SEXUAL MORALITY

In regard to sexual morality the Graeco-Roman world into which Christianity was born strongly resembled our modern permissive societies: casual, and especially premarital, sex were normal, accepted behaviour; so normal, in fact, that to question their morality would have struck many people as very strange, almost unthinkable.

Cicero, the famous Roman politician, lawyer, barrister, philosopher, moralist and author (106–43 BC), was himself inclined to the stricter moral standards of the early Roman Republic. But in 56 BC he undertook to defend a certain Marcus Caelius Rufus in the high court at Rome. In his early life Caelius had involved himself in violent debauchery, and now stood accused by his political enemies of having (among other things) attempted to poison his estranged mistress, Clodia, a beautiful but promiscuous celebrity belonging to the fashionable set in Rome. In the course of his defence of Caelius, Cicero argued:

> if anyone thinks young men ought to be forbidden affairs even with prostitutes, he is certainly austere (that I would not deny), but he is out of touch with our present permissive age. Indeed, he is also not in harmony with the custom of our ancestors, and the allowances which even in those times people were quite accustomed to make. For name any epoch when this was not invariably the case. When was such behaviour ever censured or forbidden? When was the permitted thing not permitted?[4]

Now by the first century AD the Greek city of Corinth had become a Roman colony, the seat of government of the Roman province of Achaia. It was famous for its sexual laxity. It was commercially very prosperous; and pleasure too, so it was said, had there become 'commercialised'. It had long had a temple to Aphrodite, the goddess of love, staffed by 1000 female slaves dedicated to her 'worship'. According to Strabo, the Greek geographer, these 'priestesses' had helped to make the city a tourist attraction, and contributed sizeably to its economic

---

[4] *Pro Caelio*, xx.47, tr. Michael Grant, *Cicero, Selected Political Speeches*, 194.

prosperity.[5] As a result, throughout the Roman Empire the Greek verb *korinthiazomai* (to adopt the lifestyle of Corinth) meant to live a life of sexual laxity.

And yet, around AD 50, as a result of the preaching of the Christian apostle, Paul, there came into existence in this very city of Corinth a Christian church. Before their conversion some of its members had followed the typically Corinthian way of life; and in a subsequent letter to them Paul reminded them of this, and pointed out what it was in their conversion experience that had changed their moral outlook and lifestyle:

> Do not be deceived: Neither the sexually immoral, nor idolaters, nor adulterers, nor male prostitutes nor homosexual offenders, nor thieves, nor the greedy, nor drunkards, nor slanderers nor swindlers will inherit the kingdom of God. And that is what some of you were. But you were washed, you were sanctified, you were justified in the name of the Lord Jesus Christ and by the Spirit of our God. (1 Cor 6:9–11 own trans.)

Nevertheless, old values and behaviour patterns die hard; and apparently there were some among Paul's professed converts who argued that the Christian gospel, with its emphasis on spiritual freedom and salvation by grace, had no reason to forbid indulgence in casual sex. Rather, it should condone, if not encourage, it. Not surprisingly, this brought a vigorous response from Paul.

Many people in our modern world hold virtually the same permissive attitude to sex as the Greeks and Romans of the first century AD; and, not being Christians themselves, nor understanding Christians' motivation, they find the Christian prohibition of sex outside marriage strange, unnatural, unhealthy maybe, or even unthinkable. Non-Christians, however, might nevertheless find it interesting and instructive to discover from Paul's response what experiences, values, and motivations actually lie behind the Christian abjuration of casual sex. They

> Throughout the Roman Empire the Greek verb *korinthiazomai* (to adopt the lifestyle of Corinth) meant to live a life of sexual laxity.

---

[5] *Geography*, VIII.6.20.

will at least find that it is not any abhorrence of sex in itself, nor any merely superficial moralising.

An exposition of 1 Corinthians 6:12–20

Slogans and replies

Here, then, is Paul arguing his case. In vigorous rhetorical style he quotes the slogans that his opponents used in order to establish their view, and one by one replies to them.[6]

First slogan (v. 12a):   '"Everything is permissible for me"
Paul's reply: 'but not everything is beneficial.'

It is perfectly true that Christianity is not a system of laws, rules and regulations that one has to keep in order to be saved: salvation is a gift and is received by faith, not earned by works (Eph 2:8–10). In that sense a believer is not under law but under grace, and is therefore free; and none championed this freedom more than Paul (see Gal 5:1).

But to suppose that true freedom sets us free to practise things that are not beneficial but, on the contrary, positively harmful and even sinful, is absurd. There is, to use an analogy, no State law forbidding citizens to put sand in their car's petrol tank. Every citizen is therefore free to do so, if he or she wishes. But what a fool anyone would be to do so. The freedom that comes through faith in Christ is not designed to allow us to harm ourselves and to sin against God with impunity. The person who thinks it is, has misread the Christian gospel (see 1 Cor 6:9–11; Gal 5:13–24). The freedom Christ gives is the freedom *not* to sin.

Second slogan (v. 12b): '"Everything is permissible for me"
Paul's reply: 'but I will not be mastered [or, enslaved] by anything'

---

[6] Ancient Greek writers did not use quotation marks when quoting someone else's statements. Translations of the Bible that follow this Greek habit in these verses make it difficult for modern readers to see which phrases are the slogans of Paul's opponents, and which are his answers. We shall use quotation marks to indicate what modern exegetes take to be the slogans used by Paul's opponents, but leave Paul's replies without quotation marks. The translation used in the course of this exposition is our own.

To use one's freedom to indulge in practices that then become overmastering habits and rob one of one's freedom, is folly indeed. Professor F. F. Bruce well brings out the play on words in Paul's Greek that highlights this folly. It depends on three cognate Greek words: *exestin* = 'it is lawful', *exousia* = 'authority', and *exousiasthēsomai* = 'to fall under someone else's authority'. Bruce translates thus: 'if all things are lawful [*exestin*] for me, I have authority [*exousia*] over them, but if I am to be enslaved [*exousiasthēsomai*] by any of them, then *they* have acquired authority over me and, instead of enjoying liberty, I have acquired a yoke of bondage'.[7]

Paul's reply, then, implies that to use one's right to freedom in order to practise fornication is to find oneself overmastered and enslaved by that practice, and no longer truly free. And the same is true of other practices such as taking drugs. Paul, therefore, protests that he, for one, is determined not to use his right to freedom in order to indulge in vices that would overmaster him and destroy his freedom.

Third slogan (v. 13): '[*a*] "Food for the stomach and the stomach for food;
[*b*] and God will destroy both stomach and food."'

Paul's reply: '[*a*] but the body is not for fornication, but for the Lord, and the Lord for the body' (v. 13).
'[*b*] and God both raised the Lord and will also raise us through his power' (v. 14).

At first sight the libertines' third slogan seems to be concerned simply with food. But Paul's immediate reply shows that he understood the first part of this third slogan to be intended as an analogy: desire for food is a natural desire, and food is nature's provision for satisfying that desire. Moreover, it makes no *moral* difference what kind of food we take to satisfy our hunger, nor with how many different people we share a meal from time to time. Similarly, on this analogy, the desire for sex would be a perfectly natural desire, and it would make no *moral* difference with how many different partners we satisfied that desire from time to time. Fornication would be simply one natural way among others for the satisfaction of our sexual urge.

---

[7] Bruce, *1 and 2 Corinthians*, 62.

Paul first answers this third slogan negatively: he denies the appropriateness of the suggested analogy between the stomach and the body. The stomach is for food from whatever source it comes; but the body, he says, is not for fornication. It matters immensely, both morally and spiritually, with whom one satisfies one's sexual desires.

Christ himself made this same distinction between the stomach and food on the one hand, and the body and fornication on the other:

> nothing that enters a man from the outside can make him 'unclean'. For it doesn't go into his heart but into his stomach... What comes out of a man is what makes him unclean. For from within, out of men's hearts, come evil thoughts, fornications, thefts, murders adulteries... All these evil things proceed from within, and defile. (Mark 7:18–23)

Food and the stomach are (along with other internal organs) merely nature's way of keeping the body alive by supplying its necessary nutrients. But the body itself, its significance and purpose, belong to an altogether higher level of morality and spirituality.

Next Paul answers the slogan positively, deliberately copying the form of the slogan, so as to make it clear that he is rebutting the analogy suggested by the slogan:

> "'Food is for the stomach and the stomach for food'"
>
> BUT
>
> 'The body is... for the Lord, and the Lord for the body.'

This is the prime purpose of the body. What that means, Paul will explain in a moment. But the slogan contained two parts; he has answered the first part, he will now answer the second before going further.

The second part ran: 'and God will destroy both stomach and food' (v. 13b). In making this point these would-be Christians were doubtless influenced by a strand of thought common to various schools of Greek philosophy. This stated that the only morally and spiritually important part of a human being was the soul, for that was eternal and survived death. The body, including the stomach and all other organs, was not eternal, but only a temporary phenomenon. God himself had arranged it that the body and all its functions would at death perish forever. The physical body, therefore, was not morally or spiritually significant.

But Paul immediately denied this basic disparagement of the significance of the human body. The body was not a merely temporary phenomenon. The very heart of the Christian gospel was that God raised the body of Christ from the dead, and will one day similarly raise the bodies of all believers from the dead. Paul did not imagine that material food would be necessary to maintain the resurrection body in existence (see 1 Cor 15:35–49), nor that marriage would continue to be practised in heaven as here on earth. But a believer's body itself, he pointed out, will not only be raised from the dead, but even now in this life is of eternal moral and spiritual significance; and he proceeded to give the reasons for this, and in so doing reminded them of basic Christian facts which they seemed to have forgotten—or had never grasped.

Basic facts about the body

Basic fact 1: *believers' bodies are even now in this life members of Christ* (1 Cor 6:15). It is, as Christians regard it, a glorious part of the Christian gospel that immediately upon a person's repentance and faith in Christ, Christ comes by his Spirit to dwell in the body of that believer. That body thus becomes a member of Christ, a vehicle for Christ to use to express his character, to exhibit the love and grace, holiness and compassion, that he showed when here on earth. Paul described the process in this way:

> I have been crucified with Christ; and yet I live; yet no longer I, but Christ lives in me; and that life which I now live in the flesh, I live in faith, the faith which is in the Son of God who loved me and gave himself up for me. (Gal 2:20 RV)

That being so, Paul argued, for believers to remove their bodies from their function as members of Christ and make them members of a prostitute would be outrageous (1 Cor 6:15).

Imagine a beautiful limousine, dedicated to the service of the president. Suppose, then, that the chauffeur, responsible for the driving and upkeep of the president's limousine, were surreptitiously to take it on one occasion and use it to transport his pigs to market! That would be a small outrage compared with a Christian using his body, a member of Christ, for intercourse with a prostitute.

Basic fact 2: *sexual intercourse is never a merely mechanical, impersonal event* (1 Cor 6:16–18). It is true that permissiveness tends ever more to regard casual sex as if it were nothing more than a mere physical act, like the temporary connecting up of two aircraft in flight for the purpose of aerial refuelling. Paul, however, reminded his friends in Corinth of something that they had either forgotten or ignored: the sexual union of a man and a woman, according to the Creator (see Gen 2:24), is the blending of two human bodies and two personalities. The man who is joined to a prostitute becomes one with that prostitute (1 Cor 6:16). Similarly, the person who is joined to the living Christ is one spirit with him (v. 17). The two 'joinings' are utterly incompatible.

It is for this reason, Paul argued, that a believer must flee fornication. Fornication is an assault on the very purpose, function and dignity of a believer's body (v. 18). And to show his friends how that was, Paul reminded them of another basic fact.

Basic fact 3: *the purpose of God's redemption of the human body is to make that body a temple of God's own Holy Spirit* (see 1 Cor 6:19–20). Humankind's redemption has been an infinitely heavy cost upon God's love. God has willingly paid that cost, but not merely for the negative purpose of forgiving and blotting out of the human race's sins. He has paid it for the infinitely higher, positive, purpose of making each redeemed person's body, soul and spirit a temple of the glory of his own divine presence. Since he has paid the price of redemption, he regards believers' bodies as his own purchased property and will insist on the eventual complete fulfilment of his purpose for them.

These, then, are the basic facts and motivations behind the Christian attitude to sex. Understandably, they will mean very little, and perhaps be incomprehensible, to those who take a completely secular view of life. But there seems little doubt which view values the human body more highly.

CHAPTER 12

ETHICAL ISSUES RAISED BY SCIENCE AND TECHNOLOGY

When it comes to the transmission of life, science and technology have raised both new possibilities, and new ethical questions. . . . Isn't it enough to say that, if a process can lead to great benefits in health, it should be done, and no further questions need be raised about what techniques are employed to achieve it?

NEW POSSIBILITIES AND NEW QUESTIONS

When it comes to the transmission of life, science and technology have raised both new possibilities, and new ethical questions, both at the start of life and at its end. We will now consider both, beginning with new possibilities arising at the start of life.

Some of these possibilities are (1) helping couples who have not been able to have children, to have them; (2) genetic screening to eliminate the possibility of children being born with serious defects; (3) stem-cell research and therapeutic cloning for the potential alleviation or cure of serious illnesses like Parkinson's and Alzheimer's diseases.

The question is, what has ethics to say to these procedures, if anything at all? Isn't it enough to say that, if a process can lead to great benefits in health, it should be done, and no further questions need be raised about what techniques are employed to achieve it? Questioning the ethics of such potentially beneficial techniques is surely mere theoretical pettiness.

This overlooks the fact that this attitude already presumes an ethical stance. It says that if the result is good, then the means used to produce it must automatically be good. This, we may remember, is the policy advocated by utilitarianism. It says that our main aim in life should be to produce the maximum pleasure and welfare for the maximum number of people. But it also says that if, in order to achieve that maximum benefit, one has to destroy an innocent life, then one should go ahead, destroy it, and not ask any further questions. In other words, the morality of an act depends, not on the quality of the act itself but on the results it achieves.

Other philosophers like Kant would deny that view outright, regarding it as contrary to common sense morality. The end, they maintain, does not justify the means. If an act is in itself morally repugnant, then whatever good results it might achieve, it remains an immoral act and should not be done.

ISSUES AT THE START OF LIFE

In light of this debate, let us now look at some of the problems that are raised by advances in modern science and technology in connection with the transmission of life.

In vitro fertilisation

Sometimes the sperm of a husband and the eggs of his wife are perfectly healthy, but there is some physical blockage that prevents fertilisation occurring. In vitro fertilisation (IVF) is a procedure in which sperm from the prospective father is used in the laboratory to fertilise an egg taken from the prospective mother. The fertilised egg is then implanted in the womb, and the fetus develops normally.

Of course, there are practical problems concerned with this procedure, but these are not our concern here, which is with ethics.[1]

There is no doubt that this technique, where successful, brings joy to many couples who, without it, would have no hope of having their own biological child. From the ethical point of view, there are two things to be said. First of all, the technique in itself does not infringe the integrity of the marriage; it merely assists the completion of natural processes that are otherwise blocked. It is true that some ethicists feel that to produce an embryo artificially is already undue manipulation of a new life. More serious, however, is the objection that in the course of in vitro fertilisation, more embryos are normally produced than can be implanted.[2] The rest are destroyed; and if an embryo is already a human life, to produce it and then destroy it is a serious offence. This, then, raises the important and much debated topic of the status of embryonic life. We shall discuss it in a moment.

---

[1] The IVF technique (which is expensive and not always successful—only about 25–30% of those treated give birth to a child in any one cycle of the treatment, see 'Fertility Treatment 2014, p. 39) is not without risk of birth defects: about twice the risk of babies born naturally (Hansen et al., 'The Risk of Major Birth Defects', see Sanders, 'Eutychus', 17).

[2] It is possible to only fertilise as many eggs as will actually be implanted, and this procedure is sometimes, though relatively less often, practised.

Third-party involvement through donation

The use of third-party involvement through sperm or egg donation arises when either husband or wife is, for some reason or other, infertile. Let us suppose it is the husband that is infertile. In times past, the only way of overcoming this problem was for another man to take the first man's wife and have sexual relationships with her. That would have been regarded as adulterous, because it infringes the integrity of the sacred union of a man and his wife.

Nowadays, this problem is solved in a very different way. Men anonymously contribute their sperm to a sperm bank, where the sperm is stored. When the husband is infertile, a couple can apply to this bank for the sperm of some anonymous donor that can be used by the in vitro technique to fertilise the wife's egg. The woman then produces a child in the normal way. Many argue that since this satisfies the wife's natural desire for a child and brings joy to her, why should any objection be made?

It is the fact, of course, that this process of in vitro fertilisation has long since been used on animals, where the identity of the donor bull does not matter to the cow, and no moral issues are involved. Ethical problems arise, however, when this technique is applied to human generation. Let's examine these briefly.

Ethical problems arising

This process intervenes in, and destroys the uniqueness of, the marriage bond between a man and his wife. It is not the same as when a man marries a widow who already has children. By definition, the widow's former husband by whom she had the children is now dead, and the man who marries her is aware from the start (and so are the children, if they are old enough) that they are her children, and not his. There is no infringement of the marriage bond.

It depersonalises the process of the transmission of life. For in this case the wife's conception and bearing of the child is no longer the result of her intimate relations with her own husband. The process thus reduced to a mechanical function, the danger is that we begin to think of human beings as merely biological machines with the power to replicate.

It imperils the child's identity. It is a part of a child's identity as a human being that he or she should know who his or her parents are. It is the sad fact that some children can never know this. Perhaps as babies they were orphaned of both parents. Perhaps they were unwanted at birth, and given into the care of the State or to adoptive parents. Couples who adopt children out of compassion in this way are generally very careful to let the children know that they are not their physical parents, when the children are able to bear the information. The discovery of this fact may be accepted with no difficulty by some children, whereas others find it traumatic, and feel they can never rest until they know who their birth parents were. The trauma is increased when, say, the physical mother of the child still lives, but refuses to let her identity be known to the child that she gave up. The birth mother may feel it too painful to have to admit to her child the reason for which she gave it away; she may also by this time have long since been married to another man and would be embarrassed if he discovered her past history.

But with in vitro fertilisation by donor sperm, the case is different. In many countries the anonymity of the donor is guaranteed by the State. The reason for that is that, if anonymity were not preserved and their identity could be known by the resultant children, the number of donors would significantly decrease. Moreover, what an embarrassment it would be to the receptors, if a donor turned up one day and announced in front of the child's family that he was the father of the child, and not the person the child thought was his or her father.

Suppose, on the other hand, it is the wife who is infertile. Modern techniques make it possible for another woman to donate eggs, and for those eggs to be fertilised by sperm from the wife's husband and implanted in the wife's womb. This, in part, satisfies the wife's longings to have a child; but it is the inescapable fact that, strictly speaking, the child is not her genetic child.[3]

---

[3] As a result of these considerations, there are many couples who think that coming to terms with childlessness (however painful), or adoption, are much better options than altering the basic genetic structure of the family unit. Adoption has not only brought joy to many couples, but also to many children; for it means giving children who already exist, and who through no fault of their own have no parents to care for them, the opportunity of growing up in a home with caring parents. There are still many such children in the world today.

Not only that, but egg donation raises all the same ethical problems that we considered in connection with sperm donation. But in addition to all this, we are again faced with the fact that the process of in vitro fertilisation involves the destruction of spare embryos. It is this ethical question that becomes ever more prominent, when we consider the new procedures that have become available to modern medicine. We must, therefore, turn now to consider the status of human life and the question: when does life begin? And these points we will put across in a somewhat different style.

When does life begin?

In what follows we are going to imagine that a group of medical scientists, engaged in front-line research on issues connected with the transmission of life, has invited an ethicist to address them on the relevance of ethics to their work. We file in and stand, as it were, at the back of the lecture theatre as the ethicist responds as follows.

> Ladies and gentlemen! The first thing I wish to do is to thank you sincerely for your invitation, and I gladly respond to it. Secondly, I should like to express my admiration for the brilliance of mind, and the ingenuity of experiment, that have combined to give us such magnificent insights into the workings of human life. I come before you with some trepidation, for in answering your questions I must of necessity trespass somewhat upon your territory, where my unsure grasp of all the technicalities will be at once evident to you. For this, I am sure, in your gracious way, you will readily make due allowance. What we have in common, however, as scientists on the one hand and ethicists on the other, is that we share a common interest in the more profound questions about human life, such as: When does it begin? What is its essential value? What moral constraints, if any, must govern our manipulation of human life?
>
> As the philosophers and social scientists have frequently reminded us, none of us comes to these questions with a completely open mind. We all have our presuppositions and preconceived value

systems. Some of you, for instance, hold that life is little more than the unplanned result of millennia of mindless evolution. But, since that mindless process has by some quirk of nature produced highly intelligent brains, there can be no ethical objection to these brains now turning round and taking charge of the process of evolution, thereby improving the system more than evolution, left to itself, could have done. On these presuppositions, morality does not enter the question.

On the other hand, many of you—if not most of you—will hardly agree with this evaluation. The human race, you will argue, has developed complex societies that in turn have by mutual consent set the values that should be attributed to life. It follows from this, that the answer to the question of what ethics has to do with medical and scientific research should be that it must be left to society to decide what is morally acceptable.

But even as I say so, none of us can forget what some totalitarian societies have done with the right they have claimed, to enforce their estimate of the value of human life. They have not stopped with the manipulation—and, if need be, the destruction—of embryos and fetuses: they have demanded the right to eliminate whole populations of adults.

It is considerations of this kind that convince many that the value of human life cannot be safely established without some transcendental reference point. They will contend that it is the Creator himself who has established the intrinsic value of human life, by the fact that he has created it in his own image, and ultimately human life belongs to him. On that understanding, to destroy an innocent human life is an affront to the Creator himself.

Of course, I may not assume that all of you would accept that human life has this transcendental significance. On the other hand, I am sure that all of you would agree that intentionally to destroy an innocent human life is in fact a crime, described by the ugly term 'murder'. But that simply brings us to the basic question: when exactly does human life begin?

Here, of course, views diverge. The issue was forcefully brought to our attention some decades ago, long before the advent of the spectacular insights of molecular biology and genetic engineering. It was raised over the issue of the legality of abortion. At that time many governments decided that abortion was ethically acceptable up to about the 28th week of pregnancy. At that point, it was argued, the fetus became a viable human being, that could, if need be, exist outside the womb. Therefore intentionally to abort it after that, would be tantamount to homicide. Before the 28th week, however, the fetus was thought not to be fully human, and therefore might be eliminated without any pang of conscience.

But, ladies and gentlemen, your own research into intensive care methods has undercut that view, and has shown that nowadays a fetus is viable after 24 weeks or so; and can, with suitable intensive care, survive outside the womb, and eventually become a fully mature adult. Yet, even where these intensive care facilities exist (and they do not exist everywhere in the world), it is still thought legitimate to abort fetuses up to the 28th week, and in some countries even beyond it. So, if viability is to be the criterion of what is fully human-life—in the sense that, after that, it would be a crime to destroy it—a startling fact emerges. We are still aborting fetuses that have full human status.

Incidentally, to this layman, it seems highly ironic that in one theatre of a hospital, doctors could be vigorously attempting to maintain the life of a 24-week-old premature baby while, at the same time, doctors in another theatre are destroying a fetus of the same age. But in any case, our recent advances in genetics require us to raise the question of the status of human life at much earlier stages of its development. Whether or not a fetus of 24 weeks old or earlier can be acknowledged as a human being, many will argue that the embryo that is formed at fertilisation surely cannot be regarded as already possessing the full status of human life. Then we must ask: what is it? It certainly has life; and there is absolutely no doubt what that life will develop into. It will not develop into a frog or a chimpanzee! Its life is not frog-life, or chimpanzee-life.

It must be human life; for only human life can develop into a human being.

Moreover, ladies and gentlemen, we know why that is. Your own medical research, if I have understood it correctly, has shown us that the zygote, once formed by fertilisation, contains all the information necessary for the development of a human life. No subsequent information will be added: the information is complete at conception.

'Yes,' the retort will be, 'but while it is a human life, it does not yet have developed personhood, and therefore, though it must be treated with respect, it cannot be given full human status.' But that raises another question: at what stage does human life attain fully developed personhood? At 28 weeks the fetus is not yet a fully developed human person—indeed, a newborn infant is not yet a fully developed human person. Nor will personhood be fully developed until many years have gone by, and life's experience has brought the person to full maturity.

How safe is it, then, to argue that the status of human life depends on the *development* of human personality? If this were true, we should have to ask: at what stage in the development of the human personhood a human life attains full status, such that intentionally to destroy it should be regarded as murder. At five years old? Or twenty-five? Or fifty? Moreover, at the age of seventy onwards, the ravages of time can begin to diminish the peak of personhood that was attained in mid-life. Does that mean that this, still viable but now diminished, human life may be eliminated with impunity, because in lacking full human personhood it lacks full human status?

A startling view on this topic is propounded by leading pro-abortionist, Mary Ann Warren. She suggests that the characteristics central to personhood are sentience, the capacity to feel emotions, the ability to reason, the capacity to communicate, self-awareness and the capacity to apply moral principles to one's own actions. Because a fetus does not have the capacity to do these things, she argues that 'fetuses are neither persons nor members of the moral community. Furthermore, neither a fetus's resemblance to a person, nor its potential for becoming a person, provides an adequate basis for the claim that it has a full and equal right to life.'[4] But why not?

One of her criteria for a full and equal right to life is the ability to reason and the capacity to apply moral principles to one's own actions. It seems clear to me, and I think, to you as well, that a newborn baby does not possess the ability to reason; and some years will pass before it has the capacity to apply moral principles to itself. According to these considerations, then, a baby of five years old does not have a full and equal right to life.

Perhaps Mary Ann Warren would not wish to extend her argument that far. But some philosophers would, and do. Peter Singer, for instance, states that the life of a newborn baby is of less value to it than the life of a pig.[5]

More convincing, to my mind at any rate, is the argument put forward by the theologian and ethicist, John Breck:

> the age-old debate over the time at which the fetus can be said to be human, and more specifically to be a personal being, is fundamentally misleading. It is based on the erroneous presupposition that the criteria for determining personhood are to be agreed upon by other people and then fulfilled by the fetus, whether those criteria include conception, implantation, quickening or birth ... *personhood is conferred by God* and not by physiological development, medical analysis or social convention.[6]

This, of course, is the standard biblical position, and the awareness of its implications is delightfully expressed in the poetry of the ancient Hebrew lyricist:

> For you [God] formed my inward parts; you knitted me together in my mother's womb. I praise you, because I am fearfully and wonderfully made. Wonderful are your

---

[4] 'On the Moral and Legal Status of Abortion', 139–40.
[5] See the quotation from Singer and discussion of it in Ch. 10.
[6] *The Sacred Gift of Life*, 149.

works, my soul knows it very well. My frame was not hidden from you, when I was being made in secret, intricately woven in the depths of the earth. Your eyes saw my unformed substance; in your book were written, every one of them, the days that were formed for me, when as yet there was none of them. (Ps 139:13–16)

Moreover, Christians, in common with people of some other faiths, hold that there is another dimension to human life that is apposite to this topic. That is that human life contains a non-material component. Sometimes it is called 'soul', and sometimes 'spirit'; but it is held to be an essential part of human life.[7] Admittedly, people of this persuasion disagree about the exact point in the development of the embryo and of the fetus, at which this spiritual element enters in. Some have believed that it occurs at the moment of birth, when the infant takes its first breath. Others have held that it takes place at the time of 'quickening', when the mother first feels the fetus move in her womb. These views, I understand, have largely been abandoned.

Still others hold that this 'ensoulment', as they call it, takes place at some indeterminate time, between the formation of the zygote, and the appearance of the primitive streak, that will later develop into the nervous system. But there seems to be no firm evidence to prove this timing, rather than others.

It is my contention, ladies and gentlemen, that from the very beginning new life has a non-material component. I speak as a Christian, and draw this conclusion in part from my belief in the incarnation of the Son of God, whose very conception as a human being was by the Holy Spirit (Luke 1:35). If, then, you ask me what ethics has to say, in the context of all the possibilities opened up by modern science, in connection with the transmission of life, I reply that our prime consideration must be the inviolability of human life from the very moment of its conception.

---

[7] Hindus and Buddhists will also insist that there is something spiritual and eternal in a human being right from the moment of conception, though they base their beliefs on very different premises.

The popular attitude that, if anything can be done it should be done, because the end justifies the means, is the shallow ethical view of act utilitarianism. Utilitarianism tells us that whether an act is good or evil is determined solely by whether that act does, or does not, produce a large good for the maximum number of people. If it does produce such good, then the act itself is by definition good; even though, by any objective standard, it was patently unethical. This theory seems to me, and not to me only, to be altogether false: good results do not justify unethical acts. I know that this conclusion has far-reaching implications: if the zygote is already alive, and its life is human life, and if human life (simply by virtue of being human life) is inviolable and sacred, then to damage or destroy it intentionally, is to be deprecated as profoundly unethical. I deliberately say 'intentionally', for I am well aware of the difficult decisions that medical doctors must take on occasions, when their effort to relieve intolerable pain indirectly—but not intentionally—involves the ending of a human life. But all will agree, that even in ethical dilemmas, care must be taken to avoid shallow ethical thinking.

To return for the moment, then, to the question of abortion: it is often argued that the decisive consideration must always be the rights of the pregnant woman, rather than the rights of the unborn child. Of course, it is widely agreed that if the woman's life is threatened by, say, an ectopic pregnancy, or some other potentially lethal development, then the woman's life must take precedence. But in the literature on this topic another, very different, argument is frequently urged, namely, that a woman has the right to do what she likes with her body: the fetus, so it is said, is part of her body, and therefore she owns it. She has complete rights over the fetus, and if for any reason she wishes to end the pregnancy, she has the full right to abort it.

But this reasoning is surely open to question. The fetus within her is not simply a part of her body, as her arm or even her heart and lungs are. It is a separate person, with a brain and heart of its own. And, being a separate person with its own body, it too has its rights. It is also questionable whether it is true to say that she owns the fetus. Indeed, for a woman to argue that she owns the fetus, and therefore can do what she likes with it, sounds too much like the kind of argument with which slavery was supported for centuries. After all, the essence of slavery was that it was right for one person to own another. Moral philosopher D. D. Raphael has reminded us that:

> A child 'belongs' to his parents, biological or adoptive, in the sense that they rather than anyone else have the right and the duty to nurture him, on the understanding that they will accept the duty. If they do not accept the duty, they lose the right to exclude others from the position of caring for the child and determining his future. Children are not the property of their parents. If I own a material object, perhaps one that is beautiful or rare, I am entitled to destroy it or to mar it by neglect or ill-use, however much other people may deplore my behaviour. This is not the position of parents in relation to their children. The religious doctrine that human life belongs to God may be questionable for its ban on suicide but not for its more general implication that no human life belongs to, is at the disposal of, another human being.[8]

I shall not need to point out to this audience the shallowness of another argument that is used in favour of abortion on demand. It claims that every child has a right to be wanted; therefore, no unwanted child should be allowed to come to term and be born. Put as a syllogism, this argument runs: Every child has a right to be wanted. Many children, however, are denied this right and are unwanted. Therefore, one should also deprive them of their right to life as well. To my ears, the logic sounds distinctly odd.

Ladies and gentlemen, thank you! I wish you every success in your ongoing research endeavours.

---

[8] *Moral Philosophy*, 145.

PROBLEMS AT THE END OF LIFE

We move now from issues that arise in relation to the beginning of life, to issues that arise when we consider life's end. Improvements in nutrition and advances in medical science mean that, in many countries, people live longer now than they did in times past. In addition, technology can often keep people artificially alive, who otherwise would die. This results in increased burdens, both on families as they have to care for elderly people longer and on the State as more resources get used up by an increasingly elderly population. The problems that these burdens raise have to be faced, especially by the relatives of the patients, and the doctors who are treating them. It is in that context that we discuss them.

A good death?

These burdens, then, have led in recent years to an ever-growing demand on the part of some people for the legalisation of euthanasia. To understand the problems that this raises, we must first consider the exact meaning of the word *euthanasia*. Literally translated, it simply means 'a good death', and in itself that sounds inoffensive. But, in fact, it is generally used to describe the *intentional killing* of people; either on the part of the doctors treating them or in the sense of giving them help to end their own lives. It is also sometimes described as 'mercy killing', since the alleged purpose of killing the patient is to relieve him or her of unnecessary and hopeless suffering. But, whatever the motive involved in euthanasia, it is important that we notice that it implies an act of intentional killing.

A further distinction must be made between voluntary euthanasia and involuntary euthanasia. Voluntary euthanasia is when the patient asks to be killed, or for help to terminate his or her own life. Involuntary euthanasia is when the patient is killed, without his or her consent, or without even being consulted.

What does ethics have to say, then, about this situation? Is euthanasia a duty that any merciful doctor must perform? Or is intentional killing of any patient, for whatever reason, a criminal offence?

Some argue that, just as we are prepared to use humane 'mercy-killing' on animals in pain; so we should be prepared to do the same for human beings who are suffering so intensely that to go on living is almost intolerable. One feels compassion also for the close relatives—often a wife or daughter, who can be utterly worn out by the necessity of tending for the sick day and night for weeks on end.

On the other hand, the ending of a human life is a very serious thing indeed. For anyone who believes that it is God who gives life, and that it is God's sole prerogative to end it, any intentional killing of a patient by anyone else must be wrong. But it is not only believers in God who see this danger. Many people, both in the medical profession and outside it, protest strongly against euthanasia, since it goes against all that they think medicine stands for. For instance, the Hippocratic oath for long centuries forbade the prescription of lethal drugs for assisted suicide.

Furthermore, many governments in civilised societies still refuse to legalise euthanasia; and their reason is the sheer difficulty in proving in any one case that the euthanasia was, as far as the patient was concerned, voluntary.

The slippery slope

Actual experience in countries that take a lenient view of euthanasia shows a clear danger of a 'slippery slope': a gradual descent from permitting euthanasia in cases where there is a clearly expressed and consistent desire for it on the part of the patient, to using it in cases where consent is not given. Such a slide towards involuntary euthanasia can readily occur in a hedonistic society, since the care of the elderly will increasingly get in the way of the pleasure of the young and middle-aged. In addition, an elderly patient may have money or property, which her relatives would like to have for themselves; so any means of hastening her death would be welcome to them. On the basis of the utilitarian principle of the maximum pleasure for the maximum number of people, there may well be, not only a temptation to pressurise the patient to agree to voluntary euthanasia, but also a temptation to pressurise doctors to use non-voluntary euthanasia to get rid of them. In any case, since the elderly are also a burden on the resources of the State, it is not hard to see how governments could connive at the practice.

Ethics will challenge our values here. It is a sad comment on society when the demand for pleasure on the part of some devalues the lives of others—particularly the lives of those to whom we owe our own life. In the ancient world at large, matricide and patricide were regarded as the most appalling crimes and sins. Moreover, one of the Ten Commandments is 'Honour your father and your mother' (Exod 20:12). Intuitionist ethics would point out that we have an evident duty to honour and protect at the end of their lives those who transmitted life to us, and nurtured and protected us while we were young.

The stress of decision

In any case, a patient's decision to accept euthanasia would almost always be taken at a time of great stress. The patient might well be in a state of clinical depression (not uncommon in terminal cases) and request euthanasia. By what criteria could doctors assess this request? A patient, if depressed, might come out of the depression, change her mind and wish to live longer. The difficulty with the statement, 'my life is no longer worth living,' is that it is highly subjective; and if it were allowed as a reason for euthanasia, why should it not be claimed in other situations? Think, for example, of a jilted teenager, who feels that life is intolerable; or a woman with post-natal depression.

Some people try to avoid the problem of making such decisions under stress by writing what is called a 'living will'. They give directions in advance to their physician. If, for example, they should have an incurable and irreversible condition, which is causing such pain and discomfort so that their life seems no longer worth living, the physician should apply euthanasia.

The state-directed T4 Euthanasia Programme, embarked upon by Nazi Germany just before the Second World War led to the murder of 70,000 people, including handicapped children and the mentally ill, in the two years it operated openly, and a total of as many as 200,000.

But even here there are real dangers. Firstly, such wills are sometimes made in complete ignorance of the medical conditions that may eventually ensue; and so interpretation of them by doctors and relatives may not be easy. Moreover, it is one thing to agree to euthanasia when one is reasonably healthy; it is another thing to desire it when one is ill. Experience often shows that when patients are in danger of losing life, the more they want to cling on to it; and they change their minds about euthanasia. The living will, therefore, provides no guarantee of avoiding the slippery slope. Indeed, following the terms of a living will may result in action being taken that is not in the interests of the patient at all.

For many people, the danger of a slide towards non-voluntary euthanasia carries with it sinister memories of the state-directed T4 Euthanasia Programme, embarked upon by Nazi Germany just before the Second World War. It led to the murder of 70,000 people, including handicapped children and the mentally ill, in the two years it operated openly, and a total of as many as 200,000 when the years of its covert phase up until the end of the war are added.[9] This horrific programme helped prepare the way for the attempted genocide of the Jewish race, and the elimination of many millions of others—Slavs, Poles, gypsies, and so on. After the war, the Declaration of Geneva reinforced the Hippocratic tradition and committed the medical profession to resist euthanasia with renewed vigour.

The management of pain

The idea that death is normally preceded by severe pain is a misconception; and so is not valid as an argument for euthanasia. Drugs have been developed that can control most pain and free most terminal patients from acute discomfort. In some countries there are hospices where such patients can receive palliative care and come to terms with death.

In this connection, there are two other considerations. The first is the so-called 'law of double effect'. This refers to cases of patients with a terminal illness, where a painkiller is used with the intention of making them comfortable. But, because of the intensity of the pain, the dosage has to be increased to such an extent that it may have the secondary effect of causing the death of the patient. The crucial point here is that the intention of the doctors is not to kill: it is to carry out their duty to alleviate the pain. This is, therefore, not euthanasia.[10]

The second consideration has to do with the new ethical problems, created by the development of sophisticated modern technology for artificially keeping patients alive, who, before the discovery of such techniques, would have died. The question is: has a doctor the duty to start such treatment when the outlook is hopeless? Or should he allow

---

[9] Michael Berenbaum, 'T4 Program'.
[10] Sadly, of course, there are from time to time malevolent doctors who abuse their position to administer lethal doses of painkiller, sometimes for financial gain.

nature to take its course? And again, when a doctor has used such a machine to keep someone artificially alive—but it is not doing anything more than keeping him or her breathing—is the doctor morally and legally free to switch it off, and let the patient die?

In Britain, for example, the Government Select Committee that argued against euthanasia, nevertheless supported the right of doctors to decide not to start (or, having started, to withdraw) artificial devices for maintaining life, when the case is hopeless.

Allowing a terminally ill patient to die, in cases when further medical intervention is clearly useless, is not euthanasia. There is no intention to kill. Sometimes the term *passive euthanasia* is used in this connection; but passive euthanasia is a contradiction in terms, since euthanasia always involves intention. It is also misleading to use this term, since its use can have the effect of slowly eroding the distinction between intentional killing, and allowing nature to take its course, in cases where further medical treatment is useless.

CHAPTER 13

EXERCISES IN ETHICS

Perceiving that there are ethical problems in a situation, which at first sight seemed straightforward, often goes a long way towards deciding what the answer to the problems should be. At other times the ethical problem will be clear enough. The main question will be: what ought we to do in this situation, and how would we justify our decision?

PUTTING ETHICS INTO PRACTICE

Up to this point in our discussion we have thought much about ethical principles from a theoretical point of view. Now in this chapter we ask ourselves practical questions such as are likely to arise in various areas of day-to-day living. As we think through what answers ought to be given, and discuss them in class or other group settings, we shall have opportunity to apply the theoretical principles we have encountered.

Sometimes the main point of the discussion will be to discern what ethical problem or problems are raised in a complex situation. Perceiving that there are ethical problems in a situation, which at first sight seemed straightforward, often goes a long way towards deciding what the answer to the problems should be. At other times the ethical problem will be clear enough. The main question will be: what ought we to do in this situation, and how would we justify our decision?

Some of the following situations may seem merely theoretical, because so far in life we have never met them; but discussing them now will help us to come to responsible decisions when later on in life we encounter them.

SPORT

A professional foul

Sometimes the only way to stop an opponent scoring a goal would be deliberately to foul him. This is called a 'professional foul'.

    (*a*) Would you commit a professional foul?
        i. if not, why not?
        ii. if yes, how would you justify it?

(b) Would you argue that it is better to foul, incur a penalty and take the risk that the player who took the penalty kick might miss, than let the other side score a certain goal, if not fouled? If you would use that argument, then answer the next question.

(c) You owe a large sum of money. You cannot pay. If you don't pay you will certainly be sent to prison. But you work for a bank. You have the opportunity to steal a lot of money that would cover your debt. If you are caught, you will be sent to prison. But you may not be caught! And therefore you take the risk and steal the money. What is the difference between (b) and (c)?

Honesty in playing a game

In a famous international football match the man who scored the winning goal and won the cup for his national team had in the process handled the ball without being seen by the referee. Would you argue:

(a) that, ethically speaking, he ought to have pointed out his fault to the referee? Or,

(b) that, if you can commit an offence and get away with it without being seen, it is ethically OK? Or,

(c) that so long as you win the game, it does not matter whether you keep the rules or not? Or,

(d) that everybody breaks the rules, so why shouldn't I? Or,

(e) that you haven't really *won* the game, if you've cheated?

Deliberate match-fixing

Sometimes a goalkeeper is in a position where he can make sure his team unexpectedly loses a match that everybody beforehand thought it was going to win. He can pretend to be doing his utmost to save a goal, while in actual fact he deliberately fumbles the ball and lets it into the net. When this happens people suspect that the goalkeeper has been bribed by a betting-syndicate. Consider:

(a) Why would a betting-syndicate do this? Is it wrong?

(b) The betting-syndicate did not compel anyone to bet on the outcome of the match; but their business depends on the betters losing. Why shouldn't they do their best to ensure that the betters lose?

(c) Why blame the goalkeeper? What is wrong with his making a bit of money on the side? It was only a game, wasn't it?

(d) Or do you think that the betting-syndicate should be fined a very large sum of money and the goalkeeper banned for life from playing football? If so, why?

Drug-taking by athletes

Some athletes who have tested positive for drugs at the Olympics have been subsequently stripped of their medals.

(a) Is there anything ethically wrong in an athlete taking an artificial substance to help himself or herself win a medal? If so, what?

(b) An athlete argues that many people take drugs for their own pleasure, and he just took them for the pleasure of winning a medal. What would you say to his argument?

(c) What ethical right has the Olympic committee to interfere with people's personal lives and forbid them to take drugs if they want to?

The commercialisation of sport: merchandising

In many countries famous football teams sell copies of their shirts to the public. They charge very high prices for them. These shirts are very popular with children. The football clubs deliberately change their style of shirt twice a year, with the result that children put pressure on their parents to buy them the latest shirt, even though it is often the case that the parents cannot really afford it. But if a child goes to school with an outdated shirt, the other children will tease and mock him. Is this:

(a) a sound, shrewd and necessary way of making money on the part of the clubs, in order to be able to buy expensive players and entertain the public better? Or,

(b) a cynical and unethical use of children to pressurise parents to buy shirts they cannot really afford, in order to make excessive profits for the clubs?

Argue the pros and cons for both views.

The commercialisation of sport: big business

In days gone by, the point of sport was that it was a game. People liked to win, of course; but winning was not the important thing: the game, and the sheer interest of it, were the chief things. In the original Olympic games, the winner's prize was simply a laurel wreath. Commercialisation of sport has made significant changes: it has turned sport into a money-making business. What effects has this had? Do any of them raise ethical questions? Adjudicate between the following views:

(a) It has greatly increased the skill and standard of play. It thus gives greater pleasure to the fans. It is therefore good.
(b) When so much money is at stake the profit motive has led to a deterioration in the ethical behaviour of the players on the field. It is therefore bad.
(c) It is ethically wrong to pay a star footballer far more in a week than a nurse earns in a year.
(d) It is the public who ultimately pays the salaries of star footballers, and the public has a right to pay more for what it enjoys more. Ethics doesn't come into it.

ADVERTISING

Preliminary questions

What is, or should be, the proper purpose of advertising?

(a) to let people know that a product exists that will definitely benefit them?
(b) to describe the qualities of the product?
(c) to saturate people's minds with the brand name of a product so that they automatically think of a product under this

name? For example, 'Kodak' was originally the brand name of a certain make of camera. In many countries 'Kodak' became the actual word for 'camera'.
(d) to exert psychological pressure on people to buy the product?
(e) to make people feel they need the product, when in fact they don't really need it at all?
(f) to maintain a factory and the jobs of the employees, and the profits of the shareholders?

An ethical dilemma

Science has shown beyond all doubt that smoking is a major cause of lung cancer. Is it ethical for cigarette manufacturers to advertise their products? The ethical dilemma is that if they fail to sell their cigarettes, thousands of their employees will lose their jobs. On the other hand, if people buy their cigarettes and smoke them, thousands of them will die prematurely of lung cancer. In the light of this, answer the following questions, and give your reasons:

(a) Would you ban all cigarette advertising and thus save many people's lives? Or allow cigarette advertising and save many people's jobs?
(b) Nicotine is an addictive drug. If manufacturers increase the level of nicotine in their cigarettes, they will get more people hooked on smoking and so increase their sales. Would there be anything ethically wrong in their doing so?
(c) Have advertisers a duty to tell the *whole* truth? For instance, it is in the commercial interests of cigarette manufacturers to get people addicted to smoking at the earliest age possible. So they publish large advertisements showing attractive film stars smoking the manufacturer's brand cigarettes, thus suggesting to young people that to start smoking is a grown-up and glamorous thing to do.
  i. Have they a duty to tell the young people the whole truth that smoking may also kill them prematurely? Or may they rightly leave the young people to find that out for themselves later on in life?
  ii. Should the government make it illegal to place cigarette

advertisements near schools? Or would that be a denial of human freedom?

Advertising techniques

(a) An advertisement for a new car consists of a picture of the car with a very attractive, scantily dressed, woman sitting on the bonnet. At the top of the picture in large writing it says: 'With this car you could be the envy of everyone in the neighbourhood.' The advertisement is, of course, aimed at you as well as at the general public.
   i. What is it in you that the advertisement is designed to appeal to? And what psychological devices is it using to make you feel you want to buy the car?
   ii. Is this an ethically proper way to treat you as a person?
   iii. How relevant is the advertisement to the quality of the car itself?

(b) Many manufacturers and shopkeepers entice people to buy, say, furniture by advertising: 'Buy now, pay later! Minimal deposit required. First year interest free.' This means that people can get immediate possession of the furniture, without waiting for a long time to save up the money to buy it with. But then, after the first year they find that they have to pay not only a regular instalment but also a very high interest rate. As a result many people run into serious debt. If they cannot pay, the shopkeeper will take the furniture back, even though the customer has already paid a large amount for it. In cases like this would you:
   i. blame the customer only, on the ground that he or she should have had more sense?
   ii. blame the shopkeeper as well for enticing people to buy things they could not afford?

(c) Too much fat in food is nowadays thought to contribute to disease of the arteries and heart. Manufacturers, therefore, know that customers will prefer food with less fat in it. A label on a particular packet of food simply announces: 'This product contains 5% less fat.' Is the manufacturer being totally honest? What additional information would the label need to give in order to let the customer decide whether the product was safe to eat?

PROFESSIONAL ETHICS

Let's consider several scenarios.

An exam. Harriet is doing an important university entrance examination in mathematics and gets stuck with a question. She realises that she can just see the solution already done by Oliver sitting next to her. Harriet copies Oliver's solution, gets through the examination and is accepted by the university.

Another girl, Maria, is just as clever as Harriet, but she too gets stuck with the same question. She is sitting on the other side of Oliver. She too could see Oliver's solution if she tried to. But she feels it would be cheating, and therefore unethical. She refuses to try, and in consequence fails the examination.

(a) Would you say that Harriet has shown initiative, knows how to get on in the world, and deserves to succeed?
(b) Would you think that Maria is a fool for not doing what Harriet did?
(c) Would you hold that everyone has a right to cheat a little bit, if his or her career is at stake?
(d) How would you describe the ethical principle that Maria has follows: Kantianism? Ethical Egoism? Utilitarianism?
(e) What effect would it have on the value of a university degree, if every student cheated like Harriet?
(f) Would you trust a surgeon to operate on you if you knew he had cheated his way through all his examinations?

A resumé. Richard is filling in a CV as an applicant for a job. Quite rightly he wishes to put his abilities, qualifications and experience in the best possible light. But he has exaggerated some things, and included others that strictly speaking are not altogether true. He shows you what he has written and asks what you think. What practical advice would you give him? What ethical principles would you insist on?

A controlled study. Vera, a scientist, is hired by a drug firm to set up and supervise an experiment to test a new drug. The aim is to discover whether the new drug will arrest the progress of cancer. One hundred cancer patients are chosen for the test. Some of the patients are given the drug, the rest are given a placebo. Early on, Vera notices that the drug has significant beneficial effects, but it is not yet sufficiently tested to qualify for government recognition. In order to get that approval, the test must be completed, but Vera feels that she ought immediately to give the drug to all the other patients to arrest the cancer and prolong their lives. However, if she does so, the trial will be invalidated. What is the right thing for Vera to do?

A conference paper. A representative of a drug firm approaches a scientist working in a certain area of medicine. He asks the scientist: 'Would you like to present a paper in your subject at a prestigious international conference in your field? We would give you a handsome honorarium, pay your first-class fare and all hotel expenses, and, incidentally, you would not even need to write the paper, our scientists would write it for you.' Would you accept the offer, or would you suspect that the motives of the drug firm were unethical? If so, in what way might they be unethical?

Scientific research. The progress of science depends on the honesty of scientists in the recording of their data and the accuracy of the results they publish. At the same time, a young scientist is under pressure from his university to get results. And, of course, his desire to become famous in his field urges him, likewise, to get results. What ethical dangers lie in this situation, both for himself and for the reputation of science?

Trade secrets. Joyce is a secretary to the director of a firm engaged in research on developing an altogether new kind of car engine. She has access to a secret file containing the specification of the prototype. Her boyfriend works for a rival firm. Joyce loves him very much and hopes soon to marry him, as she is getting older. He puts pressure on Joyce to get him a copy of the file, which she could easily do without anyone knowing that it was she who had done it. He threatens her that, if she does not do it, he will break off his friendship. On what grounds should Joyce make her decision?

Disease control. Suppose you work with animals on a farm, and you realise that one of the cows has a serious infectious disease. You inform the farm manager, who tells you to kill and bury the animal without telling anyone. However, you know that the animal was bought in a certain market just a few days before, and you realise that, if you do not tell the authorities, there could be a serious outbreak of disease in many places. On the other hand, if you do tell the authorities, the farm on which you work will be isolated, and many animals may have to be destroyed. In addition, your relationship with the manager might be difficult, to say the least. What ethical issues are involved here? What would you do?

COMMERCIAL ETHICS

Has morality anything to do with business? If so, what? Does it matter by what methods it makes its profits, as long as it provides jobs for many people? Is it responsible to serve the best interests of the public?

Gifts, tips and bribes. What is the difference between these three things?

(a) In many countries the waiters and porters in a big hotel receive so many voluntary tips from the guests for having given them good service that this is regarded as part of their wages. Their employers, therefore, pay them only a small wage; and yet people compete with each other to be employed by the hotel.

(b) In some countries police officers are paid such a small wage that in order to make a living they stop cars on the road, and threaten to charge the drivers with an offence, unless they give them a bribe.

(c) In some countries government officials, although they receive a wage, obstruct applications by the public for things such as passports, or for custom's clearance, unless they are given a bribe.

(d) In some countries, when the government invites tenders from large civil engineering companies to build, say, a dam, one of the government officials will choose the company that is prepared to pay him personally a very large bribe.

Consider the four situations above. Are they all the same? Which, if any, of them is justified?

Sales perks. You are the sub-manager of a big firm. You meet a wealthy foreign businessman who invites you to spend a holiday with him and his family yachting in the South Pacific, all expenses paid. Would you accept his hospitality? Or, suspecting his motives, would you decline?

Vested interest. An application arrives with a city council for planning permission for a large shopping development in an area that has up until now been restricted to housing. Council member Felix makes a long speech in favour of granting planning permission, and votes in favour of the motion, which is then passed. But at the time Felix does not declare that he himself is a shareholder in the company doing the developing. Would you wish to raise any ethical questions about this situation, and if so, what are they, and on what grounds would you raise them? Suppose Felix argues that he is a citizen, like anyone else, and has a right to look after his own interests. How would you respond to his argument?

Outright bribery. You are the head of a company that makes aircraft. You are responsible for getting enough sales to maintain a work force of ten thousand. You are negotiating with an airline to secure an order for fifty jet airliners. The representative of the airline says that he can guarantee the order, if you make it worth his while. Would you refuse to bribe him? Or would you argue that the employment of ten thousand people is at stake; and so the bribe is legitimate? What are the ethical issues involved?

Company property. You are the foreman in a factory, and you have noticed that from time to time various tools are going missing. You report it to the manager. He tells you to find out who is taking them. Eventually you detect who is doing it. But then you discover that his wife is sick and needs expensive medicines, and he is hard up for cash. You feel sorry for him. If you report him, he loses his job. If you don't report him, you might be suspected of conniving with him, and you might lose your job. You believe, however, that stealing tools is wrong. What would you do?

(a) Report him, and so make sure you keep your job?
(b) Organise a collection among his fellow workers in the factory, to help him pay for his wife's medicines?
(c) Persuade the man to admit what he has done?
(d) Explain the situation to the manager and intercede with him to have mercy and allow the man to pay back the value of the tools, in small instalments?

What would virtue ethics and Christian ethics tell you to do?

Private property. You have inherited a large house from your grandmother, and you wish to sell it. You advertise all its good points and a prospective buyer comes to view it and likes it very much. However, the ground on which the house is built is subject to subsidence, and there is dry rot in the roof. Moreover there is a wood-pulp factory in the vicinity that, when the wind is in the wrong direction, fills the house with an objectionable odour. You know that if you point out these faults to the prospective buyer you will lose the sale. What should you do?

(a) Are you ethically obliged to tell the buyer these faults? Or is it the buyer's responsibility to find them out for himself?
(b) If you were the buyer, what would you like the owner to do? Is that a guide to what you as the seller ought to do?

Competition. A supermarket, backed by a large company, opens on the edge of the town, and in order to gain business sells some products at very low prices—so-called 'loss leaders'. The small shops in the town cannot compete with these prices. As a result they are forced out of business. The supermarket then raises its prices. Is this kind of competition ethical? If not, why not?

CRIME AND PUNISHMENT

In order to help us think about this topic, let's listen in as three students discuss their views on crime and punishment. Ramesh is all for the reformation of offenders: 'Punishment is always wrong,' he says. 'If prison is just for punishing offenders, they will re-offend when you let them go. What you must do is have plenty of trained counsellors, psychological help and rehabilitation facilities, so that offenders receive the necessary therapy to enable them to fit back in to normal society without re-offending. That is the only way to deal with crime successfully.'

'Yes, but surely there is a role for real punishment,' says Lee. 'Isn't there a clear need to have some kind of deterrent to prevent the offender from re-offending, and to stop others from committing the same offence? After all, Ramesh, you are in danger of painting a picture of rehabilitation centres that makes going to them sound like going to school or university to get a good training! If that is what they are for, then everybody would want to go! No, your view is totally inadequate: there must be a real element of punishment to deter people. And that means making the punishment really severe so that it will act as a deterrent. Can't you see that the harder the punishment is, the less likely people are to want to offend? Be really hard on offenders, and you will soon solve the problem of the overcrowding of our prisons, is what I say!'

'Hold on,' interjects Juliana. 'Both of you are forgetting two very important things. Sure, we need to deter people from committing crimes, and to reform them when they do so that they don't commit any more crimes when they are let out of prison. But these are only secondary reasons for imprisoning and punishing people. The basic and only ethical reason for punishing people in the first place must be that they *deserve* to be punished, and therefore must be punished whether it deters them from committing further crimes, or not, and whether or not it reforms them. Let's hope it does both. But if a person does not *deserve* to be punished in the first place, you've no right to imprison or punish him in order either to reform him or to deter him.

'Moreover, your view, Ramesh, is very dangerous. You say punishment is always wrong, and that the reason for imprisoning people is to give them the necessary therapy to make them fit better in normal society when they are released. But that's just what tyrants have often said. If somebody's political views didn't please the tyrant, he did not always charge them with having committed a crime, for perhaps they had not *done* anything wrong, they had only *thought* the wrong things and held the wrong ideas. No, the tyrant said they were mentally sick and needed "therapy". So he had them imprisoned in a psychiatric "hospital", and "treated" until they were "cured". No one, of course, could say in advance how long it would take to "cure" them; and, anyway, who was to say when these "patients" were cured and normal again? It wasn't a question of making them stay in this "hospital" as long as they *deserved* to be there: they were forced to stay until they were "cured", however long that was.

'I know, Ramesh, that punishing someone because he deserves it sounds barbarous to you. But it is safer and kinder than your idea. If a man is punished because he deserves to be punished then at least the severity of his punishment and the length of his stay in prison must be commensurate with the seriousness of his crime, no more and no less; and when he has served his sentence, he must be let out whether he is reformed or not. Of course, if he is in prison because he deserves to be there, for, say, six years, then by all means use the time and every medical, educational and spiritual device you can to help him change his way of life, and deter him from committing more crime. But you may only do that, if he has *deserved* to be in prison to start with.'

'Yes, Juliana,' interjects Lee, 'I agree with you. It's not enough to try to reform people in prison. They must be punished in order to deter them from offending again. That's what I said. Why do you make out that I have forgotten something important?'

'Because', replies Juliana, 'you forgot to say that you mustn't use somebody's punishment as a deterrence *unless* that somebody has deserved the punishment in the first place. The severity of the punishment must depend on how much punishment the crime deserved. If you forget the question of *desert*, and think only of using the punishment as a deterrence, then the greater the punishment, the greater the deterrent effect. Then why not put people in solitary confinement for stealing sausages, or imprison them for life for driving carelessly? Indeed, why wait until people *deserve* to be punished? Why not punish them in advance in order to deter them from ever committing a crime?'

But at that Ramesh and Lee both protest: 'Now you're carrying things to an extreme!'

ENVIRONMENTAL ETHICS

Industrialisation. As a result of the Industrial Revolution some countries have become wealthy. However, the Industrial Revolution had a devastating effect on the environment—the destruction of huge areas of forest, pollution of ground, rivers and atmosphere, etc. In recent years, these same industrialised nations have put in place legislation to regulate and reduce the destruction of the environment. They also put pressure on the developing countries to impose similar restrictions on their infant industries. Those developing nations, however, point out that the industrialised nations are thereby effectively denying them the right to enrich themselves by following the methods that those same industrialised nations used to get their wealth in the first place.

What is your response to this? Is it fair? It is, of course, the fact that, if developing countries copy the methods by which the industrialised nations built up their economies, they will do a lot of environmental damage. In your opinion, what are the ethical issues raised by this? How ought the technologically advanced nations to help the less advanced nations?

Natural resources. Large pharmaceutical companies in the industrialised world have begun to realise the importance of traditional medicine. Some of these firms are now using their wealth to strip the rain forests of suitable plants to get the raw material for the medicines they hope to develop and sell in order to make huge profits. The indigenous population, however, not only see little or none of this money, they lose the source of their own meagre revenues. Is this fair? What should be done about it?

Loss of habitat. Is the destruction of animal habitats ever ethically justified? Give your reasons.

Livestock enhancement. Pig farmers are naturally interested in producing pigs of the best possible quality and weight. They have found that injecting the pigs with antibiotics, when it is not necessary for curing the pigs of any diseases, nevertheless helps them put on weight. But this means that the people who eat the meat are in danger of absorbing high levels of antibiotic residues, and reducing their own resistance to disease. How would you adjudicate the ethics of this situation?

Space exploration. The objection has been raised: 'It is unethical to spend billions on space research, when millions of people on earth are dying of hunger.' In this context, discuss the pros and cons of space research.

Animal fur. Animal rights activists in some countries have been known to insult women in the streets for wearing animal-fur coats. Discuss the ethical issues raised.

Climate change. There is mounting evidence that exhaust gases from cars and aircraft contribute to global warming. Others argue that, whereas this may be so, it is merely a consequence of the evolutionary process that nature has always used, and in which humans, as part of nature, are now involved. It therefore should not, and cannot be stopped. Is this true, or do humans have a moral responsibility towards the biosphere? If so, what is that moral responsibility, in your opinion?

Mass starvation. Every few years a situation arises in which thousands of people, perhaps a million or more, in a given country are about to die of hunger because of a nationwide famine brought about partly by natural causes like drought or flooding, partly by destructive wars, and partly because earlier relief funds were not used for building up the nation's infrastructures. What moral duty have the other nations to such a country in these circumstances?

CHAPTER 14

BEYOND ETHICS

Ethics, being a normative discipline, aims to tell us what we ought to do, what is right and what is wrong, and why what is right, is right, and why what is wrong, is wrong. But there are two, more fundamental, problems: why do we do wrong in the first place? And, secondly, what can be done to put us right, so that we don't continue doing wrong?

ETHICS REVEALS THE PROBLEMS

Compared with the enormous amount of ethical thinking that has gone on in the course of the centuries, and the vast proliferation of the resultant literature, our study of ethics has been all too brief. What we have attempted to do, however, is to sketch in some of the most famous and influential theories, and particularly the major theories current in the modern world; and then to point out where more ethical thinking still needs to be done.

But long before any of us has reached the end of thinking about ethics—if we ever do—we shall have discovered, what perhaps we have already surmised, that ethics by itself is not enough to solve our major ethical problems. Ethics, being a normative discipline, aims to tell us what we ought to do, what is right and what is wrong, and why what is right, is right, and why what is wrong, is wrong. But there are two, more fundamental, problems: why do we do wrong in the first place? And, secondly, what can be done to put us right, so that we don't continue doing wrong?

SOCRATES' ANSWERS

Socrates had not been studying moral philosophy long before he found himself asking the first question: why do people do wrong? He had early come to the conclusion that, when we do wrong, we actually injure our own souls more than we injure the person we have wronged. But what man in his right mind, he asked, would do what was wrong if he really knew it would injure himself? Socrates concluded, therefore, that it was ignorance that led a man to do wrong, ignorance, that is, of what wrongdoing really is, and of what injury it does to himself. No one, he argued, knowingly and willingly does wrong.

But then Socrates had to answer the second question: what can, and must be, done to put us right? His answer followed from his diagnosis: if ignorance of the truth was the reason why we do wrong, the way to put us right was to get us to search for the truth. We should then come to know what justice is, and courage and holiness and all the other virtues. We should also come to see the damage we do to our own souls when we do wrong; and once we knew all that, we should cease doing wrong and harming ourselves and others.

ARISTOTLE'S VIEW

Aristotle disagreed with Socrates.[1] He considered that Socrates' view contradicted the observed facts: people do indeed do wrong, knowing it to be wrong. There is, he maintained, in spite of Socrates' denial, such a thing as lack of self-control: a man who knows that something is wrong, can nevertheless through lack of self-control go and do it.

He distinguished, of course, between lack of self-control and self-indulgence. A self-indulgent man, that is, a man who rejects any moral restraint, knows that certain acts are generally considered wrong; but he goes ahead and does them deliberately. He doesn't care whether they are right or wrong: he is determined to do what he wants to do. This is unrestrained evil.

It is different with a man who lacks self-control. He knows what is right and what is wrong, and wants to do what is right, but loses his self-control and does what is wrong, in spite of knowing it is wrong. How does this happen? Such a man, Aristotle observed, does not suddenly change his mind and *think* that he now *ought* to do what before he thought was wrong. Why, then, does he do it? Aristotle analysed the problem and came up with a number of explanations. Here are two of them.

Two of Aristotle's explanations for deliberate wrongdoing

Explanation 1
It is possible for a person in one sense to have knowledge, and yet in another sense not to have it.[2] As illustrations of this point Aristotle cites the condition of people asleep, mad or drunk. It is easy to see the point

---

[1] See his *Nicomachean Ethics*, VII.2.1 ff.
[2] *Nicomachean Ethics*, VII.3.7

of the analogy. A man knows that it is wrong to pick a quarrel with somebody, or smash up the furniture or throw his beer mug through a glass window. But when he gets drunk, his knowledge does him no good whatever. Aristotle suggests, therefore, that when people are under the influence of passions such as outbursts of anger, or of sexual passion, they are like people asleep, or mad or drunk. In a certain sense they have a knowledge of right and wrong, but that knowledge has no controlling effect as long as the passion lasts.

It is no argument to the contrary, says Aristotle, that people who are misbehaving as a result of lack of self-control, can mouth ethical terms and speak as if they had genuine moral knowledge. Drunk men can quote phrases from Empedocles, he says, or cite scientific proofs. It's like those who have just begun to learn a science. They can 'string together its phrases, but do not yet know it; for it has to become part of themselves, and that takes time; so that we must suppose that the use of language by men in a state of loss of self-control means no more than its utterance by actors on the stage.'[3]

Explanation 2

The second explanation is concerned with *the different effect on people's behaviour of knowledge of a universal principle on the one hand, and of perception of immediate particular facts on the other.* This has to do, not so much, or, at least, not alone, with our internal powers of self-control, but with our perception of the reality of external things. Let's take an easy illustration.

It is a scientifically demonstrated, universal, fact that all hard drugs eventually injure the brain, which we can render as a syllogism:

Major premise: All hard drugs eventually injure the brain and should not be taken.
Minor premise: This is a hard drug.
Conclusion: This drug should not be taken.

Those facts ought to lead to that conclusion. But suppose a girl who knows the objective universal principle, that all hard drugs eventually injure the brain and should not be taken, is invited to a party. She is there offered an actual hard drug. She has it pointed out to her that all

---

[3] *Nicomachean Ethics*, VII.3.8.

the people at the party are on hard drugs, and 'look how happy they are!' Now she is faced, not with a (to her) remote universal principle, 'all hard drugs injure the brain and should not be taken', but with an immediate perception of a particular situation; an apparently marvellously happy party. Basing her judgment on this immediate perception, she now thinks:

1. *All hard drugs make you feel wonderful.*
2. *This is a hard drug . . .*

And at this point desire for feeling wonderful takes over. The remote universal scientific principle is pushed into the back of her mind, and she takes the drug with all its potential danger.

In the same way, Aristotle argues, we can know universal moral principles, and yet in a particular situation be moved to act by more immediate, but fallacious, arguments and appearances that appeal to our feelings and appetites.

The root cause and the cure of wrong behaviour

We have not the space here to discuss all the details of Aristotle's extensive analysis of how it is that people do wrong in spite of knowing what is right; we must rather ask what, according to him, the original and root cause of human bad behaviour is, and then what proposals he makes for its cure.

As to the root cause, he seems to think that it goes back to humankind's primitive state. In the course of describing the various forms of moral delinquency, he mentions that there are in the remote (to the Greeks of that time) parts of the world human beings who are completely brutish and behave no better than animals. According to some Greeks, this is how humankind began, and how human nature was, and is, in its raw state. Behaviour improved as people gradually learned to live in cities and to submit themselves to laws and conventions necessary in city life. Bad, and near brutish, behaviour that could still be met with even in cities, was a hangover from—or a return to—the human race's primitive condition.

It was perhaps natural for Greeks to think like this. They had witnessed in their day the growth of city-states and the flowering of brilliant cultures that often graced those cities. They could certainly feel proud of the progress that had been achieved. But what would they now say two and a half millennia later, if they could see the widespread crime and moral corruption in our most modern cities, and that in spite of our modern education and 'civilisation'? Education, by itself, obviously does not eradicate evil behaviour.

What, then, was Aristotle's hope for solving the problem of the moral weakness common to us all? It was simply the moral training of children, and then the rigorous self-discipline of adults. Like archers aiming at the bull's-eye, people must practise aiming at the virtuous 'mean', and not err in the direction of either of the attendant vices at each extreme. The way to become virtuous is simply by training oneself to do virtuous acts. In other words, in the end all that ethics can say is: do the best you can.

But Aristotle was under no illusion as to the difficulty of his proposed solution. He poignantly remarks:

> it is possible to fail in many ways (for evil belongs to the class of the unlimited... and good to that of the limited) while to succeed is possible only in one way (for which reason also one is easy and the other difficult—to miss the mark is easy, to hit it difficult)... For men are good in but one way, but bad in many.[4]

This, then, is the verdict of one of the greatest Greek philosophical ethicists in the ancient world. Now let us put alongside of that the confession of one of the greatest religious moralists of all time.

THE CONFESSION OF THE APOSTLE PAUL

Saul of Tarsus, who later became the Christian apostle, Paul, was brought up in the strictest of Jewish religious traditions. For him ethics was a matter of dutifully keeping God's law. As a young man therefore he made a rigorous conscientious and sustained attempt to keep all the rules and regulations of the whole Old Testament, in addition to the Ten Commandments. Looking back in later life, he tells us that there was a time when he genuinely thought that he had

---

[4] *Nicomachean Ethics*, II.6.14.

succeeded in keeping the law to the point where he was, if not faultless, 'as to righteousness under the law, blameless' (Phil 3:6). Through the practical experience of life he eventually came to see things very differently, and in a detailed confession that has since become famous he has described exactly how that came about, and the moral and spiritual struggle that ensued. Here is that confession, which we quote in full so that we can sympathetically enter in to the inner struggle through which the writer had passed:

> What then shall we say? That the law is sin? By no means! Yet if it had not been for the law, I would not have known sin. For I would not have known what it is to covet if the law had not said, 'You shall not covet.' But sin, seizing an opportunity through the commandment, produced in me all kinds of covetousness. For apart from the law, sin lies dead. I was once alive apart from the law, but when the commandment came, sin came alive and I died. The very commandment that promised life proved to be death to me. For sin, seizing an opportunity through the commandment, deceived me and through it killed me. So the law is holy, and the commandment is holy and righteous and good....
>
> For we know that the law is spiritual, but I am of the flesh, sold under sin. For I do not understand my own actions. For I do not do what I want, but I do the very thing I hate. Now if I do what I do not want, I agree with the law, that it is good. So now it is no longer I who do it, but sin that dwells within me. For I know that nothing good dwells in me, that is, in my flesh. For I have the desire to do what is right, but not the ability to carry it out. For I do not do the good I want, but the evil I do not want is what I keep on doing. Now if I do what I do not want, it is no longer I who do it, but sin that dwells in me.
>
> So I find it to be a law that when I want to do right, evil lies close at hand. For I delight in the law of God, in my inner being, but I see in my members another law waging war against the law of my mind and making me captive to the law of sin that dwells in my members. Wretched man that I am! Who will deliver me from this body of death? (Rom 7:7-12, 14-24)

Paul writes here with all the fervour and feeling of an oriental, but with an unusual honesty that is prepared to disclose his inner feelings and his ethical turmoil. We can discern four elements in his experience:

1. He came to realise that the law is spiritual.
2. He found that awareness of the demand of the law made things worse, not better.
3. He found his inner resources inadequate to overcome his weakness.
4. He came to feel like a captive in his own castle.

Let's look at each of these briefly in turn.

The law is spiritual

It was not enough that his outward behaviour conformed to the letter of the law. He found it was not enough not to steal, lie, or commit adultery, to honour his parents, and refrain from idolatry. He discovered that the law is spiritual and is meant to control not our outward acts merely, but our inner desires, motives and thoughts. The particular commandment that 'killed' him, as he put it (v. 11), was the one that addressed a person's inner motives and dispositions: 'You shall not covet.' Try as he might, he found he could not stop himself coveting.

Let's take another example. A man is filled with jealousy and hatred for a rival. He could readily injure or even murder him. The only reason he doesn't is that he lacks the opportunity and is afraid of the consequences. Now it is certainly good that he is thus restrained from injuring his rival. But we have to ask what he would do if like an ancient emperor, or a modern dictator, he could do what he liked with impunity. In this case the inner passion, secretly entertained, is virtually as bad as the act committed.

The demand of the law made things worse, not better

Religious though he was, when this particular commandment convicted him that he was not the perfect saint he had until that point imagined he was, it stirred up in him a kind of rebellion that made him do all the more what the law forbade (7:7–8). It was not that he now felt that the law was unreasonable or bad (7:10–13). But the law by itself could not save him from his moral weakness; on the contrary, it concentrated his attention upon it and made it worse.

Inner resources inadequate to overcome weakness

In his struggle he summoned intellect to help him. 'With my mind', he says, 'I serve the law of God' (7:25 own trans.). It was, he felt, the only rational way to behave. But he adds: 'I see in my members another law waging war against the law of my mind and making me captive to the law of sin that dwells in my members' (7:23). It was the same with his emotions and his will. 'I delight in the law of God in my inner being,' he says; for he saw it as a delightful way to live, if only he could keep the law of God. What is more he could honestly say 'the willing is present with me, (v. 18b, literally translated). But intellect, emotions, and will together, he found, were unequal to the task of overcoming his moral weakness.

A captive in his own castle

Listen again to what Paul says,

> I do not do what I want, but I do the very thing I hate. . . . I have the desire to do what is right, but not the ability to carry it out. For I do not do the good I want, but the evil I do not want is what I keep on doing. . . . Wretched man that I am! Who will deliver me from this body of death? (7:15, 18–19, 24)

We find, then, that both the Greek philosopher Aristotle and the Hebrew religionist Paul confess, each in his own way, the limitations of ethics. Ethics can show us what is wrong and tell us to avoid it. Ethics can point us in the direction of what is right, and urge us to aim at it. But when experience shows us that we constantly fall short of true ethical standards, ethics itself can give us no help to attain those standards other than the repeated advice: try again! And the higher the standard set and aimed at, the greater will be the internal sense of coming short, and of frustration. The person who is perfectly content with the standard he or she has attained is suffering either from a defective moral conscience or else from a severe form of Pharisaism.

Paul's honest confession of his failure is famous; but if it had been his last word on the topic, we might never have heard of that confession or of him either. Elsewhere, however, in his writings he tells us that he eventually found a solution to his problem, which he describes in terms of putting on 'the new self, which is being renewed in knowledge' (Col 3:10). However, before we consider what this might mean, we should look at a similar insight from a very different source.

A MARXIST INSIGHT

No economic, political, social and ethical theory was ever worked out so rigorously and in such detail, or applied with such thoroughness to every facet of life, including art, music and literature, as was Marxism. But as late as 1961 the Communist Party confessed:

> The moulding of the new man is a long and complicated process. ... Communist education presupposes the emancipation of the mind from the religious prejudices and superstitions that still prevent some Soviet people from displaying their creative ability to the full. A more effective system of scientific atheist propaganda is needed, one that will embrace all sections and groups of the population, and will prevent the dissemination of religious views, especially among children and adolescents. Nor must it be forgotten that the survivals of capitalism in the minds of people have to be overcome and a new man educated under conditions of a fierce ideological struggle.[5]

This confession is instructive. It shows the Party's awareness, learned perhaps by experience, that it was not enough to educate the people systematically in the principles of Marxist ethics and to exhort them to conform their outward behaviour to the strict letter of Marxist theory. What was necessary was nothing less than the moulding and education of 'the new man'.

The language of this confession is striking. It is almost religious, and remarkably parallels that of the New Testament. It talks of 'the new man',

---

[5] Documents of 22nd Congress of the CPSU, 1:176–78.

and so does the New Testament, as we have just seen (Eph 4:24; Col 3:10). Interestingly enough, the New Testament agrees with Marxism, in this particular at least, that religious rituals and disciplines and moral effort are all insufficient: nothing avails except the creation of a 'new man'. The Apostle Paul expresses the desire, that you 'be renewed in the spirit of your minds, and put on the new man' (Eph 4:23–24); and 'Do not be conformed to this world, but be transformed by the renewal of your mind' (Rom 12:2). 'He [God] saved us . . . by . . . renewal of the Holy Spirit' (Titus 3:5).

These resemblances, however, do but highlight the obvious, crucial, differences between Marxism and Christianity both in the diagnosis of the root cause of man's defective behaviour, and in the formulation of its cure. For Marx, God and religion were part of the apparatus that had connived at, and helped to perpetuate, man's alienation from the means of production. The cure of man's alienation, therefore, and the way to spiritual and moral renewal and to the proper education of the 'new man', was to set mankind free from, among other things, the tyranny of God, and of the very concept of God.

> For Marx, God and religion were part of the apparatus that had connived at, and helped to perpetuate, man's alienation from the means of production.

It is a simple fact of history that in the place of the 'tyranny of God' communism substituted the complete dominance of a totalitarian Party over every department of life, as though sheer force could change people's hearts and produce a 'new man', spiritually and morally renewed. But many people who reject totalitarianism as a method for the moral improvement of society nevertheless agree with Marxism to this extent at least, that they also reject God both as the authority behind morality and also as the source of humankind's possible moral regeneration and renewal. They fear that to introduce God into ethics is simply to impose another form of totalitarian authority and so to diminish human dignity and freedom. They claim it treats human beings morally as children rather than as adults who are quite capable of setting and obeying their own ethical rules.

Moreover, in the opinion of some, religion sets impossibly high standards, and this inevitably leads to a psychologically unhealthy obsession with failure and guilt, which wrecks human personality and undermines confidence in human progress.

In the light of these fears and allegations, therefore, surely the rational thing to do is to investigate exactly what Christian ethics actually says about the cause of humankind's universal moral weakness, and, more particularly, what strategy it proposes for producing its version of what the Communist Party called 'the new man'.

THE PLACE OF ETHICS IN CHRISTIAN DOCTRINE

A major statement of the place of ethics in Christian doctrine is contained in a treatise written by the Apostle Paul, and known as the Epistle to the Romans. It consists of four main parts:

1. 1:1–5:11   God's provision for man's reconciliation and acceptance with God, and for the renewal of man's fellowship with him.
2. 5:12–8:39   God's programme for the remaking of man's character and final glorification.
3. 9:1–11:36   God's strategy for the nation of Israel's eventual restoration and salvation.
4. 12:1–16:27   Christian ethics.

The first thing to notice here is the position given to ethics: it comes last in the treatise! That is not because ethics is deemed to be unimportant. The reason for it is twofold:

1. Ethics is a second order, and not a first order, exercise.
2. Christian ethics flow from, and are motivated by, the mercies of God in restoring humankind to fellowship with God.

Ethics is a second order exercise

Let's take an analogy. No one buys a car for the purpose of being able to observe all the traffic rules and regulations. Nor does anyone consider he has achieved the final goal and purpose of possessing a car, when at last he has been able to drive it in complete conformity with the traffic code. The purpose of having a car is to travel, to transport oneself and other people. Keeping the traffic code is simply a way of driving safely for oneself and other people.

Parents do not beget a child for the purpose of being able to teach it ethics. They beget a child so that they can have someone who is their very own, someone whom they can love and treasure, and someone who can love them in return. Of course, little by little they teach it to behave, and why it should behave in this way and not in that, because it is the best way of expressing the purpose for which it was born.

Similarly, God did not create humankind so that he could have creatures on whom he could impose rules and regulations. He made man (that is, man and woman) in his own image and likeness, a moral and spiritual being, capable of sustaining a relationship with God who is spirit, so that man could enjoy God, and God could enjoy man. Of course he taught man ethics through his laws and commandments; but that was so that man should properly express the image and likeness of God in his behaviour towards God and other human beings.

Herein, therefore, lies humanity's tragedy: it is not the simple fact that humans do wrong, and often evil, things; it is our alienation from God and the consequent rupture of fellowship between us and our Creator that lie behind these acts.

This was poignantly depicted by Christ in his famous parable of the Prodigal Son (Luke 15:11–32). It was not merely that when the prodigal got to the far country he squandered his property (given to him by his father) in reckless living (15:13), or as his elder brother put it 'devoured your property with prostitutes' (15:30). It was the rejection of his father that lay behind his going off to the 'far country' in the first place, until, as the father put it, his son was, as far as fellowship with his father was concerned, 'dead' and 'lost' (15:32).

Christian ethics are motivated by the mercies of God

This is why the last part of Paul's treatise, the part that deals with ethics, strictly so called, begins with the exhortation:

> I urge you, therefore, brothers, by the mercies of God, to present your bodies as a living sacrifice, holy and acceptable to God, which

is your reasonable [or, rational; the Gk. *logikos*] service. Do not conform any longer to the pattern of this world, but be transformed by the renewing of your mind. Then you will be able to test and approve what God's will is—his good, pleasing and perfect will. (Rom 12:1–2 own trans.)

Paul does not hesitate in what follows in the next five chapters to remind his fellow Christians in great detail that they have a binding ethical duty to live to please God with all their physical, mental, emotional and spiritual powers; and further that in order to do this they will need a transformation of their outlook, values and behaviour by a continual renewing of their minds— the very thing that the Communist Party's manifesto declared to be indispensable. But Paul does not spell out what these ethical duties are until he has spent the first eleven chapters of his treatise expounding to them the mercies of God. In Christian doctrine and thinking this order is supremely important. It is not that ethical duties come first, and that, if humans make an honest attempt to perform them as best they can, they may hope that in the end God will have mercy on them. It is the other way round. God's mercies come first, and both motivate and empower humans to fulfil their ethical duties.

> It is not that ethical duties come first, and that, if humans make an honest attempt to perform them as best they can, they may hope that in the end God will have mercy on them. It is the other way round.

The first two major parts of Paul's treatise

These two parts of the treatise (1:1–5:11 and 5:12–8:39) have much in common. Both describe in great detail the mercies of God; and each comes to its climax with an extended statement of the nature and logic of God's love and of the deductions that can be made from it.

Part 1

> God's love has been poured into our hearts through the Holy Spirit who has been given to us. For while we were still weak, at just the right time, Christ died for the ungodly. For one will scarcely die for a righteous person—though perhaps for a good person one

would dare even to die—but God demonstrates his love for us in that while we were still sinners, Christ died for us. Since, therefore, we have now been justified by his blood, much more shall we be saved by him from the wrath of God. For if while we were enemies we were reconciled to God by the death of his Son, much more, now that we are reconciled, shall we be saved by his life. More than that, we also rejoice in God through our Lord Jesus Christ, through whom we have now received the reconciliation. (Rom 5:5–11 own trans.)

Part 2

What then shall we say in response to these things? If God is for us, who can be against us? He who did not spare his own Son, but gave him up for us all, how will he not also with him graciously give us all things? Who shall bring any charge against God's chosen ones? It is God who justifies. Who is to condemn us, when Christ Jesus is the one who died—more than that, who was raised—who is at the right hand of God, who indeed is interceding for us? Who shall separate us from the love of Christ? Shall tribulation, or distress, or persecution, or famine, or nakedness, or danger, or sword? ... No, in all these things we are more than conquerors through him who loved us. For I am convinced that neither death nor life, nor angels nor rulers, nor things present nor things to come, nor powers, nor height nor depth, nor anything else in all creation, will be able to separate us from the love of God in Christ Jesus our Lord. (Rom 8:31–39 own trans.)

Differences of theme

But while these two parts of the treatise share many similarities, the major theme of each part is significantly different.

Part 1 deals with God's strategy for the reconciliation to him of men and women until now alienated and hostile to God, and sinful in addition, and their re-introduction into complete acceptance and fellowship with God.

Part 2 deals with God's provision and timetable for the remaking of people's characters, with their empowerment to learn to live as adult sons and daughters of God, and with their eventual glorification.

Once more the order of these two parts is significant. Both are concerned with the creation of the 'new man', but the first stage in the process is the introduction of the individual person into full acceptance and fellowship with God, with reconciliation and total security of relationship. Part 2 then describes the second stage in the process, that is, the moral and spiritual remaking of the person's character and lifestyle.

This order of the stages in the process needs to be emphasised, for popular thought (if people think about it at all) tends to reverse this order. People imagine that first one must make serious effort to reform one's character and lifestyle by endeavouring to live according to the Christian ethic; and then, if at life's end one has been reasonably successful, one may perhaps (but who knows?) achieve acceptance with God. This makes one's sense of acceptance with God depend on one's moral performance and attainment; and the standard of Christian ethics being so high, it induces in people who sincerely attempt to attain acceptance with their Creator on these terms, an inevitable sense of inward insecurity. Unless they are hardened Pharisees, their failures make them think that Christian ethics are unrealistically demanding, and that God must be a slave driver.

> . . . first reconciliation and acceptance with God, and then the remaking of character and lifestyle.

The fact is that the order of God's programme for 'creating the new man' is the other way round: first reconciliation and acceptance with God, and then the remaking of character and lifestyle.

The parable of the Prodigal Son revisited

Once more the parable of the Prodigal Son illustrates the principle that Paul's treatise is making. The prodigal's return to the father began with a profound change of mind. 'He came to himself', says the story (Luke 15:17). He repented, not merely of this or that sinful act, but of his fundamental decision to reject his father. He had demanded to be given his part of the inheritance before his father was dead. In the society of the time this was a scandalous thing to do. It was tantamount to saying to his father, 'You're living too long. You're in my way. Give me my inheritance now so that I can get you out of my life and go and enjoy myself.' This was at heart the same fundamental sin as that of Adam and Eve. They wanted to keep the paradise God had built for them; but they wanted to be independent of God's moral judgment, and to know and decide, apart from God, what was good and evil.

The prodigal's repentance, then, was a radical reversal of his previous attitude. It was followed by action: he arose and returned to the father; and then by confession: 'Father, I have sinned against heaven and before you. I am no longer worthy to be called your son' (15:21). He had originally intended to add: 'Treat me as one of your hired servants', willing now to work to earn his way back into his father's favour. But his father would have none of that suggestion. Nor did the father insist on some programme of reform and retraining *before* he was welcomed back and accepted. There and then, as he stood bankrupt, destitute and in his smelly clothes, he was embraced and unconditionally accepted and reinstated in the fellowship of his father. After that he would learn to live as a true adult son of his father.

> The prodigal's repentance was a radical reversal of his previous attitude.

Part 1 of the treatise revisited

Further detail from Part 1 of the treatise is worth considering. It first describes man's alienation from God and the folly of his attempts to be independent of God:

1. His suppression of the evidence, supplied by creation, of the power and Godhood of God (1:18–32).
2. His refusal to acknowledge that the warnings of the moral law written on his heart by the Creator are reminders that one day he must give account to God and that he needs to repent towards God (2:1–16).
3. The abuse of religion, as though man has such independence of God that he can by his own effort, buy acceptance with God by keeping his law, and thus regards himself superior to those who fail to keep God's law—while all the time the fact is that he, like everybody else, has sinned and still falls short of God's standards (2:17–3:20).

Part 1 then goes on to explain God's provision for the first stage of humanity's regeneration, namely, reconciliation, acceptance and peace with God (3:21–5:11). This is brought about:

1. *on God's side*: by the gift of his Son as the atoning sacrifice for sins that makes it possible for God to remain righteous and yet justify the person who puts his or her faith in Jesus (3:24–26).
2. *on the human side*: not on the ground of man's keeping God's law (which he has broken and still comes short of), but solely by faith apart from the works of the law, as man receives his justification as a free gift of God's grace through Jesus Christ (3:21–30).

The resultant peace with God and the sense of acceptance and security in the love of God are eloquently set out, by logical argument, in the passage already quoted (5:1–11). But the immediate point is this: when the person thus justified and accepted by God then sets out on the long process of the remaking of his or her character and lifestyle, as described in Part 2 of the treatise, and begins to practise the Christian ethic detailed in Part 4, he or she does so, not in order to gain acceptance, but because they have already been accepted; not in slavish fear of failure and ultimate rejection, but in God-given confidence of being saved from the wrath of God through Christ and of attaining the glory of God (5:1–2, 9–11).

Part 2 of the treatise revisited

Part 1, we remember, has just maintained that justification and acceptance with God cannot be achieved by man's work, but only by faith in God's work of redemption. That, Paul maintains, does not undercut the authority of God's law, but rather establishes it (3:31). It insists that God cannot overlook our shortcomings. The authority of his law and the values it stands for, must be upheld, its penalties enforced; and they were enforced in Christ's propitiatory death (3:25).

Now Part 2 carries that emphasis further. Though acceptance with God cannot be achieved by one's keeping of God's law, acceptance with God leads to subsequent behaviour that fulfils the righteous requirement of that law.

> There is therefore now no condemnation for those who are in Christ Jesus. For the law of the Spirit of life has set you free in Christ Jesus from the law of sin and death. . . . in order that the righteous requirement of the law might be fulfilled in us who walk not according to the flesh but according to the Spirit. (Rom 8:1–2, 4)

We have not the space here to cover all the detail of Part 2 which describes the empowerment of the believer to fulfil the righteous requirement of the law; or what happens when he or she temporarily fails. Nor can we dwell on the final goal of this process, which is the achievement of the believer's glorification and conformity to the image of God's Son (8:26–30). Our concern here is to notice how the contents of this Part 2 are related to the practice of Christian ethics as detailed in Part 4.

The situation is not as it is with many ethical systems, in which the would-be practitioner is first given a theoretical system of principles and then exhorted to do his or her best to put them into practice. Part 2, by contrast, describes first the practical provision that God makes for the regeneration and renewal of the person, so that that person may be enabled realistically to begin to practise Christian ethics first as a child of God, and then as his adult son or daughter, and not find it a form of slavery. That provision is the regenerating power and indwelling of the Spirit of God.

> So then, brothers, we are debtors, not to the flesh, to live according to the flesh. For if you live according to the flesh you will die, but if by the Spirit you put to death the deeds of the body, you will live. For all who are led by the Spirit of God are sons of God. For you did not receive the spirit of slavery to fall back into fear, but you have received the Spirit of adoption as sons, by whom we cry, 'Abba! Father!' The Spirit himself bears witness with our spirit that we are children of God, and if children, then heirs—heirs of God and fellow heirs with Christ, provided we suffer with him in order that we may also be glorified with him. (8:12–17)

A summary of part 4 of Paul's treatise

Part 4, which deals with practical Christian ethics, is also too detailed to study here in depth, but a bird's-eye view may provide an idea of its extent. John Stott gives the following summary:

12:1–2	Our relationship to God: consecrated bodies and renewed minds.
12:3–8	Our relationship to ourselves: thinking soberly about our gifts.
12:9–16	Our relationship to one another: love in the family of God.
12:17–21	Our relationship to our enemies: not retaliation but service.
13:1–7	Our relationship to the state: conscientious citizenship.
13:8–10	Our relationship to the law: neighbour-love as its fulfilment.
13:11–14	Our relationship to the day: living in the 'already' and the 'not yet'.
14:1–15:13	Our relationship to the weak: welcoming, and not despising, judging or offending them.[6]

OBJECTIONS TO CHRISTIAN ETHICS

William K. Frankena raises thoughtful objections to the adoption of ethical systems based on Christianity or any other religion. The first is its potential divisiveness:

> But then one is impelled to wonder also if there is anything to be gained by insisting that all ethical principles are or must be logically grounded on religious beliefs. For to insist on this is to introduce into the foundation of any morality whatsoever all of the difficulties involved in the adjudication of religious controversies, and to do so is hardly to encourage hope that mankind

---

[6] Headings in *The Message of Romans* for 12:1–15:13.

can reach, by peaceful and rational means, some desirable kind of agreement on moral and political principles.[7]

There are several answers to this problem. First, people loyal to Christ's prohibition on the use of force to defend or promote his teaching would never dream of using other than peaceful and rational means to persuade other people to adopt Christian ethics. People cannot be forced by violence genuinely to believe truth. Religions that use violence to promote their cause thereby raise serious doubts about the truth of their doctrines.

Secondly, Christian ethics, based on, and motivated by, personal experience of the mercies of God, are strictly speaking, only for those who have had such experience. Nonetheless, in many situations Christian ethical principles coincide with principles based on other systems of ethics. Many systems of ethics, and not only Christian ethics, hold, for example, that it would be wrong to execute innocent people, to torture children, or to rob the poor.

Thirdly, as R. M. Adams points out, there is nothing in the history of modern secular moral theory to suggest that, if only religion were left out of ethics, general agreement would soon be reached on a single comprehensive moral theory. History teaches the opposite. Adams concludes:

> The development and advocacy of religious ethical theory, therefore, does not destroy a realistic possibility of agreement that would otherwise exist.[8]

There is no rational reason, therefore, for denying peacefully expressed religious views a voice among the conflicting theories of secular ethics.

William K. Frankena, however, remarks:

> However deep and sincere one's own religious beliefs may be, if one reviews the religious scene, contemporary and historical, one cannot help but wonder if there is any rational and objective method of establishing any religious belief against the proponents of other religions or of irreligion.[9]

---

[7] 'Is morality logically dependent on religion?', 313.
[8] 'Religious ethics in a pluralistic society', 93.
[9] 'Is morality logically dependent on religion?', 313

The same could be said of any system of philosophy, or even science. All such systems are based, as Aristotle said, on first principles that have to be accepted on faith without logical demonstration; but then they proceed to make truth-claims, the truth of which must be demonstrated by evidence and cogent argument. Religions cannot claim exemption in this regard. They all make truth claims, which similarly must be capable of being supported by evidence and cogent argument. Democracy demands, moreover, that all religions should be free, peacefully to argue for the truth of their beliefs. We, the authors of this book, however, are Christians, and are not qualified properly to represent other religions. We must, therefore, content ourselves to speak for the truth of Christ, and let others speak for their convictions. The specifics of our own convictions about the truth of Christ are set out in more detail in Book 5 of this series, which we would invite you to read as we continue on our quest.[10]

---

[10] *Claiming to Answer: How One Person Became the Response to Our Deepest Questions.*

APPENDIX: THE SCIENTIFIC ENDEAVOUR

The doing of successful science follows no set of cosy rules. It is as complex as the human personalities that are involved in doing it.

THE CLEAR VOICE OF SCIENCE

Science rightly has the power to fire the imagination. Who could read the story of how Francis Crick and James D. Watson unravelled the double helix structure of DNA without entering at least a little into the almost unbearable joy that they experienced at this discovery? Who could watch an operation to repair someone's eye with a delicately controlled laser beam without a sense of wonder at human creativity and invention? Who could see pictures from space showing astronauts floating weightless in the cabin of the International Space Station or watch them repair the Hubble telescope against the background of the almost tangible blackness of space without a feeling akin to awe? Science has a right to our respect and to our active encouragement. Getting young people into science and giving them the training and facilities to develop their intellectual potential is a clear priority for any nation. It would be an incalculable loss if the scientific instinct were in any way stifled by philosophical, economic or political considerations.

But since one of the most powerful and influential voices to which we want to listen is the voice of science, it will be very important for us, whether we are scientists or not, to have some idea of what science is and what the scientific method is before we try to evaluate what science says to us on any particular issue. Our aim, therefore, first of all is to remind ourselves of some of the basic principles of scientific thinking, some of which we may already know. Following this, we shall think about the nature of scientific explanation and we shall examine some of the assumptions that underlie scientific activity—basic beliefs without which science cannot be done.

Then what is science? It tends to be one of those things that we all know what it means until we come to try to define it. And then we find that precise definition eludes us. The difficulty arises because we use the word in different ways. First of all, *science* is used as shorthand for:

1. sciences—areas of knowledge like physics, chemistry, biology, etc.;
2. scientists—the people who work in these areas;
3. scientific method—the way in which scientists do their work.

Often, however, the word *science* is used in expressions like 'Science says...', or 'Science has demonstrated...', as if science were a conscious being of great authority and knowledge. This usage, though understandable, can be misleading. The fact is that, strictly speaking, there is no such thing as 'science' in this sense. Science does not say, demonstrate, know or discover anything—scientists do. Of course, scientists often agree, but it is increasingly recognised that science, being a very human endeavour, is very much more complex than is often thought and there is considerable debate about what constitutes scientific method.

SCIENTIFIC METHOD

It is now generally agreed among philosophers of science that there is no one 'scientific method', so it is easier to speak of the kind of thing that doing science involves than to give a precise definition of science. Certainly observation and experimentation have primary roles to play,

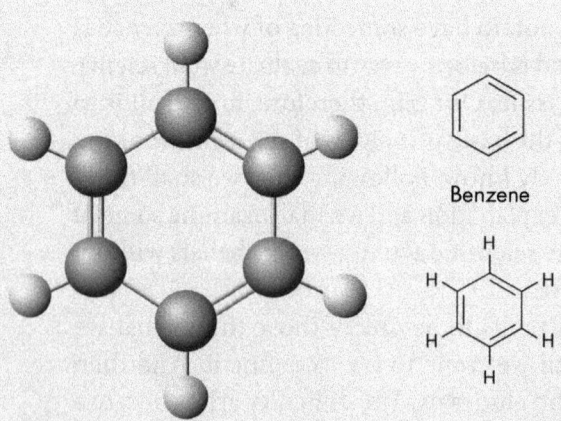

FIGURE Ap.1. Benzene Molecule.

In 1929 crystallographer Kathleen Lonsdale confirmed Kekulé's earlier theory about the flat, cyclic nature of benzene, an important milestone in organic chemistry.

Reproduced with permission of ©iStock/hromatos.

as well as do the reasoning processes that lead scientists to their conclusions. However, a glance at the history of science will show that there is much more to it than this. We find, for example, that inexplicable hunches have played a considerable role. Even dreams have had their place! The chemist Friedrich August Kekulé was studying the structure of benzene and dreamed about a snake that grabbed its own tail, thus forming itself into a ring. As a result he was led to the idea that benzene might be like the snake. He had a look and found that benzene indeed contained a closed ring of six carbon atoms! The doing of successful science follows no set of cosy rules. It is as complex as the human personalities that are involved in doing it.

Observation and experimentation

It is generally agreed that a revolution in scientific thinking took place in the sixteenth and seventeenth centuries. Up to then one main method of thinking about the nature of the universe was to appeal to authority. For example, in the fourth century BC Aristotle had argued from philosophical principles that the only perfect motion was circular. Thus, if you wanted to know how the planets moved, then, since according to Aristotle they inhabited the realm of perfection beyond the orbit of the moon, they must move in circles. In a radical departure from this approach, scientists like Galileo insisted that the best way to find out how the planets moved was to take his telescope and go and have a look! And through that telescope he saw things like the moons of Jupiter which, according to the Aristotelian system, did not exist. Galileo comes to embody for many people the true spirit of scientific enquiry: the freedom to do full justice to observation and experimentation, even if it meant seriously modifying or even abandoning the theories that he had previously held. That freedom should be retained and jealously guarded by us all.

Data, patterns, relationships and hypotheses

In summary form, the most widespread view, often attributed to Francis Bacon and John Stuart Mill, is that the scientific method consists of:

1. the collection of data (facts, about which there can be no dispute) by means of observation and experiment, neither of them influenced by presuppositions or prejudices;
2. the derivation of hypotheses from the data by looking for patterns or relationships between the data and then making an inductive generalisation;
3. the testing of the hypotheses by deducing predictions from them and then constructing and doing experiments designed to check if those predictions are true;
4. the discarding of hypotheses that are not supported by the experimental data and the building up of the theory by adding confirmed hypotheses.

Scientists collect data, experimental observations and measurements that they record. As examples of data, think of a set of blood pressure measurements of your class just before and just after a school examination, or of the rock samples collected by astronauts from the surface of the moon.

There are, however, many other things that are equally real to us, but which scarcely can count as data in the scientific sense: our subjective experience of a sunset, or of friendship and love, or of dreams. With dreams, of course, heart rate, brain activity and eye movement can be observed by scientists as they monitor people who are asleep and dreaming, but their subjective experience of the dream itself cannot be measured. Thus we see that the scientific method has certain built-in limits. It cannot capture the whole of reality.

Scientists are in the business of looking for relationships and patterns in their data and they try to infer some kind of hypothesis or theory to account for those patterns. Initially the hypothesis may be an intelligent or inspired guess that strikes the scientists from their experience as being a possible way of accounting for what they have observed. For example, a scientist might suggest the (very reasonable) hypothesis that the blood pressure measurements in your class can be accounted for by the fact that examinations cause stress in most people! To test the hypothesis a scientist will then work out what he or she would expect to find if the hypothesis were true and then will proceed to devise an experiment or a series of experiments to check if such is indeed the case. If the experiments fail to confirm expectation, the hypothesis may be modified or discarded in favour of another and the process repeated. Once a hypothesis has been successfully tested by repeated experimentation then it is dignified by being called a theory.[1]

It is now generally agreed by scientists themselves and philosophers of science that our account so far of what the scientific method is, is not only highly idealised but also flawed. In particular, contrary to what is asserted about observation and experimentation above, it is now widely accepted that no scientist, however honest and careful, can come to his or her work in a completely impartial way, without presuppositions and assumptions. This fact will be of importance for our understanding of science's contribution to our worldview. It is easier, however, to consider that topic after we have first had a look at some of the logical concepts and procedures that underlie scientific argumentation and proof.

Induction

Induction is probably the most important logical process that scientists use in the formulation of laws and theories.[2] It is also a process that is familiar to all of us from a very early age whether we are scientists or not, though we may well not have been aware of it. When we as young children first see a crow we notice it is black. For all we know, the next crow we see may well be white or yellow. But after observing crows day after day, there comes a point at which our feeling that any other crow we see is going to be black is so strong that we would be prepared to say that all crows are black. We have taken what is called an inductive step based on our own data—we have seen, say, 435 crows—to make a universal statement about all crows. Induction, then, is the process of generalising from a finite set of data

---

[1] The terms *hypothesis* and *theory* are in fact almost indistinguishable, the only difference in normal usage being that a hypothesis is sometimes regarded as more tentative than a theory.
[2] Note for mathematicians: the process of induction described above is not the same as the principle of mathematical induction by which (typically) the truth of a statement $P(n)$ is established for all positive integers n from two propositions:
(1) $P(1)$ is true;
(2) for any positive integer k, we can prove that the truth of $P(k+1)$ follows from the truth of $P(k)$.
The key difference is that (2) describes an infinite set of hypotheses, one for each positive integer, whereas in philosophical induction we are generalising from a finite set of hypotheses.

to a universal or general statement.

A famous example of the use of induction in science is the derivation of Mendel's laws of heredity. Gregor Mendel and his assistants made a number of observations of the frequency of occurrence of particular characteristics in each of several generations of peas, like whether seeds were wrinkled or smooth, or plants were tall or short, and then made an inductive generalisation from those observations to formulate the laws that now bear his name.

> Induction, then, is the process of generalising from a finite set of data to a universal or general statement.

But, as may well have occurred to you, there is a problem with induction. To illustrate this, let's turn our minds to swans rather than the crows we thought about just now. Suppose that from childhood every swan you have seen was white. You might well conclude (by induction) that all swans are white. But then one day you are shown a picture of an Australian black swan and discover that your conclusion was false. This illustrates what the problem with induction is. How can you ever really know that you have made enough observations to draw a universal conclusion from a limited set of observations?

But please notice what the discovery of the black swan has done. It has proved wrong the statement that all swans are white, but it has not proved wrong the modified statement that if you see a swan in Europe, the high probability is that the swan will be white.

Let's look at another example of induction, this time from chemistry.

Particular observations:

Time	Date	Substance	Litmus test result
0905	2015-08-14	sulphuric acid	turned red
1435	2015-09-17	citric acid	turned red
1045	2015-09-18	hydrochloric acid	turned red
1900	2015-10-20	sulphuric acid	turned red

Universal or general statement (law): litmus paper turns red when dipped in acid.

This law, based on induction from the finite set of particular observations that are made of particular acids at particular times in particular places, is claimed to hold for all acids at all times in all places. The problem with induction is, how can we be sure that such a general statement is valid, when, in the very nature of things, we can only make a finite number of observations of litmus paper turning red on the application of acid? The story of the black swan makes us aware of the difficulty.

Well, we cannot be absolutely sure, it is true. But every time we do the experiment and find it works, our confidence in the litmus test is increased to the extent that if we dipped some paper in a liquid and found it did not go red we would be likely to conclude, not that the litmus test did not work, but that either the paper we had was not litmus paper or the liquid was not acid! Of course it is true that underlying our confidence is the assumption that nature behaves in a uniform way, that if I repeat an experiment tomorrow under the same conditions as I did it today, I will get the same results.

Let's take another example that Bertrand Russell used to illustrate the problem of induction in a more complex situation: Bertrand Russell's inductivist turkey. A turkey observes that on its first day at the turkey farm it was fed at 9 a.m. For two months it collects observations and notes that even if it chooses days at random, it is fed at 9 a.m. It finally concludes by induction that it always will be fed at 9 a.m. It therefore gets an awful shock on Christmas Eve when, instead of being fed, it is taken out and killed for Christmas dinner!

So how can we know for certain that we have made enough observations in an experiment? How many times do we have to check that particular metals expand on heating to conclude that all metals expand on heating? How do we avoid the inductivist turkey shock? Of course we can see that the problem with the turkey is that it did not have (indeed could not have) the wider experience of the turkey farmer who could replace the turkey's incorrect inductivist conclusion with a more complicated correct one: namely the law that each turkey will experience a sequence of days of feeding followed by execution!

The point of what we are saying here is not to undermine science by suggesting that induction is useless, nor that science in itself cannot lead us to any firm conclusions. It simply teaches us to recognise the limits of any one method and to found our conclusions, wherever possible, on a combination of them.

The role of deduction

Once a law has been formulated by induction, we can test the validity of the law by using it to make predictions. For example, assuming Mendel's laws to be true, we can deduce from them a prediction as to what the relative frequency of occurrence, say, of blue eyes in different generations of a family, should be. When we find by direct observation that the occurrence of blue eyes is what we predicted it to be, our observations are said to confirm the theory, although this sort of confirmation can never amount to total certainty. Thus deduction plays an important role in the confirmation of induction.

> Deduction plays an important role in the confirmation of induction.

It may be that what we have said about induction has given the impression that scientific work always starts by looking at data and reasoning to some inductive hypothesis that accounts for those data. However, in reality, scientific method tends to be somewhat more complicated than this. Frequently, scientists start by deciding what kind of data they are looking for. That is, they already have in their mind some hypothesis or theory they want to test, and they look for data that will confirm that theory. In this situation deduction will play a dominant role.

For example, as we mentioned above regarding observation and experimentation, in the ancient world, Greek philosophers supposed as a hypothesis that the planets must move in circular orbits around the earth, since, for them, the circle was the perfect shape. They then deduced what their hypothesis should lead them to observe in the heavens. When their observations did not appear to confirm their original hypothesis completely, they modified it. They did this by replacing the original hypothesis by one in which other circular motions are imposed on top of the original one (epicycles, they were called). They then used this more complicated hypothesis from which to deduce their predictions. This theory of epicycles dominated astronomy for a long time, and was overturned and replaced by the revolutionary suggestions of Copernicus and Kepler.

Kepler's work in turn again illustrates the deductive method. Using the observations the astronomer Tycho Brahe had made available, Kepler tried to work out the shape that the orbit of Mars traced against the background of 'fixed' stars. He did not get anywhere until he hit on an idea that was prompted by geometrical work he had done on the ellipse. That idea was to suppose as a hypothesis that the orbit of Mars was an ellipse, then to use mathematical calculations to deduce what should be observed on the basis of that hypothesis, and finally to compare those predictions with the actual observations. The validity of the elliptical orbit hypothesis would then be judged by how closely the predictions fit the observations.

This method of inference is called the deductive or hypothetico-deductive method of reasoning: deducing predictions from a hypothesis, and then comparing them with actual observations.

Since deduction is such an important procedure it is worth considering it briefly. Deduction is a logical process by which an assertion we want to prove (the conclusion) is logically deduced from things we already accept (the premises). Here is an example of logical deduction, usually called a syllogism:

P1: All dogs have four legs.
P2: Fido is a dog.

C: Fido has four legs.

Here statements P1 and P2 are the premises and C is the conclusion. If P1 and P2 are true then C is true. Or to put it another way, to have P1 and P2 true and C false, would involve a logical contradiction. This is the essence of a logically valid deduction.

Let's now look at an example of a logically invalid deduction:

P1: Many dogs have a long tail.
P2: Albert is a dog.

C: Albert has a long tail.

Here statement C does not necessarily follow from P1 and P2. It is clearly possible for P1 and P2 to be true and yet for C to be false.

It all appears to be so simple that there is danger of your switching off. But don't do that quite yet or you might miss something very important. And that is that deductive logic cannot establish the truth of any of the statements involved in the procedure. All that the logic can tell us (but this much is very important!) is that if the premises are true and the argument is logically valid, then the conclusion is true. In order to get this clear let us look at a final example:

P1: All planets have a buried ocean.
P2: Mercury is a planet.

C: Mercury has a buried ocean.

This is a logically valid argument even though statement P1 and statement C are (so far as we know) false. The argument says only that if P1 and P2 were true, then C should be true, which is perfectly valid. This sort of thing may seem strange to us at first, but it can help us grasp that logic can only criticise the argument and check whether it is valid or not. It cannot tell us whether any or all of the premises or conclusion are true. Logic has to do with the way in which some statements are derived from others, not with the truth of those statements.

Logic has to do with the way in which some statements are derived from others, not with the truth of those statements.

We should also note that deductive inference plays a central role in pure mathematics where theories are constructed by means of making deductions from explicitly given axioms, as in Euclidean geometry. The results (or theorems, as they are usually called) are said to be true if there is a logically valid chain of deductions deriving them from the axioms. Such deductive proofs give a certainty (granted the consistency of the axioms) that is not attainable in the inductive sciences.

In practice induction and deduction are usually both involved in establishing scientific theories. We referred above to Kepler's use of deduction in deriving his theory that Mars moved in an ellipse round the sun. However, he first thought of the ellipse (rather than, say, the parabola or the hyperbola) because the observations of Brahe led Kepler to believe the orbit of Mars was roughly egg-shaped. The egg shape was initially conjectured as a result of induction from astronomical observations.

Competing hypotheses can cover the same data

But here we should notice that when it comes to interpreting the data we have collected, different hypotheses can be constructed to cover that data. We have two illustrations of this.

Illustration from astronomy. Under the role of deduction above we discussed two hypotheses from ancient astronomy that were put forward to explain the motion of the planets. Successive refinements of the epicyclic model appeared to cover the data at the expense of greater and greater complication in that more and more circles were necessary. Kepler's proposal, by contrast, covered the data by the simple device of replacing the complex array of circles by one single ellipse, which simplified the whole business enormously. Now, if we knew nothing of gravity and the deduction of elliptical orbits that can be made from it by means of Newton's laws, how would we choose between the two explanations?

At this point, scientists might well invoke the principle sometimes called 'Occam's razor', after William of Occam. This is the belief that simpler explanations of natural phenomena are more likely to be correct than more complex ones. More precisely, the idea is that if we have two or more competing hypotheses covering the same data, we should choose the one that involves the least number of assumptions or complications. The metaphorical use of the word 'razor' comes from this cutting or shaving down to the smallest possible number of assumptions. Occam's razor has proved very useful but we should observe that it is a philosophical preference, and it is not something that you can prove to be true in every case, so it needs to be used with care.

Illustration from physics. Another illustration of the way in which different hypotheses can account for the same data is given by a common exercise in school physics. We are given a spring, a series of weights and a ruler and asked to plot a graph of the length of the spring against the weight hanging on the end of it. We end up with a series, say, of 10 points on the paper that look as if they might (with a bit of imagination!) lie on a straight line. We take an inductive step and draw a straight line that goes through most of the points and we claim that there is a linear relationship between the length of spring and the tension it is put under by the weights (Hooke's law). But then we reflect that there is an infinite number of curves that can be drawn through our ten points. Changing the curve would change the relation between spring length and tension. Why not choose one of those other curves in preference to the straight

> The principle sometimes called 'Occam's razor', after William of Occam . . . is the belief that simpler explanations of natural phenomena are more likely to be correct than more complex ones.

line? That is, in the situation just described, there are many different hypotheses that cover the same set of data. How do you choose between them?

Application of Occam's razor would lead to choosing the most elegant or economical solution—a straight line is simpler than a complicated curve. We could also repeat the experiment with 100 points, 200 points, etc. The results would build up our confidence that the straight line was the correct answer. When we build up evidence in this way, we say that we have cumulative evidence for the validity of our hypothesis.

So far we have been looking at various methods employed by scientists and have seen that none of them yields 100% certainty, except in deductive proofs in mathematics where the certainty is that particular conclusions follow from particular axioms. However, we would emphasise once more that this does not mean that the scientific enterprise is about to collapse! Far from it. What we mean by 'not giving 100% certainty' can be interpreted as saying that there is a small probability that a particular result or theory is false. But that does not mean that we cannot have confidence in the theory.

Indeed there are some situations, as in the litmus-paper test for acid where there has been 100% success in the past. Now whereas this does not formally guarantee 100% success in the future, scientists will say that it is a fact that litmus paper turns red on being dipped in acid. By a 'fact', they mean, as palaeontologist Stephen Jay Gould has delightfully put it, 'confirmed to such a degree that it would be perverse to withhold provisional assent to it'.[3]

On other occasions we are prepared to trust our lives to the findings of science and technology even though we know we do not have 100% certainty. For example, before we travel by train, we know that it is theoretically possible for something to go wrong, maybe for the brakes or signalling to fail and cause the train to crash. But we also know from the statistics of rail travel that the probability of such an event is very small indeed (though it is not zero—trains have from time to time crashed). Since the probability of a crash is so small, most of us who travel by train do so without even thinking about the risk.

On the other hand we must not assume that we can accept all

---

[3] Gould, 'Evolution as Fact and Theory', 119.

proposed hypotheses arrived at by scientific method as absolute fact without testing them.

One of the criteria of testing is called falsifiability.

Falsifiability

Karl Popper put the emphasis not on the verifiability of a hypothesis but on its falsifiability. It is unfortunate that Popper's terminology can be a real source of confusion, since the adjective 'falsifiable' does not mean 'will turn out to be false'! The confusion is even worse when one realises, on the other hand, that the verb 'to falsify' means 'to demonstrate that something is false'! The term 'falsifiable' has in fact a technical meaning. A hypothesis is said to be falsifiable if you can think of a logically possible set of observations that would be inconsistent with it.

It is, of course, much easier to falsify a universal statement than to verify it. As an illustration, take one of our earlier examples. The statement 'All swans are white' is, from the very start, falsifiable. One would only have to discover one swan that was black and that would falsify it. And since we know that black swans do exist, the statement has long since been falsified.

However, there can be problems. Most scientific activity is much more complex than dealing with claims like 'All swans are white'!

For example, in the nineteenth century observations of the planet Uranus appeared to indicate that its motion was inconsistent with predictions made on the basis of Newton's laws. Therefore, it appeared to threaten to demonstrate Newton's laws to be false. However, instead of immediately saying that Newton's laws had been falsified, it was suggested by French mathematician Urbain Le Verrier and English astronomer John Couch Adams (unknown to each other) that there might be a hitherto undetected planet in the neighbourhood of Uranus that would account for its apparently anomalous behaviour. As a result another scientist, German astronomer Johann Galle, was prompted to look for a new planet and discovered the planet Neptune.

> The term 'falsifiable' has in fact a technical meaning: a hypothesis is said to be falsifiable if you can think of a logically possible set of observations that would be inconsistent with it.

It would, therefore, have been incorrect to regard the behaviour of Uranus as falsifying Newton's laws. The problem was ignorance of the initial conditions—there was a planet missing in the configuration being studied. In other words, some of the crucial data was missing. This story demonstrates one of the problems inherent in Popper's approach. When observation does not fit theory, it could be that the theory is false, but it could equally well be that the theory is correct but the data is incomplete or even false, or that some of the auxiliary assumptions are incorrect. How can you judge what is the correct picture?

Most scientists in fact feel that Popper's ideas are far too pessimistic and his methodology too counter-intuitive. Their experience and intuition tell them that their scientific methods in fact enable them to get a better and better understanding of the universe, that they are in this sense getting a tighter grip on reality. One benefit of Popper's approach, however, is its insistence that scientific theories be testable.

Repeatability and abduction

The scientific activity we have been thinking of so far is characterised by *repeatability*. That is, we have considered situations where scientists are looking for universally valid laws that cover repeatable phenomena, laws which, like Newton's laws of motion, may be experimentally tested again and again. Sciences of this sort are often called inductive or nomological sciences (Gk. *nomos* = law) and between them they cover most of science.

However there are major areas of scientific enquiry where repeatability is not possible, notably study of the origin of the universe and the origin and development of life.

Now of course we do not mean to imply that science has nothing to say about phenomena that are non-repeatable. On the contrary, if one is to judge by the amount of literature published, particularly, but not only, at the popular level, the origin of the universe and of life, for example, are among the most interesting subjects by far that science addresses.

But precisely because of the importance of such non-repeatable phenomena, it is vital to see that the way in which they are accessible to science is not the same in general as the way in which repeatable phenomena are. For theories about both kinds of phenomena tend to be presented to the public in the powerful name of science as though they had an equal claim to be accepted. Thus there is a real danger that the public ascribes the same authority and validity to conjectures about non-repeatable events that are not capable of experimental verification as it does to those theories that have been confirmed by repeated experiment.

Physical chemist and philosopher Michael Polanyi points out that the study of how something originates is usually very different from the study of how it operates, although, of course, clues to how something originated may well be found in how it operates. It is one thing to investigate something repeatable in the laboratory, such as dissecting a frog to see how its nervous system functions, but it is an altogether different thing to study something non-repeatable, such as how frogs came to exist in the first place. And, on the large scale, how the universe works is one thing, yet how it came to be may be quite another.

> How the universe works is one thing, yet how it came to be may be quite another.

The most striking difference between the study of non-repeatable and repeatable phenomena is that the method of induction is no longer applicable, since we no longer have a sequence of observations or experiments to induce from, nor any repetition in the future to predict about! The principal method that applies to non-repeatable phenomena is *abduction*.

Although this term, introduced by logician Charles Peirce in the nineteenth century, may be unfamiliar, the underlying idea is very familiar. For abduction is what every good detective does in order to clear up a murder mystery! With the murder mystery a certain event has happened. No one doubts that it has happened. The question is: who or what was the cause of it happening? And often in the search for causes of an event that has already happened, abduction is the only method available.

As an example of abductive inference, think of the following:

Data: Ivan's car went over the cliff edge and he was killed.

Inference: If the car brakes had failed, then the car would have gone over the cliff.

Abductive conclusion: There is reason to suppose that the brakes failed.

However, an alternative suggests itself (especially to avid readers of detective stories): if someone had pushed Ivan's car over the cliff, the result would have been the same! It would be fallacious and very foolish to assume that just because we had thought of one explanation of the circumstances, that it was the only one.

The basic idea of abduction is given by the following scheme:

Data: A is observed.

Inference: If B were true then A would follow.

Abductive conclusion: There is reason to suppose B may be true.

Of course, there may well be another hypothesis, C, of which we could say: if C were true A would follow. Indeed, there may be many candidates for C.

The detective in our story has a procedure for considering them one by one. He may first consider the chance hypothesis, B, that the brakes failed. He may then consider the hypothesis C that it was no chance event, but deliberately designed by a murderer who pushed the car over the cliff. Or the detective may consider an even more sophisticated hypothesis, D, combining both chance and design, that someone who wanted to kill Ivan had tampered with the brakes of the car so that they would fail somewhere, and they happened to fail on the clifftop!

Inference to the best explanation. Our detective story illustrates how the process of abduction throws up plausible hypotheses and forces upon us the question as to which of the hypotheses best fits the data. In order to decide that question, the hypotheses are compared for their explanatory power: how much of the data do they cover, does the theory make coherent sense, is it consistent with other areas of our knowledge, etc.?

In order to answer these further questions, deduction will often be used. For example, if B in the detective story is true, then we would expect an investigation of the brakes of the wrecked car to reveal worn or broken parts. If C is true we would deduce that the brakes might well be found in perfect order, whereas if D were the case, we might expect to find marks of deliberate damage to the hydraulic braking system. If we found such marks then D would immediately be regarded as the best of the competing explanations given so far, since it has a greater explanatory power than the others.

Thus, abduction together with the subsequent comparison of competing hypotheses may be regarded as an 'inference to the best explanation'. This is the essence not only of detective and legal work but also of the work of the historian. Both detective and historian have to infer the best possible explanation from the available data after the events in which they are interested have occurred.

For more on the application of abduction in the natural sciences, particularly in cosmology and biology, see the books by John Lennox noted at the end of this Appendix. Here we need to consider a few more of the general issues related to the scientific endeavour.

EXPLAINING EXPLANATIONS

Levels of explanation

Science explains. This, for many people encapsulates the power and the fascination of science. Science enables us to understand what we did not understand before and, by giving us understanding, it gives us power over nature. But what do we mean by saying that 'science explains'?

In informal language we take an explanation of something to be adequate when the person to whom the explanation is given understands plainly what he or she did not understand before. However, we must try to be more precise about what we mean by the process of 'explanation', since it has different aspects that are often confused. An illustration can help us. We have considered a similar idea in relation to roses. Let's now take further examples.

Suppose Aunt Olga has baked a beautiful cake. She displays it to a gathering of the world's top scientists and we ask them for an explanation of the cake. The nutrition scientists will tell us about the number of calories in the cake and its nutritional effect; the biochemists will inform us about the structure of the proteins, fats, etc. in the cake and what it is that causes them to hold together; the chemists will enumerate the elements involved and describe their bonding; the physicists will be able to analyse the cake in terms of fundamental particles; and the mathematicians will offer us a set of beautiful equations to describe the behaviour of those particles. Suppose, then, that these experts have given us an exhaustive description of the cake, each in terms of his or her scientific discipline. Can we say that the cake is now completely explained? We have certainly been given a description of how the cake was made and how its various constituent elements relate to each other. But suppose we now ask the assembled group of experts why the cake was made. We notice the grin on Aunt Olga's face. She knows the answer since, after all, she made the cake! But if she does not reveal the answer by telling us, it is clear that no amount of scientific analysis will give us the answer.

Thus, although science can answer 'how' questions in terms of causes and mechanisms, it cannot answer 'why' questions, questions of purpose and intention—teleological questions, as they are sometimes called (Gk. *telos* = end or goal).

However, it would be nonsensical to suggest that Aunt Olga's answer to the teleological question, that she made the cake for Sam's birthday, say, contradicted the scientific analysis of the cake! No. The two kinds of answer are clearly logically compatible.

And yet exactly the same confusion of categories is evidenced when atheists argue that there is no longer need to bring in God and the supernatural to explain the workings of nature, since we now have a scientific explanation for them. As a result, the general public has come to think that belief in a creator belongs to a primitive and unsophisticated stage of human thinking and has been rendered both unnecessary and impossible by science.

Although science can answer 'how' questions in terms of causes and mechanisms, it cannot answer 'why' questions, questions of purpose and intention.

But there is an obvious fallacy here. Think of a Ford motor car. It is conceivable that a primitive person who was seeing one for the first time and who did not understand the principles of an internal combustion engine, might imagine that there was a god (Mr Ford) inside the engine, making it go. He might further imagine that when the engine ran sweetly that was because Mr Ford inside the engine liked him, and when it refused to go that was because Mr Ford did not like him. Of course, if eventually this primitive person became civilised, learned engineering, and took the engine to pieces, he would discover that there was no Mr Ford inside the engine, and that he did not need to introduce Mr Ford as an explanation for the working of the engine. His grasp of the impersonal principles of internal combustion would be altogether enough to explain how the engine worked. So far, so good. But if he then decided that his understanding of the principles of the internal combustion engine made it impossible to believe in the existence of a Mr Ford who designed the engine, this would be patently false!

FIGURE Ap.2. Model T Ford Motor Car.

Introducing the world's first moving assembly line in 1913, Ford Motor Company built more than 15 million Model Ts from 1908 until 1927.

Reproduced with permission of ©iStock/Peter Mah.

It is likewise a confusion of categories to suppose that our understanding of the impersonal principles according to which the universe works makes it either unnecessary or impossible to believe in the existence of a personal creator who designed, made and upholds the great engine that is the universe. In other words, we should not confuse the mechanisms by which the universe works with its Cause. Every one of us knows how to distinguish between the consciously willed movement of an arm for a purpose and an involuntary spasmodic movement of an arm induced by accidental contact with an electric current.

Michael Poole, Visiting Research Fellow, Science and Religion, at King's College London, in his published debate on science and religion with Richard Dawkins, puts it this way:

> There is no logical conflict between reason-giving explanations which concern mechanisms, and reason-giving explanations which concern the plans and purposes of an agent, human or divine. This is a logical point, not a matter of whether one does or does not happen to believe in God oneself.[4]

---

[4] Poole, 'Critique of Aspects of the Philosophy and Theology of Richard Dawkins', 49.

One of the authors, in a debate with Richard Dawkins, noted how his opponent was confusing the categories of mechanism and agency:

> When Isaac Newton, for example, discovered his law of gravity and wrote down the equations of motion, he didn't say, 'Marvellous, I now understand it. I've got a mechanism therefore I don't need God.' In fact it was the exact opposite. It was because he understood the complexity of sophistication of the mathematical description of the universe that his praise for God was increased. And I would like to suggest, Richard, that somewhere down in this you're making a category mistake, because you're confusing mechanism with agency. We have a mechanism that does XYZ, therefore there's no need for an agent. I would suggest that the sophistication of the mechanism, and science rejoices in finding such mechanisms, is evidence for the sheer wonder of the creative genius of God.[5]

In spite of the clarity of the logic expressed in these counterpoints, a famous statement made by the French mathematician Laplace is constantly misappropriated to support atheism. On being asked by Napoleon where God fitted in to his mathematical work, Laplace replied: 'Sir, I have no need of that hypothesis.' Of course, God did not appear in Laplace's mathematical description of how things work, just as Mr Ford would not appear in a scientific description of the laws of internal combustion. But what does that prove? Such an argument can no more be used to prove that God does not exist than it can be used to prove that Mr Ford does not exist.

To sum up, then, it is important to be aware of the danger of confusing different levels of explanation and of thinking that one level of explanation tells the whole story.

This leads us at once to consider the related question of reductionism.

---

[5] Lennox's response to Dawkins's first thesis 'Faith is blind; science is evidence-based', 'The God Delusion Debate', hosted by Fixed Point Foundation, University of Alabama at Birmingham, filmed and broadcast live 3 October 2007, http://fixed-point.org/index.php/video/35-full-length/164-the-dawkins-lennox-debate. Transcript provided courtesy of ProTorah, http://www.protorah.com/god-delusion-debate-dawkins-lennox-transcript/.

Reductionism

In order to study something, especially if it is complex, scientists often split it up into separate parts or aspects and thus 'reduce' it to simpler components that are individually easier to investigate. This kind of reductionism, often called methodological or structural reductionism, is part of the normal process of science and has proved very useful. It is, however, very important to bear in mind that there may well be, and usually is, more to a given whole than simply what we obtain by adding up all that we have learned from the parts. Studying all the parts of a watch separately will never enable you to grasp how the complete watch works as an integrated whole.

Besides methodological reductionism there are two further types of reductionism, epistemological and ontological. *Epistemological reductionism* is the view that higher level sciences can be explained without remainder by the sciences at a lower level. That is, chemistry is explained by physics; biochemistry by chemistry; biology by biochemistry; psychology by biology; sociology by brain science; and theology by sociology. As Francis Crick puts it: 'The ultimate aim of the modern development in biology is in fact to explain all biology in terms of physics and chemistry.'[6] The former Charles Simonyi Professor of the Public Understanding of Science at Oxford, Richard Dawkins, holds the same view: 'My task is to explain elephants, and the world of complex things, in terms of the simple things that physicists either understand, or are working on.'[7] The ultimate goal of reductionism is to reduce all human behaviour, our likes and dislikes, the entire mental landscape of our lives, to physics.

> The ultimate goal of reductionism is to reduce all human behaviour, our likes and dislikes, the entire mental landscape of our lives, to physics.

However, both the viability and the plausibility of this programme are open to serious question. The outstanding Russian psychologist Leo Vygotsky (1896–1934) was critical of certain aspects of this reductionist philosophy as applied to psychology. He pointed out that such reductionism often conflicts with the goal of preserving all the basic features of a phenomenon or event that one wishes to explain. For

---

[6] Crick, *Of Molecules and Men*, 10.
[7] Dawkins, *Blind Watchmaker*, 15.

example, one can reduce water (H_2O) into H and O. However, hydrogen burns and oxygen is necessary for burning, whereas water has neither of these properties, but has many others that are not possessed by either hydrogen or oxygen. Thus, Vygotsky's view was that reductionism can only be done up to certain limits. Karl Popper says: 'There is almost always an unresolved residue left by even the most successful attempts at reduction.'[8]

Furthermore, Michael Polanyi argues the intrinsic implausibility of expecting epistemological reductionism to work in every circumstance.[9] Think of the various levels of process involved in building an office building with bricks. First of all there is the process of extracting the raw materials out of which the bricks have to be made. Then there are the successively higher levels of making the bricks, they do not make themselves; bricklaying, the bricks do not self-assemble; designing the building, it does not design itself; and planning the town in which the building is to be built, it does not organise itself. Each level has its own rules. The laws of physics and chemistry govern the raw material of the bricks; technology prescribes the art of brick making; architecture teaches the builders, and the architects are controlled by the town planners. Each level is controlled by the level above, but the reverse is not true. The laws of a higher level cannot be derived from the laws of a lower level (although, of course what can be done at a higher level will depend on the lower levels: for example, if the bricks are not strong there will be a limit on the height of a building that can be safely built with them).

Consider the page you are reading just now. It consists of paper imprinted with ink or, in the case of an electronic version, text rendered digitally. It is obvious that the physics and chemistry of ink and paper can never, even in principle, tell you anything about the significance of the shapes of the letters on the page. And this is nothing to do with the fact that physics and chemistry are not yet sufficiently advanced to deal with this question. Even if we allow these sciences another 1,000 years of development, we can see that it will make no difference, because the shapes of those letters demand a totally new and higher level of

---

[8] Popper, 'Scientific Reduction.'
[9] Polanyi, *Tacit Dimension*.

explanation than that of which physics and chemistry are capable. In fact, explanation can only be given in terms of the concepts of language and authorship—the communication of a message by a person. The ink and paper are carriers of the message, but the message certainly does not emerge automatically from them. Furthermore, when it comes to language itself, there is again a sequence of levels—you cannot derive a vocabulary from phonetics, or the grammar of a language from its vocabulary, etc.

As is well known, the genetic material DNA carries information. We shall describe this later on in some detail, but the basic idea is simply this. DNA, a substance found in every living cell, can be looked at as a long tape on which there is a string of letters written in a four-letter chemical language. The sequence of letters contains coded instructions (information) that the cell uses to make proteins. Physical biochemist and theologian Arthur Peacocke writes: 'In no way can the concept of "information", the concept of conveying a message, be articulated in terms of the concepts of physics and chemistry, even though the latter can be shown to explain how the molecular machinery (DNA, RNA and protein) operates to carry information.'[10]

In each of the situations we have described above, we have a series of levels, each one higher than the previous one. What happens on a higher level is not completely derivable from what happens on the level beneath it, but requires another level of explanation.

In this kind of situation it is sometimes said that the higher level phenomena 'emerge' from the lower level. Unfortunately, however, the word 'emerge' is easily misunderstood to mean that the higher level properties emerge automatically from the lower level properties. This is clearly false in general, as we showed by considering brick making and writing on paper. Yet notwithstanding the fact that both writing on paper and DNA have in common the fact that they encode a 'message', those scientists committed to materialistic philosophy insist that the information carrying properties of DNA must have emerged automatically out of mindless matter. For if, as materialism insists, matter and energy are all that there is, then it logically follows that they must

---

[10] Peacocke, *Experiment of Life*, 54.

possess the inherent potential to organise themselves in such a way that eventually all the complex molecules necessary for life, including DNA, will emerge.[11]

There is a third type of reductionism, called *ontological reductionism*, which is frequently encountered in statements like the following: The universe is nothing but a collection of atoms in motion, human beings are 'machines for propagating DNA, and the propagation of DNA is a self-sustaining process. It is every living object's sole reason for living'.[12]

Words such as 'nothing but', 'sole' or 'simply' are the telltale sign of (ontological) reductionist thinking. If we remove these words we are usually left with something unobjectionable. The universe certainly is a collection of atoms and human beings do propagate DNA. The question is, is there nothing more to it than that? Are we going to say with Francis Crick, who won the Nobel Prize jointly with James D. Watson for his discovery of the double helix structure of DNA: '"You", your joys and your sorrows, your memories and your ambitions, your sense of personal identity and free will, are in fact no more than the behaviour of a vast assembly of nerve cells and their associated molecules'?[13]

What shall we say of human love and fear, of concepts like beauty and truth? Are they meaningless?

Ontological reductionism, carried to its logical conclusion, would ask us to believe that a Rembrandt painting is nothing but molecules of paint scattered on canvas. Physicist and theologian John Polkinghorne's reaction is clear:

> There is more to the world than physics can ever express.
>
> One of the fundamental experiences of the scientific life is that of wonder at the beautiful structure of the world. It is the pay-off for all the weary hours of labour involved in the pursuit of research. Yet in the world described by science where would that wonder find its lodging? Or our experiences of beauty? Of moral obligation? Of the presence of God? These seem to me to be quite

---

[11] Whether matter and energy do have this capacity is another matter that is discussed in the books noted at the end of this appendix.
[12] Dawkins, *Growing Up in the Universe* (study guide), 21.
[13] Crick, *Astonishing Hypothesis*, 3.

as fundamental as anything we could measure in the laboratory. A worldview that does not take them adequately into account is woefully incomplete.[14]

The most devastating criticism of ontological reductionism is that it is self-destructive. Polkinghorne describes its programme as ultimately suicidal:

> For, not only does it relegate our experiences of beauty, moral obligation, and religious encounter to the epiphenomenal scrapheap. It also destroys rationality. Thought is replaced by electrochemical neural events. Two such events cannot confront each other in rational discourse. They are neither right nor wrong. They simply happen. . . . The very assertions of the reductionist himself are nothing but blips in the neural network of his brain. The world of rational discourse dissolves into the absurd chatter of firing synapses. Quite frankly, that cannot be right and none of us believes it to be so.[15]

BASIC OPERATIONAL PRESUPPOSITIONS

So far we have been concentrating on the scientific method and have seen that this is a much more complex (and, for that reason, a much more interesting) topic than may first appear. As promised earlier, we must now consider the implications of the fact that scientists, being human like the rest of us, do not come to any situation with their mind completely clear of preconceived ideas. The widespread idea that any scientist, if only he or she tries to be impartial, can be a completely dispassionate observer in any but the most trivial of situations, is a fallacy, as has been pointed out repeatedly by philosophers of science and by scientists themselves. At the very least scientists must already

> The widespread idea that any scientist, if only he or she tries to be impartial, can be a completely dispassionate observer in any but the most trivial of situations, is a fallacy.

---

[14] Polkinghorne, *One World*, 72–3.
[15] Polkinghorne, *One World*, 92–3.

have formed some idea or theory about the nature of what they are about to study.

Observation is dependent on theory

It is simply not possible to make observations and do experiments without any presuppositions. Consider, for example, the fact that science, by its very nature, has to be selective. It would clearly be impossible to take every aspect of any given object of study into account. Scientists must therefore choose what variables are likely to be important and what are not. For example, physicists do not think of taking into account the colour of billiard balls when they are conducting a laboratory investigation of the application of Newton's laws to motion: but the shape of the balls is very important—cubical balls would not be much use! In making such choices, scientists are inevitably guided by already formed ideas and theories about what the important factors are likely to be. The problem is that such ideas may sometimes be wrong and cause scientists to miss vital aspects of a problem to such an extent that they draw false conclusions. A famous story about the physicist Heinrich Hertz illustrates this.

Maxwell's electromagnetic theory predicted that radio and light waves would be propagated with the same velocity. Hertz designed an experiment to check this and found that the velocities were different. His mistake, only discovered after his death, was that he did not think that the shape of his laboratory could have any influence on the results of his experiment. Unfortunately for him, it did. Radio waves were reflected from the walls and distorted his results.

The validity of his observations depended on the (preconceived) theory that the shape of the laboratory was irrelevant to his experiment. The fact that this preconception was false invalidated his conclusions.

This story also points up another difficulty. How does one decide in this kind of situation whether it is the theory or the experiment that is at fault, whether one should trust the results of the experiment and abandon the theory and look for a better one, or whether one should keep on having faith in the theory and try to discover what was wrong with the experiment? There is no easy answer to this question. A great deal will depend on the experience and judgment of the scientists involved, and, inevitably, mistakes can and will be made.

Knowledge cannot be gained without making certain assumptions to start with

Scientists not only inevitably have preconceived ideas about particular situations, as illustrated by the story about Hertz, but their science is done within a framework of general assumptions about science as such. World-famous Harvard geneticist Richard Lewontin writes: 'Scientists, like other intellectuals, come to their work with a world view, a set of preconceptions that provides the framework for their analysis of the world.'[16]

And those preconceptions can significantly affect scientists' research methods as well as their results and interpretations of those results, as we shall see.

We would emphasise, however, that the fact that scientists have presuppositions is not to be deprecated. That would, in fact be a nonsensical attitude to adopt. For the voice of logic reminds us that we cannot get to know anything if we are not prepared to presuppose something. Let's unpack this idea by thinking about a common attitude. 'I am not prepared to take anything for granted', says someone, 'I will only accept something if you prove it to me.' Sounds reasonable—but it isn't. For if this is your view then you will never accept or know anything! For suppose I want you to accept some proposition A. You will only accept it if I prove it to you. But I shall have to prove it to you on the basis of some other proposition B. You will only accept B if I prove it to you. I shall have to prove B to you on the basis of C. And so it will go on forever in what is called an infinite regress—that is, if you insist on taking nothing for granted in the first place!

We must all start somewhere with things we take as self-evident, basic assumptions that are not proved on the basis of something else. They are often called *axioms*.[17] Whatever axioms we adopt, we then proceed to try to make sense of the world by building on those

---

[16] Lewontin, *Dialectical Biologist*, 267.
[17] It should be borne in mind, however, that the axioms which appear in various branches of pure mathematics, for example, the theory of numbers or the theory of groups, do not appear out of nowhere. They usually arise from the attempt to encapsulate and formalise years, sometimes centuries, of mathematical research, into a so-called 'axiomatic system'.

axioms. This is true, not only at the worldview level but also in all of our individual disciplines. We retain those axioms that prove useful in the sense that they lead to theories which show a better 'fit' with nature and experience, and we abandon or modify those which do not fit so well. One thing is absolutely clear: none of us can avoid starting with assumptions.

Gaining knowledge involves trusting our senses and other people

There are essentially two sources from which we accumulate knowledge:

1. directly by our own 'hands-on' experience, for example, by accidentally putting our finger in boiling water, we learn that boiling water scalds;
2. we learn all kinds of things from sources external to ourselves, for example, teachers, books, parents, the media, etc.

In doing so we all constantly exercise faith. We intuitively trust our senses, even though we know they deceive us on times. For example, in extremely cold weather, if we put our hand on a metal handrail outside, the rail may feel hot to our touch.

We have faith, too, in our minds to interpret our senses, though here again we know that our minds can be deceived.

We also normally believe what other people tell us—teachers, parents, friends, etc. Sometimes we check what we learn from them because, without insulting them, we realise that even friends can be mistaken, and other people may set out to deceive us. However, much more often than not, we accept things on authority—if only because no one has time to check everything! In technical matters we trust our textbooks. We have faith in what (other) scientists have done. And it is, of course, reasonable so to do, though those experts themselves would teach us to be critical and not just to accept everything on their say-so. They would remind us also that the fact that a statement appears in print in a book, does not make it automatically true!

Gaining scientific knowledge involves belief in the rational intelligibility of the universe

We all take so much for granted the fact that we can use human reason as a probe to investigate the universe that we can fail to see that this is really something to be wondered at. For once we begin to think about the intelligibility of the universe, our minds demand an explanation. But where can we find one? Science cannot give it to us, for the very simple reason that science has to assume the rational intelligibility of the universe in order to get started. Einstein himself, in the same article we quoted earlier, makes this very clear in saying that the scientist's belief in the rational intelligibility of the universe goes beyond science and is in its very nature essentially religious:

> Science can only be created by those who are thoroughly imbued with the aspiration toward truth and understanding. This source of feeling, however, springs from the sphere of religion. To this there also belongs the faith in the possibility that the regulations valid for the world of existence are rational, that is, comprehensible to reason. I cannot conceive of a genuine scientist without that profound faith.[18]

Einstein saw no reason to be embarrassed by the fact that science involves at its root belief in something that science itself cannot justify.

Allied to belief in the rational intelligibility of the universe is the belief that patterns and law-like behaviour are to be expected in nature. The Greeks expressed this by using the word *cosmos* which means 'ordered'. It is this underlying expectation of order that lies behind the confidence with which scientists use the inductive method. Scientists speak of their belief in the uniformity of nature—the idea that the order in nature and the laws that describe it are valid at all times and in all parts of the universe.

Many theists from the Jewish, Islamic or Christian tradition would want to modify this concept of the uniformity of nature by adding their conviction that God the Creator has built regularities

---

[18] Einstein, *Out of My Later Years*, 26.

FIGURE Ap.3. Milky Way Galaxy.

The Milky Way galaxy is visible from earth on clear nights away from urban areas. Appearing as a cloud in the night sky, our galaxy's spiral bands of dust and glowing nebulae consist of billions of stars as seen from the inside.

Reproduced with permission of ©iStock/Viktar.

into the working of the universe so that in general we can speak of uniformity—the norms to which nature normally operates. But because God is the Creator, he is not a prisoner of those regularities but can vary them by causing things to happen that do not fit into the regular pattern.

Here, again, commitment to the uniformity of nature is a matter of belief. Science cannot prove to us that nature is uniform, since we must assume the uniformity of nature in order to do science. Otherwise we would have no confidence that, if we repeat an experiment under the same conditions as it was done before, we shall get the same result. Were it so, our school textbooks would be useless. But surely, we might say, the uniformity of nature is highly probable since assuming it has led to such stunning scientific advance. However, as C. S. Lewis has observed: 'Can we say that Uniformity is at any rate very probable? Unfortunately not. We have just seen that all probabilities depend on *it*. Unless Nature is uniform, nothing is either probable or improbable.'[19]

---

[19] Lewis, *Miracles*, 163.

Operating within the reigning paradigms

Thomas Kuhn in his famous book *The Structure of Scientific Revolutions* (1962) pictured science as preceding through the following stages: pre-science, normal science, crisis revolution, new normal science, new crisis, and so on. Pre-science is the diverse and disorganised activity characterised by much disagreement that precedes the emergence of a new science that gradually becomes structured when a scientific community adheres to a paradigm. The paradigm is a web of assumptions and theories that are more or less agreed upon and are like the steelwork around which the scientific edifice is erected. Well-known examples are the paradigms of Copernican astronomy, Newtonian mechanics and evolutionary biology.

    Normal science is then practised within the paradigm. It sets the standards for legitimate research. The normal scientist uses the paradigm to probe nature. He or she does not (often) look critically at the paradigm itself, because it commands so much agreement, much as we look down the light of a torch to illuminate an object, rather than look critically at the light of the torch itself. For this reason the paradigm will be very resistant to attempts to demonstrate that it is false. When anomalies, difficulties and apparent falsifications turn up, the normal scientists will hope to be able to accommodate them preferably within the paradigm or by making fine adjustments to the paradigm. However, if the difficulties can no longer be resolved and keep on piling up, a crisis situation develops, which leads to a scientific revolution involving the emergence of a new paradigm that then gains the ground to such an extent that the older paradigm is eventually completely abandoned. The essence of such a paradigm shift is the replacing of an old paradigm by a new one, not the refining of the old one by the new. The best known example of a major paradigm shift is the transition from Aristotelian geocentric (earth-centred) astronomy to Copernican heliocentric (sun-centred) astronomy in the sixteenth century.

Although Kuhn's work is open to criticism at various points, he has certainly made scientists aware of a number of issues that are important for our understanding of how science works:

1. the central role that metaphysical ideas play in the development of scientific theories;
2. the high resistance that paradigms show to attempts to prove them false;
3. the fact that science is subject to human frailty.

The second of these points has both a positive and a negative outworking. It means that a good paradigm will not be overturned automatically by the first experimental result or observation that appears to speak against it. On the other hand, it means that a paradigm which eventually proves to be inadequate or false, may take a long time to die and impede scientific progress by constraining scientists within its mesh and not giving them the freedom they need to explore radically new ideas that would yield real scientific advance.

It is important to realise that paradigms themselves are often influenced at a very deep level by worldview considerations. We saw earlier that there are essentially two fundamental worldviews, the materialistic and the theistic. It seems to be the case in science that there is sometimes a tacit understanding that only paradigms which are based on materialism are admissible as scientific. Richard Dawkins, for example, says, 'the kind of explanation we come up with must not contradict the laws of physics. Indeed it will make use of the laws of physics, and nothing more than the laws of physics.'[20] It is the words 'nothing more than' that show that Dawkins is only prepared to accept reductionist, materialistic explanations.

Further reading

Books by John Lennox:

God and Stephen Hawking: Whose Design Is It Anyway? (Lion, 2011)

God's Undertaker: Has Science Buried God? (Lion, 2009)

Gunning for God: A Critique of the New Atheism (Lion, 2011)

Miracles: Is Belief in the Supernatural Irrational? VeriTalks Vol. 2. (The Veritas Forum, 2013)

Seven Days That Divide the World (Zondervan, 2011)

---

[20] Dawkins, *Blind Watchmaker*, 24.

SERIES BIBLIOGRAPHY

See also reading lists given on p. 331.

BOOKS

A

Abbott, Edwin. *Flatland: A Romance of Many Dimensions*. London, 1884. Repr. Oxford: Oxford University Press, 2006.

Ambrose, E. J. *The Nature and Origin of the Biological World*. New York: Halsted Press, 1982.

Ammon, Otto. *Die Gesellschaftsordnung und ihre natürlichen Grundlagen*. Jena: Gustav Fisher, 1895.

Anderson, J. N. D. (Norman). *Christianity: The Witness of History*. London: Tyndale Press, 1969.

Anderson, J. N. D. (Norman). *The Evidence for the Resurrection*. 1950. Leicester: InterVarsity Press, 1990.

Anderson, J. N. D. (Norman). *Islam in the Modern World*. Leicester: Apollos, 1990.

Andreyev, G. L. *What Kind of Morality Does Religion Teach?* Moscow: 'Znaniye', 1959.

Aristotle. *Metaphysics*. Tr. W. D. Ross, *Aristotle's Metaphysics: A Revised Text with Introduction and Commentary*. Vol. 2. Oxford: Clarendon Press, 1924.

Aristotle. *Nicomachean Ethics*. Tr. W. D. Ross. Oxford: Clarendon Press, 1925. Repr. Kitchener, Ont.: Batoche Books, 1999. Also tr. David Ross. Oxford: Oxford University Press, 1980.

Arnold, Thomas. *Christian Life, Its Hopes, Its Fears, and Its Close: Sermons preached mostly in the chapel of Rugby School, 1841–1842*. 1842. New edn, London: Longmans, 1878.

Ashman, Keith M. and Philip S. Baringer, eds. *After the Science Wars*. London: Routledge, 2001.

Atkins, Peter. *Creation Revisited*. Harmondsworth: Penguin, 1994.

Augustine of Hippo. *Confessions*. AD 397–400. Tr. Henry Chadwick, *The Confessions*. Oxford, 1991. Repr. Oxford World's Classics. Oxford: Oxford University Press, 2008.

Avise, John C. *The Genetic Gods, Evolution and Belief in Human Affairs*. Cambridge, Mass.: Harvard University Press, 1998.

Ayer, A. J., ed. *The Humanist Outlook*. London: Pemberton, 1968.

B

Bacon, Francis. *Advancement of Learning*. 1605. Ed. G. W. Kitchin, 1915. Repr. London: Dent, 1930. Online at http://archive.org/details/ advancementlearn00bacouoft (facsimile of 1915 edn).

Bādarāyana, Śankarācārya and George Thibaut. *The Vedānta Sūtras of Bādarāyana*. Vol. 34 of *Sacred books of the East*. Oxford: Clarendon Press, 1890.

Baier, Kurt. *The Moral Point of View: A Rational Basis of Ethics*. Ithaca, N.Y.: Cornell University Press, 1958.

Behe, Michael J. *Darwin's Black Box: The Biochemical Challenge to Evolution*. 1988. 10th ann. edn with new Afterword, New York: Simon & Schuster, 2006.

Bentham, Jeremy. *An Introduction to the Principles of Morals and Legislation*. 1780, 1789. Dover Philosophical Classics. Repr. of Bentham's 1823 rev. edn, Mineola, N.Y.: Dover Publications, 2007.

Berdyaev, N. A. *The Beginning and The End*. Tr. R. M. French. London: Geoffrey Bles, 1952.

Berlinski, David. *The Deniable Darwin and Other Essays*. Seattle, Wash.: Discovery Institute, 2009.

Bickerton, Derek. *Language and Species*. 1990. Repr. Chicago: University of Chicago Press, 1992.

Biddiss, M. D. *Father of Racist Ideology: The Social and Political Thought of Count Gobineau*. New York: Weybright & Talley, 1970.

Bouquet, A. C. *Comparative Religion*. Harmondsworth: Penguin (Pelican), 1962.

Breck, John. *The Sacred Gift of Life: Orthodox Christianity and Bioethics*. Crestwood, N.Y.: St. Vladimir's Seminary Press, 1998.

Bronowski, Jacob. *The Identity of Man*. Harmondsworth: Penguin, 1967.

Brow, Robert. *Religion, Origins and Ideas*. London: Tyndale Press, 1966.

Bruce, F. F. *1 and 2 Corinthians*. New Century Bible Commentary. London: Oliphants, 1971.

Bruce, F. F. *The New Testament Documents: Are They Reliable?* 1943. 6th edn, Nottingham: Inter-Varsity Press, 2000.

Butterfield, Herbert. *Christianity and History*. London: Bell, 1949. Repr. London: Fontana, 1958.

C

Cairns-Smith, A. G. *The Life Puzzle*. Edinburgh: Oliver & Boyd, 1971.

Caputo, John D., ed. *Deconstruction in a Nutshell: A Conversation with Jacques Derrida*. Perspectives in Continental Philosophy No. 1. 1997. Repr. New York: Fordham University Press, 2004.

Cary, M. and T. J. Haarhoff. *Life and Thought in the Greek and Roman World*. 5th edn, London: Methuen, 1951.

Chalmers, David J. *The Conscious Mind: In Search of a Fundamental Theory*. Oxford: Oxford University Press, 1996.

Chamberlain, Paul. *Can We Be Good Without God?: A Conversation about Truth, Morality, Culture and a Few Other Things That Matter*. Downers Grove, Ill.: InterVarsity Press, 1996.

Chomsky, Noam. *Knowledge of Language: Its Nature, Origin and Use*. New York: Praeger, 1986.

Chomsky, Noam. *Language and Mind*. 1972. 3rd edn, Cambridge: Cambridge University Press, 2006.

Chomsky, Noam. *Syntactic Structures*. The Hague: Mouton, 1957.

Cicero, Marcus Tullius. *Cicero, Selected Political Speeches*. Tr. Michael Grant. Harmondsworth: Penguin Books, 1969.

Cicero, Marcus Tullius. *De Natura Deorum*. Tr. H. Rackham, Loeb Classical Library, No. 268. Cambridge, Mass.: Harvard University Press, 1933.

Cicero, Marcus Tullius. *The Nature of the Gods*. Tr. H. C. P. McGregor. London: Penguin, 1972.

Cicero, Marcus Tullius. *Pro Rabirio*.

Clement of Alexandria. Stromata [or, Miscellanies]. In Kirk, G. S., J. E. Raven and M. Schofield. *The Presocratic Philosophers: A Critical History with a Selection of Texts*. 1957. Rev. edn, Cambridge: Cambridge University Press, 1983. Online at http://www.ccel.org/ccel/schaff/anf02.vi.iv.html, accessed 29 Sept. 2015.

Cornford, F. M. *Before and After Socrates*. 1932. Repr. Cambridge: Cambridge University Press, 1999. doi: 10.1017/CBO9780511570308, accessed 29 Sept. 2015.

Craig, Edward, gen. ed. *Concise Routledge Encyclopaedia of Philosophy*. London: Routledge, 2000.

Craig, William Lane. *Reasonable Faith: Christian Truth and Apologetics*. 1994. 3rd edn, Wheaton, Ill.: Crossway, 2008.

Crane, Stephen. *War Is Kind*. New York: Frederick A. Stokes, 1899. Online at http://www.gutenberg.org/ebooks/9870, accessed 11 Sept. 2015.

Cranfield, C. E. B. *A Critical and Exegetical Commentary on the Epistle to the Romans*. Vol. 1. The International Critical Commentary. Edinburgh: T&T Clark, 1975.

Crick, Francis. *The Astonishing Hypothesis: The Scientific Search for the Soul*. New York: Scribner, 1994.

Crick, Francis. *Life Itself: Its Origin and Nature*. New York: Simon & Schuster, 1981.

Crick, Francis. *Of Molecules and Men*. 1966 Jessie and John Danz Lectures. Seattle, Wash.: University of Washington Press, 1966.

Cudakov. A. *Komsomol'skaja Pravda* (11 Oct. 1988).

Culler, Jonathan. *On Deconstruction: Theory and Criticism after Structuralism*. 1982. 25th ann. edn, Ithaca, N.Y.: Cornell University Press, 2007.

D

Darwin, Charles. *The Descent of Man, and Selection in Relation to Sex*. 1871. 2nd edn, New York: A. L. Burt, 1874. Ed. James Moore and Adrian Desmond, Penguin Classics, London: Penguin Books, 2004.

Darwin, Charles. *On the Origin of Species*. 1859. Repr. World's Classics Edition, Oxford: Oxford University Press, 2008. Also cited is the 6th edn (1872) reprinted by New York University Press, 1988. Citations to one or the other edition are indicated as such.

Darwin, Francis. *The Life and Letters of Charles Darwin*. London: John Murray, 1887. doi: 10.5962/bhl.title.1416, accessed 29 June 2015.

Davies, Paul. *The Cosmic Blueprint: New Discoveries in Nature's Creative Ability to Order the Universe*. 1988. Repr. West Conshohocken, Pa.: Templeton Foundation Press, 2004.

Davies, Paul. *The Fifth Miracle: The Search for the Origin and Meaning of Life*. 1999. Repr. New York: Touchstone, 2000.

Davies, Paul. *God and the New Physics*. London: J. M. Dent, 1983. Repr. London: Penguin Books, 1990.

Davies, Paul. *The Mind of God: Science and the Search for Ultimate Meaning*. 1992. Repr. London: Simon & Schuster, 2005.

Davies, Paul and John Gribbin. *The Matter Myth: Dramatic Discoveries that Challenge Our Understanding of Physical Reality*. London, 1991. Repr. London: Simon & Schuster, 2007.

Davis, Percival and Dean H. Kenyon. *Of Pandas and People: The Central Question of Biological Origins*. 1989. 2nd edn, Dallas, Tex.: Haughton Publishing, 1993.

Dawkins, Richard. *The Blind Watchmaker*. 1986. Rev. edn, 2006. Repr. London: Penguin, 2013.

Dawkins, Richard. *Climbing Mount Improbable*. New York: Norton, 1996.

Dawkins, Richard. *Growing Up in the Universe*. The Royal Institution Christmas Lectures for Children, 1991. Five one-hour episodes directed by Stuart McDonald for the BBC. 2-Disc DVD set released 20 April 2007 by the Richard Dawkins Foundation. Available on the Ri Channel, http://www.rigb.org/christmas-lectures/watch/1991/growing-up-in-the-universe. Study Guide with the same title. London: BBC Education, 1991.

Dawkins, Richard. *River Out of Eden: A Darwinian View of Life*. 1995. Repr. London: Phoenix, 2004.

Dawkins, Richard. *The Selfish Gene*. 1976. Repr. 30th ann. edn, Oxford: Oxford University Press, 2006.

Dawkins, Richard. *Unweaving the Rainbow: Science, Delusion and the Appetite for Wonder*. 1998. Repr. London: Penguin Books, 2006.

Dawkins, Richard and John Lennox. 'The God Delusion Debate', hosted by Fixed Point Foundation, University of Alabama at Birmingham, filmed and broadcast live 3 October 2007, online at http://fixed-point.org/video/richard-dawkins-vs-john-lennox-the-god-delusion-debate/. Transcript provided courtesy of ProTorah.com, http://www.protorah.com/god-delusion-debate-dawkins-lennox-transcript/.

Deacon, Terrence. *The Symbolic Species: The Co-Evolution of Language and the Human Brain*. London: Allen Lane, 1997.

Dembski, William A. *Being as Communion: A Metaphysics of Information*. Ashgate Science and Religion. Farnham, Surrey: Ashgate, 2014.

Dembski, William A. *The Design Inference: Eliminating Chance through Small Probabilities*. Cambridge Studies in Probability, Induction and Decision Theory. Cambridge: Cambridge University Press, 1998.

Dembski, William A., ed. *Uncommon Dissent: Intellectuals Who Find Darwinism Unconvincing*. Wilmington, Del.: Intercollegiate Studies Institute, 2004.

Dennett, Daniel. *Darwin's Dangerous Idea: Evolution and the Meanings of Life*. 1995; London: Penguin, 1996.

Denton, Michael. *Evolution: A Theory in Crisis*. 1986. 3rd rev. edn, Bethesda, Md.: Adler & Adler, 1986.

Derrida, Jacques. *Of Grammatology*. 1967 (French). Tr. G. C. Spivak, 1974. Repr. Baltimore, Md.: Johns Hopkins University Press, 1997.

Derrida, Jacques. *Positions*. 1972 (French). Tr. and ed. Alan Bass, 1981. 2nd edn 2002. Repr. London: Continuum, 2010.

Derrida, Jacques. *Writing and Difference*. 1967 (French). Tr. Alan Bass, Chicago, 1978. Repr. London: Routledge Classics, 2001.

Descartes, René. *Discourse on the Method of Rightly Conducting Reason and Reaching the Truth in the Sciences*. 1637. Online at https://www.gutenberg.org/files/59/59-h/59-h.htm, accessed 11 Sept. 2015.

Descartes, René. *Meditations on First Philosophy*. Paris, 1641.

Deutsch, David. *The Fabric of Reality*. London: Penguin, 1997.

Dewey, John. *A Common Faith*. New Haven: Yale University Press, 1934.

Dostoevsky, F. *The Collected Works of Dostoevsky*. Tr. Rodion Raskolnikoff [German]. Munich: Piper, 1866.

Dostoevsky, Fyodor. *The Karamazov Brothers*. 1880 (Russian). Tr. and ed. David McDuff, Penguin Classics, 1993. Rev. edn, London: Penguin Books, 2003.

E

Eastwood, C. Cyril. *Life and Thought in the Ancient World*. Derby: Peter Smith, 1964.

Easwaran, Eknath. *The Bhagavad Gita*. 1985. Berkeley, Calif.: Nilgiri Press, 2007.

Easwaran, Eknath. *The Upanishads*. 1987. Berkeley, Calif.: Nilgiri Press, 2007.

Eccles, John C. *Evolution of the Brain, Creation of the Self*. 1989. Repr. London: Routledge, 2005.

Einstein, A. *Letters to Solovine: 1906–1955*. New York: Philosophical Library, 1987.

Einstein, A. *Out of My Later Years: The Scientist, Philosopher, and Man Portrayed Through His Own Words*. 1956. Secaucus, N.J.: Carol Publishing, 1995.

Eldredge, Niles. *Reinventing Darwin: The Great Debate at the High Table of Evolutionary Theory*. New York: Wiley, 1995.

Eldredge, Niles. *Time Frames: The Evolution of Punctuated Equilibria*. 1985. Corr. edn, Princeton, N.J.: Princeton University Press, 1989.

Ellis, John M. *Against Deconstruction*. Princeton, N.J.: Princeton University Press, 1989.

The Encyclopedia Britannica. 15th edn (*Britannica 3*), ed. Warren E. Preece and Philip W. Goetz. Chicago: Encyclopaedia Britannica, 1974–2012.

Engels, Friedrich. *Ludwig Feuerbach and the End of Classical German Philosophy*. German original first published in 1886, in *Die Neue Zeit*. Moscow: Progress Publishers, 1946.

Erbrich, Paul. *Zufall: Eine Naturwissenschaftlich-Philosophische Untersuchung*. Stuttgart: Kohlhammer, 1988.

Euripides. *The Bacchae*. Tr. James Morwood, *Bacchae and Other Plays*. Oxford World's Classics. 1999. Repr. Oxford: Oxford University Press, 2008.

Evans-Pritchard, E. E. *Nuer Religion*. 1956. 2nd edn, London: Oxford University Press, 1971.

F

Feuerbach, Ludwig. *The Essence of Christianity*. 1841. Ed. and tr. George Eliot (Mary Ann Evans). New York: Harper Torchbooks, 1957.

Feynman, Richard. *Six Easy Pieces*. 1963. Repr. London: Penguin Books, 1995.

Fischer, Ernst. *Marx in His Own Words*. Tr. Anna Bostock. London: Penguin Books, 1973.

Fish, Stanley. *Is There a Text in This Class? The Authority of Interpretive Communities*. Cambridge, Mass.: Harvard University Press, 1980.

Fish, Stanley. *There's No Such Thing as Free Speech, and It's a Good Thing Too*. New York: Oxford University Press, 1994.

Flew, Antony with Roy Abraham Varghese. *There Is a God: How the World's Most Notorious Atheist Changed His Mind*. London: HarperCollins, 2007.

Fox, S. W., ed. *The Origins of Prebiological Systems and of Their Molecular Matrices*. New York: Academic Press, 1965.

Frazer, J. G. *The Golden Bough*. 1890, 1900, 1906–15, 1937.

Fromm, Erich. *You Shall be as Gods: A Radical Interpretation of the Old Testament and its Tradition*. New York: Holt, Rinehart & Winston, 1966.

G

Gates, Bill. *The Road Ahead*. 1995. Rev. edn, Harmondsworth: Penguin, 1996.

Geisler, Norman L., and William E. Nix, *A General Introduction to the Bible* (Chicago: Moody Press, 1986), 475. Gerson, Lloyd P. *Plotinus*. London: Routledge, 1994.

Gilligan, Carol. *In a Different Voice: Psychological Theory and Women's Development*. Cambridge, Mass.: Harvard University Press, 1982.

Goldschmidt, Richard. *The Material Basis of Evolution*. The Silliman Memorial Lectures Series. 1940. Repr. Yale University Press, 1982.

Gooding, David W. and John C. Lennox. *The Human Quest for Significance: Forming a Worldview* [in Russian]. Minsk: Myrtlefield Trust, 1999.

Gould, Stephen Jay. *The Lying Stones of Marrakech: Penultimate Reflections in Natural History*. 2000. Repr. Cambridge, Mass.: Harvard University Press, 2011.

Gould, Stephen Jay. *Wonderful Life: The Burgess Shale and the Nature of History*. 1989. Repr. London: Vintage, 2000.

Grant, Michael. *Jesus: An Historian's Review of the Gospels*. New York: Scribner, 1977.

Grene, Marjorie. *A Portrait of Aristotle*. London: Faber & Faber, 1963.

Groothuis, Douglas. *Truth Decay: Defending Christianity against the Challenges of Postmodernism*. Leicester: Inter-Varsity Press, 2000.

Guthrie, W. K. C. *The Greek Philosophers from Thales to Aristotle*. 1950. Repr. London: Methuen, 2013.

Guthrie, W. K. C. *Plato: the man and his dialogues, earlier period*. Vol. 4 of *A History of Greek Philosophy*. 1875. Repr. Cambridge: Cambridge University Press, 2000.

H

Haldane, J. B. S. *Possible Worlds*. 1927. London: Chatto & Windus, 1945.

Harrison, E. *Masks of the Universe*. 1985. 2nd edn, New York: Macmillan, 2003. Citations are to the first Macmillan edition.

Harvey, William. *On the Motion of the Heart and the Blood of Animals*. 1628. Online at https://ebooks.adelaide.edu.au/h/harvey/william/motion/complete.html, accessed 4 Sept. 2018.

Hawking, Stephen. *A Brief History of Time*. 1988. Updated and expanded 10th ann. edn, London: Bantam Press, 1998.

Hawking, Stephen and Leonard Mlodinow. *The Grand Design*. New York: Bantam Books, 2010.

Hegel, G. W. F. *Hegel's Logic. Being Part One of the Encyclopaedia of the Philosophical Sciences* (1830). Tr. William Wallace, 1892. Repr. Oxford: Clarendon Press, 1984–87.

Hegel, G. W. F. *The Phenomenology of the Mind* (Spirit). 1807. 2nd edn 1841. Tr. J. B. Baillie, London, 1910. Repr. Dover Philosophical Classics, New York: Dover Publications, 2003.

Hegel, G. W. F. *The Philosophy of History*. 1861. Tr. J. Sibree, 1857. Repr. New York: Dover Publications, 1956. Repr. Kitchener, Ont.: Batoche Books, 2001. Online at Internet Archive: https://archive.org/details/lecturesonphilos00hegerich/, accessed 19 Oct. 2018.

Hegel, G. W. F. *Wissenschaft der Logik* [The Science of Logic]. Nurnberg, 1812–16.

Hemer, Colin. *The Book of Acts in the Setting of Hellenistic History*. Tübingen: J. C. B. Mohr, Paul Siebeck, 1989.

Hengel, Martin. *Judaism and Hellenism: Studies in their Encounter in Palestine during the Early Hellenistic Period*. Tr. John Bowden. London: SCM Press, 1974. Repr. Eugene, Oreg.: Wipf & Stock, 2003.

Hengel, Martin. *Studies in Early Christology*. Tr. Rollin Kearns. Edinburgh: T&T Clark, 1995.

Herodotus. *The Histories*. Tr. Robin Waterfield, 1998, Oxford World's Classics. Repr. New York: Oxford University Press, 2008.

Herzen, Alexander Ivanovich. *Byloe i dumy*. London, 1853. Tr. C. Garnett, *My Past and Thoughts, The Memoirs of Alexander Herzen*. Revised by H. Higgens, introduced by I. Berlin, 1968. Repr. London: Chatto and Windus, 2008.

Hesiod. *Theogony*. In Charles Abraham Elton, tr. *The remains of Hesiod*. London: Lackington, Allen, 1812. Also in Dorothea Wender, tr. *Hesiod and Theognis*. Harmondsworth: Penguin, 1973.

Hippolytus, *Refutation of all Heresies*. In Kirk, G. S., J. E. Raven and M. Schofield. *The Presocratic Philosophers: A Critical History with a Selection of Texts*. 1957. Rev. edn, Cambridge: Cambridge University Press, 1983.

Holmes, Arthur F. *Ethics*. Downers Grove, Ill.: InterVarsity Press, 1984; 2nd edn, 2007.

Honderich, Ted, ed. *The Oxford Companion to Philosophy*. Oxford, 1995. 2nd edn, Oxford: Oxford University Press, 2005.

Hooper, Judith. *Of Moths and Men*. New York: Norton, 2002.

Hooykaas, R. *Religion and the Rise of Modern Science*. 1972. Repr. Edinbugh: Scottish Academic Press, 2000.

Hospers, John. *An Introduction to Philosophical Analysis*. 1953. 4th edn, Abingdon: Routledge, 1997.

Houghton, John. *The Search for God—Can Science Help?* Oxford: Lion Publishing, 1995.

Hoyle, Fred. *The Intelligent Universe*. London: Joseph, 1983.

Hoyle, Fred and Chandra Wickramasinghe. *Cosmic Life-Force, the Power of Life Across the Universe*. London: Dent, 1988.

Hoyle, Fred and Chandra Wickramasinghe. *Evolution from Space: A Theory of Cosmic Creationism*. New York: Simon & Schuster, 1984.

Hume, David. *David Hume: A Treatise of Human Nature*. 1739–40. Ed. Lewis Amherst Selby-Bigge and P. H. Nidditch. Oxford: Clarendon Press, 1888. Repr. 1978. Repr. Oxford: Oxford University Press, 2014. doi: 10.1093/actrade/9780198245872.book.1, accessed 11 Sept. 2015; also online at https://davidhume.org/texts/t/, accessed 4 Sept.2018.

Hume, David. *Dialogues Concerning Natural Religion*. 1779. Repr. ed. J. C. A. Gaskin, *Dialogues Concerning Natural Religion, and The Natural History of Religion*. Oxford World's Classics. Oxford: Oxford University Press, 2008. Online at https://davidhume.org/texts/d/, accessed 2 Aug. 2017. (Abbreviated as DNR.)

Hume, David. *An Enquiry Concerning Human Understanding*. London: A. Millar, 1748. Repr. Dover Philosophical Classics, Mineola, N.Y.: Dover Publications, 2012. Online at http://www.davidhume.org/texts/e, accessed 2 Aug. 2017. (Abbreviated as EHU.)

Hume, David. *Treatise of Human Nature*. 1739–40. Eds. David Norton and Mary J. Norton, *David Hume: A Treatise of Human Nature: A critical edition*. Vol. 1 of The Clarendon Edition of The Works Of David Hume. Oxford: Oxford University Press, 2007. Online at http://www.davidhume.org/texts/t/, accessed 2 Aug. 2017. (Abbreviated as THN.)

Hunt, R. N. Carew. *The Theory and Practice of Communism*. Baltimore: Penguin Books, 1966.

Hurley, Thomas. *Method and Results: Collected Essays*. Vol. I. London: Macmillan, 1898.

Husserl, Edmund. *Ideas: General Introduction to Pure Phenomenology*. Ger. orig. *Ideen zu einer reinen Phänomenologie und phänomenologischen Philosophie. Erstes Buch:*

Allgemeine Einführung in die reine Phänomenologie (1913). Tr. W. R. Boyce Gibson. London: Macmillan, 1931.

Huxley, Julian. *Essays of a Humanist*. 1964. Repr. Harmondsworth: Penguin Books, 1969.

Huxley, Julian. *Religion Without Revelation*. New York: Mentor, 1957.

I

Isherwood, Christopher, ed. *Vedanta for Modern Man*. 1951. Repr. New York: New American Library, 1972.

J

Jacob, François. *Chance and Necessity: An Essay on the Natural Philosophy of Modern Biology*. Tr. Austryn Wainhouse. New York: Alfred A. Knopf, 1971.

Jacob, François. *The Logic of Life: A History of Heredity*. Tr. Betty E. Spillman. New York: Pantheon Books, 1973.

Jaeger, Werner. *The Theology of the Early Greek Philosophers*. The Gifford Lectures, 1936. Oxford: Oxford University Press, 1967.

James, E. O. *Christianity and Other Religions*. London: Hodder & Stoughton, 1968.

Jaroszwski, T. M. and P. A. Ignatovsky, eds. *Socialism as a Social System*. Moscow: Progress Publishers, 1981.

Jeremias, J. *New Testament Theology: The Proclamation of Jesus*. Tr. John Bowden. New York: Scribner, 1971.

Joad, C. E. M. *The Book of Joad: A Belligerent Autobiography* [= *Under the Fifth Rib*]. London: Faber & Faber, 1944.

Johnson, Phillip E. *Objections Sustained: Subversive Essays on Evolution, Law and Culture*. Downers Grove, Ill.: InterVarsity Press, 1998.

Jones, Steve. *In the Blood: God, Genes and Destiny*. London: Harper Collins, 1996.

Josephus, Flavius. *Antiquities of the Jews*. Tr. William Whiston, *The Works of Flavius Josephus*. 1737. Repr. Grand Rapids: Kregel, 1974. Repr. Peabody, Mass.: Hendrickson, 1995.

K

Kant, Immanuel. *Critique of Practical Reason*. 1788. Tr. and ed. Mary Gregor. Cambridge Texts in the History of Philosophy. 1997. Repr. Cambridge: Cambridge University Press, 2003.

Kant, Immanuel. *Critique of Pure Reason*. 1781. 2nd edn, 1787. Tr. Norman Kemp Smith. London: Macmillan, 1929. Repr. Blunt Press, 2007. Also Paul Guyer and Allen Wood, eds., Cambridge: Cambridge University Press, 1999.

Kant, Immanuel. *Groundwork of the Metaphysics of Morals*. 1785. In H. J. Paton, tr. *The Moral Law*. London: Hutchinson, 1972.

Kant, Immanuel. *The Metaphysics of Morals*. 1797. Tr. and ed. Mary J. Gregor. Cambridge Texts in the History of Philosophy. Cambridge: Cambridge University Press, 1996.

Kant, Immanuel. *Prolegomena to Any Future Metaphysics*. 1783. Tr. and ed. Gary Hatfield, *Prolegomena to Any Future Metaphysics with Selections from the Critique of Pure Reason*. Cambridge Texts in the History of Philosophy. 1997. Rev. edn, Cambridge: Cambridge University Press, 2004.

Kantikar, V. P. (Hemant) and W. Owen. *Hinduism—An Introduction: Teach Yourself*. 1995. Repr. London: Hodder Headline, 2010.

Kaye, Howard L. *The Social Meaning of Modern Biology, From Social Darwinism to Sociobiology*. 1986. Repr. with a new epilogue, New Brunswick, N.J.: Transaction Publishers, 1997.

Kenny, Anthony. *An Illustrated Brief History of Western Philosophy*. Oxford: Blackwell, 2006. First published as *A Brief History of Western Philosophy*, 1998.

Kenyon, D. H. and G. Steinman. *Biochemical Predestination*. New York: McGraw-Hill, 1969.

Kenyon, Frederic. *Our Bible and the Ancient Manuscripts*. 1895. 4th edn, 1938. Repr. Eugene, Oreg.: Wipf & Stock, 2011.

Kilner, J. F., C. C. Hook and D. B. Uustal, eds. *Cutting-Edge Bioethics: A Christian Exploration of Technologies and Trends*. Grand Rapids: Eerdmans, 2002.

Kirk, G. S., J. E. Raven and M. Schofield. *The Presocratic Philosophers: A Critical History with a Selection of Texts*. 1957. Rev. edn, Cambridge: Cambridge University Press, 1983.

Kirk, M. and H. Madsen. *After the Ball*. New York: Plume Books, 1989.

Knott, Kim. *Hinduism: A Very Short Introduction*. Oxford: Oxford University Press, 1998.

Koertge, Noretta, ed. *A House Built on Sand: Exposing Postmodernist Myths About Science*. Oxford: Oxford University Press, 1998.

Kolbanovskiy, V. N. *Communist Morality*. Moscow, 1951.

Krikorian, Yervant H., ed. *Naturalism and the Human Spirit*. 1944. Repr. New York: Columbia University Press, 1969.

Kuhn, Thomas. *The Structure of Scientific Revolutions*. 1962. 3rd edn, Chicago: University of Chicago Press, 1996.

Kurtz, Paul. *The Fullness of Life*. New York: Horizon Press, 1974.

Kurtz, Paul. *The Humanist Alternative*. Buffalo, N.Y.: Prometheus, 1973.

Kurtz, Paul, ed. *Humanist Manifestos I & II*. Buffalo, N.Y.: Prometheus, 1980.

Kurtz, Paul, ed. *Humanist Manifesto II*. Buffalo, N.Y.: Prometheus Books, 1980. Online at https://americanhumanist.org/what-is-humanism/manifesto2/, accessed 11 Sept. 2105.

L

Lamont, Corliss. *A Lifetime of Dissent*. Buffalo, N.Y.: Prometheus Books, 1988.

Lamont, Corliss. *The Philosophy of Humanism*. 1947. 8th edn, Emherst, N.Y.: Humanist Press, 1997.

Lapouge, G. Vacher de. *Les Sélections Sociales*. Paris: Fontemoing, 1899.

Leakey, Richard. *The Origin of Humankind*. London: Weidenfeld & Nicolson, 1994.

Leitch, Vincent B. *Deconstructive Criticism: An Advanced Introduction*. New York: Columbia University Press, 1982.

Lenin, V. I. *Complete Collected Works*. Tr. Andrew Rothstein. 4th Eng. edn, Moscow: Progress Publishers, 1960–78. Online at http://www.marx2mao.com/Lenin/Index.html (facsimile), accessed 11 Sept. 2015. Repr. Moscow: Progress Publishers, 1982.

Lenin, V. I. *Materialism and Empirico-Criticism*. New York: International Publishers, 1927.

Lennox, John C. *Determined to Believe: The Sovereignty of God, Freedom, Faith and Human*. Oxford: Monarch Books, 2017.

Lennox, John C. *God and Stephen Hawking: Whose Design is it Anyway?* Oxford: Lion, 2010.

Lennox, John C. *God's Undertaker: Has Science Buried God?* Oxford, Lion Books, 2007, 2009.

Leslie, John. *Universes*. London: Routledge, 1989.

Levinskaya, Irina. *The Book of Acts in its First Century Setting*. Vol. 5. Diaspora Setting. Grand Rapids: Eerdmans, 1996.

Lewis, C. S. *The Abolition of Man*. London, 1945. Repr. London: Collins, Fount, 1978.

Lewis, C. S. *Christian Reflections*. London, 1967. Repr. New York: HarperCollins, 1998.

Lewis, C. S. *God in the Dock*. London, 1979. Repr. Grand Rapids: Eerdmans, 2014.

Lewis, C. S. *Mere Christianity*. London, 1952. Rev. edn with new introduction and foreword by Kathleen Norris, New York: HarperCollins, 2001.

Lewis, C. S. *Miracles*. 1947. Repr. London: Collins, 2012.

Lewis, C. S. *The Problem of Pain*. 1940. Repr. London: Collins, 2009.

Lewis, C. S. *Transposition and other Addresses*. London: Geoffrey Bles, 1949.

Lewontin, Richard. *The Dialectical Biologist*. Cambridge, Mass.: Harvard University Press, 1987.

Locke, John. *An Essay Concerning Human Understanding*. London, 1689. Ed. Peter H. Nidditch, Oxford: Oxford University Press, 1975.

Long, A. A. *Hellenistic Philosophy*. 1974. 2nd edn, Berkeley, Calif.: University of California Press, 1986.

Lossky, N. O. *History of Russian Philosophy*. London: Allen & Unwin, 1952.

Lucretius (Titus Lucretius Carus). *De Rerum Natura*. 50 BC. Tr. A. E. Stallings as *The Nature of Things*. London: Penguin, 2007. Also tr. and ed. William Ellery Leonard. 1916. Online at: http://www.perseus.tufts.edu/hopper/text?doc=Lucr or http://classics.mit.edu/Carus/nature_things.html.

Lumsden, Charles J. and Edward O. Wilson. *Promethean Fire: Reflections on the Origin of Mind*. Cambridge, Mass.: Harvard University Press, 1983.

M

Mabbott, J. D. *An Introduction to Ethics*. Hutchinson University Library. London: Hutchinson, 1966.

McKay, Donald. *The Clockwork Image: A Christian Perspective on Science*. London: Inter-Varsity Press, 1974.

Majerus, Michael. *Melanism: Evolution in Action*. Oxford: Oxford University Press, 1998.

Margenau, Henry and Roy Abraham Varghese, eds. *Cosmos, Bios, and Theos: Scientists Reflect on Science, God, and the Origins of the Universe, Life, and Homo Sapiens*. La Salle, Ill.: Open Court, 1992.

Marx, Karl. *Marx's Theses on Feuerbach*. 1845.

Mascall, E. L. *Words and Images, a study in the Possibility of Religious Discourse*. London: Longmans, 1957.

Mascaró, Juan, tr. *The Upanishads*. Harmondsworth: Penguin, 1965.

Maslow, Abraham. *Towards a Psychology of Being*. New York: Van Nostrand Reinhold, 1968.

Masterson, Patrick. *Atheism and Alienation*. Harmondsworth: Pelican Books, 1972.

May, Rollo. *Psychology and the Human Dilemma*. Princeton, N.J., 1967. Repr. New York: Norton, 1996.

Medawar, Peter. *Advice to a Young Scientist*. New York: Harper & Row, 1979.

Medawar, Peter. *The Limits of Science*. Oxford: Oxford University Press, 1985.

Medawar, Peter and Jean Medawar. *The Life Science*. London: Wildwood House, 1977.

Metzger, Bruce. *The Text of the New Testament, its Transmission, Corruption and Restoration*. 1964. 3rd edn, Oxford: Oxford University Press, 1992.

Mill, John Stuart. *Utilitarianism*. 1861, 1863. Repr. Mineola, N.Y.: Dover Publications, 2007.

Millard, Alan. *Reading and Writing in the Time of Jesus*. Sheffield: Sheffield Academic Press, 2000.

Miller, David, Janet Coleman, William Connolly, and Alan Ryan, eds. *The Blackwell Encyclopaedia of Political Thought*. 1987. Repr. Oxford: Blackwell, 1991.

Monod, Jacques. *Chance and Necessity: An Essay on the Natural Philosophy of Modern Biology*. 1970 (French). Tr. Austryn Wainhouse, 1971. Repr. London: Penguin Books, 1997. Citations are from Vintage Books 1972 edn.

Monod, Jacques. *From Biology to Ethics*. San Diego: Salk Institute for Biological Studies, 1969.

Morris, Simon Conway. *The Crucible of Creation: The Burgess Shale and the Rise of Animals*. 1998. New edn, Oxford: Oxford University Press, 1999.

Mossner, Ernest C., ed. *David Hume, A Treatise of Human Nature*. London: Penguin Classics, 1985.

Moule, C. F. D. *The Phenomenon of the New Testament: An Inquiry into the Implications of Certain Features of the New Testament*. London: SCM, 1967.

Murphy, John P. *Pragmatism: From Peirce to Davidson*. Boulder, Colo.: Westview Press, 1990.

N

Nagel, Thomas. *The Last Word*. Oxford: Oxford University Press, 1997.

Nagel, Thomas. *Mortal Questions*. Cambridge: Cambridge University Press. 1979.

Nahem, Joseph. *Psychology and Psychiatry Today: A Marxist View*. New York: International Publishers, 1981.

Nasr, Seyyed Hossein, and Oliver Leaman, eds. *History of Islamic Philosophy*. Part 1, Vol. 1 of *Routledge History of World Philosophies*. 1996. Repr. London: Routledge, 2001.

Nettleship, R. L. *Lectures on the Republic of Plato*. London: Macmillan, 1922.

Newton, Isaac. *Principia Mathematica*. London, 1687.

Nietzsche, Friedrich. *Beyond Good and Evil: Prelude to a Philosophy of the Future*. Leipzig, 1886. 1973. Repr. tr. R. J. Hollingdale, Harmondsworth: Penguin, 1975.

Noddings, Nel. *Caring: A Feminine Approach to Ethics and Moral Education*. 1984. Repr. Berkeley, Calif.: University of California Press, 2013.

Norris, Christopher. *Deconstruction: Theory and Practice*. 1982. 3rd edn, London: Methuen, 2002.

O

Olivelle, Patrick. *The Early Upanishads: Annotated Text and Translation*. 1996. Repr. Oxford: Oxford University Press, 1998.

O'Meara, Dominic J. *Plotinus: An Introduction to the Enneads*. Oxford: Clarendon Press, 1993.

P

Paley, William. *Natural Theology on Evidence and Attributes of Deity*. 1802. Repr. Oxford: Oxford University Press, 2006.

Patterson, Colin. *Evolution*. 1978. 2nd edn, Ithaca, N.Y.: Cornstock Publishing Associates, 1999.

Peacocke, Arthur. *The Experiment of Life*. Toronto: University of Toronto Press, 1983.

Pearsall, Judy and Bill Trumble, eds. *The Oxford English Reference Dictionary*. 2nd edn, Oxford: Oxford University Press, 1996.

Pearse, E. K. Victor. *Evidence for Truth: Science*. Guildford: Eagle, 1998.

Penfield, Wilder. *The Mystery of the Mind*. Princeton, N.J.: Princeton University Press, 1975.

Penrose, Roger. *The Emperor's New Mind*. 1986. Repr. with new preface, Oxford: Oxford University Press, 1999.

Penrose, Roger. *The Road to Reality: A Complete Guide to the Laws of the Universe*. London: Jonathan Cape, 2004.

Peterson, Houston, ed. *Essays in Philosophy*. New York: Pocket Library, 1959.

Pinker, Steven. *The Language Instinct: How the Mind Creates Language*. New York: Morrow, 1994.

Plantinga, Alvin. *Warranted Christian Belief*. Oxford: Oxford University Press, 2000.

Plato. *Apology*. Tr. Hugh Tredennick, 1954. Repr. Harmondsworth: Penguin Books, 1976. Also in *The Collected Dialogues of Plato including the letters*. 1961. Repr. with corrections, Princeton, N.J.: Princeton University Press, 1973.

Plato. *The Euthyphro*.

Plato. *The Last Days of Socrates*. Tr. Hugh Tredennick. Harmondsworth: Penguin Books, 1969.

Plato. *Phaedo*.

Plato. *Republic*. Tr. Desmond Lee. 2nd edn, Harmondsworth: Penguin, 1974. Also tr. Paul Shorey, Loeb Classical Library. Cambridge, Mass.: Harvard University Press, 1930. Also in *The Collected Dialogues of Plato including the letters*, 1961. Repr. with corrections, Princeton, N.J.: Princeton University Press, 1973.

Plato. *Timaeus*.

Pliny the Younger. *Letters*. Tr. Betty Radice as *The Letters of the Younger Pliny*. Harmondsworth: Penguin Books, 1963.

Plotinus. *Enneads*. Tr. Stephen MacKenna, 1917–30. Repr. London: Penguin, 2005.

Polanyi, Michael. *The Tacit Dimension*. New York: Doubleday, 1966.

Polkinghorne, John. *One World: The Interaction of Science and Theology*. London: SPCK, 1986.

Polkinghorne, John. *Reason and Reality: The Relationship between Science and Theology*. 1991. Repr. London: SPCK, 2011.

Polkinghorne, John. *Science and Creation: The Search for Understanding*. 1988. Rev. edn, West Conshohocken, Pa.: Templeton Foundation Press, 2009.

Polkinghorne, John. *Science and Providence: God's Interaction with the World*. 1989. Repr. West Conshohocken, Pa.: Templeton Foundation Press, 2011.

Popper, Karl R. *The World of Parmenides*. London: Routledge, 1998.

Popper, Karl R. and John C. Eccles. *The Self and Its Brain: An Argument for Interactionism*. 1977. Repr. Springer Berlin Heidelberg, 2012.

Pospisil, Leopold J. *Kapauku Papuans and their Law*. Yale University Publications in Anthropology 54. New Haven, 1958.

Pospisil, Leopold J. *The Kapauku Papuans of West New Guinea*. Case Studies in Cultural Anthropology. 1963. 2nd edn, New York: Holt, Rinehart and Winston, 1978.

Powers, B. Ward. *The Progressive Publication of Matthew*. Nashville: B&H Academic, 2010.

Poythress, Vern S. *Inerrancy and the Gospels: A God-Centered Approach to the Challenges of Harmonization*. Wheaton, Ill.: Crossway, 2012.

Pritchard, J. B., ed. *Ancient Near Eastern Texts Relating to the Old Testament*. Princeton, 1950. 3rd edn, Princeton, N.J.: Princeton University Press, 1969.

Putnam, Hilary. *Reason, Truth and History*. Cambridge: Cambridge University Press, 1981.

R

Rachels, James. *Elements of Moral Philosophy*. New York: McGraw-Hill, 1986.

Ragg, Lonsdale and Laura Ragg, eds. *The Gospel of Barnabas*. Oxford: Clarendon Press, 1907.

Ramsay, William. *St. Paul the Traveller and the Roman Citizen*. London: Hodder & Stoughton, 1895.

Randall, John H. *Cosmos*. New York: Random House, 1980.

Raphael, D. D. *Moral Philosophy*. 1981. 2nd edn, Oxford: Oxford University Press, 1994.

Rawls, John. *A Theory of Justice*. Cambridge, Mass.: Harvard University Press, 1971.

Redford, Donald B., ed. *The Oxford Encyclopaedia of Ancient Egypt*. Oxford: Oxford University Press, 2001. doi: 10.1093/acref/9780195102345.001.0001.

Reid, Thomas. *An Enquiry Concerning Human Understanding*. Oxford: Clarendon Press, 1777.

Reid, Thomas. *An Inquiry into the Human Mind on the Principles of Common Sense*. 1764. Repr. Cambridge: Cambridge University Press, 2011.

Renfrew, Colin. *Archaeology and Language: The Puzzle of Indo-European Origins*. 1987. Repr. Cambridge: Cambridge University Press, 1999.

Ricoeur, Paul. *Hermeneutics and the Human Sciences*. 1981. Ed. and tr. J. B. Thompson. Repr. Cambridge: Cambridge University Press, 1998.

Ricoeur, Paul. *Interpretation Theory: Discourse and the Surplus of Meaning*. Fort Worth, Tex.: Texas Christian University Press, 1976.

Ridley, Mark. *The Problems of Evolution*. Oxford: Oxford University Press, 1985.

Rodwell, J. M., tr. *The Koran*. Ed. Alan Jones. London: Phoenix, 2011.

Rorty, Richard. *Consequences of Pragmatism: Essays, 1972–1980*. Minneapolis, Minn.: University of Minnesota Press, 1982.

Rose, Steven. *Lifelines: Biology, Freedom, Determinism*. 1998. Repr. New York: Oxford University Press, 2003.

Ross, Hugh. *The Creator and the Cosmos*. Colorado Springs: NavPress, 1995.

Ross, W. D. *The Right and the Good*. Oxford: Clarendon Press, 1930. Repr. 2002.

Rousseau, Jean Jacques. *The Social Contract*. 1762.

Russell, Bertrand. *The Autobiography of Bertrand Russell*. 1967–69. Repr. London: Routledge, 1998.

Russell, Bertrand. *History of Western Philosophy*. 1946. New edn, London: Routledge, 2004.

Russell, Bertrand. *Human Society in Ethics and Politics*. New York: Mentor, 1962.

Russell, Bertrand. *The Problems of Philosophy*. 1912. Repr. New York: Cosimo Classics, 2010.

Russell, Bertrand. *Religion and Science*. Oxford: Oxford University Press, 1970.

Russell, Bertrand. *Understanding History*. 1943. New York: Philosophical Library, 1957.

Russell, Bertrand. *Why I Am Not a Christian and Other Essays on Religion and Related Subjects*. New York: Simon & Schuster, 1957.

Russell, L. O. and G. A. Adebiyi. *Classical Thermodynamics*. Oxford: Oxford University Press, 1993.

Ryle, Gilbert. *The Concept of Mind*. London, 1949. Repr. London: Routledge, 2009.

S

Sagan, Carl. *The Cosmic Connection: An Extraterrestrial Perspective*. New York: Anchor Press, 1973.

Sagan, Carl. *Cosmos: The Story of Cosmic Evolution, Science and Civilisation*. 1980. Repr. London: Abacus, 2003.

Sagan, Carl. *The Demon-Haunted World: Science as a Candle in the Dark*. London: Headline, 1996.

Sandbach, F. H. *The Stoics*. 1975. Rev. edn, London: Bloomsbury, 2013.

Sartre, Jean-Paul. *Being and Nothingness: An Essay on Phenomenological Ontology*. 1943. Tr. Hazel E. Barnes. 1956. Repr. New York: Pocket Books, 1984.

Sartre, Jean-Paul. *Existentialism and Human Emotions*. Tr. Bernard Frechtman. New York: Philosophical Library, 1957.

Sartre, Jean-Paul. *Existentialism and Humanism*. Tr. and ed. P. Mairet. London: Methuen, 1948.

Sartre, Jean-Paul. *The Flies*. 1943 (French). Tr. Stuart Gilbert. New York: Knopf, 1947.

Schaff, Adam. *A Philosophy of Man*. London: Lawrence and Wishart, 1963.

Scherer, Siegfried. *Evolution. Ein kritisches Lehrbuch*. Weyel Biologie, Giessen: Weyel Lehrmittelverlag, 1998.

Schmidt, W. *The Origin and Growth of Religion*. Tr. J. Rose. London: Methuen, 1931.

Scruton, Roger. *Modern Philosophy*. 1994; London: Arrow Books, 1996.

Searle, John R. *The Construction of Social Reality*. London: Penguin, 1995.

Searle, John R. *Minds, Brains and Science*. 1984 Reith Lectures. London: British Broadcasting Corporation, 1984.

Selsam, Howard. *Socialism and Ethics*. New York: International Publishers, 1943.

Sen, Amartya and Bernard Williams, eds. *Utilitarianism and Beyond*. Cambridge: Cambridge University Press, 1982. 8th repr. in association with La Maison Des Sciences De L'Homme, Paris, 1999.

Shakespeare, William. *As You Like It*.

Sherrington, Charles S. *The Integrative Action of the Nervous System*. 1906. Repr. with new preface, Cambridge: Cambridge University Press, 1947.

Sherwin-White, A. N. *Roman Society and Roman Law in the New Testament*. The Sarum Lectures 1960–61. Oxford: Clarendon Press, 1963. Repr. Eugene, Oreg.: Wipf & Stock, 2004.

Simplicius. *Commentary on Aristotle's Physics* [or, Miscellanies]. In Kirk, G. S., J. E. Raven, and M. Schofield. *The Presocratic Philosophers: A Critical History with a Selection of Texts*. 1957. Rev. edn, Cambridge: Cambridge University Press, 1983.

Simpson, George Gaylord. *The Meaning of Evolution: A Study of the History of Life and of Its Significance for Man*. The Terry Lectures Series. 1949. Rev. edn, New Haven, Conn.: Yale University Press, 1967.

Singer, Peter. *Practical Ethics*. 1979. 2nd edn, Cambridge: Cambridge University Press, 1993.

Singer, Peter. *Rethinking Life and Death: The Collapse of Our Traditional Ethics.* Oxford: Oxford University Press, 1994.

Singer, Peter and Helga Kuhse. *Should the Baby Live?: The Problem of Handicapped Infants* (Studies in Bioethics). Oxford: Oxford University Press, 1985.

Sire, James. *The Universe Next Door.* Downers Grove, Ill.: InterVarsity Press, 1988.

Skinner, B. F. *Beyond Freedom and Dignity.* 1971; Harmondsworth: Penguin, 1974.

Skinner, B. F. *Lectures on Conditioned Reflexes.* New York: International Publishers, 1963.

Skinner, B. F. *Science and Human Behaviour.* New York: Macmillan, 1953.

Sleeper, Raymond S. *A Lexicon of Marxist-Leninist Semantics.* Alexandria, Va.: Western Goals, 1983.

Smart, J. J. C. and Bernard Williams. *Utilitarianism For and Against.* 1973. Repr. Cambridge: Cambridge University Press, 1998.

Smith, Adam. *An Enquiry into the Nature and Causes of the Wealth of Nations.* 1776. With introduction by Mark G. Spencer, Ware, UK: Wordsworth Editions, 2012.

Smith, John Maynard and Eörs Szathmary. *The Major Transitions in Evolution.* 1995. Repr. Oxford: Oxford University Press, 2010.

Smith, Wilbur. *Therefore Stand.* Grand Rapids: Baker, 1965.

Sober, E. *Philosophy of Biology.* 1993. Rev. 2nd edn, Boulder, Colo.: Westview Press, 2000.

Social Exclusion Unit. *Teenage Pregnancy.* Cmnd 4342. London: The Stationery Office, 1999.

Sophocles. *Antigone.* Tr. F. H. Storr, *Sophocles* Vol. 1. London: Heinemann, 1912.

Spencer, Herbert. *Social Statics.* New York: D. Appleton, 1851.

Stalin, Joseph. *J. Stalin Works.* Moscow: Foreign Languages Publishing House, 1953.

Stam, James H. *Inquiries into the Origin of Language: The Fate of a Question.* New York: Harper & Row, 1976.

Starkey, Mike. *God, Sex, and the Search for Lost Wonder: For Those Looking for Something to Believe In.* 1997. 2nd edn, Downers Grove, Ill.: InterVarsity Press, 1998.

Stauber, Ethelbert. *Jesus—Gestalt und Geschichte.* Bern: Francke Verlag, 1957.

Storer, Morris B., ed. *Humanist Ethics: Dialogue on Basics.* Buffalo, N.Y.: Prometheus Books, 1980.

Stott, John R. W. *The Message of Romans.* Leicester: Inter-Varsity Press, 1994.

Strabo. *Geography.* Tr. with introduction Duane W. Roller as *The Geography of Strabo*, Cambridge: Cambridge University Press, 2014. Tr. H. C. Hamilton and W. Falconer, London, 1903. Online at Perseus, Tufts University, http://www.perseus.tufts.edu/hopper/text?doc=Perseus%3Atext%3A1999.01.0239, accessed 11 Sept. 2015.

Strickberger, Monroe. *Evolution.* 1990. 3rd edn, London: Jones and Bartlett, 2000.

Strobel, Lee. *The Case for Christ: A Journalist's Personal Investigation of the Evidence for Jesus.* Grand Rapids: Zondervan, 1998.

Suetonius. *Lives of the Caesars*. Tr. Catharine Edwards. 2000. Repr. Oxford World's Classics. Oxford: Oxford University Press, 2008.

Sunderland, Luther D. *Darwin's Enigma*. Green Forest, Ark.: Master Books, 1998.

Swinburne, Richard. *The Existence of God*. 1979. Repr. Oxford: Oxford University Press, 2004.

Swinburne, Richard. *Faith and Reason*. 1981. Repr. Oxford: Clarendon Press, 2002.

Swinburne, Richard. *Is There a God?* Oxford: Oxford University Press, 1996.

Swinburne, Richard. *Providence and the Problem of Evil*. Oxford: Oxford University Press, 1998.

T

Tacitus, Cornelius. *Annals*. Tr. Alfred John Church and William Jackson Brodribb as *Complete Works of Tacitus*. New York: Random House, 1872. Repr. 1942. Online at Sara Byrant, ed., Perseus Digital Library, Tufts University, Medford, MA: http://www.perseus.tufts.edu/hopper/text?doc=Perseus:text:1999.02.0078, accessed 2 Aug. 2017.

Tada, Joni Eareckson and Steven Estes. *When God Weeps: Why Our Sufferings Matter to the Almighty*. Grand Rapids: Zondervan, 1997.

Tax, Sol and Charles Callender, eds. *Issues in Evolution*. Chicago: University of Chicago Press, 1960.

Thaxton, Charles B., Walter L. Bradley and Roger L. Olsen. *The Mystery of Life's Origin*. Dallas: Lewis & Stanley, 1992.

Thibaut, George, tr. *The Vedānta Sūtras of Bādarāyana* with the Commentary by Śankara, 2 Parts. New York: Dover, 1962.

Torrance, T. F. *The Ground and Grammar of Theology*. Belfast: Christian Journals Limited, 1980; and Charlottesville: The University Press of Virginia, 1980. Repr. with new preface, Edinburgh: T&T Clark, 2001.

Torrance, T. F. *Theological Science*. Oxford: Oxford University Press, 1978.

U

Unamuno, Don Miguel de. *The Tragic Sense of Life*. Tr. J. E. Crawford. 1921. Repr. Charleston, S.C.: BiblioBazaar, 2007.

V

Von Neumann, John. *Theory of Self-Reproducing Automata*. Ed. and completed by Arthur W. Burks, Urbana: University of Illinois Press, 1966.

W

Waddington, C. H., ed. *Science and Ethics: An Essay*. London: Allen & Unwin, 1942.

Wallis, R. T. *Neoplatonism*. 1972. Repr. London: Duckworth, 1985.

Ward, Keith. *God, Chance and Necessity*. 1996. Repr. Oxford: Oneworld Publications, 2001.

Warner, Richard, and Tadeusz Szubka. *The Mind-Body Problem*. Oxford: Blackwell, 1994.

Weiner, Jonathan. *The Beak of the Finch*. London: Cape, 1994.

Welch, I. David, George A. Tate and Fred Richards, eds. *Humanistic Psychology*. Buffalo, N.Y.: Prometheus Books, 1978.

Wenham, John. *Easter Enigma—Do the Resurrection Stories Contradict One Another?* Exeter: Paternoster Press, 1984. Repr. as *Easter Enigma: Are the Resurrection Accounts in Conflict?*, Eugene, Oreg.: Wipf & Stock, 2005.

Wesson, Paul. *Beyond Natural Selection*. 1991. Repr. Cambridge, Mass.: Massachusetts Institute of Technology Press, 1997.

Westminster Shorter Catechism. 1647. [Widely available in print and online.]

Wetter, Gustav A. *Dialectical Materialism*. Westport, Conn.: Greenwood Press, 1977.

Whitehead, Alfred North. *Process and Reality*. Gifford Lectures 1927–28. London: Macmillan, 1929. Repr. New York: The Free Press, 1978.

Wilson, Edward O. *Consilience*. London: Little, Brown, 1998.

Wilson, Edward O. *Genes, Mind and Culture*. Cambridge, Mass.: Harvard University Press, 1981.

Wilson, Edward O. *On Human Nature*. Cambridge, Mass.: Harvard University Press, 1978.

Wilson, Edward O. *Sociobiology: The New Synthesis*. Cambridge, Mass.: Harvard University Press, 1975.

Wimsatt, William K. and Monroe Beardsley. *The Verbal Icon: Studies in the Meaning of Poetry*. 1954. Repr. Lexington, Ky.: University of Kentucky Press, 1982.

Wippel, John F., ed. *Studies in Medieval Philosophy*. Vol. 17 of *Studies in Philosophy and the History of Philosophy*. Washington D.C.: Catholic University of America Press, 1987.

Wittgenstein, L. *On Certainty*. Ed. G. E. M. Anscombe and G. H. von Wright; tr. Denis Paul and G. E. M. Anscombe. Oxford, 1969. Repr. New York: Harper & Row, 1972.

Wolpert, Lewis. *The Unnatural Nature of Science*. London: Faber & Faber, 1992.

Wolstenholme, Gordon, ed. *Man and His Future*. A Ciba Foundation Volume. London: J. & A. Churchill, 1963.

Wolters, Clifton, tr. *The Cloud of Unknowing*. 1961. Repr. London: Penguin, 1978.

Wolterstorff, Nicholas. *Divine Discourse: Philosophical Reflections on the Claim that God Speaks*. 1995. Repr. Cambridge: Cambridge University Press, 2000.

X

Xenophon. *Memorabilia*. Tr. E. C. Marchant. *Memorabilia. Oeconomicus. Symposium. Apology*. Vol. 4. Loeb Classical Library, Vol. 168. 1923. Repr. Cambridge, Mass.: Harvard University Press, 1997.

Y

Yancey, Philip. *Soul Survivor: How my Faith Survived the Church*. London: Hodder & Stoughton, 2001.

Yockey, Hubert. *Information Theory and Biology*. Cambridge: Cambridge University Press, 1992.

Z

Zacharias, Ravi. *Jesus Among Other Gods: The Absolute Claims of the Christian Message*. Nashville, Tenn.: Thomas Nelson, 2000.

Zacharias, Ravi. *The Real Face of Atheism*. Grand Rapids: Baker, 2004.

Zaehner, Z. C., ed. *The Concise Encyclopedia of Living Faiths*. 1959. 2nd edn, 1971. Repr. London: Hutchinson, 1982.

ARTICLES, PAPERS, CHAPTERS AND LECTURES

A

Adams, R. M. 'Religious Ethics in a Pluralistic Society.' In G. Outka and J. P. Reeder, Jr., eds. *Prospects for a Common Morality*. Princeton, N.J.: Princeton University Press, 1993.

Alberts, Bruce. 'The Cell as a Collection of Protein Machines: Preparing the Next Generation of Molecular Biologists.' *Cell* 92/3 (6 Feb. 1998), 291–4. doi: 10.1016/S0092-8674(00)80922-8.

Almond, Brenda. 'Liberty or Community? Defining the Post-Marxist Agenda.' In Brenda Almond, ed. *Introducing Applied Ethics*. Oxford: Wiley Blackwell, 1995.

Alpher, R. A., H. Bethe and G. Gamow. 'The Origin of Chemical Elements.' *Physical Review* 73/7 (Apr. 1948), 803–4. doi: 10.1103/PhysRev.73.803.

Anscombe, G. E. M. 'Modern Moral Philosophy.' *Philosophy* 33 (1958), 1–19.

Asimov, Isaac (interview by Paul Kurtz). 'An Interview with Isaac Asimov on Science and the Bible.' *Free Enquiry* 2/2 (Spring 1982), 6–10.

Auer, J. A. C. F. 'Religion as the Integration of Human Life.' *The Humanist* (Spring 1947).

Austin, J. L., P. F. Strawson and D. R. Cousin. 'Truth.' *Proceedings of the Aristotelian Society, Supplementary Volumes*, Vol. 24, Physical Research, Ethics and Logic (1950), 111–72. Online at http://www.jstor.org/stable/4106745. Repr. in Paul Horwich, ed. *Theories of Truth*. Aldershot: Dartmouth Publishing, 1994.

B

Bada, Jeffrey L. 'Stanley Miller's 70th Birthday.' *Origins of Life and Evolution of Biospheres* 30/2 (2000), 107–12. doi: 10.1023/A:1006746205180.

Baier, Kurt E. M. 'Egoism.' In P. Singer, ed. *A Companion to Ethics*. Oxford: Blackwell, 1991. Repr. 2000, 197–204.

Baier, Kurt E. M. 'Freedom, Obligation, and Responsibility.' In Morris B. Storer, ed. *Humanist Ethics: Dialogue on Basics*. Buffalo, N.Y.: Prometheus Books, 1980, 75–92.

Baier, Kurt E. M. 'The Meaning of Life.' 1947. In Peter Angeles, ed. *Critiques of God*, Buffalo, N.Y.: Prometheus Books, 1976. Repr. in E. D. Klemke, ed. *The Meaning of Life*. New York: Oxford University Press, 1981, 81–117.

Baker, S. W. 'Albert Nyanza, Account of the Discovery of the Second Great Lake of the Nile.' *Journal of the Royal Geographical Society* 36 (1866). Also in *Proceedings of the Royal Geographical Society of London* 10 (13 Nov. 1856), 6–27.

Bates, Elizabeth, Donna Thal and Virginia Marchman. 'Symbols and Syntax: A Darwinian Approach to Language Development.' In Norman A. Krasnegor, Duane M. Rumbaugh, Richard L. Schiefelbusch and Michael Studdert-Kennedy, eds. *Biological and Behavioural Determinants of Language Development*. 1991. Repr. New York: Psychology Press, 2014, 29–65.

Behe, Michael J. 'Reply to My Critics: A Response to Reviews of *Darwin's Black Box: The Biochemical Challenge to Evolution*.' *Biology and Philosophy* 16 (2001), 685–709.

Berenbaum, Michael. 'T4 Program.' In *Encyclopaedia Britannica*. Online at https://www.britannica.com/event/T4-Program, accessed 2 Nov. 2017.

Berlinski, David. 'The Deniable Darwin.' *Commentary* (June 1996), 19-29.

Bernal, J. D. 'The Unity of Ethics.' In C. H. Waddington, ed. *Science and Ethics: An Essay*. London: Allen & Unwin, 1942.

Black, Deborah L. 'Al-Kindi.' In Seyyed Hossein Nasr and Oliver Leaman, eds. *History of Islamic Philosophy*. Part 1, Vol. 1 of *Routledge History of World Philosophies*. 1996. Repr. London: Routledge, 2001, 178-97.

Boghossian, Paul A. 'What the Sokal hoax ought to teach us: The pernicious consequences and internal contradictions of "postmodernist" relativism.' *Times Literary Supplement*, Commentary (13 Dec. 1996), 14-15. Reprinted in Noretta Koertge, ed. *A House Built on Sand: Exposing Postmodernist Myths about Science*. Oxford: Oxford University Press, 1998, 23-31.

Briggs, Arthur E. 'The Third Annual Humanist Convention.' *The Humanist* (Spring 1945).

Bristol, Evelyn. 'Turn of a Century: Modernism, 1895-1925.' Ch. 8 in C. A. Moser, ed. *The Cambridge History of Russian Literature*. 1989. Rev. edn, 1992. Repr. 1996, Cambridge: Cambridge University Press, 387-457.

C

Caputo, John D. 'The End of Ethics.' In Hugh LaFollette, ed. *The Blackwell Guide to Ethical Theory*. Oxford: Blackwell, 1999, 111-28.

Cartmill, Matt. 'Oppressed by Evolution.' *Discover* Magazine 19/3 (Mar. 1998), 78-83. Reprinted in L. Polnac, ed. *Purpose, Pattern, and Process*. 6th edn, Dubuque: Kendall-Hunt, 2002, 389-97.

Cavalier-Smith, T. 'The Blind Biochemist.' *Trends in Ecology and Evolution* 12 (1997), 162-3.Chaitin, Gregory J. 'Randomness in Arithmetic and the Decline and Fall of Reductionism in Pure Mathematics.' Ch. 3 in John Cornwell, ed. *Nature's Imagination: The Frontiers of Scientific Vision*. Oxford: Oxford University Press, 1995, 27-44.

Chomsky, Noam. 'Review of B. F. Skinner.' *Verbal Behavior*. *Language* 35/1 (1959), 26-58.

Chomsky, Noam. 'Science, Mind, and Limits of Understanding.' Transcript of talk given at the Science and Faith Foundation (STOQ), The Vatican (Jan. 2014). No pages. Online at https://chomsky.info/201401__/, accessed 3 Aug. 2017.

Coghlan, Andy. 'Selling the family secrets.' *New Scientist* 160/2163 (5 Dec. 1998), 20-1.

Collins, Harry. 'Introduction: Stages in the Empirical Programme of Relativism.' *Social Studies of Science* 11/1 (Feb. 1981), 3-10. Online at http://www.jstor.org/stable/284733, accessed 11 Sept. 2015.

Collins, R. 'A Physician's View of College Sex.' *Journal of the American Medical Association* 232 (1975), 392.

Cook, Sidney. 'Solzhenitsyn and Secular Humanism: A Response.' *The Humanist* (Nov./Dec. 1978), 6.

Cookson, Clive. 'Scientist Who Glimpsed God.' *Financial Times* (29 Apr. 1995), 20.

Cottingham, John. 'Descartes, René.' In Ted Honderich, ed. *The Oxford Companion to Philosophy*. Oxford, 1995. 2nd edn, Oxford: Oxford University Press, 2005.

Crick, Francis. 'Lessons from Biology.' *Natural History* 97 (Nov. 1988), 32–9.

Crosman, Robert. 'Do Readers Make Meaning?' In Susan R. Suleiman and Inge Crosman, eds. *The Reader in the Text: Essays on Audience and Interpretation*. Princeton, N.J.: Princeton University Press, 1980.

D

Davies, Paul. 'Bit before It?' *New Scientist* 2171 (30 Jan. 1999), 3.

Dawkins, Richard. 'Put Your Money on Evolution.' Review of Maitland A. Edey and Donald C. Johanson. *Blueprint: Solving the Mystery of Evolution*. Penguin, 1989. *The New York Times Review of Books* (9 Apr. 1989), sec. 7, 34–5.

Dembski, William. 'Intelligent Design as a Theory of Information.' *Perspectives on Science and Christian Faith* 49/3 (Sept. 1997), 180–90.

Derrida, Jacques. 'Force of Law: The "Mystical Foundation of Authority".' In Drucilla Cornell, Michel Rosenfeld and David Gray Carlson, eds. *Deconstruction and the Possibility of Justice*. 1992. Repr. Abingdon: Routledge, 2008.

Dirac, P. A. M. 'The Evolution of the Physicist's Picture of Nature.' *Scientific American* 208/5 (1963), 45–53. doi: 10.1038/scientificamerican0563-45.

Dobzhansky, Theodosius. 'Chance and Creativity in Evolution.' Ch. 18 in Francisco J. Ayala and Theodosius Dobzhansky, eds. *Studies in the Philosophy of Biology: Reduction and Related Problems*. Berkeley, Calif.: University of California Press, 1974, 307–36.

Dobzhansky, Theodosius. Discussion of paper by Gerhard Schramm, 'Synthesis of Nucleosides and Polynucleotide with Metaphosphate Esters.' In Sidney W. Fox, ed. *The Origins of Prebiological Systems and of Their Molecular Matrices*, 299–315. Proceedings of a Conference Conducted at Wakulla Springs, Florida, on 20–30 October 1963 under the auspices of the Institute for Space Biosciences, the Florida State University and the National Aeronautics and Space Administration. New York: Academic Press, 1965.

Dobzhansky, Theodosius. 'Evolutionary Roots of Family Ethics and Group Ethics.' In *The Centrality of Science and Absolute Values*, Vol. I of *Proceedings of the Fourth International Conference on the Unity of the Sciences*. New York: International Cultural Foundation, 1975.

Documents of the 22nd Congress of the Communist Party of the Soviet Union. 2 vols. Documents of Current History, nos. 18–19. New York: Crosscurrents Press, 1961.

Dose, Klaus. 'The Origin of Life: More Questions Than Answers.' *Interdisciplinary Science Reviews* 13 (Dec. 1988), 348–56.

Druart, Th.-A. 'Al-Fārābī and Emanationism.' In J. F. Wippel, ed. *Studies in Medieval Philosophy*. Vol. 17 of Studies in Philosophy and the History of Philosophy. Washington D.C.: Catholic University of America Press, 1987, 23–43.

Dyson, Freeman. 'Energy in the Universe.' *Scientific American* 225/3 (1971), 50–9.

E

Eddington, Arthur. 'The End of the World: From the Standpoint of Mathematical Physics.' *Nature* 127 (21 Mar. 1931), 447–53. doi: 10.1038/127447a0.

Edwards, William. 'On the Physical Death of Jesus Christ.' *Journal of the American Medical Association* 255/11 (21 Mar. 1986), 1455–63.

Eigen, Manfred, Christof K. Biebricher, Michael Gebinoga and William C. Gardiner. 'The Hypercycle: Coupling of RNA and Protein Biosynthesis in the Infection Cycle of an RNA Bacteriophage.' *Biochemistry* 30/46 (1991), 11005–18. doi: 10.1021/bi00110a001.

Einstein, Albert. 'Physics and Reality.' 1936. In Sonja Bargmann, tr. *Ideas and Opinions.* New York: Bonanza, 1954.

Einstein, Albert. 'Science and Religion.' 1941. Published in *Science, Philosophy and Religion, A Symposium*. New York: The Conference on Science, Philosophy and Religion in Their Relation to the Democratic Way of Life, 1941. Repr. in *Out of My Later Years*, 1950, 1956. Repr. New York: Open Road Media, 2011.

Eysenck, H. J. 'A Reason with Compassion.' In Paul Kurtz, ed. *The Humanist Alternative*. Buffalo, N.Y.: Prometheus Books, 1973.

F

Feynman, Richard P. 'Cargo Cult Science.' Repr. in *Engineering and Science* 37/7 (1974), 10–13. Online at http://calteches.library.caltech.edu/51/2/CargoCult.pdf (facsimile), accessed 11 Sept. 2015. (Originally delivered as Caltech's 1974 commencement address in Pasadena, Calif.)

Fletcher, J. 'Comment by Joseph Fletcher on Nielsen Article.' In Morris B. Storer, ed. *Humanist Ethics: Dialogue on Basics*. Buffalo, N.Y.: Prometheus Books, 1980, 70.

Flew, Anthony. 'Miracles.' In Paul Edwards, ed. *The Encyclopedia of Philosophy*. New York: Macmillan, 1967, 5:346–53.

Flew, Anthony. 'Neo-Humean Arguments about the Miraculous.' In R. D. Geivett and G. R. Habermas, eds. *In Defence of Miracles*. Leicester: Apollos, 1997, 45–57.

Flieger, Jerry Aline. 'The Art of Being Taken by Surprise.' *Destructive Criticism: Directions. SCE Reports* 8 (Fall 1980), 54–67.

Fodor, J. A. 'Fixation of Belief and Concept Acquisition.' In M. Piattelli-Palmarini, ed., *Language and Learning: The Debate Between Jean Piaget and Noam Chomsky*. Cambridge, Mass.: Harvard University Press, 1980, 143–9.

Fotion, Nicholas G. 'Logical Positivism.' In Ted Honderich, ed. *The Oxford Companion to Philosophy*. 2nd edn, Oxford: Oxford University Press, 2005.

Frank, Lawrence K. 'Potentialities of Human Nature.' *The Humanist* (Apr. 1951).

Frankena, William K. 'Is morality logically dependent on religion?' In G. Outka and J. P. Reeder, Jr., eds. *Religion and Morality*. Garden City, N.Y.: Anchor, 1973.

G

Genequand, Charles. 'Metaphysics.' Ch. 47 in Seyyed Nossein Nasr and Oliver Leaman, eds. *History of Islamic Philosophy*. Vol. 1 of *Routledge History of World Philosophies*. London: Routledge, 1996, 783–801.

Genné, William H. 'Our Moral Responsibility.' *Journal of the American College Health Association* 15/Suppl (May 1967), 55–60.

Gilbert, Scott F., John Opitz and Rudolf A Raff. 'Resynthesizing Evolutionary and Developmental Biology.' *Developmental Biology* 173/2 (1996), 357–72.

Ginsburg, V. L. *Poisk* 29–30 (1998).

Gould, Stephen Jay. 'Evolution as Fact and Theory.' In Ashley Montagu, ed. *Science and Creationism*. Oxford: Oxford University Press, 1984.

Gould, Stephen Jay. 'Evolution's Erratic Pace.' *Natural History* 86/5 (May 1977), 12–16.

Gould, Stephen Jay. 'Evolutionary Considerations.' Paper presented at the McDonnell Foundation Conference, 'Selection vs. Instruction'. Venice, May 1989.

Gould, Stephen Jay. 'In Praise of Charles Darwin.' Paper presented at the Nobel Conference XVIII, Gustavus Adolphus College, St. Peter, Minn. Repr. in Charles L. Hamrum, ed. *Darwin's Legacy*. San Francisco: Harper & Row, 1983.

Gould, Stephen Jay. 'The Paradox of the Visibly Irrelevant.' *Annals of the New York Academy of Sciences* 879 (June 1999), 87–97. doi: 10.1111/j.1749-6632.1999.tb10407.x. Repr. in *The Lying Stones of Marrakech: Penultimate Reflections in Natural History*. 2000. Repr. Cambridge, Mass.: Harvard University Press, 2011.

Gribbin, John. 'Oscillating Universe Bounces Back.' *Nature* 259 (1 Jan. 1976), 15–16. doi: 10.1038/259015c0.

Grigg, Russell. 'Could Monkeys Type the 23rd Psalm?' *Interchange* 50 (1993), 25–31.

Guth, A. H. 'Inflationary Universe: A Possible Solution to the Horizon and Flatness Problems.' *Physical Review D* 23/2 (1981), 347–56.

Guttmacher Institute. 'Induced Abortion in the United States', Fact Sheet. New York: Guttmacher Institute, Jan. 2018. Online at https://www.guttmacher.org/fact-sheet/induced-abortion-united-states, accessed 1 Feb. 2018.

H

Haldane, J. B. S. 'When I am Dead.' In *Possible Worlds*. [1927] London: Chatto & Windus, 1945, 204–11.

Hansen, Michèle; Jennifer J. Kurinczuk, Carol Bower and Sandra Webb. 'The Risk of Major Birth Defects after Intracytoplasmic Sperm Injection and in Vitro Fertilization.' *New England Journal of Medicine* 346 (2002), 725–30. doi: 10.1056/NEJMoa010035.

Hardwig, John. 'Dying at the Right Time: Reflections on (Un)Assisted Suicide.' In Hugh LaFollette, ed. *Ethics In Practice*. Blackwell Philosophy Anthologies. 2nd edn, Oxford: Blackwell, 1997, 101–11.

Hawking, S. W. 'The Edge of Spacetime: Does the universe have an edge and time a beginning, as Einstein's general relativity predicts, or is spacetime finite without boundary, as quantum mechanics suggests?' *American Scientist* 72/4 (1984), 355–9. Online at http://www.jstor.org/stable/27852759, accessed 15 Sept. 2015.

Hawking, S. W. Letters to the Editors. Reply to letter by J. J. Tanner relating to article 'The Edge of Spacetime'. *American Scientist* 73/1 (1985), 12. Online at http://www.jstor.org/stable/27853056, accessed 15 Sept. 2015.

Hawking, S. W. and R. Penrose. 'The Singularities of Gravitational Collapse and Cosmology.' *Proceedings of the Royal Society London A* 314/1519 (1970), 529–48. doi: 10.1098/rspa.1970.0021.

Hocutt, Max. 'Does Humanism Have an Ethic of Responsibility?' In Morris B. Storer, ed. *Humanist Ethic: Dialogue on Basics*. Buffalo, N.Y.: Prometheus Books, 1980, 11–24.

Hocutt, Max. 'Toward an Ethic of Mutual Accommodation.' In Morris B. Storer, ed. *Humanist Ethics: Dialogue on Basics*. Buffalo, N.Y.: Prometheus Books, 1980, 137–46.

Hookway, C. J. 'Scepticism.' In Ted Honderich, ed. *The Oxford Companion to Philosophy*. Oxford, 1995. 2nd edn, Oxford: Oxford University Press, 2005.

Hoyle, Fred. 'The Universe: Past and Present Reflections.' *Annual Reviews of Astronomy and Astrophysics* 20 (1982), 1–35. doi: 10.1146/annurev.aa.20.090182.000245.

Hursthouse, Rosalind. 'Virtue theory and abortion.' *Philosophy and Public Affairs* 20, 1991, 223–46.

Huxley, Julian. 'The Emergence of Darwinism.' In Sol Tax, ed. *The Evolution of Life: Its Origins, History, and Future*. Vol. 1 of *Evolution after Darwin*. Chicago: University of Chicago Press, 1960, 1–21.

Huxley, Julian. 'The Evolutionary Vision: The Convocation Address.' In Sol Tax and Charles Callender, eds. *Issues in Evolution*. Vol. 3 of *Evolution after Darwin*. Chicago: University of Chicago Press, 1960, 249–61.

I

Inwood, M. J. 'Feuerbach, Ludwig Andreas.' In Ted Honderich, ed. *The Oxford Companion to Philosophy*. Oxford, 1995. 2nd edn, Oxford: Oxford University Press, 2005.

J

Jeeves, Malcolm. 'Brain, Mind, and Behaviour.' In Warren S. Brown, Nancey Murphy and H. Newton Malony, eds. *Whatever Happened to the Soul: Scientific and Theological Portraits of Human Nature*. Minneapolis: Fortress Press, 1998.

Johnson, Barbara. 'Nothing Fails Like Success.' *Deconstructive Criticism: Directions*. *SCE Reports* 8 (Fall 1980), 7–16.

Josephson, Brian. Letters to the Editor. *The Independent* (12 Jan. 1997), London.

K

Kant, Immanuel. 'Beantwortung der Frage: Was ist Aufklärung?' *Berlinische Monatsschrift* 4 (Dec. 1784), 481–94. Repr. in *Kant's Gesammelte Schriften*. Berlin: Akademie Ausgabe, 1923, 8:33–42.

Khrushchev, Nikita. *Ukrainian Bulletin* (1–15 Aug. 1960), 12.

Klein-Franke, Felix. 'Al-Kindī.' In Seyyed Hossein Nasr and Oliver Leaman, eds. *History of Islamic Philosophy*. Vol. 1, Part 1 of *Routledge History of World Philosophies*. 1996. Repr. London: Routledge, 2001, 165–77.

Kurtz, Paul. 'A Declaration of Interdependence: A New Global Ethics.' *Free Inquiry* 8/4 (Fall 1988), 4–7. Also published in Vern L. Ballough and Timothy J. Madigan, ed. *Toward a New Enlightenment: The Philosophy of Paul Kurtz*. New Brunswick, N.J.: Transaction Publishers, 1994 (ch. 3, 'The Twenty-First Century and Beyond: The Need for a New Global Ethic and a Declaration of Interdependence').

Kurtz, Paul. 'Does Humanism Have an Ethic of Responsibility?' In Morris B. Storer, ed. *Humanist Ethics: Dialogue on Basics*. Buffalo, N.Y.: Prometheus Books, 1980, 11–24.

Kurtz, Paul. 'Is Everyone a Humanist?' In Paul Kurtz, ed. *The Humanist Alternative*. Buffalo, N.Y.: Prometheus Books, 1973.

L

Lamont, Corliss. 'The Ethics of Humanism.' In Frederick C. Dommeyer, ed. *In Quest of Value: Readings in Philosophy and Personal Values*. San Francisco: Chandler, 1963, 46–59. Repr. from ch. 6 of Corliss Lamont. *Humanism as a Philosophy*. Philosophical Library, 273–97.

Larson, Erik. 'Looking for the Mind.' (Review of David J. Chalmers. *The Conscious Mind: In Search of a Fundamental Theory*.) *Origins & Design* 18/1(34) (Winter 1997), Colorado Springs: Access Research Network, 28–9.

Leitch, Vincent B. 'The Book of Deconstructive Criticism.' *Studies in the Literary Imagination* 12/1 (Spring 1979), 19–39.

Lewis, C. S. 'The Funeral of a Great Myth.' In Walter Hooper, ed. *Christian Reflections*. Grand Rapids: Eerdmans, 1967, 102–116.

Lewis, C. S. 'The Weight of Glory.' In *Transposition and other Addresses*. London: Geoffrey Bles, 1949. Repr. in *The Weight of Glory and Other Addresses*. HarperOne, 2001.

Lewontin, Richard C. 'Billions and Billions of Demons.' *The New York Review of Books* 44/1 (9 Jan. 1997).

Lewontin, Richard C. 'Evolution/Creation Debate: A Time for Truth.' *BioScience* 31/8 (Sept. 1981), 559. Reprinted in J. Peter Zetterberg, ed. *Evolution versus Creationism*. Phoenix, Ariz.: Oryx Press, 1983. doi: 10.1093/bioscience/31.8.559, accessed 15 Sept. 2015.

Lieberman, Philip and E. S. Crelin. 'On the Speech of Neanderthal Man.' *Linguistic Inquiry* 2/2 (Mar. 1971), 203–22.

Louden, Robert. 'On Some Vices of Virtue Ethics.' Ch. 10 in R. Crisp and M. Slote, eds. *Virtue Ethics*. Oxford: Oxford University Press, 1997.

M

Mackie, J. L. 'Evil and Omnipotence.' *Mind* 64/254 (Apr. 1955), 200–12.

McNaughton, David and Piers Rawling. 'Intuitionism.' Ch. 13 in Hugh LaFollette, ed. *The Blackwell Guide to Ethical Theory*. Oxford: Blackwell, 2000, 268–87. Ch. 14 in 2nd edn, Wiley Blackwell, 2013, 287–310.

Maddox, John. 'Down with the Big Bang.' *Nature* 340 (1989), 425. doi: 10.1038/340425a0.

Marx, Karl. 'The Difference between the Natural Philosophy of Democritus and the Natural Philosophy of Epicurus.' In *K. Marx and F. Engels on Religion*. Moscow: Foreign Languages Publishing House, 1955.

Marx, Karl. 'Economic and Philosophical Manuscripts.' In T. B. Bottomore, tr. and ed. *Karl Marx: Early Writings*. London: Watts, 1963.

Marx, Karl. 'Theses on Feuerback.' In Frederick Engels, *Ludwig Feuerback*. New York: International Publishers, 1941.

May, Rollo. 'The Problem of Evil: An Open Letter to Carl Rogers.' *Journal of Humanistic Psychology* (Summer 1982).

Merezhkovsky, Dmitry. 'On the Reasons for the Decline and on the New Currents in Contemporary Russian Literature.' 1892 lecture. In Dmitry Merezhkovsky. *On the reasons for the decline and on the new currents in contemporary Russian literature*. Petersburg, 1893.

Meyer, Stephen C. 'The Explanatory Power of Design: DNA and the Origin of Information.' In William A. Dembski, ed. *Mere Creation: Science, Faith and Intelligent Design*. Downers Grove, Ill.: InterVarsity Press, 1998, 114–47.

Meyer, Stephen C. 'The Methodological Equivalence of Design and Descent.' In J. P. Moreland, ed. *The Creation Hypothesis*. Downers Grove, Ill.: InterVarsity Press, 1994, 67–112.

Meyer, Stephen C. 'Qualified Agreement: Modern Science and the Return of the "God Hypothesis".' In Richard F. Carlson, ed. *Science and Christianity: Four Views*. Downers Grove, Ill.: InterVarsity Press, 2000, 129–75.

Meyer, Stephen C. 'The Return of the God Hypothesis.' *Journal of Interdisciplinary Studies* 11/1&2 (Jan. 1999), 1–38. Online at http://www.discovery.org/a/642, accessed 3 Aug. 2017. Citations are to the archived version, which is repaginated, and online at http://www.discovery.org/scripts/viewDB/filesDB-download.php?command=download&id=12006, accessed 3 Aug. 2017.

Miller, J. Hillis. 'Deconstructing the Deconstructors.' Review of Joseph N. Riddel. *The Inverted Bell: Modernism and the Counterpoetics of William Carlos Williams*. *Diacritics* 5/2 (Summer 1975), 24–31. Online at http://www.jstor.org/stable/464639, accessed 3 Aug. 2017. doi: 10.2307/464639.

Monod, Jacques. 'On the Logical Relationship between Knowledge and Values.' In Watson Fuller, ed. *The Biological Revolution*. Garden City, N.Y.: Doubleday, 1972.

N

Nagel, Ernest. 'Naturalism Reconsidered.' 1954. In Houston Peterson, ed. *Essays in Philosophy*. New York: Pocket Books, 1959. Repr. New York: Pocket Books, 1974.

Nagel, Thomas. 'Rawls, John.' In Ted Honderich, ed. *The Oxford Companion to Philosophy*. 1995. 2nd edn, Oxford: Oxford University Press, 2005.

Nagler, Michael N. 'Reading the Upanishads.' In Eknath Easwaran. *The Upanishads*. 1987. Repr. Berkeley, Calif.: Nilgiri Press, 2007.

Neill, Stephen. 'The Wrath of God and the Peace of God.' In Max Warren, *Interpreting the Cross*. London: SCM Press, 1966.

Newing, Edward G. 'Religions of pre-literary societies.' In Sir Norman Anderson, ed. *The World's Religions*. 4th edn, London: Inter-Varsity Press, 1975.

Nielsen, Kai. 'Religiosity and Powerlessness: Part III of "The Resurgence of Fundamentalism".' *The Humanist* 37/3 (May/June 1977), 46–8.

O

The Oxford Reference Encyclopaedia. Oxford: Oxford University Press, 1998.

P

Palmer, Alasdair. 'Must Knowledge Gained Mean Paradise Lost?' *Sunday Telegraph*. London (6 Apr. 1997).

Penzias, Arno. 'Creation is Supported by all the Data So Far.' In Henry Margenau and Roy Abraham Varghese, eds. *Cosmos, Bios, Theos: Scientists Reflect on Science, God, and the Origins of the Universe, Life, and Homo Sapiens*. La Salle, Ill.: Open Court, 1992.

Pinker, Steven, and Paul Bloom. 'Natural Language and Natural Selection.' *Behavioral and Brain Sciences* 13/4 (Dec. 1990), 707–27. doi: 10.1017/S0140525X00081061.

Polanyi, Michael. 'Life's Irreducible Structure. Live mechanisms and information in DNA are boundary conditions with a sequence of boundaries above them.' *Science* 160/3834 (1968), 1308–12. Online at http://www.jstor.org/stable/1724152, accessed 3 Aug. 2017.

Poole, Michael. 'A Critique of Aspects of the Philosophy and Theology of Richard Dawkins.' *Christians and Science* 6/1 (1994), 41–59. Online at http://www.scienceandchristianbelief.org/serve_pdf_free.php?filename=SCB+6-1+Poole.pdf, accessed 3 Aug. 2017.

Popper, Karl. 'Scientific Reduction and the Essential Incompleteness of All Science.' In F. J. Ayala and T. Dobzhansky, ed. *Studies in the Philosophy of Biology, Reduction and Related Problems*. London: MacMillan, 1974.

Premack, David. '"Gavagai!" or The Future History of the Animal Controversy.' *Cognition* 19/3 (1985), 207–96. doi: 10.1016/0010-0277(85)90036-8.

Provine, William B. 'Evolution and the Foundation of Ethics.' *Marine Biological Laboratory Science* 3 (1988), 27–8.

Provine, William B. 'Scientists, Face it! Science and Religion are Incompatible.' *The Scientist* (5 Sept. 1988), 10–11.

R

Rachels, James. 'Naturalism.' In Hugh LaFollette, ed. *The Blackwell Guide to Ethical Theory*. Oxford: Blackwell, 2000, 74–91.

Randall, John H. 'The Nature of Naturalism.' In Yervant H. Krikorian, ed. *Naturalism*, 354–82.

Raup, David. 'Conflicts between Darwin and Palaeontology.' *Field Museum of Natural History Bulletin* 50/1 (Jan. 1979), 22–9.

Reidhaar-Olson, John F. and Robert T. Sauer. 'Functionally Acceptable Substitutions in Two α-helical Regions of λ Repressor.' *Proteins: Structure, Function, and Genetics* 7/4 (1990), 306–16. doi: 10.1002/prot.340070403.

Rescher, Nicholas. 'Idealism.' In Jonathan Dancy and Ernest Sosa, eds. *A Companion to Epistemology*. 1992. Repr. Oxford: Blackwell, 2000.

Ridley, Mark. 'Who Doubts Evolution?' *New Scientist* 90 (25 June 1981), 830–2.

Rogers, Carl. 'Notes on Rollo May.' *Journal of Humanistic Psychology* 22/3 (Summer 1982), 8–9. doi: 10.1177/0022167882223002.

Rorty, Richard. 'Untruth and Consequences.' *The New Republic* (31 July 1995), 32–6.

Ruse, Michael. 'Is Rape Wrong on Andromeda?' In E. Regis Jr., ed. *Extraterrestrials*. Cambridge: Cambridge University Press, 1985.

Ruse, Michael. 'Transcript: Speech by Professor Michael Ruse,' Symposium, 'The New Antievolutionism', 1993 Annual Meeting of the American Association for the Advancement of Science, 13 Feb. 1993. Online at http://www.arn.org/docs/orpages/or151/mr93tran.htm, accessed 3 Aug. 2017.

Ruse, Michael and Edward O. Wilson. 'The Evolution of Ethics.' *New Scientist* 108/1478 (17 Oct. 1985), 50–2.

Russell, Bertrand. 'A Free Man's Worship.' 1903. In *Why I Am Not a Christian*. New York: Simon & Schuster, 1957. Also in *Mysticism and Logic Including A Free Man's Worship*. London: Unwin, 1986.

Russell, Colin. 'The Conflict Metaphor and its Social Origins.' *Science and Christian Belief* 1/1 (1989), 3–26.

S

Sanders, Blanche. *The Humanist* 5 (1945).

Sanders, Peter. 'Eutychus.' *Triple Helix* (Summer 2002), 17.

Sayre-McCord, Geoffrey. 'Contractarianism.' In Hugh LaFollette, ed. *The Blackwell Guide to Ethical Theory*. Oxford: Blackwell, 2000, 247–67. 2nd edn, Wiley Blackwell, 2013, 332–53.

Scruton, Roger. *The Times* (Dec. 1997), London.

Searle, John. 'Minds, Brains and Programs.' In John Haugeland, ed. *Mind Design*. Cambridge, Mass.: Cambridge University Press, 1981.

Sedgh, Gilda, et al., 'Abortion incidence between 1990 and 2014: global, regional, and subregional levels and trends.' *The Lancet* 388/10041 (16 July 2016), 258–67. doi: 10.1016/S0140-6736(16)30380-4.

Shapiro, James A. 'In the Details . . . What?' *National Review* (16 Sept. 1996), 62–5.

Simpson, George Gaylord. 'The Biological Nature of Man.' *Science* 152/3721 (22 Apr. 1966), 472–8.

Singer, Peter. 'Hegel, Georg Wilhelm Friedrich.' In Ted Honderich, ed. *The Oxford Companion to Philosophy*. Oxford, 1995. 2nd edn, Oxford: Oxford University Press, 2005.

Skorupski, John. 'Mill, John Stuart.' In Ted Honderich, ed. *The Oxford Companion to Philosophy*. Oxford, 1995. 2nd edn, Oxford: Oxford University Press, 2005.

Slote, Michael. 'Utilitarianism.' In Ted Honderich, ed. *The Oxford Companion to Philosophy*. Oxford, 1995. 2nd edn, Oxford: Oxford University Press, 2005.

Slote, Michael. 'Virtue Ethics.' In Hugh LaFollette, ed. *The Blackwell Guide to Ethical Theory*. Oxford: Blackwell, 2000, 325–47.

Sokal, Alan D. 'Transgressing the boundaries: towards a transformative hermeneutic of Quantum Gravity.' *Social Text* (Spring/Summer 1996), 217–52.

Sokal, Alan D. 'What the Social Text Affair Does and Does Not Prove.' In Noretta Koertge, ed. *A House Built on Sand: Exposing Postmodernist Myths About Science*. Oxford: Oxford University Press, 1998, 9–22.

Solzhenitsyn, Alexander. 'Alexandr Solzhenitsyn—Nobel Lecture.' *Nobelprize.org*. Nobel Media AB 2014. Online at https://www.nobelprize.org/nobel_prizes/literature/laureates/1970/solzhenitsyn-lecture.html, accessed 15 Aug. 2017.

Spetner, L. M. 'Natural selection: An information-transmission mechanism for evolution.' *Journal of Theoretical Biology* 7/3 (Nov. 1964), 412–29.

Stalin, Joseph. Speech delivered 24 April 1924. New York, International Publishers, 1934.

Stolzenberg, Gabriel. 'Reading and relativism: an introduction to the science wars.' In Keith M. Ashman and Philip S. Baringer, eds. *After the Science Wars*. London: Routledge, 2001, 33–63.

T

Tarkunde, V. M. 'Comment by V. M. Tarkunde on Hocutt Article.' In Morris B. Storer, ed. *Humanist Ethics: Dialogue on Basics*. Buffalo, N.Y.: Prometheus Books, 1980, 147–8.

Taylor, Robert. 'Evolution is Dead.' *New Scientist* 160/2154 (3 Oct. 1998), 25–9.

W

Walicki, Andrzej. 'Hegelianism, Russian.' In Edward Craig, gen. ed. *Concise Routledge Encyclopedia of Philosophy*. London: Routledge, 2000.

Wallace, Daniel, "The Majority Text and the Original Text: Are They Identical?," *Bibliotheca Sacra*, April-June, 1991, 157-8.

Walton, J. C. 'Organization and the Origin of Life.' *Origins* 4 (1977), 16–35.

Warren, Mary Ann. 'On the Moral and Legal Status of Abortion.' Ch. 11 in Hugh LaFollette, ed. *Ethics in Practice: An Anthology*, 1997, 72–82. 4th edn, Oxford: Blackwell, 2014, 132–40.

Watters, Wendell W. 'Christianity and Mental Health.' *The Humanist* 37 (Nov./Dec. 1987).

Weatherford, Roy C. 'Freedom and Determinism.' In Ted Honderich, ed. *The Oxford Companion to Philosophy*. Oxford, 1995. 2nd edn, Oxford: Oxford University Press, 2005.

Wheeler, John A. 'Information, Physics, Quantum: The Search for Links.' In Wojciech Hubert Zurek. *Complexity, Entropy, and the Physics of Information*. The Proceedings of the 1988 Workshop on Complexity, Entropy, and the Physics of Information, held May–June, 1989, in Santa Fe, N. Mex. Redwood City, Calif.: Addison-Wesley, 1990.

Wigner, Eugene. 'The Unreasonable Effectiveness of Mathematics in the Natural Sciences', Richard Courant Lecture in Mathematical Sciences, delivered at New York University, 11 May 1959. *Communications in Pure and Applied Mathematics*, 13/1 (Feb. 1960), 1–14. Repr. in E. Wiger. *Symmetries and Reflections*. Bloomingon, Ind., 1967. Repr. Woodbridge, Conn.: Ox Bow Press, 1979, 222–37.

Wilford, John Noble. 'Sizing Up the Cosmos: An Astronomer's Quest.' *New York Times* (12 Mar. 1991), B9.

Wilkinson, David. 'Found in space?' Interview with Paul Davies. *Third Way* 22:6 (July 1999), 17–21.

Wilson, Edward O. 'The Ethical Implications of Human Sociobiology.' *Hastings Center Report* 10:6 (Dec. 1980), 27–9. doi: 10.2307/3560296.

Y

Yockey, Hubert. 'A Calculation of the Probability of Spontaneous Biogenesis by Information Theory.' *Journal of Theoretical Biology* 67 (1977), 377–98.

Yockey, Hubert. 'Self-Organisation Origin of Life Scenarios and Information Theory.' *Journal of Theoretical Biology* 91 (1981), 13–31.

STUDY QUESTIONS FOR TEACHERS AND STUDENTS

SECTION 1: THE STATUS, BASIS AND AUTHORITY OF ETHICS

CHAPTER 1: QUESTIONS FOR ETHICAL THEORIES

Introduction

1.1　What is your impression of the attitude of your contemporaries to ethics and morality? Would you say:
  (a)　that they have a common core of moral values? If so, what is it? Or
  (b)　that there is no general consensus on ethics. If so, why is that?

1.2　What do you understand by liberalism, its original principles and its present difficulties? Would you agree with Brenda Almond's criticism cited in the text?

1.3　What special difficulties does the modern world pose both for the formation of a coherent moral theory and for the practical ethical decisions that have to be made?

1.4　Do you think that human beings have rights? If so, what are they, and who grants them?

1.5　Do you think that human beings have duties? If so, who or what imposes them?

1.6　There is a difference between human rights and civil rights. What is it?

1.7　What is meant by saying that information is not necessarily knowledge, and knowledge is not necessarily understanding? Debate the question.

1.8　Discuss the fourfold analysis of ethical theory given in the text.
  (a)　What is the special concern of each of its four levels?
  (b)　How, do you think, is an understanding of the first three levels likely to affect decisions at level four?

1.9　What can we learn from the Hippocratic oath about the importance of the distinction between the four levels of ethical theory?

CHAPTER 2: WHAT SHOULD WE DO, AND WHY?

The status of ethics

2.1　What do we mean by calling ethics a 'normative' discipline?

2.2　Explain the emotivist theory of ethics, and discuss its merits and demerits.

2.3　Is the theory of cultural relativism absolutely true, or only partly true?

2.4　'The theory of cultural relativism is in the end incoherent.' Discuss.

2.5　Can a moral statement ever be objectively true, or is it never more than an expression of opinion?

2.6 Is intolerance always wrong? What attitude would you have taken to Pol Pot's ethical theory and practice?

The inadequacy of subjectivism

2.7 All of us are conditioned and prejudiced by our cultural background. Does that mean that it is impossible for us:
   (a) ever to come to see that we could be wrong and another culture be right?
   (b) ever to perceive that some truths are objective and universal?

2.8 In practical affairs do people sometimes prefer to rely on guidance from some objective source rather than trust their own subjective impressions and judgments? Give examples.

2.9 Is it true to say that if morality were subjective, it would reduce morality to a question of taste? What would it matter if it did?

2.10 'If there were no objective standards of morality, we should have to abandon all idea of moral progress.' Why is that so?

2.11 In comparatively recent times enormous social and cultural pressure used to be brought to bear on Hindu widows to immolate themselves on their husbands' funeral pyres (the practice was known as *suttee*). Would you:
   (a) have argued that, since it was cultural, the practice should be tolerated? Or
   (b) have joined with those who campaigned to get the government to make the practice illegal? If so, on what ground would you have done so?

2.12 'Subjectivism tends to be self-refuting.' Discuss, and cite an example.

2.13 'It is difficult for moral subjectivists to behave consistently with their theory in daily life.' Give examples to show how this is.

Arguments against objectivism

2.14 If you object that something is not fair, do you expect people to know what you mean by 'fair'? If so, why?

2.15 Sometimes when family members come to divide up the possessions of a deceased relative, they seriously disagree over what division is fair. Does that mean that the concept 'fairness' is of no practical use and should be abandoned?

2.16 'If there is no such thing as justice, then in the end the most powerful will control the rest.' Discuss.

2.17 'Moral laws are like the laws of arithmetic: no one invented them.' Discuss.

2.18 What evidence is there that moral values are universal?

2.19 Cite any culture you know of in which deceit is normal, expected, and acceptable behaviour. Would you condone it? If not, why not?

2.20 What mistakes are involved in claiming that the differing funeral customs of the Greeks and Callatiae are evidence that moral values are not universal and objective, but relative?

2.21 'The fact that we had to be taught moral values by our parents and school teachers shows that those values are merely a cultural tradition.' Is this necessarily true? Debate the question.

CHAPTER 3: THE SOURCE OF OBJECTIVE MORAL VALUES

On what are objective moral values grounded?

3.1 Give the reasons for agreeing, or not agreeing, with the theory that materialistic evolution can explain the existence of universal, objective moral values.

3.2 What is sociobiology? Is it true that our genes control our behaviour?

3.3 Can we rebel against our genes?

3.4 How would you account for altruism?

3.5 What is ethical naturalism?

3.6 To what extent would the Bible agree with ethical naturalism?

3.7 What is the logical difficulty in deriving an 'ought' of duty from a statement of bare fact, without some additional adequate 'bridging' reason?

3.8 Discuss Rachels's suggestion that our personal interests are enough to ground an adequate ethic.

3.9 'Instinct is the source and base of all ethics.' Argue for and against this view.

Universal, objective moral values are grounded in the character and will of God

3.10 Why must any moral theory be able to give a valid explanation of why we have a duty to keep the moral law?

3.11 Why did the ancients (and why do some moderns) call on God, or the gods, to witness their statements, promises and covenants?

3.12 What did contractarianism mean to Socrates?

3.13 How was political contractarianism applied in the sixteenth and seventeenth centuries?

3.14 What was the difference between Hobbes's application of contractarianism and Rousseau's?

3.15 What is modern moral contractarianism? What is the motivation behind it?

3.16 What are the good features of moral contractarianism?

3.17 What are its weaknesses?

3.18 What is meant by 'The Divine Command Theory of Morality'? What is its basis? What are its implications?

3.19 Explain the Euthyphro problem in your own words. Do you think there is a satisfactory answer to it?

3.20 What was the old covenant? What was its background according to Exodus 19:1–6? What were its terms and conditions?

3.21 What does Christ offer to do for us through the new covenant?

SECTION 2: MAJOR CONTEMPORARY ETHICAL SYSTEMS

CHAPTER 4: CHRISTIAN ETHICS

Introduction

4.1 On what is Christian ethics based and what authority does it claim?

4.2 What is its attitude to Nature?

4.3 What do Christians mean by saying that obedience to the moral law is ultimately obedience to a person? Why do they think this is important?

4.4 From what sources do Christians derive their knowledge of the moral law?

4.5 Name and explain four of the major goals of Christian ethics.

4.6 What are the four general principles that underlie and motivate Christian ethical behaviour?

4.7 What action-spheres do the Ten Commandments cover?

4.8 What attitude does the New Testament take to the Ten Commandments of the Old Testament? What part do they play in its ethical theory?

4.9 What is meant by saying that Christian ethics presuppose a personal experience of salvation?

4.10 'Christ's ethical demands are higher than mere justice.' Give an example of this.

4.11 Why are both justice and love necessary in sound ethical practice?

4.12 What sources of guidance are available to Christians when the Bible itself does not explicitly indicate what decision ought to be taken?

4.13 Name some objections to Christian ethics. How cogent do you consider them to be? Give your reasons.

CHAPTER 5: ACT UTILITARIANISM

Then and now

5.1 On what theory of man's psychological make-up did Bentham base his theory?

5.2 What, according to utilitarianism, is man's supreme good and goal, and what general principle does it advocate for the achievement of that goal?

5.3 What was Bentham's hedonic calculus? What was it for?

5.4 How did Bentham apply his theory to the question of punishment and prison reform?

5.5 What specific rule did Bentham lay down for all action-spheres?

5.6 What was Bentham's 'Principle of Utility'?

5.7 Why is this theory called 'act utilitarianism'?

5.8 Do you agree with Bentham that the end justifies the means? Does it matter if an act is evil in itself, if it produces a good result?

5.9 What did Bentham mean by claiming that in our decisions we should always be neutral and impartial in calculating the maximum amount of pleasure for the maximum number of people? Should this rule be invariably applied in all cases?

5.10 In the case of the hospital fire would you blame the electrician for saving his wife rather than the surgeon? If not, what is the difference between the electrician and the chief of police who let his brother go free?

An evaluation of utilitarianism: its practical difficulties

5.11 What attractive features do you find in utilitarianism?

5.12 J. S. Mill said: 'It is better to be a Socrates dissatisfied, than a fool satisfied.' What bearing has this remark on Bentham's theory of pleasure?

5.13 What are the difficulties involved in putting Bentham's hedonic calculus into practice?
5.14 Who should be the judge of what kind of pleasure/good should be aimed at:
   (a) in a family?
   (b) in a school?
   (c) in the State?
5.15 Is it sufficiently fair and just to aim simply at maximising pleasure/good for the maximum number in the State?
5.16 In what did J. S. Mill say that human rights are grounded? Do you agree with him?
5.17 What is the difference between human rights and civil rights? Do they both have the same source? What duties do civil rights carry with them?
5.18 Is it fair and just to make the morality of an act depend solely on its future results? If not, why not?
5.19 On what would you make the question of whether an act is morally right or wrong depend?
5.20 How far into the future must we look before we can decide whether a proposed act should be carried out or not? Ought nuclear reactors ever to have been built?
5.21 If in assessing the morality of an act, one has to consider the agent's motives and intentions as well as the nature of the results, how does that undermine the basic principle of act utilitarianism?
5.22 If in addition to immediate, bad results an evilly intentioned act eventually leads to good results, should that act be regarded as morally good?
5.23 When Christians say that all things work together for good, what good are they referring to? (Read Rom 8:28–30)
5.24 What modifications have modern utilitarians made to the original theory?

An evaluation of utilitarianism: its moral problems

5.25 In what sense did Bentham think that Nature, pain and pleasure dictate man's moral duty?
5.26 What is meant by saying that pleasure is something you find when you are looking for something else? Do you agree?
5.27 Is all pleasure morally good? If not, how do you decide which is good and which isn't?
5.28 What are the dangers of making pleasure the supreme good in life?
5.29 Is it always right to give people what would please them?
5.30 Think for a moment about your own motivations. Would it be true to say that you are driven solely by pain and pleasure? If not, what other motives drive you?
5.31 Would you ever be moved by loyalty to the truth to tell people things they would be very displeased to hear?
5.32 Would you ever be moved by love to look after an aged parent, even when caring for that parent caused you much pain and no pleasure?

5.33 What is the weakness of basing our duty to society simply on the facts of impersonal nature?

Utilitarianism's general principle

5.34 What specific rules would you bring to bear upon the rightness or wrongness of cutting down the world's rainforests?

5.35 If directors of a business find that by telling lies they can make more profit, maintain more employees and keep their shareholders happy, is there anything wrong with that? If so, what?

5.36 If the institution of marriage and family life were to break down and its place be taken by promiscuity, would it increase or decrease the happiness of all concerned? Give reasons for your answers.

5.37 Why do we need specific rules for the various action-spheres of life?

5.38 Where did J. S. Mill think that we get the rules and norms of moral behaviour from? What authority did he think they have?

5.39 What is the difference between direct-consequentialism and rule-consequentialism?

5.40 In the past century the rule 'You shall not murder innocent people' has been broken millions of times. Cite historical examples to support your view that (*a*) it has increased, or (*b*) it has not increased, the sum of human happiness.

5.41 What is meant by distributive justice?

5.42 Why and how do J. S. Mill and John Rawls demand that utilitarianism must be modified in order to achieve distributive justice?

5.43 The theory of act utilitarianism that the end justifies the means runs clean counter to common sense morality. Why is that? Do you agree? Give examples in support of your own moral opinion.

5.44 What do you consider to be the role and function of the family in society, and our duty towards our close relatives? To what extent should that duty take priority over other duties and loyalties?

CHAPTER 6: INTUITIONISM

The 'end' and the 'ought'

6.1 What is the difference between a teleological ethical theory and a deontological one?

6.2 Which of the two is Intuitionism, and why?

6.3 By what process do intuitionists come to perceive what they call the basic duties?

6.4 What, according to Ross, are the basic duties?

6.5 What do intuitionists mean by calling some duties derivative? Cite two examples of derivative duties, and explain what they are derived from.

6.6 What did Ross mean by calling the basic duties prima facie duties?

6.7 What did Ross say should happen when in a given situation two basic duties conflict?

An evaluation of intuitionism: its strengths and weaknesses

6.8 Would you agree that intuitionism has some features that are superior to utilitarianism and consequentialism? If so, give your reasons.

6.9 'Intuitionism is marked by a strong emphasis on our duties to the past.' Explain what this means and what its significance is.

6.10 Intuitionism gives reasons for thinking that our special care for parents and relatives is morally appropriate. Comment on this, and contrast it with utilitarianism.

6.11 'Anthony Kenny's criticism of consequentialism shows by contrast the rightness of intuitionist doctrine.' Explain what this means.

6.12 Many philosophers criticise Ross's list of basic duties. Why?

6.13 Many argue that Ross's claim that the basic duties are self-evident cannot be true. On what ground do they argue this?

6.14 Intuitionism has no supreme goal, nor any overarching principle. Is this true? If so, why is it a disadvantage?

6.15 What is meant by saying that intuitionism's ethics have no base and therefore no ultimate authority? Is it true?

6.16 What is the difference between 'a reason to do something' and 'a duty to do something'?

6.17 What weaknesses beset the idea that it is society itself that originates our basic ethical standards?

6.18 'People who do not believe in God have difficulty in suggesting an adequate ethical substitute.' Debate this assertion.

CHAPTER 7: KANTIAN ETHICS

The first formulation of the Categorical Imperative

7.1 'Kant's approach to ethics was that of a rationalist rather than an empiricist.' Explain what this means.

7.2 What is meant by saying that Kant's ethical system is severely deontological? How does it contrast with utilitarianism?

7.3 What did Kant mean by the term 'good-will', and what part did it play in his ethical system?

7.4 If you gave a gift to the poor out of compassion, or because you found such generosity enjoyable, Kant would have regarded your act as not truly moral. Why? Would you agree with him?

7.5 What, according to Kant, was unsatisfactory with the morality of the grocer?

The three formulations of the Categorical Imperative

7.6 What is the difference between a hypothetical imperative and a categorical imperative?

7.7 Kant holds that there is only one categorical imperative and that it is the basic principle of true moral decision. What is this categorical imperative, and how does it affect behaviour?

7.8 What does Kant mean when he says 'Act only according to that maxim by which you can at the same time will that it should become a universal law'? How would you evaluate this principle?

7.9 What reason does Kant give for saying that it would be wrong of me to borrow money, promising to repay it, but knowing in advance that I would not be able to repay it?

7.10 Explain exactly why, according to Kant's second example, it is wrong for a well-off man to refuse to help those in need. Then answer the following questions:

(a) What do you understand by the Golden Rule? In your opinion, is Kant teaching by his second example something similar to the Golden Rule?

(b) In this second example, has Kant inadvertently gone over to a utilitarian principle?

7.11 What do the terms 'means' and 'end' mean?

7.12 What is the difference between using other people as a means, and using other people *simply* as a means?

7.13 What is meant by saying that each individual human being is an end in himself and herself?

7.14 What in practice does treating people as ends involve?

7.15 What implications does this principle carry:

(a) in private life?

(b) in industry?

(c) in the State?

7.16 What does the Bible say is man's chief end?

7.17 'The third formulation of the Categorical Imperative puts the balance to the first two.' What does this mean? And why is it important?

7.18 What should happen when reasonable people disagree over what principles and rules should be universalised?

A critical assessment of Kantian ethics

7.19 What does Raphael mean when he says that the capacity for imaginative sympathy is what enables us to judge and act as moral beings? How will it affect our attitude to other people if we use this capacity?

7.20 'The empiricist version gives a positive psychological explanation of the feeling of obligation to others but fails to give us good reason for making a normative judgment' (Raphael). What does Raphael mean, and why is it important?

7.21 What is the fundamental difference between Christian ethics and secular ethics?

7.22 What made Kant believe in God, the life-to-come and the final judgment?

7.23 'Kant's "autonomous will" puts man and man's reason, rather than God and God's Word, at the centre of morality.' Discuss.

7.24 What similarity, if any, do you see between Kant and Sartre?

CHAPTER 8: VIRTUE ETHICS

A different emphasis

8.1 What is virtue ethics? How does it differ from the ethical theories you have so far studied?

8.2 How does the kind of person we are inwardly affect our outward behaviour? Give illustrations.

8.3 How do inner motives and intentions alter the moral significance of an act? Give examples.

8.4 What, according to the Bible, is the all-important inner virtue? What are its characteristic features?

8.5 What is quietism? Why does the Bible not approve of it?

8.6 What is the New Testament's attitude to the development of inner virtues?

8.7 What exactly is a virtue? How would you distinguish between a virtue and a motive or an intention?

8.8 What, according to Aristotle, are the three parts of the human make-up? To which part do the moral virtues pertain, and to which the intellectual virtues?

Aristotle's ethics

8.9 What was the original meaning of the Greek word for 'virtue' (*aretē*)? What does it mean when applied in the moral realm?

8.10 Put in your own words Aristotle's doctrine of 'the mean'. How does his analogy with food help us to understand it?

8.11 Is fear a bad thing in itself? What purpose does it serve in the human make-up?

8.12 What does Aristotle mean by saying that courage is the mean between cowardice and rashness?

8.13 Is pleasure always a good thing? If not, in what ways can it become a bad thing?

8.14 According to Aristotle, what would be the right attitude, and what the wrong attitudes, to:
  (a) the getting and giving of money?
  (b) ambition?
  (c) self-assessment?
  (d) other people?

8.15 List each of the following series of three qualities in the order: (1) deficiency; (2) excess; (3) mean:
  (a) patience, irascibility, lack of spirit.
  (b) magnanimity, timidity, vanity.
  (c) shyness, uninhibitedness, modesty.

8.16 By what method do we decide in any one situation what the mean is? By logic? If not, how?

8, 17 How is learning to act virtuously like learning to drive a car?

8.18 How does one become virtuous?
  (a) What does Aristotle say about it?

(b) What does the Bible say about it?

8.19 What do you think Peter means when he says that God 'has granted to us all things that pertain to life and godliness' (2 Pet 1:3)?

Unfair criticisms of Aristotle

8.20 'Courage and love should be practised with large-hearted abandon, not with penny-pinching calculations of a grocer weighing out packets of tea.' Is this a fair criticism of Aristotle's ethical theory?

8.21 'In respect of its substance and the definition which states its essence, virtue is a mean, with regard to what is best and right, an extreme.' What did Aristotle mean by this?

8.22 Does Aristotle think that all vices are either an excess or a deficiency of some virtue? What was his attitude to envy, spite, and theft?

8.23 He says in regard to adultery and murder and suchlike things: 'It is not possible ever to be right with regard to them; one must always be wrong ... simply to do any of them is to go wrong ... however they are done, they are wrong.' How does he differ from act utilitarianism in this regard?

8.24 What would Aristotle say to modern advocates of permissiveness? On what ground, if at all, would they dispute his view?

8.25 What, according to Aristotle, are the intellectual virtues? What is the difference between them?

8.26 What aim do the intellectual virtues have in common?

8.27 Why must practical wisdom itself be virtuous if it is to do its job properly?

8.28 What does Aristotle mean by saying that 'vice is destructive of the originating causes of action'?

8.29 What is the function of the scientific power of the intellect?

8.30 When Aristotle says that we grasp the 'first principles', not by scientific proof, but by intuition, what does he mean? And how does this resemble what the Bible says?

8.31 Would you agree that the functioning of our intuition is influenced by our prior dispositions?

8.32 How is Aristotle's concept of happiness (*eudaimonia*) affected by his contemporary culture?

8.33 What was Aristotle's concept of ideal, supreme happiness?

8.34 What difference would it have made to Aristotle's ethical theory if he had thought of love, not reason, as the highest thing in the universe?

Modern virtue ethics

8.35 'Modern virtue ethics owes much of its good features to women philosophers.' Comment and explain.

8.36 Compared with Utilitarianism and Kantianism what is virtue ethics' distinguishing principle?

8.37 How do you understand Slote's 'rough' characterisation of virtue ethics?

8.38 'Some virtue-ethicists are against rules. They hold that in making moral decisions all should be left to the sensitivities, or moral connoisseurship, of the virtuous individual.' What does this mean? And what ground do they have for saying so?

8.39 What, according to Hursthouse, determines whether an act is wrong or right?

8.40 'Acts count as right because a virtuous person would choose them.' What is ambiguous about this statement?

8.41 Is a painting good because an expert art critic chooses it? Or does he choose it because it is good?

8.42 What difficulty does Robert Louden find with virtue ethics' need to assess the morality of an agent? Would you agree with him?

8.43 Why would it be dangerous to define what is right as 'what virtuous people choose to do'?

8.44 'Virtue ethics, in spite of what it appears to say, ultimately assumes and depends on the objectivity of moral standards and of absolute values.' Is this comment fair?

8.45 What does Hursthouse say is the goal of ethics? Why doesn't Slote like it?

8.46 What is the difference between the two footballers' attitude to playing football, in the illustration in the text?

8.47 What does Slote mean by claiming that virtue ethics must be self-standing and must not have a goal beyond itself?

8.48 Why do Christians say that living virtuously is not sufficient by itself, and that it must have a goal beyond itself? What is that goal?

Slote's version of virtue ethics

8.49 Slote tells us of his search for one basic principle to unify virtue ethics as a theory. What two principles does he suggest and which does he prefer?

8.50 What does Slote mean by saying that ethical theory must be agent-based?

8.51 If universal benevolence were chosen as the basic unifying principle, how then would the virtuousness of an agent be measured?

8.52 What is meant by the claim that universal benevolence is not grounded in any more basic thing, principle or moral law?

8.53 Why, in the end, does Slote reject universal benevolence as the basic unifying principle? Why does he think that it would be as inhuman as Bentham's utilitarianism?

8.54 What have Carol Gillingham and Nel Noddings contributed to Slote's version of virtue ethics?

8.55 What problem does an ethic of caring solve, according to Slote?

8.56 How does Slote apply the example of the loving father's care for both his sons to the question of humanitarian aid?

8.57 'Virtue ethics excludes all deontic notions and concentrates solely on aretaic values.' What does this mean? What are its implications?

8.58 Caring for people is certainly an admirable virtue, if we have it; but do we have a *duty* to care for others? If so, why? On what is it based?

8.59 Have large firms a *duty* to care for their employees?

8.60 When Cain asked, 'Am I my brother's keeper?', what did God actually say in reply? (Gen 4).

CHAPTER 9: EGOISM

Extremism in ethical theory and practice

9.1 In what sense does virtue ethics represent an extreme position?

9.2 In what respect do act utilitarianism and Kantianism stand at opposite extremes; and in what sense do they both stand at the same extreme?

9.3 What does the term 'egoist' mean? Can you cite any famous egoists in history?

9.4 What is the difference between 'self-interest' and selfishness?

9.5 Can mixed motives sometimes be morally acceptable?

9.6 If we are creatures of a creator, why must it logically be in our interest to serve the will and purpose of our creator?

9.7 If on the other hand we are the product of mindless forces, is it *necessarily* in our interests to serve anything or anyone? Or should our basic motive be the survival of the fittest?

9.8 Is 'seeking one's personal salvation', as the Bible puts it, an unworthy, selfish aim? If not, how is it not?

9.9 Does Christianity teach people to be good for what they get out of it? If not, what does it teach?

9.10 What does the Bible mean by 'denying oneself'? Why did Christ teach his disciples that they must be willing to do so?

9.11 What is the Christian motivation for daily work meant to be? Necessity? Enjoyment? Disinterested philanthropy? Selfish ambition? Self-interest? Money and goods?

Christian ethics and the wrongness of selfishness

9.12 What is selfishness?

9.13 What is meant by saying that a selfish man is guilty of a gross abuse of the basic conditions of human life and society? Do you agree?

9.14 Summarise the lessons drawn from the analogy of the human body for our individual behaviour in society. How do they combine self-interest with unselfish service?

9.15 When Christians talk about serving Christ and others in hope of reward, what kind of reward are they looking forward to?

9.16 What attitudes and motives does Christ as a role-model inculcate in his disciples?

Ethical egoism

9.17 What is ethical egoism?

9.18 In what basic principle is it grounded? Name some of the serious implications of its being grounded in this one solitary principle.

9.19 'If one attempts to universalise ethical egoism, it becomes logically self-contradictory.' Give an example to show how this is.

9.20 Why could it be immoral to advise someone to act on the basic principle of ethical egoism?

9.21 Construct a practical example to show how the general practice of ethical egoism in society would lead to a widespread breakdown in trust.

Entrepreneurial egoism

9.22 What do you understand entrepreneurial egoism to be?

9.23 Argue, with examples, both for and against the idea that the wealth created by entrepreneurial egoism 'trickles down' to society at large. State your own solution to the problem.

Psychological Egoism

9.24 'Psychological egoism is not a moral theory.' What is it then? And how does it impinge on ethical theory?

9.25 It is a basic tenet of ethical theory that 'ought' implies 'can'. What does this mean, and what moral implication for man's ethical duty follows from psychological egoism, if it is true?

9.26 On what scientific basis does the theory of psychological egoism claim to be founded?

9.27 'One example to the contrary would demolish the theory of psychological egoism.' How is that? Can you think of any such examples in history or in modern times?

9.28 What is your estimate of the explanation that psychological egoism gives of the behaviour of the man who saved the children from the house on fire?

9.29 'A theory which gives the same explanation both for a thing and for its opposite is worthless.' Is this a fair comment?

9.30 Is it true that human beings are motivated by one single motive? If you think not, give reasons for your view.

9.31 Have you any sympathy with the writer of Romans 7:18–19?

SECTION 3: WHAT USE IS ETHICS?

CHAPTER 10: DETERMINING THE VALUE OF A HUMAN BEING

Introduction

10.1 In what sense are ethics based on values?

10.2 Is it true to say that all people have ethical views, whether they know it or not?

10.3 From the list of ethical theories given in the text, which values would you make your own?

10.4 'A newborn baby is worth less than a pig.' Discuss.

10.5 What is meant by saying that it is impossible to build a satisfactory ethic without a transcendental dimension?

CHAPTER 11: THE ETHICS OF THE TRANSMISSION OF LIFE

11.1 What, according to nature, is the necessary framework for the transmission of new life?

11.2 What is the significance of marriage?

11.3 What is meant by the double function of sex within marriage?

11.4 If marriage is an ideal, what are the ethical conditions for its maintenance?

11.5 What are some of the effects of divorcing sex from marriage? In your opinion, are these effects good or bad? Give your reasons.

11.6 'The irresponsible attitude of some men towards their wives makes marriage a misery.' What would intuitionism and virtue ethics say about this?

11.7 'Marriage was invented to justify the tyranny of men over women.' Comment.

11.8 What pressures do you feel are put upon young people in relation to sexual activity?

11.9 The media moguls make vast sums of money by commercialising sex. Is this ethical? Give your reasons.

11.10 What attitude does Christianity take to casual sex? What reasons and motivations does it give for this attitude?

CHAPTER 12 ETHICAL ISSUES RAISED BY SCIENCE AND TECHNOLOGY

Science, technology and new possibilities

12.1 'If it can be done, it should be done.' Would it be ethically safe to apply this principle to all the possibilities opened up by science and technology? If not, why not?

12.2 The use of sperm and egg donors raises a range of ethical problems. What are they? How valid do you think they are?

12.3 What does 'infringing the integrity of the marriage relationship' mean?

12.4 Do you think that children have a right to know about their genetic ancestry? Why does it matter?

12.5 What effect do you think it could have on a child to discover that its conception involved an anonymous donor?

12.6 Why do you think donors demand anonymity? Why would parents not wish their children to know who the donor was?

When does life begin?

12.7 Write an essay critiquing the arguments used in this speech.

Problems at the end of life

12.8 What is the definition of euthanasia?

12.9 What is the difference between voluntary and involuntary euthanasia?

12.10 'Passive euthanasia is a contradiction in terms.' Comment.

12.11 What attitude did the Hippocratic tradition maintain and why?

12.12 Why do many governments still refuse to legalise euthanasia? What is the 'slippery slope' argument? Do you see it as a danger? Why?

12.13 Has a doctor a duty always to use the latest medical technology to keep a patient alive?

12.14 What difference does a religious faith make in determining the attitude towards euthanasia?

12.15 Why are the doctor's intentions important when she administers a pain-killing drug?

CHAPTER 13: EXERCISES IN ETHICS

13.1 The labels that are normally put on the three views of punishment discussed under the heading 'Crime and Punishment' are 'deterrence', 'retribution' and 'reform'. But which label applies to which view?

13.2 Choose three students from the class or study group to play the roles of Ramesh, Lee, and Juliana. Let each one argue for his or her position, and get the class or group to respond.

13.3 'The prime purpose of retributory punishment is to uphold the values expressed by the law. The law against murder seeks to uphold the value of human life. If this law can be broken with impunity, the value it seeks to uphold is destroyed.' Argue for and against this view.

13.4 'You cannot have true liberty in society without justice.' Is this true?

13.5 'If a person knew that what he was doing was wrong when he did it, then to say that he could not help doing it, and should not be held responsible, is to treat him as less than fully human, and more like an animal or a cabbage. The true and kindest way to help him is to train him to take responsibility for his actions.' Debate this view.

13.6 Suppose two men, Raul and Ivan, commit identical crimes. However, Raul gets much more enjoyment out of the crime than Ivan. The utilitarian theory of punishment suggests that Raul should be punished more than Ivan. Do you agree?

13.7 Read Deuteronomy 25:1–3. What principles of justice are enunciated here? How should they be interpreted and applied in our modern world?

13.8 Do you think it is ethical for parents to punish their children? Include in your answer what you feel are the dangers, if any, of excessive punishment, or of no punishment at all.

CHAPTER 14: BEYOND ETHICS

Ethics reveals the problems

14.1 What are the two questions that ethics as a normative system cannot answer by itself?

14.2 What did Socrates think to be the reason why people did wrong, and what did he think the cure was?

14.3 Have you ever done anything wrong, knowing it to be wrong? If so, why did you do it?

Aristotle's view

14.4 On what grounds did Aristotle disagree with Socrates over this question?

14.5 According to Aristotle, what was the difference between a person who lacks self-control and a self-indulgent person?

14.6 'Can a person who does what he knows to be wrong, be said really to know that it is wrong?' What answer did Aristotle give to this question, and how did he illustrate it?

14.7 What theory of Aristotle is the story of the girl who took the hard drug meant to illustrate? Is it true to life?

Aristotle on the root cause and the cure of wrong behaviour

14.8 'Aristotle's theory about the root-cause of humankind's defective moral behaviour has much in common with social evolutionary theory.' Comment.

14.9 How convincing is Aristotle's theory in the light of the enormous amount of corruption in our modern cities, and in view of the behaviour of the civilised nations of the world during the last century and up to the present?

14.10 What was Aristotle's suggestion for the cure of defective moral behaviour? To what extent is it realistic?

14.11 What did Aristotle mean by saying that there are many ways to be bad but only one way to be good?

14.12 Would you agree with Aristotle that it is difficult to be good?

The confession of the Apostle Paul

14.13 At one stage in his life the Apostle Paul felt that he could keep, and had in fact kept, the Ten Commandments satisfactorily. What changed his mind?

14.14 When Paul says that the law is spiritual, what does he mean?

14.15 What does it mean to covet?

14.16 In what sense can the fostering of hatred for someone in one's heart and mind be said to be tantamount to murder?

14.17 Paul says that sometimes the law's prohibition of something made him want to do it all the more. In your experience is this true to life? If so, how is that?

14.18 Do you think that intellect and sheer willpower are sufficient to stop oneself from doing or thinking wrong?

14.19 'The person who is perfectly content with the moral standard that he or she has attained is suffering either from a defective moral conscience or else from a severe form of Pharisaism.' What does this mean? Would you agree?

A Marxist insight

14.20 Comment on the similarity between the language used in the Communist Party's statement of 1961 and the language of the New Testament. Have they any substantial ideas in common?

14.21 Is it true that some people disapprove of bringing God into ethics? If so, why?

14.22 Do you think that taking the ethical standards of religion seriously is psychologically unhealthy? Why or, why not?

The place of ethics in Christian doctrine

14.23 What is meant by saying that ethics is a second order, and not a first order, exercise? Illustrate your answer.

14.24 'God did not create humankind so that he could have creatures on whom he could impose rules and regulations.' What did he create us for, then?

14.25 How does the parable of the Prodigal Son illustrate what the Bible regards as lying at the root of humankind's wrong-doing?

14.26 'Christian ethics flow from, and are motivated by, the mercies of God.' What mercies?

14.27 Why does Paul leave the statement of Christian ethics to the last part of his treatise?

14.28 The climaxes to Parts 1 and 2 of Paul's treatise resemble each other. In what respect?

14.29 What is the difference in major theme between Part 1 and Part 2?

14.30 Why is the order of these two Parts in the treatise significant? What would be the effect on the message of the treatise if this order were reversed?

14.31 How does the parable of the Prodigal Son illustrate the point that Paul is making by insisting that reconciliation and acceptance with God precede the moral remaking of a person's character?

14.32 In what was the Prodigal Son's initial behaviour like that of Adam and Eve in the Genesis story?

14.33 What, according to Romans 1:18–3:20, are the symptoms of humankind's alienation from God?

14.34 What, according to Romans 3:21 ff., is the provision God has made for man's reconciliation? On what principles is it offered?

14.35 How does that provision affect the second stage in the process of producing the 'new man'?

14.36 Part 1 of Paul's treatise teaches that a person is justified by faith apart from the works of the law (3:28). What does this mean?

14.37 Part 2 teaches that it is God's intention that the righteous requirements of the law should be fulfilled. How? And at what stage in a person's experience?

14.38 'Christian ethics is not merely a matter of determined self-effort.' How and why is it not?

14.39 What in Christianity as distinct from Marxism is the means of creating and educating the 'new man'?

14.40 'Christian ethics does not produce a slave-like mentality and behaviour. It is the lifestyle of God's free-born grown-up sons and daughters.' How, according to Romans 8, is this so?

14.41 What areas of life does Christian ethics cover, according to Part 4 of the treatise?

14.42 Frankena argues that to attempt to ground ethics on religious beliefs divides society, and stops mankind from reaching agreement on moral and political principles. What answers do Christian ethicists give to this objection?

14.43 In what sense and to what extent must the truth-claims of all religions be treated like those of philosophy and science?

APPENDIX: THE SCIENTIFIC ENDEAVOUR

Scientific method

A.1 In what different ways have you heard the word 'science' used? How would you define it?

A.2 How is induction understood as part of our everyday experience and also of the scientific endeavour?

A.3 In what ways does deduction differ from induction, and what role does each play in scientific experiments?

A.4 Do you find the idea of 'falsifiability' appealing, or unsatisfactory? Why?

A.5 How does abduction differ from both induction and deduction, and what is the relationship among the three?

Explaining explanations

A.6 How many levels of explanation can you think of to explain a cake, in terms of how was it made, what was it made from, and why was it made? What can scientists tell us? What can 'Aunt Olga' tell us?

A.7 In what ways is reductionism helpful in scientific research, and in what ways could it be limiting, or even detrimental, to scientific research?

A.8 How do you react to physicist and theologian John Polkinghorne's statement that reductionism relegates 'our experiences of beauty, moral obligation, and religious encounter to the epiphenomenal scrapheap. It also destroys rationality'?

The basic operational presuppositions of the scientific endeavour

A.9 What is meant by the statement 'Observation is dependent on theory'?

A.10 What are some of the axioms upon which your thinking about scientific knowledge rests?

A.11 What does trust have to do with gaining knowledge?

A.12 What does belief have to do with gaining knowledge?

A.13 According to physicist and philosopher of science Thomas Kuhn, how do new scientific paradigms emerge?

SCRIPTURE INDEX

OLD TESTAMENT

Genesis
1:26	218
2:24	223, 234
9:6	218–19
37–50	121
39:9	100–1
50:20	121

Exodus
19:1–8	90–1
20:1–24	90–1
20:1–17	101–2
20:12	251
20:13–15	130
21–23	102
24:1–11	90–1

Leviticus
11:44–45	90
19:2	90
19:18	100
20:7	90

Deuteronomy
6:5	100

Psalms
16:11	127
96:9–13	64
111:2	19
139:13–16	245–6

Proverbs
book	102

Song of Songs
book	224

Amos
3:2	64

Micah
6:8	100

NEW TESTAMENT

Matthew
5–7	103
5:43–45	104
5:44	99
5:45	99
5:48	99
7:12	157
16:21	197
16:24–27	197
22:37	100
22:39–40	100

Mark
7:18–23	232
10:42–44	200–1
10:45	201
12:30–31	130

Luke
1:35	246
13:24	196
13:25	196
13:28	196
15:11–32	286, 289–90
15:17	289
15:21	290
22:20	91

John
1:1–2	26
4:10	196
4:34	195
5:22–23	98
11:50	135 n. 21
15:20	197

Acts
13:1–3	105

Romans
1:1–5:11	285, 287–8, 290–1
1:18–32	290
1:20	177
1:31	77
2:1–16	290
2:14–15	105, 147
2:17–3:20	290–1
3:21–5:11	291
3:21–30	291
3:24–26	291
3:25	291
3:31	291
5:1–11	291
5:5–11	287–8
5:12–8:39	285, 287, 288–9, 291–2
7:7–12	280–3
7:7–8	281
7:10–13	281
7:14–24	280–3
7:25	282
7:18–19	208
8:1–2	292
8:3–4	103–4
8:4	292
8:12–17	292
8:14–15	105
8:26–30	292
8:28	122
8:29–30	99
8:31–39	288
9:1–11:36	285
11:36	99
12:1–16:27	285, 291, 292, 293
12:1–2	286–7, 293
12:2	284
12:3–8	293
12:9–16	293
12:17–21	293
13:1–7	293
13:1	126
13:7	126
13:8–10	293

Romans
- 13:9 — 126
- 13:10 — 100
- 13:11–14 — 293
- 14:1–15:13 — 293
- 14:5–12 — 106

1 Corinthians
- 6:9–11 — 229, 230
- 6:12–20 — 230–4
- 10:31 — 99
- 10:32–33 — 105
- 11:14 — 105
- 12:12–31 — 199 n. 3
- 13:3–7 — 168
- 13:5 — 208
- 15:35–49 — 233

2 Corinthians
- 3:2–18 — 91
- 5:14–15 — 101

Galatians
- 2:20 — 233
- 5:1 — 230
- 5:13–24 — 230
- 5:16–25 — 103–4
- 5:22 — 168
- 6:10 — 126

Ephesians
- 2:8–10 — 230
- 2:8–9 — 196
- 4:23–24 — 283–4
- 4:25 — 104
- 4:28 — 198
- 5:11 — 130
- 5:25–31 — 224

Philippians
- 2:4–8 — 201
- 2:8–11 — 99
- 3:6 — 279–80

Colossians
- 3:10 — 283, 283–4
- 3:12–13 — 104
- 3:23–24 — 200

2 Thessalonians
- 3:10 — 198

1 Timothy
- 2:1–2 — 126
- 4:7 — 174
- 5:4 — 136
- 5:8 — 136
- 6:11 — 174

2 Timothy
- 2:13 — 90
- 2:22 — 226
- 3:3 — 77
- 3:4 — 128

Titus
- 1:2 — 90
- 3:5 — 284

Hebrews
- 8:6–12 — 91
- 10:14–18 — 91
- 11 — 105
- 12:10 — 99

1 Peter
- 1:16 — 90

2 Peter
- 1:5–7 — 174

1 John
- 3:2–3 — 99
- 3:18 — 168

OTHER ANCIENT LITERATURE

Aristotle
Nicomachean Ethics — 11, 171
- I.13.19 — 169
- II.6.14 — 279
- II.6.17 — 174–5
- II.6.18 — 175
- VI.2.6 — 176
- VI.5.6 — 177
- VI.6.1–2 — 177
- VII.2.1 — 276
- VII.3.7 — 276
- VII.3.8 — 277
- X.6.8 — 178

Cicero
Pro Caelio
- XX.47 — 228

Herodotus
The Histories
- III.38.3–4 — 68

Livy
Ab urbe condita
- II.32.8–12 — 199 n. 3

Lucian of Samosata
Vera Historia — 25

Plato
- *Euthyphro* — 89–90
- *Timaeus* — 11
- *Republic* — 62–3

Sophocles
Antigone — 69 n. 10

Strabo
Geography
- VIII.6.20 — 228–9

Theophrastus
On Stone — 32

GENERAL INDEX

A
abduction 313–15
abortion 69–70, 129, 225, 242, 243, 247–8
acceptance with God 285, 288–9, 290–2
act consequentialism 145. *See also* CONSEQUENTIALISM
act utilitarianism 109–36, 139, 145, 191, 247
 authority of 112
 basis of 112–13, 123–6
 evaluated 117–36
 general principle of 112, 113–15, 117, 128–32
 goal of 112, 113–15
 guidance of 112, 116–17, 135–6
 modified 117, 122–3
 moral problems of 123–36
 practical difficulties of 117–23
 specific rule of 112, 115–16, 130, 132–5
 status of 112
Adams, John Couch 311
Adams, R. M. 294
adoption (legal) 240 n. 3
advertising 260–3
afterlife 14–15
agency 315–18
agent-based morality 184–7
alienation 284, 286, 288, 290
Almond, Brenda 45–6
altruism 76–7, 81, 162, 203
Anscombe, Elizabeth (G. E. M.) 169, 178–9
antibiotics 225
aretē 170, 176, 179, 187
Aristotle 11, 21, 48, 158, 159, 169–80, 181, 183, 191, 276–9, 282, 295, 301
 doctrine of the mean 170–4, 176, 179–80, 279
 evaluated 174–5, 177–8
artificial life support 252–3

astorgos 77
astronomy 28, 306–7, 308–9, 311–12, 329–30
atheism 74, 162–3, 316. *See also* GOD: INDEPENDENCE FROM
 and God as Creator 24
authority 112, 149–50, 284, 300, 301, 313, 326
 ethical/moral 48, 50, 85–6, 164
 ultimate/supreme xii
axioms 325–6

B
Bacon, Francis 26, 301–2
Baier, Kurt 192
benevolence, universal 184–7, 188
beneficence 67, 142, 143, 147
Bentham, Jeremy 111, 112–15, 117, 118–19, 122–6, 127, 133, 146, 184, 191
 hedonic calculus 114–15
Big Bang theory 36
biology 315, 319
Body of Christ 104, 199
body (human) 231–4
Book of the Dead, Egyptian 67–8
Brahe, Tycho 306–7, 308
Breck, John 245
bribery 265–6. *See also* CORRUPTION
Bronowski, Jacob 38
Bruce, F. F. 231
Buddhism 246 n. 7

C
Caelius Rufus, Marcus 228
Calderone, Mary 227
Caputo, John D. 213
caring, ethic of 185–8
Carnegie, Andrew 198
causation 176–7, 278–9, 317
Chamberlain, Paul 60
character 167–8, 169–70, 179, 288–9

chemistry 319
Christian ethics 95–107, 183, 188, 192–3, 195–201, 285–95. *See also* ETHICS; VIRTUE ETHICS
   authority of 98
   basis of 98
   demands of 104
   general principles of 100–1
   guidance 104–6
   motivation of 104
   objections to 106–7
   and self-interest 195–8
   and selfishness 198–201
   specific rules 101–4
   status of 98
   supreme goal of 99–100
Christian service 200–1
Christianity 14, 82
   supreme goal 147
   and Marxism 284
Cicero, Marcus Tullius 64, 228
Collins, Francis S. 28
commerce 204–5, 265–7
common sense morality 134–5, 213
Communist Party Manifesto 287
compassion 77, 90, 104, 153–4, 167, 169, 192, 194, 233, 240, 249–50
compromise 161
conscience 105
consciousness in direct experience 34
consequences 131–2, 139, 181
consequentialism 111, 139, 145–7, 154
   act 145
   direct 131
   rule 131
contraception 225
contractarianism 83–8, 126, 148, 150, 162–3, 216
   moral 85–8, 90
   political 84–5
contradiction(s)
   in law of nature 156–7
   in will 157
Copernican revolution 319, 320
Copernicus, Nicolas 306
correctness, moral 191
corruption 88. *See also* BRIBERY
courage 171, 173–4
covenant
   new 91
   old 90–1
Crick, Sir Francis 75, 299, 319, 322
crime 127, 267–9. *See also* PUNISHMENT
culture 105

D

Darwin, Charles 26–7, 74–5
Darwinism, Social 74–5, 82
data collection 302–3, 308–11
Dawkins, Richard 75–6, 317–18, 319, 330–1
death 14, 15. *See also* ABORTION; EUTHANASIA; LIFE: AFTER DEATH
decision making, ethical 49, 50, 105, 179–80, 213
deduction/inference 302, 306–8, 313–15
   defined 302
deontology 153, 179, 188, 191. *See also* DUTY/DUTIES
   theories, defined 139–40
dependence, cultural 56–7
design 13
determinism 17, 34
   genetic 75–6
development, moral 59–60, 105–6
dialectical materialism 23
dignity, human 159
direct consequentialism 131. *See also* CONSEQUENTIALISM
Divine Command Theory of Morality 88–9
divine revelation 24–9, 163
DNA 28, 299, 321–2
Dobzhansky, Theodosius 82 n. 17
drugs 259
duty/duties xiii, 7, 9, 14, 140, 148, 161, 187–8, 191–3, 194–5, 217, 248. *See also* DEONTOLOGY
   absolute 162–3
   basic 142–4, 147
   of beneficence 67, 142, 143, 147
   conflict of 144
   derived 143, 147
   family 67, 135–6, 145
   of fidelity 142, 143, 144, 145
   of gratitude 132, 142, 143, 145
   of justice 142, 145, 147
   moral 45, 77, 78–81, 82–3, 85, 87, 88, 98, 113, 123, 125–6, 135–6, 139, 153–4, 178, 205–6, 287

duty/duties
   of non-maleficence 143, 144, 147
   to past 2, 132, 145
   of reparation 142, 145
   self-evident 147
   of self-improvement 142

E
education 3-4, 279, 283, 284
egoism 189-208
   commercial 204-5
   entrepreneurial 204-5
   ethical 191-3, 201-4. *See also*
      CHRISTIAN ETHICS; ETHICS;
      VIRTUE ETHICS
      basic principle of 202-3
      status of 202
   psychological 205-8
      evaluated 207-8
   self-interest 191-201
   selfishness 192, 193-201
Egyptian Book of the Dead 67-8
Einstein, Albert 28, 327
emergence 321-2
emotivism 55-8
empiricism 153, 161-2
end justifies the means 145
ends 158-62, 217
Enlightenment, the 153, 164, 178, 191
environment 270-1
Epicurianism 48, 113
eternal life 195-6, 197
ethical systems 219
   assessment of 97
ethics. *See also* CHRISTIAN ETHICS;
   EGOISM: ETHICAL; NATURALISM;
   VIRTUE ETHICS
   in advertising 260-3
   application of principles 49, 50-1,
      68-70, 202-3
   authority 48, 50
   basis for 48, 123-6, 162-3, 218
   biblical 130
   commercial 265-7
   and daily life 49
   difficulties 46-7
   environmental 270-1
   exercises in 255-71
   goal of 48-9, 50
   limitation of 275

   in making decisions 49, 50
   medical 49-51, 237
   in New Testament 103-4
   in Old Testament 101-3
   practical application of 213
   professional 263-5
   and science 235-53
   sexual 223-34
   in sport 257-60
   status of 48
   and technology 46, 235-53
   of transmission of life 221-34, 237-48
   teleogy in 191
ethnocentrism 57-88
eudaimonia 170, 177, 183
euthanasia 215, 249-53
Euthyphro problem 89-90, 106-7
evolution, organic 13-14, 28, 82, 214,
   219-20, 242
Ewing, A. C. 140
exestin 231
existentialism (and existentialists) 38,
   61, 164
exousia 231
exousiasthēsomai 231
experience xi, xiii, xiv, 4, 9, 26, 34, 58, 76,
   104, 105, 113, 127, 130-1, 161-2,
   173, 179-80, 207, 213, 280, 283, 294,
   302, 312, 322, 324, 325-6
   conversion 229
   sexual 223-7
   spiritual 280-3
   subjective 6, 302
experimentation 301, 302, 305, 330
explanation 315-23
extremism 191-3

F
fairness 62, 64. *See also* JUSTICE
faith 163, 197, 230, 233, 291, 326, 327
falsifiability 311-12
feelings 55-6
fellowship with God 285, 288-9
fidelity 142, 143, 144, 145
final judgment 163
Fish, Stanley 64-6
Foot, Philippa 169
foresight 120-2
fornication 231-2, 234. *See also* SEX
Fotion, Nicholas 23

Frank, S. L. 140
Frankena, William K. 293-4
free will 17, 34, 164, 322. *See also* WILL
freedom 90-1, 230-1, 284

G
Galileo Galilei 17, 301
Galle, Johann 311
genes 75-6
Gilligan, Carol 185
glorification 99-100, 288-9, 291, 292
God. *See also* GOD AS CREATOR
  acceptance with 285, 288-9, 291-2
  as basis for ethics 124, 126, 130, 145, 163
  character of 82, 90, 148, 163
  existence of 106, 316-18
  fellowship with 285, 288-9
  glory of 147
  image of 14, 218-19
  independence from 290
  Kant's view of 163-4
  law of 101-4, 279-83, 290, 291-2
  love of 287-8
  mercies of 285, 286-7, 294
  reconciliation to 285, 288, 289, 291
  and revelation 26-9
  as tyrant 89-91, 284
  will of 82, 88-91, 148, 163, 195
  wrath of 288, 291
God as Creator 26-9, 82, 88, 98, 177, 316-17. *See also* GOD
  aim of 103-4
  atheism and 24
  of humanity 14-15, 26, 218, 242
  of rationality 14
  and science 26-9
  of universe 327-8
Golden Rule 157
good will 153-4, 155
gratitude 101, 142, 143, 145, 194
guidance 104-6
  moral 130, 213
guilt 34

H
happiness 112-13, 115-16, 123, 125, 126, 170, 177-8, 216-17. *See also* PLEASURE
  maximum 129-32

Hardwig, John 215
heaven 15, 196
hēdonē 113
hedonism 250
Hegel, Georg Wilhelm Friedrich 23
Heidegger, Martin 61
Hero of Alexandria 22
Herodotus 68-9
Hertz, Heinrich Rudolf 325
Hinduism 246 n. 7
Hippocrates 50 n. 2
Hippocratic oath 49-51
history 22-4, 33
Hobbes, Thomas 85, 87
holiness 89-90, 178
Holmes, Arthur E. 168
Holy Spirit 105, 233, 234, 246, 284, 287, 292
human rights 14-15, 17
humanity. *See also* MAN
  biblical view of 160
  dignity of 159
  individual significance of 35-6
  make-up of 169
  nature of 14-15
  origin of 36, 312
  personhood 243-5
  purpose of 14, 15, 36-8, 160
  rights of 14-15, 17, 119-20
  superior to non-personal beings 34-5
  value 211-20, 242
Hume, David 78-9, 80, 162-3
hunger 271
Hursthouse, Rosalind 169, 180-4
hypotheses 301-3, 306-7, 308-11, 314-5
hypothetico-deductive method 302, 306-8, 313-15
  defined 302

I
idolatry 101, 128
ignorance 275
illusion 29-30
impartiality 116-17. *See also* PARTIALITY
imperative
  categorical 154-61
  hypothetical 154-5
in virto fertilisation 238-41
inconsistency, logical 156

induction 207, 302, 303–5, 306, 308, 327
  intuitive 141
infanticide 215
inference. *See* DEDUCTION
information 46–7, 320–2
instinct 81–2
intention(s) 120–2, 131, 167–8, 177
interests 79–80, 81
intolerance 57. *See also* TOLERANCE
intuition 17–18, 34–5, 140, 141, 148, 184
intuitionism 137–50, 162–3, 217, 251
  basis of 148
  ethical 140–2
  evaluated 145–50
  strengths of 145–7
  supreme goal of 147–8
  weaknesses of 147–50
intuitivists 140
'is'/'ought' problem 78–81, 125–6. *See also* OUGHT
Islam 14, 82, 327–8
Israel 285
IVF 238–41

J

Jesus Christ
  as the Bread of Life 195
  crucifixion 99, 128, 197, 233
  death of 106, 135, 287–8, 291
  and ethics xiv, 163
  glorification of 99
  hostility to 195
  incarnation of 98, 246
  influence of 23–4
  as judge 98, 105–6
  kingdom of 197, 200–1
  and law of God 98
  love for 101, 200
  and rationality 26
  resurrection of 98, 106, 197, 233, 288
  as revealer of God 24, 26, 163
  as sacrifice for sins 91, 291
  second coming of 197
  and self-denial 197–8
  and serving God/Christ 195, 200–1
  and spiritual satisfaction 195–6
  and truth 56–7
Judaism 82, 140, 327–8
Judas Iscariot 182
judgment
  final 64, 163
  subjective 58
  value 213–14, 219
justice 62–70, 100, 104, 129, 142, 145–7, 185. *See also* FAIRNESS
  distributive 133
  objective 63–6
  universal 63–4
justification (theological) 288, 291

K

Kant, Immanuel 153–64, 193, 194, 237
Kantian ethics/Kantianism 140, 151–64, 179, 181, 184, 191–2, 217–18
  assessed 161–4
Kekulé, Friedrich August 300, 301
Kenny, Anthony 146–7, 149
Kepler, Johannes 306–7, 308–9
Kierkegaard, Søren 61
kingdom of God/Christ 200–1
knowledge 4–8
  moral 276–8
korinthiazomai 229
Kuhn, Thomas 329–31
Kuhse, Helga 215

L

Laplace, Pierre-Simon 318
law
  of God 101–4, 279–83, 290, 291–2
  of nature (natural) 64, 67, 146, 156–7
  of non-affirmability 34
  universal 155–8
Le Verrier, Urbain 311
Lewis, C. S. 67, 328
Lewontin, Richard 325
liberalism 45–6
liberty 90–1, 120, 230–1
life
  after death 14–15. *See also* HEAVEN
  beginning of 241–8
  eternal 195–6, 197
  ethics of transmission of 221–34, 237–47
  origin of 36
  sacredness of 102
  support (artificial) 252–3
  value of 241–2
logical positivism 23
logikos 287

Logos 14, 26, 98. *See also* REASON/REASONING
Lonsdale, Kathleen 300
Lossky, N. O. 140
Louden, Robert 182
love 100, 168, 178, 185, 208
 of God 287–8
Lucian of Samosata 25

M
Mabbott, J. D. 61
MacIntyre, Alasdair 169
man. *See also* HUMANITY
 in image of God 218–19
 as machine 37–8, 322
Marcel, Gabriel 61
marriage 45–6, 102, 127, 129, 223–7, 238–40
Marx, Karl 23
Marxism 48–9, 132, 200, 283–5
 and Christianity 284
materialism 12–13, 75–6, 214, 330–1
 dialectical 23
 non-moral 74
McDowell, John 169
McNaughton, David 140, 141–3, 148
means 158–60
mechanism 315–8
Medawar, Sir Peter B. 20
medical ethics 49–51, 237
memory 34, 322
Mendel, Gregor 304, 306
mercies of God 285, 286–7, 294
metaphysics 330
Mill, John Stuart 45, 118, 119–20, 123, 130–2, 133, 216, 301–2
Monod, Jacques 75
Moore, G. E. 140
morals
 absolute 60, 61, 131, 182
 basis of 162–3, 196
 objective 55–58, 59, 62–6, 70, 71–91, 182
 source of 70, 71–91
 subjective 58–61, 63–4
 ultimate authority 163–4
 universal principles 60, 61, 63–4, 66–70, 71–91

motivation/motive(s) 104, 167–8, 178, 179, 186–7, 188, 194–5, 200, 204, 207–8, 286–7

N
Nagel, Thomas 133
naturalism, ethical 77–81, 82, 125, 162–3, 215–16
Nature 105, 123–5, 126, 135–6, 148, 163
'new man' 283–5, 289
Noddings, Nel 185
nomos 312
non-rationality/the non-rational 14, 35, 36. *See also* RATIONALITY
norms 130–2
Nussbaum, Martha 169

O
objectivism 60, 61–70
observation 301, 303–5, 306, 324, 330
'Occam's razor' 309, 310
organic evolution 13–14, 28, 82, 214, 219–20, 242
'ought' 60, 78–81, 188, 125–6, 201, 276. *See also* 'IS'/'OUGHT' PROBLEM

P
pain 112–15, 117, 123–5, 126–8, 132–3, 252–3
Palmer, Alasdair 74
parable of the Prodigal Son 286, 289–90
paradigm shift 301, 329–31
partiality 156, 157, 184–5. *See also* IMPARTIALITY
Paul (Apostle)
 on law of God 279–83
Peacocke, Arthur 321
peer pressure 226–7
Peirce, Charles Sanders 313
perception 179–80
permissiveness 228–9, 234
persecution (of Christians) 197
personhood 243–5
Phillips, William D. 28
philosophy 15, 16, 20–2, 23
phronēsis 176
physics 309–10, 319–21
Plato 11, 21, 48, 63, 64, 135

pleasure 112-15, 116, 117-18, 123-5,
    126-8, 132-3, 147, 172, 175, 184-5,
    191-2, 224, 225, 237. *See also*
    HAPPINESS
  as idolatry 128
  maximum 123, 250
  and moral wrong 128
  quality of 118, 119-20, 123
  quantity of 118, 119-20, 123
pluralism 46-7
Polanyi, Michael 313, 320
Polkinghorne, John 322-3
Poole, Michael 317
Popper, Karl R. 23, 311-12, 320
positivism, logical 23
pragmatism 139
Prance, Ghillean 28
prayer 105
prediction(s) 22-3, 74, 302, 306-7, 311,
    313, 324
preference(s) 7, 37, 55-6, 58-9, 309
pregnancy, unwanted 129, 225
presuppositions 14-16, 21, 241-2, 295,
    302, 303, 323-31
  and axioms 325-6
  and intelligibility of universe 327-8
  and observation 324
  and paradigms 329-31
Pritchard, H. A. 140
probability 310, 328
progress, moral 59-60, 105-6, 105-6,
    278-9
prohibition, absolute 146, 149-50
promiscuity 228. *See also* SEX
Provine, William B. 74
punishment 115, 267-9. *See also* CRIME
purpose 14, 15
  of humanity 36-8

Q
quietism 168

R
Rachels, James 77, 79-81, 193
Raphael (Raffaello Sanzio da Urbino) 11
Raphael, D. D. 161-2, 248
rationalism 153, 161
rationality 14, 25-7, 34-5, 327. *See also*
    NON-RATIONALITY; REASON/
    REASONING

Rawls, John 133
reality 29-35
  definition/meaning 29
  external 29-30
  and history 33
  ultimate 34-5
  vs. counterfeit 30-3
reason/reasoning 17, 21-2, 24-5,
    153, 161, 207-8, 217-18. *See also*
    RATIONALITY
  human 163-4
reconciliation 195-6, 285, 288, 289, 291
redemption 15, 234
reductionism 319-23, 330-1
regeneration 291, 292
relationship(s) 223-5, 293. *See also*
    MARRIAGE
  casual 225
  with God 286, 289, 293
  permanent 223-4
relativism, cultural 56-8, 68-9
religion 15, 46, 69, 112, 124, 283-5,
    290-1, 293-5
repeatability 312-15
repentance 289-90
revelation
  divine 24-9, 163
  Two Book view of 26-7
revolution 84-5
  industrial 160, 270
  in scientific thinking 301, 306
  sexual 225, 227
reward 193, 195, 197, 200-1
rights (moral) 45. *See also* HUMANITY:
    RIGHTS
  human 14-15, 17
  individual 216
  negative 45
  positive 45
RNA 321
Rorty, Amélie 169
Rose, Steven 76
Ross, W. D. 140, 141-4, 147, 149
Rousseau, Jean-Jacques 84-5
rule consequentialism 131. *See also*
    CONSEQUENTIALISM
rule utilitarianism 111, 121. *See also*
    UTILITARIANISM
rules xii, 8, 21, 37, 130-2, 168, 173,
    179-80, 230, 286, 301, 320

Ruse, Michael 75
Russell, Bertrand 20, 305

S

Sagan, Carl 28
salvation 195-6, 230
Sartre, Jean-Paul 61, 164
Sayre-McCord, Geoffrey 86, 87, 150
Schaff, Adam 36-7
science 4, 15-16, 18-20, 26-9, 297-331.
   See also SCIENTIFIC METHOD
  defined 299-300
  and ethics 235-53
  explanation 315-23
  and God as Creator 26-9
  limitation of 19-20, 36-7, 302, 316, 320, 327
  presuppositions 323-31. *See also* PRESUPPOSITIONS
scientific method 300-15. *See also* SCIENCE
  abduction 313-15
  axioms 325-6
  data collection 302-3
  deduction/inference 302, 306-8, 313-15
  defined 302
  experimentation 301, 302, 305, 330
  explanation 315-23
  falsifiability 311-12
  hypotheses 301-3, 306-7, 308-11
  induction 207, 302, 303-5, 306, 308, 327
    intuitive 141
  observation 301, 304, 306, 324
  paradigm shift 301, 329-31
  repeatability 312-15
  trust 326
self 46
self-assessment 172
self-consciousness 34
self-control 172, 276, 277
self-denial 193, 196-7
self-discipline 279
self-improvement 142
self-indulgence 276
self-interest 154, 158, 162, 191-201, 204-8, 216
self-preservation 80-2

selfishness 69, 192, 193-201, 206, 207.
   See also EGOISM
Sen, Amartya 111
sense (experience, perception) 29-30, 326
Sermon on the Mount 103
service, Christian 200-1
SETI 28
sex 129, 221-34. *See also* FORNICATION; PERMISSIVENESS
  casual 226, 228, 229-30, 234
  education programmes 227
  extra-marital 229
  pleasure in 224, 225, 225-6
  premarital 226, 227, 228
  repression 225, 227
  US Sex Information and Education Counsel 227
sexual revolution of 1960s 225, 227
sexually transmitted disease(s) 225
significance, individual 35-6
sin 230, 234, 289-91, 292
Singer, Peter 215, 219-20, 245
Skorupski, John M. 120, 133
slavery 48, 69, 86, 90, 106, 159, 178, 200-1, 230-1, 247-8, 292
Slote, Michael 112, 134, 169, 179, 180, 181, 183, 184-8
  ethic of caring 185-8
Smart, J. J. C. 111, 134-5
Smith, Adam 204
Social Darwinism 74-5, 82
sociobiology 75-7, 82
sociology 4, 319
Socrates 9, 11, 21, 56, 80, 84, 89, 128, 143, 275-6
sophia 176
soul 246
space exploration 271
Spencer, Herbert 75
sport 257-60
Starkey, Mike 226
State, the 17, 48, 135-6, 216
stewardship 218-19
Stocker, Michael 169
Stoicism (and Stoics) 48, 64
Stott, John 293
Strabo 228-9
'struggle for survival' 74

subjectivism 58–62
suffering 249
suicide 248
   assisted 215
summum bonum 21
supernatural, the 86, 316
survival
   'struggle for s.' 74
   's. of the fittest' 74
   's. of the species' 76–7
syllogism 307
sympathy 162, 194, 208

T

taste 59
technology 46, 235–53
teleogical theories 139
teleogy 191
telos 139, 316
Ten Commandments 90–1, 101–3
theism xiii, 13, 16, 24–9, 327–8
   worldview 330–1
theology 103, 319
   moral 163–4
Theophrastus 32
theory/theories 139–40, 302–3, 306, 308, 324–5
tolerance 61. *See also* INTOLERANCE
totalitarianism 135, 216, 242, 284
touchstone 32–3
transcendental values 219
trust 203, 217, 326
truth 102, 275–6, 295
   necessary 141, 177
   objective 46–7, 55–58
   self-evident 141–2
Two Book view of revelation 26–7

U

ultimate reality and individuals 34–5. *See also* REALITY
uncertainty 45, 121–2
uniformity 327–8
US Sex Information and Education Counsel 227
utilitarianism 111, 139, 145–8, 153, 154, 157, 162–3, 175, 178–9, 181, 184, 186, 216–17, 237, 250. *See also* ACT UTILITARIANISM
   atheistic 121–2
   outcome u. 123
   rule u. 111, 121
   satisficing u. 123
   supreme goal 147
utilitas 115
utility 115–16
utopia 14–15, 23, 132, 200

V

vacuum, moral 45–6
Verification Principle 23, 311
virtue ethics 165–88, 218. *See also* CHRISTIAN ETHICS; EGOISM: ETHICAL; ETHICS
   Aristotle 169–78
   basis of 186
   general principle 181–2
   goal of 183–4
   modern 178–88
virtue(s) 169–77, 191, 275–6, 279
   developing 173–4
   intellectual 169, 176–7
   moral 169–71
   theoretical 179–80
Vygotsky, Leo 319–20

W

Warren, Mary Ann 244–5
Watson, James D 299, 322
welfare 49, 86–7, 116–17, 126, 129, 216–7, 237
Westminster Shorter Catechism 99
Whitehead, Sir Alfred North 27
will (human) 157. *See also* FREE WILL
Williams, Bernard 111, 134–5
Wilson, Edward O. 75
Wilson, John A. 67
wisdom
   philosophic 176
   practical 176
   scientific 176, 177
work 101, 197–8, 200
worldview 3–9, 15–29
   defined 8–9
   theism 330–1
wrongdoing 275–9, 282

ABOUT THE AUTHORS

David W. Gooding is Professor Emeritus of Old Testament Greek at Queen's University Belfast and a Member of the Royal Irish Academy. He has taught the Bible internationally and lectured on both its authenticity and its relevance to philosophy, world religions and daily life. He has published scholarly articles on the Septuagint and Old Testament narratives, as well as expositions of Luke, John, Acts, Hebrews, the New Testament's use of the Old Testament, and several books addressing arguments against the Bible and the Christian faith. His analysis of the Bible and our world continues to shape the thinking of scholars, teachers and students alike.

John C. Lennox is Professor Emeritus of Mathematics at the University of Oxford and Emeritus Fellow in Mathematics and the Philosophy of Science at Green Templeton College. He is also an Associate Fellow of the Saïd Business School. In addition, he is an Adjunct Lecturer at the Oxford Centre for Christian Apologetics, as well as being a Senior Fellow of the Trinity Forum. In addition to academic works, he has published on the relationship between science and Christianity, the books of Genesis and Daniel, and the doctrine of divine sovereignty and human free will. He has lectured internationally and participated in a number of televised debates with some of the world's leading atheist thinkers.

David W. Gooding (right) and John C. Lennox (left)

Photo credit: Barbara Hamilton.

The Quest for Reality and Significance

Being Truly Human: *The Limits of our Worth, Power, Freedom and Destiny*

In Book 1, Gooding and Lennox address issues surrounding the value of humans. They consider the nature and basis of morality, compare what morality means in different systems, and assess the dangerous way freedom is often devalued. What should guide our use of power? What should limit our choices? And to what extent can our choices keep us from fulfilling our potential?

Finding Ultimate Reality: *In Search of the Best Answers to the Biggest Questions*

In Book 2, they remind us that the authority behind ethics cannot be separated from the truth about ultimate reality. Is there a Creator who stands behind his moral law? Are we the product of amoral forces, left to create moral consensus? Gooding and Lennox compare ultimate reality as understood in: Indian Pantheistic Monism, Greek Philosophy and Mysticism, Naturalism and Atheism, and Christian Theism.

Questioning Our Knowledge: *Can we Know What we Need to Know?*

In Book 3, Gooding and Lennox discuss how we could know whether any of these competing worldviews are true. What is truth anyway, and is it absolute? How would we recognize truth if we encountered it? Beneath these questions lies another that affects science, philosophy, ethics, literature and our everyday lives: how do we know anything at all?

The Quest for Reality and Significance

Doing What's Right: *Whose System of Ethics is Good Enough?*

In Book 4, Gooding and Lennox present particular ethical theories that claim to hold the basic principles everyone should follow. They compare the insights and potential weaknesses of each system by asking: what is its authority, its supreme goal, its specific rules, and its guidance for daily life? They then evaluate why even the best theories have proven to be impossible to follow consistently.

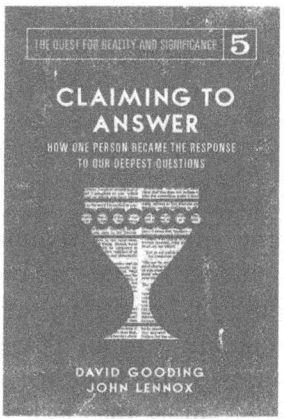

Claiming to Answer: *How One Person Became the Response to our Deepest Questions*

In Book 5, they argue it is not enough to have an ethical theory telling us what standards we ought to live by, because we often fail in our duties and do what we know is wrong. How can we overcome this universal weakness? Many religions claim to be able to help, but is the hope they offer true? Gooding and Lennox state why they think the claims of Jesus Christ are valid and the help he offers is real.

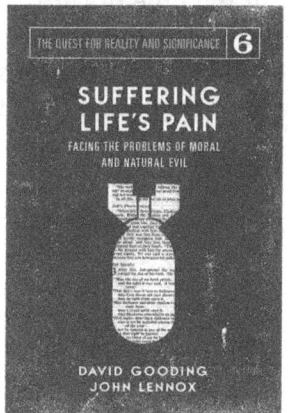

Suffering Life's Pain: *Facing the Problems of Moral and Natural Evil*

In Book 6, they acknowledge the problem with believing in a wise, loving and just God who does not stop natural disasters or human cruelty. Why does he permit congenital diseases, human trafficking and genocide? Is he unable to do anything? Or does he not care? Gooding and Lennox offer answers based on the Creator's purpose for the human race, and his entry into his own creation.

Myrtlefield Encounters

Key Bible Concepts
How can one book be so widely appreciated and so contested? Millions revere it and many ridicule it, but the Bible is often not allowed to speak for itself. Key Bible Concepts explores and clarifies the central terms of the Christian gospel. Gooding and Lennox provide succinct explanations of the basic vocabulary of Christian thought to unlock the Bible's meaning and its significance for today.

The Definition of Christianity
Who gets to determine what Christianity means? Is it possible to understand its original message after centuries of tradition and conflicting ideas? Gooding and Lennox throw fresh light on these questions by tracing the Book of Acts' historical account of the message that proved so effective in the time of Christ's apostles. Luke's record of its confrontations with competing philosophical and religious systems reveals Christianity's own original and lasting definition.

Myrtlefield Encounters

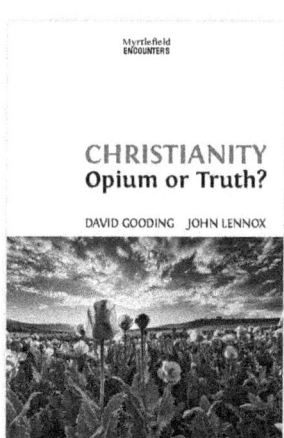

Christianity: Opium or Truth
Is Christianity just a belief that dulls the pain of our existence with dreams that are beautiful but false? Or is it an accurate account of reality, our own condition and God's attitude toward us? Gooding and Lennox address crucial issues that can make it difficult for thoughtful people to accept the Christian message. They answer those questions and show that clear thinking is not in conflict with personal faith in Jesus Christ.

The Bible and Ethics
Why should we tell the truth or value a human life? Why should we not treat others in any way we like? Some say the Bible is the last place to find answers to such questions, but even its critics recognize the magnificence of Jesus' ethical teaching. To understand the ethics of Jesus we need to understand the values and beliefs on which they are based. Gooding and Lennox take us on a journey through the Bible and give us a concise survey of its leading events and people, ideas, poetry, moral values and ethics to bring into focus the ultimate significance of what Jesus taught about right and wrong.

Myrtlefield Expositions

Myrtlefield Expositions provide insights into the thought-flow and meaning of the biblical writings, motivated by devotion to the Lord who reveals himself in the Scriptures. Scholarly, engaging, and accessible, each book addresses the reader's mind and heart to increase faith in God and to encourage obedience to his Word. Teachers, preachers and all students of the Bible will find the approach to Scripture adopted in these volumes both instructive and enriching.

- The Riches of Divine Wisdom: *The New Testament's Use of the Old Testament*
- According to Luke: *The Third Gospel's Ordered Historical Narrative*
- True to the Faith: *The Acts of the Apostles: Defining and Defending the Gospel*
- In the School of Christ: *Lessons on Holiness in John 13–17*
- An Unshakeable Kingdom: *The Letter to the Hebrews for Today*

www.myrtlefieldhouse.com

Our website, www.myrtlefieldhouse.com, contains hundreds of resources in a variety of formats. You can read, listen or watch David Gooding's teaching on over 35 Bible books and 14 topics.

You can also view the full catalogue of Myrtlefield House publications and download e-book editions of the *Myrtlefield Expositions*, *Encounters* and *Discoveries* series.

The website is optimized for both computer and mobile viewing, making it easy for you to access the resources at home or on the go.

For more information about any of our publications or resources contact us at: info@myrtlefieldhouse.com

THE QUEST FOR REALITY AND SIGNIFICANCE

Clear, simple, fresh and highly practical—this David Gooding/John Lennox series is a goldmine for anyone who desires to live Socrates' 'examined life'.

Above all, the books are comprehensive and foundational, so they form an invaluable handbook for negotiating the crazy chaos of today's modern world.

Os Guinness, author of *Last Call for Liberty*

These six volumes, totalling almost 2000 pages, were written by two outstanding scholars who combine careers of research and teaching at the highest levels. David Gooding and John Lennox cover well the fields of Scripture, science, and philosophy, integrating them with one voice. The result is a set of texts that work systematically through a potpourri of major topics, like being human, discovering ultimate reality, knowing truth, ethically evaluating life's choices, answering our deepest questions, plus the problems of pain and suffering. To get all this wisdom together in this set was an enormous undertaking! Highly recommended!

Gary R. Habermas, Distinguished Research Professor & Chair, Dept. of Philosophy, Liberty University & Theological Seminary

David Gooding and John Lennox are exemplary guides to the deepest questions of life in this comprehensive series. It will equip thinking Christians with an intellectual roadmap to the fundamental conflict between Christianity and secular humanism. For thinking seekers it will be a provocation to consider which worldview makes best sense of our deepest convictions about life.

Justin Brierley, host of the *Unbelievable?* radio show and podcast

I would recommend these books to anyone searching to answer the big questions of life. Both Gooding and Lennox are premier scholars and faithful biblicists—a rare combination.

Alexander Strauch, author of *Biblical Eldership*

Book 4 – DOING WHAT'S RIGHT: *Whose System of Ethics is Good Enough?*

Navigating the enduring questions about the good and the right, justice and value, scrutinizing their goal, guidance, and ground, David Gooding and John Lennox—with characteristic clarity, courage, and common sense—adroitly unveil both what's timely and timeless along the moral terrain. The rigorous honesty of their relentless pursuit of a moral account sufficient for both theoretical and practical purposes yields important dividends: insights not just into the human condition and the manifest limitations of materialism, but how morality objectively and robustly construed points beyond itself, intimating of promise and potential we can scarcely imagine.

Dr. David Baggett, co-author of *The Morals of the Story*

www.ingramcontent.com/pod-product-compliance
Lightning Source LLC
Chambersburg PA
CBHW071732150426
43191CB00010B/1553